*Institute of Social and Religious Research*

# THE PROTESTANT CHURCH AS A SOCIAL INSTITUTION

H. Paul Douglass and Edmund deS. Brunner

The Institute of Social and Religious Research, which is responsible for this publication, was organized in January, 1921, as an independent agency to apply scientific method to the study of socio-religious phenomena.

# The Protestant Church as a Social Institution

By

H. PAUL DOUGLASS

and

EDMUND deS. BRUNNER

Published for

THE INSTITUTE OF SOCIAL AND RELIGIOUS RESEARCH

by

HARPER AND BROTHERS

NEW YORK AND LONDON

# PREFACE

Beginning with the *Church and Community Survey of Salem County, New Jersey*, published in 1922, and following with some twenty volumes, large and small, which conserved and completed surveys undertaken by the Interchurch World Movement, the Institute of Social and Religious Research up to the present writing (July, 1934) has carried out forty-eight research projects published in seventy-eight volumes. About a dozen of these volumes were brought out by other publishers; the rest appeared under the Institute's own auspices.

Justifying the Institute's title, all of the above projects may more or less aptly be described as social studies. Eight were sociological in primary interest. The remainder dealt directly with organized religion and its processes; and the primary purpose even of the sociological studies was to supply a background for the understanding of religious problems. In short, the religious volumes were social studies in form, and the sociological studies were religious in purpose.

The fields of organized religion most continuously explored by the Institute have been those of the rural and urban church, home and foreign missions, Christian education, racial aspects of organized religion, and the coöperation and unity of religious forces. Research in the rural field and urban church fields has especially been governed by the idea of continuity. One project has built upon another. Cumulative results have begun to appear through the improvement of techniques, and the extension of research over periods of time has permitted the comparison of earlier and later data so as to establish trends.

As was the case with the first group of Interchurch World Movement projects, the majority of subsequent Institute studies have been undertaken on direct request from agencies of organized religion, largely the interdenominational ones. The Institute has not so much initiated research as it has discriminated between researches desired by others. The interested agencies, however, frequently conceived the researches required in rather narrow and particularistic ways. In such cases the Institute has habitually worked over the project into more generalized form, so that the results might have the widest applicability. It has also sometimes deliberately originated research projects in order to fill a gap not recognized by others. Since, however, the Institute has generally served demand, its total output, while impressive, in no sense covers the entire field of organized religion;

and it cannot pretend to be distributed in any balanced fashion. It does not constitute a unit; nevertheless it is broadly representative of a wide range of the current interests of organized religion, and its cumulative value has been generously recognized.

This series of Institute studies constitutes the main source of the present book.

In addition it has drawn upon Institute data used by staff members or other collaborators in books published under other initiative. Several staff members, for example, collaborated with President Hoover's Research Committee in the study of *Recent Social Trends in the United States*, also in important publications of the Federal Council of Churches and of the Home Mission Councils. They have also assisted in the set-up of numerous localized researches with which they have sometimes exchanged data. Such collateral sources have also been made use of in the present volume.

The volume also introduces considerable unpublished data gathered by the Institute in connection with various projects and utilizes still other results presented elsewhere from a specialized viewpoint but capable of a wider application.

With such sources one might have summarized by making abstracts or selections from each of the forty-eight studies and presenting them, under some scheme of topical organization, as a source book in organized religion in America.

But, as already pointed out, the differences in the scales and proportions adopted by the several studies precluded the use of such a method. Some studies were much more specialized than others; for example, special investigations of the rural "hinterlands" of the church, of churches of foreign populations in their urban setting, or of Negro churches as compared with white, represented more intensified research in these limited fields than it had been possible to give to the rural and urban church in general.

Others of the Institute projects had set themselves to solve highly specific problems, such as that of the relation between the church and environmental forces, reported on in *The Strategy of City Church Planning*. As a total such intensive studies could not be put on the same level with more basic and general ones.

But it was not merely the disproportionate distribution of the available data that prevented the direct transcription of selections from the sources into a summary volume. An even more important consideration was the omission of topics necessary to anything like a comprehensive and balanced study of the church as a social institution. These omissions were represented in the files of the Institute by scores of outlines of proposed studies which had never been reached. Many of them had had preliminary development as to scope and methodology and had been classified as to relative importance. The priorities of some had even been fixed in a scheme of future research, now destined never to be completed. The sense of the many areas of the church's life which remain entirely unexplored makes it impossible for the writers simply to draw upon their assimilated data and call the results a book.

On the other hand, here, at least, is the largest body of objective research of its kind. No other set of data concerning the churches as social institutions exists, which was gathered from so nearly a common viewpoint, developed according to anything like similar techniques, and covers so large a part of the field.

The temptation was consequently very strong to tease out the material so as to cover the chief omitted points, and to present as balanced and comprehensive a report as possible on the Protestant church as a social institution.

This was the method finally adopted. The present volume, then, is essentially a fresh composition, based on the sources previously described and attempting to draw on them somewhat proportionately. It finds its central phenomena and principle of balance in the modal church, rural and urban respectively, as revealed by cumulative researches. It is thus able to relate exceptional variations in church characteristics to the two major types as objectively revealed and thus to do all aspects of the story relative justice without neglecting the central theme.

The preparation of a volume on these lines was committed to the two members of the Institute staff who had most continuously directed projects in the respective fields of the rural and the urban church. It was planned by them in common, and they are in entire agreement as to its content. In the actual writing, however, Dr. Brunner's contribution is confined to the rural sections, while Dr. Douglass is responsible for the rest of the volume. The book consists of four parts. The first includes two introductory chapters, one analytical, the other historical. Part II reviews the major institutional factors and processes internal to the church, in eight chapters. Part III deals with three outstanding external factors which condition the church, namely, its environment, its integrating tendencies, and the intellectual and religious climate of the age to which it belongs. The last part ventures into the field of prophecy on the basis of established tendencies projected into the future. It forecasts the prospects of the church and the policies indicated as conditions of success; and emphasizes the promise of unity as one of the most valid grounds of hope for the church as an institution.

The following method of reference to sources has been adopted: In sections depending essentially upon a single source direct documentation by means of footnotes is often used. On topics which draw on several Institute studies, sources are indicated only by the chapter bibliographies, which also make sparing references to related researches by others.

# CONTENTS

ix

# TABLES

# CHARTS

PART ONE

INTRODUCTION

# CHAPTER I

## *The Church as a Social Institution*

The historic significance of the church and, no less, its essential present meanings, hinge upon belief in a cosmic situation consisting of mundane and supra-mundane aspects in intercommunication. The validation of any concept of this sort is essentially religious. It is based upon the reliability of subjective insights. It holds for religious people. It asserts realities of a spiritual order. In religious language, it must be "apprehended by faith."

The specific characteristics of the church originate in its relation to the spiritual order and bear the marks of their source. But a vast institutional fabric and an extensive system of secondary mores have built themselves about these central ideas and convictions and have accumulated bulk, prestige and variety throughout the ages.

### THE CHURCH A PHASE OF HUMAN SOCIETY

Whatever, then, the church may be specifically, generally it is a social institution and bears the marks of the class of phenomena to which it belongs. The studies of the Institute of Social and Religious Research have primarily addressed themselves to the institutionalized aspects of religion. They have treated the church as an aspect and phase of human society. They have dealt effectively with whatever habitual behaviors, practices, attitudes, and experiences they have found grouped under the term religious as traits of human groups. These they have observed and sometimes measured, but without raising any question of the validity of the conceptions and beliefs underlying them.

The reasons for this limitation have been two: first, the belief that the Institute had a distinctive contribution to make to the understanding of the church; and that this involved the maintenance of a distinctive point of view. Everyone else was regarding the church religiously. It was time for someone to regard it scientifically. Here was a novel enterprise in the field of institutional religion. It adopted the rules of the scientific game. It confined itself to the objective viewpoint to see what would happen. What happened was at least this: some new ability to direct the church toward its own higher goals.

In the second place, however, no other basis than the scientific one would have been possible in the nearly fifty studies relating to the church. The more or less representative persons who sponsored, directed and carried out the studies could never have agreed on any set of postulates with respect to the church as a phase of a supra-mundane society. Acceptable generalizations could be made and tentative conclusions reached about the church and its external aspects. But the research students were in no position to choose between the competing religious interpretations offering conflicting accounts of the specific inner aspects of the phenomena in question. However limited the objective vision of the church might appear to the eye of faith, it at least made research possible for whatever it might be worth. The unity and comparability of the studies grow out of their confinement to the objective viewpoint and to scientific methods of investigation.

## Object of Study Versus Object of Faith

Now at the end of fourteen years' experience in making objective studies of the church as a social institution the Institute has to testify that its effort has been under continuous suspicion and has frequently aroused resistance and opposition. The religious point of view has been habitually jealous for the specific character which a church gets from its supra-mundane realm, and has resented examination and comparison with other societies.

This assertion is not contradicted by the fact, set forth in the Preface, that most of the Institute's projects were undertaken upon definite request of ecclesiastical leaders or agencies and that their results have been often used and greatly valued, especially by those in charge of the affairs of the church as an institution. Moreover, this has been true even when the facts disclosed have constituted a criticism of the church's management.

Opposition to objective studies merely carries the issue a step farther back. The more aggressively religious mood within the church is at outs with the viewpoints of practical administration quite as truly as it is at outs with the scientific attitude. The ecclesiastical leaders are themselves suspected of being more concerned with externals of the church as an institution than with the great realities behind it.

This acute and continuing conflict between the view that the church as an object of faith is not amenable to objective study and the effort to make objective studies has, in a very real sense, conditioned the success of the effort. To be sure, the studies have gone right on. They have been backed by extensive private resources which have given them freedom from any and all ecclesiastical agencies for support or control. They have had no other interference. But in spite of these extraordinary advantages they have all along had to struggle against undercurrents of resistance. Virtually all the Institute's studies were first-hand studies. As such, they have had to depend upon the willingness of the object of study to stand examination. Would the church do this? Would it open its books and permit observance of its processes? Generally, though often with some pressure, it would! The religious viewpoint has, nevertheless, presented many real obstacles with reference both to the comprehension of what was intended and the readiness to give serious coöperation. It has shut many doors and opened others but narrowly.

Opposition has naturally been more definite with respect to some projects than to others. In general, little objection has been raised to territorial or community studies directly concerned with local church units, especially when their results pointed out remedies for already acknowledged evils. When it came, however, to studies touching the organization or functioning of the church in general or of its ministry, objections began to be more vocal.

Moreover, in the last analysis, attention to the published studies and the willingness to follow their conclusions were even more conditioned by suspicion of or dissent from the objective viewpoint with respect to the churches. The studies indeed might be made, but would the religious viewpoint prevent many from reading the reports or taking them seriously?

All told, then, resistance to the scientific study of the church from church sources has been thrown into relief as a major phenomenon by fourteen years of experience. This is itself data of first significance as to the frequent conflict of the scientific attitude and the religious spirit.

The actual objections which objective church studies have had to meet did not all draw the issue in such single theoretical terms as has been done in the preceding pages. Each objection had its own tone and expressed itself in its own version. The further functions of the present introductory chapter are therefore two: (1) to examine the grounds of the resistances encountered in their variety as well as in their common insistence upon a special viewpoint; and (2) to confess and make explicit the ways in which the Institute, in its own mind, had met them.

## Sources of Resistance

Ignoring private individualists whose criticisms were simply the indulgence of their temperaments, and also ignoring the occasional person who was palpably affronted by the discovery of unwelcome facts about his particular institution, we find that two continuously significant sources of resistance to objective studies of the church based on the religious viewpoint have made themselves manifest.

### SHOCKED AND GRIEVING PIETY

The first consists of a rather large number of simple-minded and sincerely religious folks who have been now shocked and now grieved by the attempt to take a scientific attitude with respect to something as holy to them as the church is. They have never heard of the like before and they suspect the scientific approach of failure to sense the inner values which they apprehend. The church, to them, remains a society projected into the supramundane sphere,—something whose dominant aspect is out of sight or, perhaps better, something too dazzling for sight to bear—something incandescent and glorious. Nevertheless, familiarly known in its human aspect, it possesses dear and revered qualities. The devout believer is sure that the power to stir his emotions is something resident in the phenomena themselves, not merely something imported by his own mind. The scientific viewpoint is consequently charged, first, with ignoring the invisible part and aspect of the church, and, secondly, with illicitly treating the visible part as though it were mere cold phenomenon; whereas the religious person has inside knowledge that the phenomenon is not cold, but warm and palpitating. Piety, therefore, inclines to conclude that no true account of the realities of a religious institution can be given by one who thinks of it merely as an objective entity.

The scientific viewpoint as such has obviously no applicable answer to difficulties which arise in subjective feeling and sentiment. It can only point out that science has been most successful when its mood has been most completely divorced from the private concerns of individual human beings. A giant lens is to be poured from molten glass. If successful, it will bring the planets twice as near as they have ever been before. Success means profits to investors, credit and fame to technicians and craftsmen and the satisfaction of insatiable curiosity to pure scientists. These motivations of the hearts of men may rage passionately behind the event. But the more forgotten they are for the moment, the steadier the hand that pours the flood of glass into the mold.

Science may challenge piety to recognize a sort of twin in single-handed and complete dedication to truth, as well as a genuine morality in the stern discipline of concentration upon an honest accounting with observable facts. Investigators in the objective realm acknowledge compelling loyalties in behalf of which they know labor and anguish. This is the best, perhaps the only hopeful ground of appeal for understanding as between the scientific spirit and naïve piety.

RATIONALIZED OBJECTIONS

When it comes to answering resistances coming from the second source, namely, a varied group of criticisms alleging rational objections, the scientific attitude is on more accustomed ground.

These criticisms arise out of: (1) special versions of the nature of the church in its religious and universal aspect; (2) special evaluations of the actual present church; and (3) general attitudes toward the whole tendency to institutionalize religion. Objective studies of the church have been criticized, for example, for not taking sides in controversies as to its nature; for being diverted by an interest in institutional phenomena when they ought to spend the time calling upon an unfaithful church to repent; and for not repudiating institutionalism, root and branch, instead of possibly bolstering it up with facts, the knowledge of which may lead to greater institutional efficiency.

Now, in view of the rationalized objections and resistances which it has all along met, the long series of Institute studies represent more than mere persistence in a scientific undertaking. Implicitly they constitute an answer to criticism. Repeated objection has forced repeated reappraisal of the theory of objective studies as related to the church, in connection with which a definite attitude toward the church as an institution has matured. The church has been observed and considered objectively for fourteen years. For the observer, after all this time, to have experienced no change of attitude and reached no fresh generalization would be less than scientific. A well-developed attitude derived from steady attention to objective considerations might rightfully be anticipated. The Institute, in some measure, has acquired such an attitude. In order to exhibit it concretely, it is appropriate to note how it meets the main points of rationalized objection. In this way the grounds upon which its persistence in objective studies finally justifies itself may be made clear.

THE NATURE OF THE CHURCH

Among sources of rationalized challenge to the validity of the objective studies of the church, one has first to consider conflicting versions of the nature of the church.

The divisions of American religious opinion among the historic doctrines of the church were intensively explored in the series of Institute studies on church coöperation and unity. The results showed the persistence and currency of deep-rooted differences between Protestant and Catholic viewpoints.[1]

To the radical Protestant, religion consists of direct and unique personal relations between God and the individual. The sum total of the persons who have realized these relationships constitutes the church, which is to be described as an essentially spiritual entity, and only very secondarily as a social institution.

In the characteristic Catholic viewpoint, on the contrary, the essence of religion is found in God's corporate relations to men effectualized through the church as an ordained channel of life. The church is definitely a divinely constituted social institution. Its sacraments convey grace, its priesthood is essential to the valid performance of the church's saving functions. Both of

---

[1] See chapter xv, p. 332.

these views are easily turned into grounds of objection to scientific studies of the church.

## HIGH-CHURCH RESISTANCE

The consequences drawn from the high-church version of the church ought logically to be favorable to objective studies. The divine authority ascribed to the external institutions should permit free examination of it, since its authority is beyond challenge from any conclusions which investigation may reach. The really robust Catholic mind has never hesitated to put a Pope or two in hell, because the private character of popes makes no difference to the sanctity of the church. The scientist surely can do it no greater damage.

Nevertheless the priestly consciousness does not easily consent to any curious and unabashed inquiry into its functions, especially one which might throw light upon its inner psychology. The prestige of religious professionals suffers from any exhibition of shortcoming in their institutions. Ministers of religion, consequently, have often shown extreme sensitiveness with respect to objective studies. Curiously, however, this sensitiveness does not follow denominational lines. The objection of ministers to keeping time schedules or to having their work examined in its aspects as a job, their resentment against a consideration of employer-employé relations as involving themselves or of equity as between the superior and the subordinate members of a staff, are quite as prevalent among the common or garden type as they are among convinced high-churchmen. The former, with no claim to be priests, have appropriated a personal high-church attitude.

## PROTESTANT RESISTANCE

Historic Protestantism in its most characteristic version intended no absolute break with Catholic tradition and took middle ground in defining the church as both spiritual and corporate. It is the total body of those who are inwardly in vital relations with God; outwardly it is the set of institutions which both symbolize and realize this fact.

In consulting the opinion of the American religious public, the actual crux of the difference between this and the Catholic position was located in the varying consequences drawn from the assertion that the church is both spiritual and corporate. If it is corporate, one should be able to list its invariable marks as an institution. But to this proposal an overwhelming majority of opinion replied that "the church can be identified by spiritual marks only." In tests on this point nine-tenths of 624 church leaders responding affirmed the proposition in this form. The proportion of agreement reached more than eight-tenths with all denominations except the

Protestant Episcopal, which historically reflects a somewhat diluted Catholic tradition.[2]

Studies of church unity have further established the fact that the religious masses of the United States habitually contrast the external and organic aspects of the church with the spiritual aspects. They deliberately stress the subordination of the church to the gospel. They fear institutional mechanics as an obstacle to the Holy Spirit. They are unimpressed by objective measurements of church phenomena because they wish to devote all their stress to the imponderables. These tendencies reflect a deeply-rooted folk-attitude. The majority of American Christians fear too close an identification of the church with the visible institution bearing that name. This fear reflects a burnt-finger attitude toward the church as an institution, based on experience of the evils of institutionalism in the past. Its concrete index is found in traditional opposition to the Roman Catholic church.

Minds holding this point of view are naturally hard to interest in objective investigations of the church as a social institution. It is not so much that such investigations wrong the church as that they touch no important point or aspect of the church as religiously understood and defined.

It turns out, then, that both the superiority complex of professionals and the burnt-finger attitude of the Protestant masses are in instinctive rebellion against objective studies of the church and are inclined to give them grudging coöperation, if any.

### EVALUATION OF THE PRESENT CHURCH

A second source of rationalized challenge to objective studies of the church is found in a considerable body of Protestant opinion which has reached a highly unfavorable estimate of the religious values of the present church. At this point the low theoretical estimate accorded the visible church by the Protestant masses is reinforced by a very poor opinion of its current quality. Not content with depreciating the church in theory in order to exalt the gospel, opinion is widespread in many circles that the church has very largely failed the gospel, either in proclaiming or in living it. This opinion is echoed from many sides and by spiritually-minded and socially-minded people alike. Both are grieved by the discrepancy between the dream and the reality; both regard the visible church with a certain irritation as an institution that has somehow contrived to let religion down. In particular, stress upon church organization is regarded as a hindrance to the appreciation of its need of recovering inner values. Such views come naturally to persons of the fundamentalist frame of mind, as contrasted with institutionalists, according to Professor Kirsopp Lake's apt distinction. And

---

[2] Douglass, *Church Unity Movements in the United States*, p. 260.

they are especially numerous among people belonging to that party in the church which labels itself Fundamentalist.

All told, the prevalence in many Protestant circles of a scolding mood with respect to the church constitutes a rather curious and portentous phenomenon. It contrasts sharply with the invariable pity awakened in Catholics in behalf of the church "sore oppressed." The church as an institution is a sort of Protestant whipping-boy. It is beaten as disappointed heathens beat their idols. In extreme cases this position carries over into an almost Manichean mood, as though the embodiment of religion in an institution were a sort of pollution. Such a viewpoint inclines to envisage the unholy church throughout the world, in eternal conflict with the inner and unorganized virtues of the spirit. To teach tricks of institutional survival and efficiency to such an apostate or defiled church is to do a disservice to true religion. Such attitudes are in implicit resistance, if not in vocal opposition, to objective "engineering" studies of the church; and, from this viewpoint, such studies as the Institute's have often been berated as a waste of money and mistaken expenditure of effort.

CRITICAL ANTI-INSTITUTIONALISM

In addition, however, to popular, professional, and doctrinaire resistance to scientific methods of studying the church, others are to be distinguished which may be denominated critically anti-institutionalist. These positions have no quarrel with the scientific method as such; indeed, some of those holding this view believe themselves to have something of a monopoly on that method as applied to religion. These include doctrinal and ethical radicals, people perhaps with confessed humanistic leanings; also unconventional mystics who keep their religion in one mental compartment in order that they may be strictly scientific in another. Neither of these groups can be thought of as motivated by traditional religious qualms. From both, nevertheless, objections to scientific studies of the church as an institution have been heard; because, it is alleged, these studies assume or at least do not preclude the perpetuation of the church in its present institutional forms.

Radical anti-institutionalism, from the standpoint of advanced doctrinal and social thinking, is well expressed, for example, in a pamphlet, issued by the Community Church of New York, entitled "Religion Without a Church." Religion, it is conceded, cannot exist without social expression. Indeed it is inherently social. But a fatal choice was made when it was attempted to embody religion primarily in an ecclesiastical institution and to put it in custody of organized agencies. The same error, it is held, applies to medicine, law, teaching, and economic enterprises. All have developed separate, segregated and rival institutions without power to generate the ideals necessary to control themselves or the society to which they belong.

Religion confined within a specialized institution is equally powerless. Religion, it is held, must be released from the church and diffused through all the agencies of the community. The church naturally resists such a recall and redistribution of its prerogatives. But this is what must happen if religion is to rule society. The present churches can only be regarded as vestigial growths surviving beyond their time and possibly as centers of infection rather than of helpful life.[3]

The attitude of such a viewpoint toward objective studies is in effect this: "In not taking sides against the present churches, your studies are in fact helping them to succeed. We want them to fail. The more you show them how to survive, the more damage they are in position to do to truth and progress." Such a statement is an almost literal transcription of explanations actually given of unwillingness to coöperate in studies of the church as an institution.

From a different and essentially mystical standpoint a highly attractive alternative to the present church has appeared in the vision of a church without ecclesiasticism. This makes especially persuasive appeal in what may be called its cosmopolitan-liberal form. Such a viewpoint controlled certain passages of *Rethinking Missions*, the recent Laymen's Foreign Missions Inquiry report. Convinced of the impertinence of much of the baggage of western ecclesiasticism as imposed upon Oriental Christians by missionaries; and impressed by widespread revolt of nationalism against "cultural imperialism" as it is expressed in the western church, many of the finest minds of the present generation take very kindly to the notion of a free fellowship in religion, in which historic forms shall be completely subordinated to personal relationships of spiritually kindred spirits. Within such a fellowship, it is hoped, the essential genius of religion would find untrammeled expression. The following quotations from the Laymen's report eloquently express such moods:

". . . Many times during the history of western Christianity men's hearts have turned from the rigidity of the ecclesiastical institution in which the spirit of Christ's religion seemed to them to be smothered, from the stiff and hardened phrases in which the living faith of the Founder seemed to be stifled, and they have longed for what a medieval prophet called the Eternal Gospel, expressed in free ways through a universal Church, vital, spiritual, and growing and expanding with the life of men.

". . . The approach might thus have been the charm and attractive power of a great personal life rather than metaphysical statements about his essential nature.

". . . Experiments in number have been tried to effect a return to the simplicity of the Gospel, and to inaugurate a movement free enough and spiritual enough

---

[3] McAfee, *Community Religion; Religion Without a Church* (New York, The Community Church of New York, 1928), No. 2.

to grow into a universal Church. Every such experiment in the West, however, finds itself in rivalry with the churches of the ecclesiastical type already holding the field.

". . . The freer type of church might well have brought over into itself the most important leaders of life and thought in all three [Oriental] lands and have marked the beginning of a new era in the life of Christianity."[4]

Such viewpoints find very little to impress them in objective studies of the church as an institution; since the very institutionalization of religion is viewed as something artificial and unhealthy.

All types of anti-institutionalist argument sooner or later appeal to the long story of struggle between the ecclesiastical and prophetic elements in religion. Institutionalism has always stoned the prophets. It is easy to bring forward plenty of terribly convincing evidence on this point.

All these varied evidences of the sensitiveness of the church to the objective approach to its phenomena, and of its habitual and quick resort to defense mechanisms, confirm what was earlier insisted upon, namely, that the widespread and reiterated fact of resistance to objective studies is one of the most important data which these studies reveal.

PIECE-MEAL REPLY TO OBJECTIONS

Now the projects of the Institute, each in its own particular order and detail, have had to overcome more or less resistance from one or another or sometimes from all the sources catalogued above. Each project has turned criticism aside and has gone ahead on the plea of having limited objectives. Each has said in effect: We are not dealing with the church in general; we only want to discover something about this narrow group of facts and to appraise them on their own merits. Your religious qualms are not properly involved; since we have no bias against you and do not pretend to penetrate into the realms in which your qualms originate.

Explanations of this sort have never fully satisfied objections to particular projects, and they cannot well satisfy as an explanation of the persistence of the Institute in the total body of its objective research.

Now that this total product is being reviewed and summarized in the present volume, it seems permissible to dramatize the situation as implying a sort of convergence, at one time, of all the objections which have been made separately to the several projects. Imagine, then, all the objectors uniting in the demand to know what, after so many years of research, is the underlying implication with respect to the church of the continued use of scientific method. The Institute studies have repeatedly exposed unacknowledged assumptions on the part of the subjects of their investigations.

---

[4] *Rethinking Missions: Report of the Commission of Appraisal of the Laymen's Foreign Missions Inquiry* (New York: Harper and Brothers, 1932), Chapter V, pp. 3, 4, 5.

Is it not fair for the Institute to take its own medicine at least to the extent of trying to explain what, now at length and at the end of the process, it has arrived at by way of basic conclusions with respect to the church as an institution, and with respect to the institutionalization of religion which turned out to be the crucial point of nearly all of the objections.

## REAPPRAISAL OF INSTITUTIONALIZED RELIGION

In response to an actually persistent demand thus dramatized no literal consultation of the entire group of those who have made the Institute's researches has been or could have been held. It thus remains for the writers to make as representative a generalization as they can in behalf of the entire series of studies.

With respect to the institutionalization of religion, that generalization may be expressed in a word, as follows: institutionalization is inevitable, dangerous, yet manageable. Institutionalized religion may conceivably be made to serve the interests of modern society, and no less the ends apprehended and professed by religious insight.

### INEVITABILITY OF INSTITUTIONALIZATION

To state the grounds of this conclusion carries one back into some of the fairly familiar commonplaces of social psychology and sociology. Institutions are simply the more important and deeply rooted of the social habits of men, and are as inherent and inescapable as are any set of habits. Psychology reveals that even the most casual meetings of groups resolve themselves into milder or less mild struggles between personalities for ascendancy, as measured by attention or admiration. But these struggles from their most primitive beginnings have always been controlled by convention which defines behavior: as for example between the older and the younger, the male and the female; and which varies according to the particular kinds of occasions within which the casual grouping takes place. These examples show the all but universal formalization of social conduct which is the root of institutionalization.

Sociology goes on to show that virtually all religious types exhibit highly developed stages and degrees of formalization. Those most critical of what they consider the institutionalism of the church themselves exhibit it. Sects, for example, like the Primitive Baptist, representing extreme anti-ecclesiastical attitudes, maintaining the utmost simplicity and freedom in worship and an unpaid ministry, are genuinely shocked by the excesses of the Holy Rollers as the latter appear in mountain communities. Yet the truth is that the mountain preacher who most loudly proclaims that he receives his sermon by direct inspiration of God is asserting a highly-developed religious convention. Even in the most informal intercourse of his group he is subject to the dead hand of social ritualism. In the mountain community the father-character is so formalized that the intimate life of the family, generation after generation, is terribly robbed of spontaneity. The intercourse of loafers seated on the village lumber pile has a special ritual of greeting and for the conduct of conversation. Peculiar religious diction and intonation are universally employed in primitive religious services to signify the inter-communion between the human and the divine members of a common society. One who has witnessed the "speaking with tongues" of the wilder religions is sure to have been impressed by the imitative manner of vocaliza-tion. Institutionalization, then, has no exclusive connection with prayer-books or a sacerdotal order of clergy.

Moreover, in religious groups whose ecclesiasticism is least developed, formalized group judgments defining and evaluating the person are more frequent and burdensome than in the ritualistic churches. As marks of the individual, the fulfillment of religious obligations like churchgoing and Bible reading completely outrank intelligence and interestingness. The conventicle type of religious organization, which lodges authority in the local congregation and denies the necessity of any universal church, is heavier handed and more capricious in the discipline and control of its members than an ecclesiastical inquisition ever was. In short, the doctrine which denies the corporate reality of the church in the interest of its spiritual nature becomes locally corporate with a vengeance. "Presbyter" is simply "Priest writ large."

Even if religion originates in a person-to-person relation between God and the individual, it is logically and historically inevitable that a duplica-tion of that relation between God and many men will involve person-to-group relations. This takes place as soon as the social implications of individual religious ties develop. New Testament history accurately points out the crucial character of the moment when believers begin to multiply in number. As has often been observed, religions newly originating with a lone prophet and his disciples cannot outlast a single generation in pure and original form; since every successful attempt of a religion to perpetuate itself involves means of propaganda, education and discipline, and these are impossible without institutionalization.

All American sects have continuously become more churchly in doctrine, ethics and administration, particularly as social isolation has broken down. Even in the freest churches prayer becomes stereotyped. Testimony repeats old patterns. The religious originality of the first generation slips down into the institutionalized custom of succeeding ones. The ecclesiasticism of the sect is a different sort from that of the established church, but it is not a whit less institutionalized.

The attempt, then, to conceive of a non-institutionalized religion for modern man is sociologically infantile. It is an attack on rationality and ethical stability themselves. Religion cannot have currency without developing some generalized form, and generalized form implies habits resistant to change which are the essence of institutionalization.

## DANGER OF INSTITUTIONALISM

On the other hand, no extensive and objective study of the church as an institution can have failed to impress the minds of those making the study with the dangers of institutionalism.

Probably no body of data ever assembled constitutes so staggering an indictment of the actual evils and futilities of current religious institutionalism as the Institute's studies of the American church. The utter incoherence and colossal wastefulness of the church and its impotence to lift itself out of its pitiable traditional entanglements have never been so dispassionately set forth nor in so impressive factual terms.

The church, in other words, is often like a spider trapped in its own web. Moreover, the difficulty of the situation is that it is paradoxical. Thus Professor George A. Coe defines institutionalism as the "defect of a virtue." Its virtue is to give permanence and power to the creative religious insights of prophetic spirits. Its defect is to give these insights a hold-over authority after they have ceased to have pertinence and timeliness.

". . . Institutions," Dr. Coe goes on to say, "*qua* institutions, have an inherent gravitation away from creativity toward self-imitation.

"The church is a permanent necessity; if what we call churches should disappear, some institution that bears a different name would assume their functions. . . . But churches, in common with all other institutions, acquire a momentum that is repetitious and mechanical rather than personal and creatively variant. Religion comes to mean being loyal and obedient to the partial insight and the institutional creation of yesterday. Precedents, the product of a particular time, place, and state of mind, become controlling assumptions, as though they were the eternal truth, the will of God, or a finished creation."[5]

There is nothing novel about this conclusion, but the Institute's studies, in their total import, would seem to justify it.

## MANAGEABILITY OF INSTITUTIONALISM

Nevertheless, it is also a fair conclusion from these studies that, in the large, the desirable possibilities of institutionalism outweigh its evils; and that, inevitable as it is, it is subject to control.

Objective studies of the church have contributed much to the understanding of the possibility and technique of change. The scientific method, in turn, has been a discipline in fair-mindedness, helping one to see the fre-

---

[5] *What Is Christian Education?* (New York: Charles Scribner's Sons, 1929), pp. 240, 241.

quent need of change. Its consequent mood brings anything but joy to the standpatter; and its results almost inevitably constitute an apologetic for institutional plasticity.

The scientific viewpoint has also increasingly made possible a temperate account of specialization in religion; and of the necessity of dividing, concentrating and relating undifferentiated religious functions under some relatively stable scheme of organization; yet without delivering religion over to monopolistic implications at the hands of a specialized clergy nor to hard and fast forms in doctrine, rites and ethical practices. In brief, institutionalization with plasticity gives the maximum power to religious values.

As to the implementation of such a conclusion the further verdict of Professor Coe appears sound and significant:

". . . Nothing, in fact, could be more religious, than finding and putting into operation a method for the continuous self-criticism (which means self-testing and judging) of religion and of religious institutions."[6]

In no defense, then, of the existing churches beyond the strength of facts objectively discovered, and on express condition that radical self-criticism shall continuously be exercised, the result of long experience in objective studies may easily be that one comes to a renewed belief in the church; that is to say, in the institutionalized aspect of religion, a church whose naturalness and inevitability are accepted, whose dangers and paradoxes are recognized, and whose processes and results are critically evaluated and controlled.

### Practical Value of Studies of Institutionalized Religion

Having thus dealt faithfully with both emotional and rational objections to the theoretical basis of objective studies of the church, and having offered a positive apologetic for such studies, the way should be open to emphasize their secondary but very real practical values. Besides the fact that they are on the side of institutional plasticity and self-criticism, one quickly thinks of several obvious contributions of objective studies to the value of the church as an aspect of modern civilization.

(1) The period of the world's history during which these studies have been in process has served to emphasize the central importance as a social force of the phenomena with which they have been concerned. Russia, Italy, China, Germany in turn have found in organized religion the strongest challenge to their respective versions of a totalitarian state. The national and international implications of the organized church for politics were never more pronounced nor acute: all the more reason then for attempting to understand it.

(2) The church has obviously been a badly-conducted institution in many

---

[6] *Ibid.*, pp. 241, 242.

respects. Its duplicatory congregations and plants and much of the cost of its propagation have been socially wasteful. These factors, coupled with the sectarian division of community life by the churches, have often rendered it positively demoralizing. Nothing can be more shocking than such a situation as chapter vi reveals in which Christian ministers in the United States are compelled to serve superfluous churches on salaries that are below any decent standards of living and even below the present meager economic levels of the working classes. Anything that adds reason and expertness to the conduct of so chaotic an enterprise must be reckoned as of the highest social utility.

(3) The wobbly character and the failure of the church at so many points is a burden not merely to the purse but also to the faith of multitudes of poor and pious people. Unnecessary failure, the failure of unwise and futile organization saddled upon them by religious tradition or by the deliberate drive of denominational zeal, has proved in the long run a terribly undermining influence in religious morale. As chapter x shows, the cost per individual of churches of inferior quality is frequently actually greater than that of the best churches. This religious overcharge, at the expense of those least able to bear it, never can be brought to light so long as the church is allowed to shelter itself behind the skirts of ecclesiastical sanctity. Objective studies immediately reveal it for what it is, an atrocious scandal.

(4) One of the most useful services of objective studies of the church has been to reveal the vital possibilities of coöperation and unity among the sadly divided religious fragments politely generalized under the term, the American church. A tracing of progress made in this line and a demonstration of the possibilities of rapid farther progress stand among the most valuable discoveries of studies using the scientific approach to religion.

(5) Objective studies of the church show the infinite importance of good institutional techniques in the agency which after all creates the best opportunity that the inner values of religion have to take hold of the individual. The school can only expose the pupil to education; its high percentage of failure is proverbial; yet in no other way can he be so well and thoroughly exposed. Similarly the church can only expose the individual to religion; but it can do this; and objective studies of its institutionalized methods help to show how this may be done in the most effective way.

Finally, the scientific viewpoint on the whole strengthens the conviction that the inner and outer aspects of religion are but two sides of a single whole. Institutionalized religion really symbolizes and in a sense measures the energy of the inner meanings for which the religious viewpoint contends. Something beyond a consistently fair-minded attitude toward religion may thus easily eventuate from long attention to objective studies. At most they do not contradict a warmly sympathetic attitude toward religion. At best they may serve to confirm faith in the treasure of the spirit which lies within the earthen vessels of institutionalism and in those imponderable values which multitudes testify to, as more real to them than all objective facts.

# CHAPTER II

*History and Evolution of the Church in the United States*

The nearly fifty Institute studies upon which this volume is based, have involved the gathering of ample and authentic data concerning the history and evolution of many hundreds of churches of all denominations and in all parts of the United States. Some of the studies have gone back to the generation of the Pilgrim Fathers, while numerous others have traced the very beginnings of organized religion in the older Colonial areas and from zone to zone across the progressing West. Still others dealt elaborately with religious origins among the newer streams of immigration both in city and in country and in a great variety of economic environments, also with such special populations as Negroes, Southern highlanders and American Indians. Studies of another type have traced the history of denominations and of denominational organizations, as well as the course of coöperative movements and agencies. The whole body of historical data thus gathered constitutes an extraordinarily rich collection of source material.

The circumstance, however, that the data were gathered piecemeal in connection with so many different studies and from no single point of view, makes them difficult to generalize. Time has not permitted a fresh going over of the total material with a view to its unification. What one has is an extensive series of historical vistas which cannot immediately be combined into a broad survey.

The best that can be done in such premises probably is to borrow some of the most outstanding historical and sociological concepts which have characterized the studies in question and to apply them to the data as organized within a simple and obvious framework. This the present historical chapter does. It is backed by multitudinous facts, but does not pretend to be exclusively the result of generalization from freshly gathered data.

The history of the church in the United States exhibits two phenomena of the greatest significance. The first is that of cultural migration, expressed in the importation of organized religion from other countries and its transfer from zone to zone in connection with the peopling of the continent; the second, that of cultural variation under new opportunity and stimulus.

Churching has been an integral phase of the peopling of the United States. The various immigrant strains invariably brought distinctive cultures, including religious concepts and traditional forms of religious organization. Church origins in the United States were merely the conservative reaffirmation of these aspects of transplanted religious culture. Whatever more ultimate social and economic interpretation may be necessary to explain them, they were actually brought as mature cultural deposits, in which even the original theology had become a somewhat remote element. The extraordinary variety of religion in the United States merely reflects the multiplicity of the cultures developed by the stocks and varieties of the people who made up the nation.

At the same time the break-up of medieval solidarity, the evolution of nationalistic cultures, Protestantism, and individualism—that galaxy of forces which largely created the variety of human materials assembled in the new world—were all augmented and carried much farther in the American environment. The independence of the United States, its imperial expanse of virgin resources, and the corresponding release of new habits and energies, all meant opportunity and stimulus for further cultural variation in which organized religion measurably shared.

At the outset migratory religion was essentially conservative. Each group carried its church to its new home in order to preserve familiar values against the new and wild environment with its powerful pressure in favor of change. The Sunday school, for example, was the frontier's popular and essentially lay device to provide scattered communities with a minimum of religious privilege. Later immigrants have habitually used the church to help them to resist the corrosive influence upon their group habits of the tradition of the American majority.

On the other hand, frontier schisms and the rise of new religions have represented prophetic exceptions to the prevailingly conservative forces of religion. Change of location, social revolution, technical and material advance, have helped to make room for new religions, and have all favored at least moderate innovation such as permits something of new meaning to be read into old forms and keeps the church at least partially in tune with the evolution of the national spirit.

Secondary directive forces have been amply recognized in the gathering of historical data; but they take a distinctly minor place in the total picture. Official propagation and maintenance of churches by denominational missions and other ecclesiastical activities are, for example, ancillary rather than primary forces. Every people which has come to America has brought with it a habit and tradition of religious organization. The church as a whole is the assertion of these existing habits rather than a creation brought about by anyone's deliberate action.

From another viewpoint the church of the United States has been a vast experiment whose results have been controlled less by policy than by the operation of large social forces. For example, the churching of the nation has taken place according to the principle of profusion. Far more churches than can well be sustained have been organized. This has brought about acute competition between them; and the ultimate control of the situation rests in the hands of a selective mortality, by which the more superfluous and less efficient are dying off while the stronger and more useful survive.

Within the circle of these concepts, and as subject to and limited by such forces as have just been suggested, the evolution of the church in the United States is now to be reviewed. The division of the nation's story into historic periods or epochs adopts and follows familiar usage.

## The Colonial Period

The story of the nation begins familiarly with explorers dedicating newly discovered western lands to country and king. Kings, in turn, grant them to favorites, relatives, and business partners. A competitive capitalistic exploitation of America by the leading European nations ensues. Variant religious groups, drawn into close solidarity by persecution, furnish apt materials for the venture of colonization. Such groups, however, are a minority, the main feature of the story being the highly speculative and unstable mixture of the elements which undertook the New World adventure.

Capitalists hold out religious toleration as a bait to attract new settlers. The religious groups, however, establish themselves as cultural conservatives and immediately attempt to enforce their particular mores by law. Still more significant is the fact that commercial colonization as well immediately resorts to the enforcement of a tradition essentially identical with that held by the religious groups, as the balance wheel of life in the New World. Church and state come to be closely associated in the majority of the colonies and, between the two, later-coming religious variants are made decidedly uncomfortable if indeed they are not banished. Each in turn goes out to find freedom in colonizing its own wilderness. It happens, therefore, that to a large extent people of different faiths are settled in separate geographical areas, first on different latitudes and next on successive western frontiers.

Colonies composed of mixed religious elements experience successions of political crises as one element after another becomes temporarily ascendant.

In the long run an equilibrium is reached over most of the colonial area and some "established order" enters upon a long supremacy as a provincial faith. It is 150 years—half of the total life of the civilized man in the United States—before any second church arises in many New England communities. In Spanish and French colonies Catholicism similarly enjoys a long era of undisputed control. In brief, the civilization and cultural standards of the respective European nations from which colonies came, and especially those of the English stock, are successfully transplanted to western shores. They are maintained by social tradition, by active contact with the older world, and by cultural agencies such as the early founded colleges.

It is only gradually during the Colonial period that a considerable cultural distinction grows up between seaboard and frontier. The seaboard has acquired moderate wealth, has kept up world contacts by reason of its sea trade, has acquired an incipient urbanness and is ripe for conservative reaction as soon as contrary frontier tendencies begin to be clear-cut.

In 150 years, settlement has penetrated only as far as the western boundary of Massachusetts, or has just begun to trickle through the passes of the Southern Alleghenies. On the western fringe a ruder and more spontaneous manner of life is developing. This breaks forth religiously in passionate revivals which challenge the coldness and conventionality of existing religious custom and result in sectarian parties. Especially does it contend with the older cultural tradition with respect to an educated ministry. Convinced "that every brother that is qualified by God for the same has a right to preach according to the measure of faith and that knowledge of the tongues and liberal sciences are not necessary," sectarian preachers begin to invade the exclusive parishes of the established churches and thus establish exceptions which are later to become the rule in American religion.

In the final event, however, the Colonial period sees religious conservatism challenged by sectarian and individualistic tendencies rather than essentially changed. Up to the end of the period the church is closely identified with established social order and government. The thirteen colonies have acquired some 3,000 churches of twenty-eight denominations, eighteen imported and ten indigenous; but scarcely 5 per cent. of the population is in active church-membership. This circumstance lays upon all churches, both publicly supported and sectarian, the necessity of active propaganda to win support, and produces in them something of a common character which is later to prove itself the basic American church type.

### EARLIER NATIONAL PERIOD

The earlier decades of the nation's independent life are characterized by the second of the tendencies which have continuously presided over the destinies of the American church. It is preëminently the period of opportunity and incentive for religious innovation.

A profound social revolution is initiated by and follows the Revolutionary War, which breaks the inherited system of traditional rank and enfranchises the common man. The corresponding religious revolution overthrows the established order of the church and permanently fixes organized religion in the United States upon a voluntary basis.

Intensive studies of the peopling of local areas on the fringes of the older Colonial territory reveal the characteristic methods by which organized religion spreads. Thus when the establishment of churches ceases to be the business of local government in New England, responsibility falls to individual settlers. Pioneer leaders of the patriarchal type rally their scattered companions and set up the majority of churches in the new territory on their individual initiative. They speedily find leadership in the itinerant ministries of the multiplying sects and get some aid from missionary societies established in the older territories.

The results of belated efforts to maintain the exclusive sway of an old religious order when its day has passed, is seen in the case of a group of New Hampshire settlers who moved to the Vermont frontier late in the 18th century. Rehearsing that "different parties and sectaries in religion often prove very detrimental to the growth and well-being of societies," they agree as the basis of their venture, "that this proprietary will use every prudent and reasonable measure to discourage and hinder the introducing of such persons as settlers, etc. who may be likely to create parties and divisions in said town, and that so far as may be, we will adhere to what is commonly called the Congregational form of worship and church government in said township."[1] In spite of the high resolve of the founders the new town had five denominational churches by 1816.

Similar evidence of the growth of religious freedom appears both in northern cities and on southern plantations. The new impulse permits Negro slaves blessed with gifts of religious fervor and eloquence to win wide popular recognition, and frequently personal liberty as well as the right to preach the gospel.

Even more striking, however, than the breaking out and spread of new religious bodies and doctrines in the wake of the new freedom, is the rapid assimilation of the divided churches to a common type. Numerous communities erect union meeting houses, occupied more or less peaceably by four or five competing sects in rotation. Religious bodies like the Protestant Episcopal and Lutheran, which up to the present maintain positions somewhat distinct from those of the main body of Protestants, are swept into the common current and become more like the average than before or since.

On the other hand, the new nation has embarked with redoubled vigor upon the conquest of the continent. In connection with the greatly accelerated rate of settlement men of action press into the wilderness far in advance of the forces of culture. This schooling of the frontier for one hundred years fixes the most authentic characteristics of the young nation. If the revolution had broken the forms of the old order, the frontier transforms the

---

[1] Hooker, *Hinterlands of the Church* (New York: Institute of Social and Religious Research, 1931), p. 288.

spirit of the new, and brings about the final breach between America and the Old World.

The frontier furnishes the maximum opportunity and incentive for religious innovation. Under the doctrine of human equality, extreme individualism and emotionalism permit men under religious tension to regard their spiritual "hunches" as evidences of divine leadership and to take the initiative in organized religion, with complete abandon.

Behind the frontier a new balance of national forces is continuously forming. With the passing of a few decades the West comes into the saddle politically. Here develops the most authentic and characteristic type of American culture, one from which the rest of the United States has since taken its reputation.

Material development as well goes forward with unparalleled strides. Each economic advance is directly reflected in new crops of churches. One who follows the story by way of local history finds typical evidence in the all-but-certain appearance of sectarian preachers among the mongrel populations clustered about the water powers, where infant industries are springing up. Another crop of sectarians marks the appearance of the steamboat on the Hudson, the Ohio and the Mississippi. Finally, the railroad becomes the vehicle of the migration of types of religion which had lacked the genius for pioneering. It brings a third crop of religious institutions to supplement those which had come via the canoe and the steamboat. These water-power churches, steamboat churches and railroad churches all represent further religious variation, every significant advance in economic activity grouping peoples in new ways, and each calling forth a new type of religious organization.

The most prolific source of religious variation is, however, the unequal exposure of areas and elements of population to frontier experience, and the subsequent uneven cooling-off of the mood of religion after its frontier excesses. While the average spirit of the West goes far beyond the religious conventions of the older settled territories and leaves them ripe for conservative reaction, the characteristic West is unable to keep up with its own wilder spirits. Consequently all the major denominations experience extreme tensions in opposite directions, and most of them suffer two-way splits which divide into reactionary, radical and middle-of-the-road divisions.

Later immigration introduces a new crop of conservative religious groups from Europe. They find here semi-Americanized people of their own national stocks, who have moved beyond them, culturally speaking; consequently the latest-come can find no comfort even in the churches of their own tradition. At the same time the more advanced elements of these same stocks have abandoned their earlier traditions and have gone over to the more distinctive frontier types. This principle is repeatedly illustrated by populations of German antecedents, whose most recent immigrants remain unassimilated to the main group, while its younger element has deserted to Methodistic ways. Such unequal evolution of people of the same religious tradition still remains a prime cause of religious division.

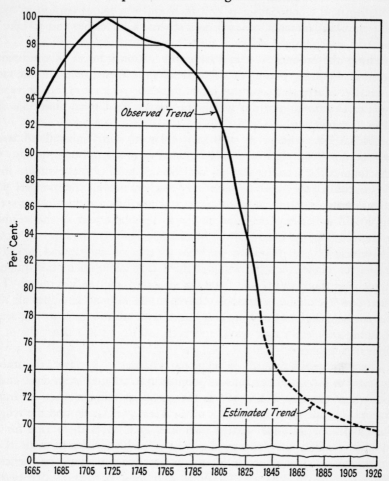

CHART I—PER CENT. OF COLLEGE GRADUATES AMONG CONGREGATIONAL MINISTERS IN NEW ENGLAND—BY DECADES 1665 TO 1835, AND IN 1926

The gradual abolition of slavery in the North similarly gives opportunity for the appearance of separate Negro churches, which mark the Negro's participation in the freer religious opportunity of the nation.

On the other hand, this, the period *par excellence* of sectarian separation, is not without its tendencies to increasing homogeneity. The separate churches are increasingly based upon the same assumptions and follow the same methods. Revivalism, which has been the mother of sects, is conventionalized as a method employed by all the churches and is increasingly used in union meetings. The early 19th century begins also to develop something of a national outlook in religion. This is expressed in more or less comprehensive surveys of the religious needs of the West on the part of interdenominational missionary societies representing the eastern churches, by interdenominational Sunday-school movements, and by the beginning of inter-church coöperation as exemplified in the not wholly satisfactory Congregational-Presbyterian plan of union.

By 1835 the young nation may have had 25,000 locally organized churches of some seventy-five denominations. Credible estimates make it probable that some 14 per cent. of the population was connected with them. It is at least certain that organized religion on the voluntary basis had significantly increased its hold upon the nation during the earlier period. The churches had taken on new vitality. At the same time their cultural level had strikingly declined, the educational quality of the ministry suffering a catastrophic slump between 1700 and 1835 from which it has never since completely recovered.[2]

### FARM AND VILLAGE CIVILIZATION

From the first crossing of the Alleghenies, a farm and village type of civilization has rapidly formed itself behind the advancing frontier. This becomes dominant by 1835 or 1840 and remains the typical version of American life up to 1890.

Sturdy individualism has possessed the continent and rewarded the masses with widely diffused land-ownership and increasing material comforts. Culturally conservative forces have won in the struggle with the frontier. The nation becomes a place of homes, schools and churches. Cultural tradition is fixed about these marks of the dominant American type.

As territorial expansion shakes itself free from the eastern forested belt and presses forward on the prairies and plains, it proceeds at an ever-increasing rate, speeded by improved communication and new tools for agricultural production. The older communities experience urban foreshadowing, in the beginnings of the factory system clustered about water power. Thus, after nearly 200 years of un-differentiated life, a New England city erects a second Congregational church "for the people of the armory village." New class distinctions grow up on the basis of the developing economic order, crossed by more subtle social differentiations than those which had formerly divided people of different racial stocks.

---

[2] May, *The Education of American Ministers* (New York: Institute of Social and Religious Research, 1934), Vol. II, p. 21.

On the whole, however, the trend of the period is strongly toward religious and cultural uniformity. Increasingly the divided churches make the same assumptions and use the same methods. The nation is rapidly developing the aspect of sameness which still strikes foreign observers as characteristic of American life.

Nevertheless the surviving frontier continues to bring forth sectarian divisions. The nation is too quickly tamed to suit its wilder spirits. Thus, the anti-missionary and anti-Sunday-school reaction of the earlier frontier becomes a permanent mark of churches upon poor land and in more isolated regions. The less favored rural communities continue the religious habits of an earlier day.

New types of immigration also bring a new variety of imported religions. German Protestants, now coming in great streams, transplant their distinctive Lutheran cultures on a large scale; but much of the mid-century immigration is Roman Catholic—Irish and German, and in New England, French Canadian. Fresh crops of churches follow in the wake of these population movements. Synagogues of German and Polish Jews begin to appear in the cities of the West. Protestant minorities from Catholic countries receive aid from American churches of the same families, and systematic missions for immigrants begin to be developed.

The unequal assimilation to the American type of older and newer immigrant streams from the same countries brings about a repetition of the three-way tensions experienced by the earlier religious groups. This is particularly illustrated within the Lutheran bodies, and results in numerous party divisions.

The sectional divergence of North and South, arising in conflicting economic interests and reaching crisis in the controversy over slavery, splits the major denominations into sectional churches. Increased opportunity, brought to the Negro masses by emancipation, coupled with pressure for racial segregation, opens the way for a rapid development of the great Negro churches, which still constitute the chief institutional achievement of the race.

The acute competition of western lands with the farms of the colonial area, together with new ease of communication, bring about a belated diffusion of religious types which had avoided pioneering. Denominational zeal and the development of home-missionary agencies systematize the expansion process. The sectarian church almost inevitably follows the migration of any distinct type of religion to any part of the country.

The rapid growth of major cities carries still farther forward premonitions of the urban age. Large quantities of new suburban churches appear, marking a new frontier as the end of the religious occupation of the continent begins to be seen.

By the end of the era, marked by the virtual exhaustion of free land open to homesteading by 1890, the United States has acquired some 165,000 churches of 143 denominations. These churches have 20,000,000 members, 14,000,000 of whom are classified as evangelical. This is 20 per cent. of the population. But the nation is decreasingly prepared to support these hordes of new churches at the economic and cultural level reached in the earlier settled areas, and there is a continually decreasing proportion of educated ministers.

## THE URBAN ERA

The period from 1890 onward bears obvious marks of an urban era. It is characterized by the rapid growth of the cities, which culminates in the transfer of the majority of the population to an urban type of immediate environment and makes urban initiative and prestige increasingly dominant. In typical cities more than half of the churches are relatively new, this giving literalness to the notion that the city constitutes the new frontier for religion. For example, more than half of the present churches in the city of Springfield, Mass., were organized in a single decade of urban expansion.

During the earlier years of the urban period, immigration reaches new magnitude and draws on new sources. The coming of races from southern and eastern Europe and from the borders of the Near East is signalized by new crops of churches, largely of Roman and Greek Catholic and Jewish faiths, and Polish, Russian and Roumanian in nationality. The new immigrants descend upon American cities in swarms and their colonies evict many of the older populations from their original seats. This eviction means the displacement and death of many of the older Protestant churches; and the repetition of the process with successive immigrant waves gives the churches' occupancy of cities the characteristics of a procession rather than of a permanent holding of territory. Other dislocations result from internal mobility and migration. Rural new-comers also throng the cities and find in the new situation opportunity for religious variation and the development of new sects. Rural Negroes follow in their wake.

With the increasing dependence of the cities upon rural migration for their growth, the unequal urbanization of denominations becomes important. The most rapidly growing are those that have the largest body of rural reinforcements to draw upon.

The time factor in religious adaptation also becomes newly important. Late-coming and but recently transplanted peasants naturally add to the reactionary pull of a church already culturally conservative. Freedom and originality in the adaptation of the church to the city is thus limited and slowed down. The church remains the most rural of the major social institutions of the United States. No such proportion of ministers is concentrated in cities as is true of all other professional classes. Growing urban-rural conflict in the economic realm adds to the tension between the conservative and progressive forces and, passing over into the realm of theology, marks one of the most definite points of religious division of the era.

At the same time specialized forms of urban church effort, especially those directed to the needs of foreign immigrants, have conspicuous development. Motivated by zeal for social welfare, but also in self-protection from the dangerous demoralization resulting when such immigrants make too violent a break with their own pasts, the older churches seek to Americanize the immigrant. When this effort involves also the proselyting of immigrants of Catholic antecedents its results are less satisfactory and raise new problems.

As the sway of urban culture over the nation increases, the tendency toward accommodation and integration in religion goes forward apace. In the main this does not reach the point of actual fusion of major religious bodies, though some scores of actual mergers of denominations occur. But a vast system of inter-church coöperative agencies develops and the integrative spirit greatly reduces the practice of schism.

There are at the present time fewer denominations per million population than at the beginning of the urban period, and dozens of additional mergers of churches are under discussion, if not in actual negotiation.

Contemporary religious developments are affected by the decidedly slowed urban growth of the last decade and the challenging of the dominance of the urban tendency by long-continued economic depression. The virtual cessation of foreign immigration has given Protestantism new advantage. The more recent rural migrants, both white and Negro, are largely Protestant. Like the Pilgrim Fathers, many Negro groups migrating to the North, bring their churches with them. Thus, a Greenwood, South Carolina, group establishes the Greenwood Baptist Church in Philadelphia, and later twenty members of the Morris Chapel Baptist Church of Greenwood organize the Morris Chapel Baptist Church in the same city. Another case is reported where twenty migrants from the rural districts of Louisiana, with their pastor, have transported their church intact from country to city.[3]

Churches of such humble groups, started on the lowliest levels of experience and economic resources, find difficulty in making headway among the highly-organized agencies of religion. It is, nevertheless, largely the religious initiative of humble people which accounts for the fact that the church exists somewhat equally on all social levels and is available to all types of communities.

---

[3] Mays and Nicholson, *The Negro's Church* (New York: Institute of Social and Religious Research, 1933), p. 35.

Matching the decreasing rate of population growth, has come a distinct decrease in the rate of establishment of new churches. The era of unlimited expansion is over and religious forces have greater leisure to consider adequacy and efficiency. Urban churches particularly evolve a considerable number of specialized types reflecting attempts at environmental and social adaptation. Under the pressure of a changing intellectual climate (associated particularly with the urban outlook) the church has developed some tendency to self-criticism, which the first chapter pointed out as the sole basis on which institutionalism can save itself from the paralyzing divergence between outward forms and inner meanings.

The remaking of the nation's economic order, which is under way at the moment of this writing, holds out certain prospects for decentralization and for a return of a larger proportion of the population to life in small communities and to the soil as a means of livelihood. It is at least possible that the next era will be less exclusively urban than the past. Nevertheless, the maturing of an urban pattern, which has gathered up the whole nation into a series of metropolitan provinces, makes it likely that America will continue to be organized about its cities and suggests the projection of present trends into the future rather than any different fundamental basis of expectancy.

Bringing the story of its history and evolution down to the date of the last Federal Census of Religious Bodies finds the United States with some 232,000 churches of 212 denominations. Fifty-five per cent. of the adult population is in church-membership, a proportion never reached before.

Whether in any sense these figures reflect a worthy extension of that supra-mundane society, which the church as a social phenomenon is presumed to reflect, still remains beyond the scope of any available evidence. This historical background, however, should add to the understanding of present institutional aspects and tendencies, and of the fortunes and prospects of the church in the United States which furnish the main theme of this book.

# PART TWO

# INSTITUTIONAL FACTORS AND PROCESSES

# CHAPTER III

## Members and Constituents

The discourse of churchmen with respect to the aims and prospects of the church invariably refers to an unspoken assumption, namely that the entire adult population of the United States ought to be enrolled in its churches, together with all children in the various ways and degrees in which the churches admit children.

From this quantitative standpoint the churches' remaining task is clear. It is to start where history has left off, namely, with 55 per cent. of the adult population in the churches, and to win the remaining 45 per cent.

Of course no branch of the church sets up a quantitative criterion in quite so crude a fashion or makes it the exclusive measure of the church's task. Indeed, as chapter I has shown, popular religious attitudes distinguish with fearful jealousy between the institution and the values it is assumed to mirror; to the extent even of exaggerated talk, as though the church had very little to do with religion. One who cited statistics of growth of church-membership would consequently very likely feel called upon to deny that these were any true measure of religious progress.

Ecclesiastics are nevertheless very sensitive to membership gains and losses, while the common man unhesitatingly judges the church in large measure by its institutional size.

The approach of objective studies of the church takes an essentially simple-minded attitude. Convinced that all mature versions of religion must inevitably find institutional form, it accepts factual indices of ecclesiastical growth as recorded by history, and factual evidences of the church's contemporary strength, as valid testimony to the substantial and increasing place of religious tradition and organization in the national life.

The scientific viewpoint is, however, in little danger of regarding size alone as the final or only criterion. It is not deeply impressed by size, and is thoroughly accustomed to taking a critical attitude toward vast enterprises, like business, the school, the courts, and indeed government itself, in order to appraise the actual vigor of the social forces behind a traditional institution.

The scientific viewpoint, at the same time, is accustomed to the use of refined techniques for the measurement of specific progress on the part of such cultural agencies as literature, schools, and churches.

None the less it does accept dependable statistics as a reasonable measure of institutional strength. It is not above thinking that, under a voluntary system of human association, the tests of the survival of an institution, of numerical growth, of gains in participation on the part of both leaders and the rank and file, of financial support, and of public recognition, constitute a battery of valid criteria for judging institutional health and power.

What the scientific viewpoint complains of is not the mundane classifications employed by statistics but that statistics exist on so few points. Thus the only items relating to religious adherence which appear in the United States Census of Religious Bodies are those concerning membership, Sunday-school enrollment, and church finances. In order, therefore, to reach anything like a comprehensive and realistic picture of the church's members and constituencies one must approach the matter by way of local church studies which have investigated a wider range of relationships. This approach is chosen in the present chapter.

## VARIETIES OF ADHERENCE

The typical church is expected to maintain a local roll of members. The turned-over corner of a card may distinguish the active from the inactive, and a blue pencil mark the resident from the non-resident. Someone in the church will have a list of Sunday-school pupils and this list may or may not show which of them are church-members. Various membership lists of subsidiary organizations, societies and clubs will be found in the hands of their respective officers, but are seldom assembled as one list. The financial authorities of the church will have their subscription list and roll of other supporters. The regularity of attendance of individuals will rarely be recorded, and there will be little agreement as to what constitutes regularity.

### DETERMINATE VERSUS INDETERMINATE ADHERENTS

All the lists thus far catalogued are those of determinate adherents, that is to say, of persons whose relationship to the church is specifically defined as belonging to this or that organization or activity.

All these lists are subject to periodic revision. They identify, first of all, certain shifting groups which together constitute the nucleus of the church. Well-organized churches maintain additional lists of marginal adherents. Or, if not, the equivalent is "carried in the head" of the pastor or deacon. Some denominations count baptized children as church-members, and all recognize younger minors as in some sense included in the religious connections of their parents. Churches that emphasize the rite of confirmation try to exercise recognized responsibility for all confirmed persons in their parishes, whether or not these persons maintain any active connection. Others identify an ill-defined group of "persons under pastoral care." As church programs develop, sponsored groups appear, as, for example, Boy Scouts or various clubs which are in the church rather than of it. Still another type of adherence is represented by the church's clients and dependents, persons to whom it more or less statedly brings charitable or other assistance, but with whom it may have no other tie.

Toward all these more indeterminate adherents who are not now by their personal behavior in active connection with the church, together with adults belonging to the families of active members, the church extends at least a diluted sense of responsibility and offers a range of service which is more or less clearly responded to by the persons concerned.[1]

REMOTER CONSTITUENCIES

Beyond the furthermost boundaries of the church's records lie multitudes of persons unknown to any church but nevertheless cherishing their own private sense of religious adherence. However little the church may value nebulous ties, which are subjectively recognized but not acted upon, it is of the highest importance for the understanding of modern societies to know that virtually everybody in the United States or Canada professes attachment to some religious faith and classifies himself accordingly. The Canadian government asks this question as a matter of course in its regular census, and only about one-half of 1 per cent. of all Canadians are unable or unwilling to answer. In American cities also, whenever individuals have been interrogated by the tens of thousands, as they have been in house-to-house canvasses, scarcely anyone is to be found unwilling to declare himself a Protestant, a Catholic, a Jew or a member of some other historic creed.

Surveys show that remote adherence is quite as characteristic of persons of Roman Catholic and Jewish antecedents as of Protestants, though the proportions for each faith are not known with any exactness. The following statement from a representative Roman Catholic source suggests the more or less typical situation:

"Perhaps the most surprising thing about our whole census undertaking was the extraordinary number of hidden and unsuspected Catholics that it revealed. We have taken up a census repeatedly in this parish and we make a very energetic effort to keep in touch with all our parishioners not only by personal contact but by mail; and yet in spite of everything, out of the 2,055 persons enumerated in our census, 910 of them were absolutely unknown to us even by name. They had never either directly or indirectly come within the notice of either my curate or myself. They had never identified themselves with any of the parish activities; they had never contributed to the collection. They were, so far as we were concerned, not yet born. That means that forty-four per cent. (44%) of our parishioners were utterly unknown to us, in spite of every reasonable and

[1] See p. 46.

energetic effort made by myself and my assistant to keep in touch with every one in the parish."[2]

REMOTE ATTACHMENT TO DENOMINATIONS

Furthermore, nearly all Protestants identify themselves as having an inner attachment or preference for some particular sect or denomination. In the extensive Springfield, Mass., survey, for example, only one-tenth of the Protestants did not know what particular denomination they preferred. In other words, the consciousness not only of attachment to a particular faith, but of a recognition of particular sectarian antecedents, is nearly universal.

For the United States in general, no figures exist to show how wide is the margin between the total number of persons listed by all the churches put together (either as determinate or as indeterminate adherents) and the total population which classifies itself according to faith and sect. While, however, the United Church of Canada reports some 1,600,000 persons under pastoral care, more than 2,000,000 report themselves as adherents to that church—a fifth more than the church knows about. Typical city surveys in the United States would place this ultra-marginal group at around 25 per cent. In Canada, three times as many persons on the average report themselves to be church adherents as the churches record as full communicant members. Such a ratio applied to the Protestants in the United States would identify virtually the entire population as in some sense adherent to some religious group.

SIGNIFICANCE OF VARYING TYPES OF ADHERENCE

All these diverse religious groupings are ways of being related to the church, and each has its own significance. Regarding the church religiously as in some sense an organ of salvation, one may puzzle as to just which one establishes the crucial saving relationship to God. To this question no decisive answer is objectively possible. From an objective standpoint, however, and as viewed by the student of society, it is obvious that, in a realistic sense, all the relationships taken together make up the actual church.

Just what significance each of these ways of adhering has, how they are related to one another, and in what sense they may combine into a single picture of nearer or remoter attachment to a religious institution one has to discover by painstaking exploration. Do they find their unity in a time sequence—in the sense that the individual's typical course is to come first in a remoter church relationship and then be brought into closer and closer ones? Does the body of indeterminate adherents constitute a reservoir from which determinate adherents, so to speak, are ladled out? Does one go

---

[2] *Revelations of a Recent Parish Census:* Reprinted, with permission, from *The Ecclesiastical Review*, March, April, July, 1930, Philadelphia, Pa., p. 5.

from the Sunday school into the church and progress from occasional attendance into regularity? Or is it rather to be conceived, as a normal expression of the Christianizing of the nation, that there should be a closely knit religious nucleus reaching out in the service of less and less closely related strata of society with an influence which permeates the whole but which is not normally to be expected to gather up the whole into an equal intensity of relationship and participation?

It is the first object of this chapter to throw the light of specific and objective studies of churches upon such generalized problems relating to church constituencies, and secondly, to show the significance of such large factors bearing upon adherence as those of age, sex, denomination, state and region.

The chapter undertakes also to show certain results of changes in time as they relate to church-membership and constituents. These are measured chiefly as losses and gains in church-membership and Sunday-school enrollment as reported for denominations and geographical areas within the nation.

While all degrees of adherence discovered in the above analysis are found in churches of all sizes and conditions, the fact that objective studies have generally been made separately for rural and urban churches, together with the fact that the smaller average size of the rural community tends to press constituents into a smaller number of molds, makes the urban and rural versions of the same story somewhat different. The chapter, accordingly, divides at this point and proceeds to consider church-members and constituencies first from the rural and then from the urban standpoint.

## RURAL MEMBERS AND CONSTITUENTS

It has been commonly believed that rural America is the stronghold of organized religion; that there is something in the quality of agriculture and its related industries and services that impels allegiance to religion on the part of those who are so engaged. Possibly this belief arose because in the early period of our national life America was nearly all rural. Possibly it is due to the fact that so large a proportion of the ministers of the church are of rural origin. Again this belief may be rooted in the fact that the rapid growth of the cities during the later 19th century and the early part of the 20th afforded a new frontier for the restless and pioneering. On this new frontier of urbanization the rural mores were altered and in some cases destroyed by the mingling of population from many localities and especially by the horde of immigrants with variant traditions and cultures, to the dismay of those who, from the relative isolation of the countryside, watched with misgiving the amazing rise of the metropolitan communities of America. The country has always viewed the city with suspicion. The conflict between the two is as old as the battle between Hamilton and Jefferson and as new as the clash between the results of the Agricultural Adjustment and the National Recovery Acts. Since, then, America was once predominantly rural, and Protestantism especially was so even longer, there may have grown up the strong feeling that the city and its life were inimical to the church.

TOWNS AND CITIES MORE RELIGIOUS THAN THE OPEN COUNTRY

The facts, however, do not sustain this well-rooted belief, at least so far as the present and immediate past are concerned. The most recent census of religious bodies in the United States, taken by the federal government in 1926, shows that 59 per cent. of the population in cities of 25,000 inhabitants or more were reported by the churches as members, whereas in places of less than 25,000, including all the rural territory, the percentage was 53. Chart II tells the story in still greater detail. It may be objected that these figures are weighted by the far larger proportion of Roman Catholics and Jews who live in urban territory as compared with rural. However, in ten of the fifteen southern states, which are the great stronghold of Protestantism, the same situation is found. It is well within the facts to state that, nationally considered, the Protestant city church is somewhat more successful than the small city or rural church when judged by the proportion of the adult population it enlists.[3]

Again, as between the churches of the towns and cities of from 2,500 to 25,000 population and those of the strictly rural areas, it is the former that are more successful in gaining adults. For the 1,500 entirely rural counties of the United States find only about 44 per cent. of their adult population in the church-membership. While the proportions vary by census regions, the trend is everywhere the same, even where, as in the South, Catholic and Jewish open-country populations are almost entirely non-existent. The importance of this fact for the future of institutionalized religion in the United States is great. For even in 1930, before the huge depression-stimulated urban-rural migration had gotten well under way, more than half the children of the nation under sixteen years of age were in rural areas, and in these areas also, depending on the region, the birth-rate among the agricultural population was from 60 to 125 per cent. higher than in the cities. The American church, and especially Protestantism, cannot with safety neglect the task of so strengthening and improving the rural church that it will become at least as efficient as the urban in its appeal to the

---

[3] When it is remembered that one-seventh of the members of rural churches are non-resident, and that house-to-house surveys have shown most of these to be urban residents, it is clear that the above statement is very conservative indeed.

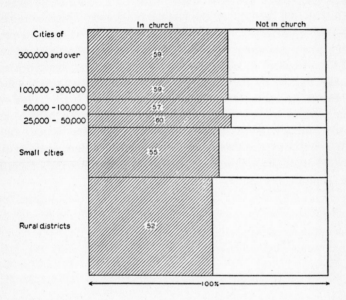

ADULT POPULATION IN CHURCH
IN PLACES OF VARYING SIZE
1926

Note  Width of bars proportional to
adult population in each group

CHART II

population.  By far the greatest amount of our population increase in the United States is now rural.

Since this is so, it is important to interpret further the hold of the rural church upon the rural population in terms of the factors that seem to influence it, such as region, type of community and of population.

### REGIONAL VARIATIONS IN THE CHURCH'S STRENGTH

The variations in the fortunes of the rural church according to the chief regions of the United States will be discussed in another chapter; but they cannot be overlooked here.  Thus, in the Mountain States, excluding Mormon areas, none shows so many as two-fifths of the adult population living outside cities of less than 25,000 population to be church-members, whereas in the seven West North-central states only one state reports less than 49 per cent. so enrolled; and half the South Atlantic states have from about two-thirds to three-fourths of their rural-small-city adult population aligned with the church.  In the main the rural church receives greatest allegiance in the states south of the Mason-Dixon line and the Ohio River and east of the Mississippi River.  It has least hold in the Pacific and Rocky Mountain states.  The problem, then, is easy to locate.  The facts have long been known, but thus far such church efforts as have been made to change the situation have made little net progress, especially in the strictly rural areas.

### RURAL CHURCHES LOSING GROUND

Indeed it seems all too likely that the church in rural America is losing rather than gaining ground.  In a large sample of village communities located in agricultural surroundings from every section of the United States, in which only one-twentieth of the churches were non-Protestant, the ratio of church-membership to population dropped from 35.3 per cent. to 32.9 per cent. between 1924 and 1930, or almost two and a half per cent.  This decline was shared in by all sections.  Indeed the South lost relatively almost as much as the Far West.  In another independent national sample, not of communities but of whole counties, the proportion of Protestant church-members to the total population fell from one-fifth to one-eighth between 1920 and 1930.

This trend seems to be comparable to that in the cities of over 25,000 population in which, as noted elsewhere,[4] the proportion of the adult population in church declined from practically 61 to 59 per cent. between the 1916 and 1926 censuses of religious bodies, whereas the places of less than 25,000 showed a slight gain.  Towns and small cities have been less studied than any other types of communities, but their populations appear to be relatively the most loyal to institutionalized religion.  In them and within

[4] P. 53.

the municipal boundaries of villages in farming areas—excluding their immediate rural hinterlands—it is the exceptional person who is outside the church. In villages, two-thirds of the adults are to be so classified. Towns and small cities do as well or better. The open country and larger city are the areas of relative deficiency and loss.

Here, then, is the second conclusion of importance. Not only does the hold of the church vary as among the major areas of the nation, but it is also far stronger in the villages and towns than it is in the open country or hamlets. Put in another way, the villages and towns, especially in the agricultural areas, are proportionately almost twice as well evangelized as is the farming population. In such places the relative isolation of the farm is overcome. In them the church begins to insist on a resident minister, as over against the itinerant who usually serves the open country. Here, too, rural mores are enforced by daily intimate contact. Public opinion is nowhere more formidable. It is strengthened in its conservative tendencies by the always disproportionately large number of elderly people in this population, in some areas relatively almost twice as many as in the cities. The 20,000,000 people living in the villages, towns and small cities of the United States are unquestionably more loyal to the church and to Protestantism than any other population groups.

### CHURCH FORTUNES IN VARYING TYPES OF RURAL COMMUNITIES

But just as it has been important to separate rural people into those living in villages and those in the open country, it is also important to realize that there are several sub-types within these two categories. Nearly one-fourth of our villages, for instance, are industrial, and in them live about 4,000,000 people. In such communities the church as a whole is but little more than two-thirds as successful as in agricultural villages. Protestantism makes a distinctly poorer record here than does Roman Catholicism, largely because Protestantism has never worked out a technique to meet the difficult problems involved in serving and supervising churches in communities that are rural only in size but that resemble in no way, save their industrial base, the huge communities of industrial workers in cities.

A second sort of rural community, in which the record of the church in enrolling members is below its general average for rural America, is that populated by people of foreign birth and foreign stock. The problem of these people is best met by denominations which, like themselves, have been transplanted. The Lutheran and Reformed churches do very well here, but the bodies of English tradition in most cases fail. The former enroll proportionately only one-eighth less of the foreign-stock population than do the general run of churches in our rural counties, but where the latter are involved they do only one-fourth as well, enrolling about 10 per cent. as against the rural average of 42 per cent.

AGE AND SEX DIFFERENCES

A final question must be considered, namely, whether the rural church appeals equally to both sexes and to the various age groups. Does it reach men as well as women, young people as well as old? Nationally 48.2 per cent. of the adult males, and 62.9 per cent. of the adult females were reported as church-members in the 1926 census. Put in another way, 55.5 per cent. of the church-membership was female, 44.5 per cent. male.

In the rural churches, as a whole, the figures show that 42.0 per cent. of the Protestant village membership is male and 58.0 per cent. female. In the country churches the comparable proportions were 44.7 and 55.3. The country churches, therefore, approximate the national average. On the other hand, the open country has a higher proportion of males in the total population than has the nation as a whole, and a considerably higher proportion than the villages. Actually, therefore, it is clear that the open-country churches are less successful than either urban or village and town churches in enlisting men in their membership. On the other hand, the proportion of men who were church-members, in all rural churches combined, rose from 40 to 42 per cent. between 1924 and 1930. The young people, too, showed no less likelihood of uniting with the church than did older persons. Apart, then, from a relative lack of success with men, the rural church seems not to fail especially with any given age or sex group.

REMOTER ADHERENTS

Membership lists, as noted in the introduction to this chapter, do not tell the whole story. Churches have followers or constituents who never formally unite with them as members of the organization. This is seen frequently in new communities where a popular minister or program will attract an average attendance of more than the church's entire membership. House-to-house religious censuses in rural communities almost invariably find more people who claim to be church-members than the churches themselves claim. In part this is because the allegiance of people is to a denomination, not necessarily to the particular church in the locality where they live. There have not been enough such house-to-house surveys to estimate the numbers and influence of these constituents. They are found more frequently in the Far West than elsewhere, and may equal from 3 to 4 per cent. of the total constituents.

But while membership lists fail to include some who are supporters of rural churches, they, on the other hand, include others who are far from active. Some of these have left the community entirely but keep their membership in the home church. Most of these live in the cities. The proportion of these non-resident members seems to be slowly increasing and amounts now to about one-seventh of the total membership of rural churches, with almost no difference between open-country and village churches.

### INACTIVE AND NON-RESIDENT

Then there are persons, in considerable numbers, who have joined rural churches but who have ceased to attend them or to contribute, even though still living in the community, and while their names are still carried on the church books. In this class there has also been an increase since 1920. Pastors describe almost one-fifth of rural church-members as inactive in this sense. In the South this proportion slightly exceeds 30 per cent. These two corrections to membership rolls mean that, outside the South, only about three-fourths of those whose names appear are at once resident, attending and contributing. In the South the comparable proportion is less than three-fifths.

The non-resident-member-ratio is a measure, not only of migration and mobility of population, but largely also of the rural church's contribution to urban population, and thus potentially to the strength of the city church. The inactive member, on the contrary, whatever the reason, is, in a sense, a measure of the church's failure locally. This failure is larger, of course, than the mere number of inactives still hopefully held on the books since it includes others formerly inactive but subsequently dropped in some "purging of the roll."

### MEMBERSHIP GAINS AND LOSSES

Thus far the discussion has concerned membership and members. The fortunes of churches as such have not been considered. But churches gain and lose ground, die and are born. More than one-half of the village churches, and more than two-fifths of the surviving open-country churches showed gains in membership between 1920 and 1930, apparently a somewhat higher proportion than between 1910 and 1920. Conversely, the proportion losing dropped from almost one-half to two-fifths.

It is rather interesting, and perhaps indicative of the conservative character of the rural church as an institution, that while church-membership rose and fell as population did, the tempo of membership change as a rule lagged markedly behind that of population, whether population was increasing or declining. Apparently new-comers to a community take a considerable time to be acclimated or perhaps welcomed religiously. Possibly also membership in a church is a tie, along with others of a social or economic nature, that makes church-members hesitant to leave a community that is only slowly losing ground. The only exception to this generalization was found in industrial villages of the mining type. Here when hard times came, church-members were the first to leave to look for work elsewhere.

It seems necessary to conclude that, for the average surviving rural churches at least, the causes of membership growth and decline are partly fortuitous. That is to say, a program or preacher who appeals to the community will attract new members and revitalize a goodly share of the inactive. Under a minimum program of itinerant preaching and little else, with an unattractive program or unpopular minister, the church lags no matter how favorable the community situation. The community situation is always an important factor, as will be shown in the next chapter, but it is often a contributive rather than a determinative influence in explaining the fortunes of a rural church.

## URBAN MEMBERS AND CONSTITUENTS

Engulfed as it is in masses of anonymous and ever-shifting populations and dazed by rapid change which turns recruiting into a desperate attempt to fill up a bottomless bucket, the individual urban church—relatively a petty institution—will scarcely credit the statistics which show that city churches, collectively speaking, are succeeding better than rural ones. How can this be true when the city church's control of the urban situation is so pitiably slight?

### THE URBAN NON-ADHERENT

Some answer to this bafflement is found in objective studies of the non-adherent Protestant element in cities. Virtually everyone brings a faith to the city when he comes, as a dip into history has already shown. With each wave of migration, the more aggressively religious elements establish churches of their own, often, to be sure, on a cultural level inferior to that of existing ones. It is in this way that cities are churched.

The less energetic elements, religiously speaking, find themselves stranded with the recession of every population wave. Yet such stranded elements do not constitute merely a hopeless and chaotic mass. Wherever they are more numerous than usual one discovers that they are new-comers to the community, either relatively or absolutely. Give them time and they will tell a better story—largely on their own initiative.

For, at any given time, nearly all new-comers to the city are under serious handicaps compared with the established populations. Some, to be sure, are sound, well-equipped and resourceful people who have merely not yet had time to place themselves religiously.

Other non-adherents consist of essentially transient groups, or people with corresponding mental attitudes. Thus, in a virtually complete survey of a suburb of 14,000 people, about one-third of the Protestant unchurched was found to consist of school teachers, domestic servants, and industrial workers living in boarding-houses. Without deep roots in the community, such groups are hard to combine with normal family constituents of the average residential church.

With still larger numbers of non-adherents in cities relative newness goes with demonstrable handicaps. They are the poorer and economically less secure peoples, and are less adjusted to the community all along the line. Being out of church simply reflects the fact that they are out of power and influence, and frequently also out of luck. Territorial religious surveys quickly identify the major components of these populations. An important element consists of rural migrants from poor land. Where such elements colonize in cities the number of Protestant unchurched mounts up. The same thing is true of recent Negro migrants from the country.

Among certain immigrant groups, newness, however, is only a relative factor in accounting for the disproportionate numbers of unchurched Protestants. In their case the break with the church comes with the first generation of Americans born of foreign parentage. Especially where the churches of such populations turn reactionary, clinging to the language and traditions of the past while their young people are rapidly assimilating to the national type, many persons will be found who hold religion as a memory but have deserted it as an active fellowship.

This principle works out all the more drastically where the Protestant group is a minority. Under such a condition a high proportion of non-adherent Protestants will be found scattered among the Roman Catholic or other preponderant populations. Such a condition naturally goes also with weak Protestant churches. To say that where Protestant churches are weak, there unchurched Protestants are many, whereas strong and prosperous churches tend to absorb a much higher proportion of persons of Protestant antecedents, is simply another way of describing a situation common alike to urban and rural territory.

Minor factors are also worthy of mention. "Irregular" churches, that is to say, those differing in some particular from the tradition of the well-established denominations, tend to gather loosely adherent groups about them. People will attend but will not enter into any stated relationship with such churches, perhaps because they sense the fact that they are a "little queer." Denominationalism, too, still tends to play a part. An area without a representative variety of churches is apt to have a disproportionate number of unchurched Protestants.

Yet not all of these factors put together account fully for the body of non-adherent Protestants. They simply tend to explain cases where the non-adherence reaches more than average proportions. The suburban survey already alluded to found that two-thirds of the unchurched differed strikingly in no particular from the churched population, except that the individuals composing the group were somewhat older in years and on the whole poorer. The immediate common-sense supposition is that the group's lack of small children may explain their failure to keep in touch with the church, while the financial burden of membership may also be a factor.

In the case of the survey just cited, virtually the entire body of Protestant ministers was assembled and confronted with the list of the Protestant unchurched of the community. Together they examined a random sampling, involving several hundred families. In many cases ministers said that they had always understood that the family in question belonged to some other church and had not felt at liberty to approach it for fear of being charged with proselyting. A limited house-to-house canvass confirmed the reputation of many such persons: their neighbors credited them with having some definite religious leanings or shadowy affiliations with some particular church. They were nevertheless outside of the most generous version of the church's own adherent lists.

There is, then, no clear-cut line of division between evangelized and unevangelized populations. Furthermore, such objective discoveries lead one to question whether any considerable proportion of the unchurched are as "gospel hardened" or as completely lapsed from the faith as the churches frequently imagine; and, except as the younger and more progressive elements of certain groups are in deliberate and conscious conflict with the reactionary morality of their fathers, no considerable element could with any justice be considered as abandoned or "living in sin."

On the contrary, such a diagnosis of the situation quite naturally explains why, in response to house-to-house canvasses, many of the unchurched multitudes should report themselves as still cherishing an attachment to some particular church or denomination. There seems no real reason why they should not keep on thinking of themselves thus since their neighbors think of them in the same way. They have the public reputation of maintaining a certain ill-defined attachment to religion and are not necessarily deceived in "cherishing a Christian hope."

An additional feature of the situation, made crucial by certain denominations, is that multitudes of such persons return to the church in the important crises of life and look to the church in the last extremity. Birth, marriage and death return them to its sacraments. Under urban conditions churches which maintain open offices for consultation, or programs offering varied forms of social service, will be sought out by many of these unchurched as casual or intermittent clients. Such occasional attachments need not be wholly without positive significance even when, from the church's standpoint they seem remote, selfish, parasitic and one-sided.

Protestantism ought to be in position to deal with these phenomena of non-adherent attachments in a frank and illuminating way. They show that the church has values for wide constituencies which lack intimate and permanent ties with it. For all of them the institution actually functions in some measure. Without being deceived, then, as to the trivial spiritual significance of some of these ties, one need not despise the least of them. From the sociological standpoint, at least, this series of increasing and decreasing attachments is an essential feature of the church's place in society.

DETERMINATE ADHERENCE

This judgment is confirmed by the discovery that the actual relationship of the average determinate adherent to his church is very slight. An urban church which offers a person of a given age or sex from six to a dozen

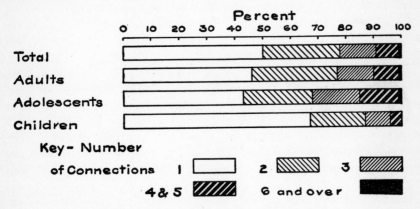

CHART III—ADHERENCE TO CITY CHURCHES: PER CENT. OF DETERMINATE ADHERENTS
WHO "BELONG" IN SPECIFIED NUMBERS OF WAYS, BY AGE GROUPS

possible ways of being connected with it—church-membership, Sunday-school enrollment, regularity of attendance, pledged financial support, membership in this and that subsidiary organization—still finds that a round half of its members belong to it in only one of these capacities and that their participation is irregular. About one-fourth have two connections, and less than one-fourth more than two. This is shown in Chart III which shows the relationships to the church of 22,149 determinate adherents. Children form the largest proportion of one-connection adherents; adolescents lead in cases of from three to five connections with the church.

On a large sampling involving 46,726 determinate adherents of twenty-six large city churches only 57 per cent. of this total was represented by full church-membership. Some of the subsidiary organizations, indeed, may be little more than the extraneous grouping of essentially non-adherent persons. Their relationship to the church is so remote and tenuous as hardly to count at all religiously, unless some magic is ascribed to the particular act of belonging to any sort of church organization.

Turning from the individual to the church, one discovers how enormously churches differ in the degree to which they are able to integrate their various groups of determinate adherents into anything like closeness of inner

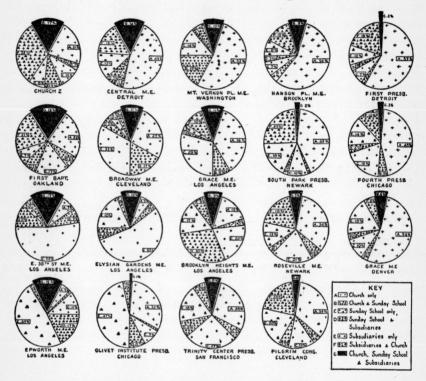

CHART IV—COMPOSITION OF CONSTITUENCIES OF NINETEEN CITY CHURCHES

relationship. Chart IV shows that in nineteen city churches the vast majority of adherents belonged to the church alone, to the Sunday school alone or to subsidiary organizations alone. The various overlappings indicating dual and triple adherence are usually represented by narrow sectors. The black area in each diagram shows the fluctuating but generally small per cent. of adherents belonging at once to church, Sunday school and subsidiary organizations.

All of these nineteen institutions of organized religion are called churches. Some of them are mainly churches. Others are mainly Sunday schools rather than churches; while in extreme cases almost half of the total adherence is through membership in subsidiaries, most of which are not religious agencies at all in the more narrowly conventional sense. Defined, then, according to the ways in which constituents are combined into a group, these organizations that go by the name of church actually reflect all sorts of different balancings of component elements, and are alike mainly in this, that the connection of the average individual adherent is a slight one.

Comprehensive figures covering the attendance of individual constituents on all occasions of public congregations and meetings of minor church groups have never been kept over a period of years by any representative group of urban churches. Totals have been compiled, but no reliable data exist to tell how frequently the individual adherent goes to church for any given purpose. Scattered data from surveys yield fragmentary results which give fragmentary insights into the situation. Thus, for the churches of a well-ordered suburban community, weekly attendance on all church gatherings equaled 80 per cent. of the combined church constituency. If every attending constituent had gone to church but once 20 per cent. would not have gone at all. The combined Sunday morning audiences of twenty-five Springfield, Mass., churches equaled one-half of the full membership; evening audiences about one-fourth. But audiences are composed very largely of irregular attendants. No generally accepted definition of regular attendance exists; but six large city churches, aggregating constituencies of 11,500 persons, claimed only 21 per cent. even of their full members as regular attendants at services. In the case of 1,400 Congregational churches, which kept records over a seven-year period ending in 1934, the figure was 21 per cent.

In twenty-eight large city churches aggregating 40,000 adherents, 42 per cent. of the total were pledged financial supporters. In other words, considerably less than half of those enrolled as having some sort of determinate attachment to the church belong to it in the two highly crucial aspects of regular attendance and financial support. Incidentally, these two factors are more closely correlated than any other aspects of adherence. The way to get a person to support the church is to make him a regular attendant. The way to make him a regular attendant is to commit him to pledged support.

Not more than from 5 to 7 per cent. of the adherents of the rather highly organized churches in question have five or more determinate attachments to them. These much-connected people include some of the church's responsible "pillars," but are more apt to be composed of religious hangers-on—persons deficient in other human relationships who find the church the easiest sphere for the expression of their personalities.

COMPLICATING CHARACTERISTICS

Of other characteristics which complicate the relationships of members and constituents to their churches the factors of age and sex have already emerged. The federal religious census has shown that relatively more men are found in the membership of city churches than of rural. Typical city surveys have shown that the proportion of men is rising. The balance of the sexes is very exact in churches which treat all baptized persons as members or otherwise bind the individual closely to the church of his fathers. It is most unequal in denominations which stress individual conversion and a personal profession of religion as the condition of membership. Women come into the church on these more personalized terms more frequently than men do.

Individual city churches often suffer from feminization. The more feminized find themselves progressively unable to make a normal appeal to men.

Except for scant data gathered in surveys, no records exist as to the age distribution of church adherents. Individual churches differ greatly on this point. Obviously a religious enterprise which consists mainly of church services is an adult enterprise. One which is mainly a Sunday school is ordinarily a child's enterprise. A few churches, often by the development of subsidiary organizations, manage to win a disproportionate number of adolescents. Still other churches are characterized by an exceptionally large percentage of young adults.

Taking the age distribution of the total population as an assumed norm, the church ought to consist of a cross-section of the population, all age and sex groups being proportionately represented. The consequences of serious unbalance in any direction are crucial. The church with too many adults has no future. The church with too many children finds it difficult to get enough support to supply its children with progressive educational facilities. A church which specializes in young adults may have great promise for the future, but, at the same time, lack present prestige and influence.

The study in a following chapter of the community roots of the church will show that the explanation for one-sided constituencies in terms of age and sex is sometimes to be found in the uneven texture of the community. Naturally where population itself departs from the normal, as in cases where unmarried men or unmarried women are concentrated in the boarding- and rooming-house sections of cities, a church which faithfully cultivates its immediate community may find itself taking over a correspondingly disproportionate distribution into its own constituency.

The factor of family status has just been alluded to. This constitutes another point on which urban churches show extreme variation. The rural or village church is essentially a group of families bound together as a fellowshiping and worshiping congregation. City populations include multitudes of unmarried and detached individuals, living outside of family relationships. When large numbers of these types get into the churches, a very different social combination ensues. Many city churches also develop second and third constituencies. The original one consists essentially of a group of families, the second of detached individuals of working age, the third of children of the neighborhood whose families are not otherwise connected with the church. In all these ways the actual composition of the constituent body of the urban church may find itself departing in an extraordinary degree from the normal distribution of population as to age, sex or family status.

Another factor in which the constituencies of urban churches differ strikingly is that of early antecedents. This has been but little explored. However, as is well known, some whole denominations are predominantly urban, others almost entirely rural. Local church surveys in cities show some churches whose adherents are mainly country-born and bred, while others consist chiefly of native urbanites. A later chapter will explore the hypothesis that many of the characteristics of the urban church are due to the holdover of rural traditions unsuited to a city environment. Obviously an individual church or a group of denominational churches, made up chiefly of rural people, and especially one composed of recent rural migrants, stands less chance of being fully adapted to urban requirements than one whose constituency is more perfectly assimilated to the city.

As to the occupational distribution of the constituencies of urban Protestant churches, relatively scant data exist. Surveys, however, have gathered enough to show that churches also differ radically in this respect. Some are professional men's churches, others churches of traders and business men, others of industrial populations. Suburban communities show other striking differences. Some of their churches are made up of commuters, many of whose interests center in the city, while others run chiefly to membership by the local population. Churches are even found in the outskirts of cities whose members are chiefly farmers and gardeners.

It is highly important, however, to note that the whole body of Protestant churches is well and proportionately distributed among all social classes and all economic levels. In typical cities there are as many Protestant churches relative to population in poor areas as in rich. If the territory of cities be analyzed with reference to comparative wealth, about equal proportions of Protestants will be found coming from the poor, the average and the wealthy sections. This creditable showing has been greatly improved by the relatively recent northward migration of Negroes who are overwhelmingly Protestant. Previously some justification might have been found for the charge that Protestants were neglecting the working classes.

As it is, those denominational families to which Negroes most largely belong or which have strong foreign antecedents make a somewhat better than average showing. Nevertheless an inventory of nearly two thousand Protestant churches, in sectors of sixteen cities painstakingly studied from the standpoint of social and economic desirability, found the churches of all the major denominations somewhat proportionately distributed among the poorest, the lower than average, the better than average, and the best territory. This is summarized in Table I.

TABLE I — DENOMINATIONAL DISTRIBUTION OF CHURCHES BETWEEN BETTER AND POORER TERRITORY

| | Number | Per Cent. in: | |
| Denomination | | Better Territory | Poorer Territory |
| --- | --- | --- | --- |
| Baptist | 221 | 46 | 54 |
| Congregational | 121 | 49 | 51 |
| Protestant Episcopal | 321 | 47 | 53 |
| Disciples | 75 | 44 | 56 |
| Methodist Episcopal | 338 | 50 | 50 |
| Presbyterian, U. S. A. | 324 | 47 | 53 |
| Lutheran | 248 | 39 | 61 |
| 28 small bodies | 322 | 42 | 58 |
| Total | 1,970 | 46 | 54 |

No denomination, then, can rightly be accused of shirking the burden of the city's need; nor can Protestantism as a whole. Fifty-one per cent. of the churches in the best areas, and 62 per cent. in the poorer returned themselves as predominantly wage-earner churches. Obviously, however, churches of the poorer areas were smaller and less amply supported than those of the richer.

Interesting experiments have been made in the classification of church constituencies according to their theological tendencies. While the available data are inadequate to justify definite conclusions, it appears that, even when theological controversy has not been acute over long periods, the churches of a denomination tend to draw selectively upon their constituencies and in the main to gather together people of some one type of doctrinal thinking. Of two churches of the same denomination in the same locality, it is sometimes notorious that one is liberal, the other conservative. In fifty Methodist churches whose pastors classified their constituencies theologically, only one-fifth were found which associated two distinctly different theological groups in the same organization.

CONSTITUENCY LOSSES AND GAINS

Only on the points of communicant membership and Sunday-school enrollment do most denominations furnish data enabling one to trace the fluctuations of adherence over a period of time. City church-membership in recent years has shared the slight net growth of membership of churches in general, its gains having a little less than kept pace with population. Sunday-school enrollment during the same period has relatively declined. The study of individual churches in representative cities shows that only by the most intense and continuous struggle is any gain at all maintained. The major denominations of Springfield, Mass., lost seventy members for every one hundred gained over a period of twenty years. A similar loss in St. Louis was seventy-six per hundred. What becomes of these people? Some die; others are formally transferred to other churches; but for 23 per cent. in Springfield, Mass., and for 41 per cent. in St. Louis the church does not know. They were lost without trace and the ultimate revision of church books dug an equal number of unmarked graves.

Turning from memberships to churches, a recent sampling of nearly 2,000 cases in representative cities found 28 per cent. losing more than 5 per cent. during the last decade, 10 per cent. stationary (losing less than 5 per cent. but not gaining as much as 5 per cent.), 16 per cent. gaining from 5 to 25 per cent., and 46 per cent. gaining more than 25 per cent. This leaves nearly four urban churches out of ten either stationary or declining. Chapter xi helps to explain these successes and failures. For the moment a single instance may serve to illuminate the sharp differentiation of fortunes when population tides are favorable to a church and when they are against it. A New Jersey church grew steadily for forty years. In the six following years it admitted 932 members; but lost 928 during the same period. In the group of churches just mentioned 49 per cent. of the Sunday schools were either stationary or declining over a period of ten years. As a concomitant of the rapid recent growth of cities, change is more radical than it used to be—more churches proportionately are dying; but more are gaining rapidly.[5]

These unequal rates of growth in individual churches work out as unequal rates of growth in denominations. No separate urban figures are available nationally at this point. In typical cities, however, denominational growth in membership has been observed over considerable periods of time and the explanation for the differences found between denominations has been sought.

The following conclusions seem justified. No one of the well-established denominations appears to grow faster than another because of superior ability or quality of church life or method as such. Differences in growth depend rather upon such objective factors as the bulk of the incoming denominational population on which it has to draw and the mobility of its

---

[5] *Springfield Church Survey* (New York: Institute of Social and Religious Research, 1926), p. 100.

adherents after they arrive. The recent growth of cities has been chiefly due to rural migration. Denominations which have large rural constituencies naturally grow faster than those which do not.

Denominations grow also by conservation of members. Where the ratio of losses to gains greatly exceeds the average they invariably fail to grow excessive. But losses appear to be closely related to the slender hold upon jobs and property which some constituencies suffer, rather than due to any special unfaithfulness in the church's pastoral efforts.

Most denominations appear to grow somewhat in proportion as they acquire large masses of remoter adherents upon which they can draw for members. This, however, is not inevitable. As has already been seen in the case of the local church, an ill-balanced constituency, in which the central core has not enough strength to assimilate the dangling subsidiaries, may even find that a surplus of remote adherents is an obstacle to increased membership.

In typical cities Protestantism grows more by direct transfer of members from other churches than it does by the transformation of remoter adherents into members for the first time. Many of those transferred to city churches by letter come from other denominations. Their coming and going as between the better-established denominations which exchange members freely result essentially in a stand-off. Each gains as much as it loses. But, though its extent has never been accurately measured, interchangeability of such masses of constituency between denominations must be recognized as an urban phenomenon of the very first magnitude. In eight large downtown churches recently studied, from one-fourth to three-fourths of all received into membership by transfer came from other denominations. In 584 city churches representing all denominations and widely distributed among cities, pastors reported that 25 per cent. of their transfers came from other denominations; 28 per cent. of them said that they got more than half from other denominations; and 8 per cent. that they got more than three-fourths.[6]

Naturally it is only the strong and successful churches that are thus able to draw largely on other denominations. Why should one leave his own denomination to go into a feeble and failing church? The inaccessibility of a church of one's own denomination naturally has something to do with the frequency of such transfers, and wealthy suburban populations cross denominational lines more frequently than generally poorer and strictly urban ones. How far such interchangeability may go is evidenced by the Reformed Church in America, a small but distinctly urban denomination originally recruited from a single nationality. In a typical group of its

---

[6] Calculated from data gathered for Sanderson, *Strategy of City Church Planning.*

urban churches 75 per cent. of total membership came from other denominations!

## Aspects Undifferentiated as Urban and Rural

In certain important aspects knowledge about church-members and constituencies does not enable one to discriminate between urban and rural churches. The federal census, for example, does not compare denominations as to their urban and rural growth separately.

Unequal denominational growth is, however, a striking phenomenon. Some part of its explanation is fairly obvious in the light of local surveys; but the great variety of factors involved has never been statistically parceled out on a national scale.

One entirely unmeasured factor is the effect of unequal birth-rates. At this point something may be inferred from racial and regional differences. It is quite certain that some denominations have larger families than others.

A more obvious explanation of recent unequal growth is unequal immigration of constituents. Thus, such denominations as several branches of the Eastern Orthodox Church, whose sources in immigration have virtually been stopped, showed greatly reduced rates of growth, if not actual losses, in the last census decade. On the other hand, denominations drawing from Northern European races, like the Finnish Lutheran, showed very rapid growth on account of their favorable immigration quotas.

Many relatively new denominations exhibit the phenomenon, all too familiar in human affairs, of slowing down and cooling off after a first burst of energy. Since they start with nothing, their first decade of existence necessarily shows enormous percentage gains. The rapid strides of the group suggest that it is about to sweep the country. In a second or third decade, however, the rate slows down until it approximates the average. Or the new sect may die out altogether. That many have done so is evidenced by their disappearance from the lists in the federal census of religious bodies.[7]

The absorption of one denomination by another is another explanation of unequal growth which naturally cannot often be repeated. Demonstrating the effects of union upon membership growth, especially when considerable minorities in one or more denominations hold out from the union, as was the case of the United Church of Canada, turns out to be an exceedingly ticklish undertaking.[8]

Apart from these uncontrollable influences upon denominational growth, considerable differences in vigor and capacity to expand themselves through

---

[7] The 1926 Census, Vol. I, p. 9.

[8] Silcox, *Church Union in Canada* (New York: Institute of Social and Religious Research, 1933), pp. 432 ff.

more normal methods appear to be registered by the well-established denominations. The most available basis of comparison is the so-called evangelistic index, that is to say, the number of persons received into membership for the first time per one hundred old members. This excludes transfer
of those already members from one denomination to another. For twelve
major denominations whose year-by-year figures were assembled for the
decade 1922-31, the evangelistic index varied from 3.3 to 5.9 with an average
of 4.89 new members per one hundred old ones, as shown in Chart V. But

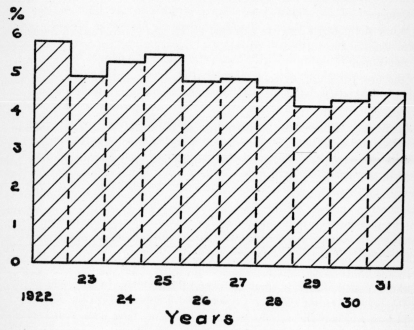

CHART V—NUMBER OF NEW MEMBERS PER 100 OLD MEMBERS IN TWELVE PROTESTANT
DENOMINATIONS, 1922-32

these denominational ratios show very little relation to the net growth of
the same denominations for the last census period. This is simply an in-
dication of the large number of factors involved and the inability of the
present state of knowledge to disentangle them. One can simply observe
the more obtrusive factors in the case of this or that denomination.

In spite, too, of enormous differences between denominations in the rate
of membership gains in recent years, the ultimate result has not greatly
modified the position of the better-established denominations relative to
the whole. Only two of the newer sects, Christian Scientists and Latter
Day Saints, have reached the status of large denominations. The great

ecclesiastical families still continue to dominate the religious situation numerically in much the same proportion from decade to decade.

As between the major faiths, the Protestant, Roman Catholic and Jewish, relatively little direct transfer of adherents has taken place.[9] Very considerable shifts of allegiance, however, have taken place between constituencies which have first drifted into the ranks of the inactive or non-adherent population. Great numbers of the posterity of such populations have been absorbed into other than their ancestral faiths. This is notably true as between Catholics and Protestants, especially in consequence of mixed marriages.

While not enough data are available to warrant generalization, numerous local studies show a strong current and reveal its direction. Thus, three recent Roman Catholic parish surveys in cities yielded the following facts: In the first parish 43 per cent. of Roman Catholic children were in public schools. Of its 521 families 20 per cent. represented mixed faiths, one parent being non-Catholic.

In the second parish the proportion of mixed marriages was 21 per cent., of which one-third were invalid from the Catholic standpoint; that is to say, they had taken place without ecclesiastical sanction. While only 10 per cent. of the parents in all-Catholic marriages failed to attend mass regularly, the proportion rose to 40 per cent. in the case of mixed marriages and to 53 per cent. in the case of the "invalid" marriages. Thirty per cent. of the children of the "invalid" mixed marriages were not baptized. When the mother only was a Catholic, only 6 per cent. were reared as Protestants, but when the father only was Catholic, 44 per cent. were reared as Protestants.

In the third parish, in the case of "invalid" marriages, 94 per cent. of Catholic parents omitted Mass, 71 per cent. of the children were baptized as Protestants and 86 per cent. were sent to the public schools.[10]

These examples are cited merely to show the magnitude of the processes involved. They work both ways. In the case of ecclesiastically valid mixed marriages where the mother is a Catholic, the children generally are carried into the Catholic Church.

SUMMARY AND FORECAST

The foregoing study of church-members and constituents may now be focused by some such general statement as the following: Under a voluntary system of religious affiliation a nation always shows large minorities which do not actively identify themselves with the church—just as multi-

---

[9] Abel, *Protestant Home Missions to Catholic Immigrants* (New York: Institute of Social and Religious Research, 1933), p. 76.

[10] "Revelations of a Recent Parish Census," reprint from *The Ecclesiastical Review*, Philadelphia, March, April and July, 1930.

tudes who classify themselves politically will not take the trouble to vote. Nevertheless the population as a whole tends to hold certain common religious ideals and to accept the traditional morality sanctioned by religion. The unchurched are a residuum deposited by population movements with which the church has not caught up.[11]     Time and the normal processes of

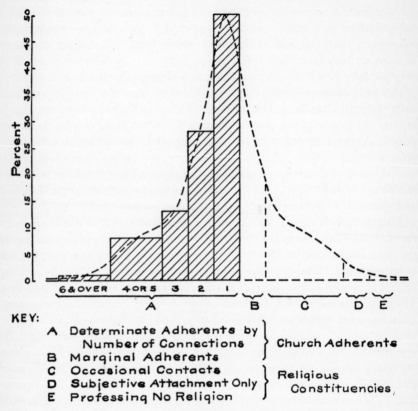

KEY:

A   Determinate Adherents by
      Number of Connections    } Church Adherents
B   Marginal Adherents
C   Occasional Contacts        } Religious
D   Subjective Attachment Only    Constituencies,
E   Professing No Religion

CHART VI—RELATIONS OF POPULATION OF THE U.S. TO THE CHURCHES

social adjustment tend to bring ever larger proportions into the church. But the later-comers, the more transient elements of any community, its socially unplaced groups at any given time, will show disproportionate numbers of non-adherents.

Non-adherents range from a scant few of professedly irreligious persons to those who definitely think of themselves as related to the church subjectively, who stand so near to the institution that they differ but little from

―――
[11] May, *The Education of American Ministers* (New York: Institute of Social and Religious Research, 1934), Vol. II, p. 226.

the majority of determinate adherents—adherents whose connection is tenuous and whose activities are intermittent. In other words, the un-churched constitute one-half of a normal distribution-curve covering a total population, the middle case of which is represented by an adherent attached to the church by one connection, but who is not regular either in partici-pation or in support. As closeness of attachment to the church increases, the number of adherents diminishes; the series ending with a few who are bound to the church by many ties to balance the few definitely ir-religious at the other end of the scale. How the two halves of the curve fit together and how each is divided is suggested by Chart VI, which is only partially based on strictly statistical evidence.

The percentage of determinate church adherents has steadily increased since the early decades of the American nation and is now just about keep-ing up with growth of population. In spite, then, of the extraordinary present mobility of the American population both rural and urban, the present losses to the church from social change are less than those which accompanied the change of position of millions from the Old World to the New and from settled Colonial areas to the frontier during the first two and one-half centuries of our history.

All the aspects of the church which subsequent chapters trace concern members and constituents as their human materials. In, behind and around the organization are always the people. They transfer from status to status as constituents. They become adherents or lapse from that status. They are organized as participants of particular church functions and activities. They are inculcated with religious traditions by appropriate cultural proc-esses, and they follow established leadership. The needs of special constitu-ents require the church to exercise special social welfare activities. As organized in the church these religious constituencies are brought into rela-tionships with other organized groups. The whole process has physical and financial aspects. The church is housed in buildings and its mainte-nance costs money. But, in whatever aspect these phenomena are dealt with, their ultimate subject-matter is the experiences of people grouped as mem-bers and constituents of the church.

## Conclusions

The data so far presented are too limited to justify any really fundamental conclusions. Before dependable inferences can be drawn, attention must shuttle back and forth between many aspects of the church until it has woven a more substantial fabric of knowledge and understanding. The present chapter's factorizing and comparisons of the phenomena of mem-bership and adherence nevertheless suggest certain preliminary insights and raise certain problems.

First, any competent understanding of the church must be keenly aware of what may be called the constituency levels as they have been developed in previous paragraphs. One may confidently affirm that it takes all of them to make up the church and that all should be envisaged as parts of the whole.

Secondly, it is highly important that the church should record and keep track of the relative proportions of its different constituencies and of their characteristics and relations to one another over a period of time. In no other way can it understand some of the most vital aspects of its own life. In view of frequently expressed suspicion of the padding of church rolls by the retention of inactive and absentee members, it is right to record that, in the main, churches are guilty of serious understatement as to the number of persons within their circles of influence. It is the extraordinary church which has really brought together in a single master-list all its varied constituents, or which can tell, in the case of a given individual, exactly what and how many relations to it he is currently maintaining. Financial statements also rarely bring together all of the money raised and spent by the church and all of its subsidiaries. Particularly do national denominational figures invariably understate the facts at this point.

Third, it is most necessary that the church understand the social processes which largely control religious adherence. Of these, migration, internal mobility as between country and city, between one region and another and within city areas, the occupation of urban territory by successive waves of population (a lower type usually following a higher one), unequal adjustment to social opportunity, and unequal assimilation to the dominant type, are factors which the church needs to recognize and ponder. Ultimately it must see that the churching of the nation is part of the whole struggle for social justice and equality of opportunity and that its outcome for multitudes depends upon the success of this struggle.

A fourth insight follows from the previous ones; the church must be content to view the winning of unchurched populations as a long process— one not ordinarily accomplished for most adults of a given population within a single generation. The individual church and the coöperative missionary efforts of churches and denominations may nevertheless do much to accelerate the equalizing processes and to bring larger numbers into closer attachment to the church than they would have if no conscious effort were made.

Beyond such tentative conclusions profounder considerations obtrude, but as problems rather than as matters on which conclusions can be stated.

For example, in what sense must each racially or economically distinctive population church itself? May this not be a more vital experience than that of being brought into the existing churches? But could this result be accomplished within some community frame-work of organized religion so as to avoid the endless heaping up of separate sects?

How far is non-adherence a form of resistance to alien mores? Obviously to considerable extent that is what it is on the part of many populations of foreign antecedents. It is keenly felt in the Orient that Christianity has unconsciously identified itself with western secular culture which it has then sought to impose upon the East under the guise of evangelization. Have Puritanism and Protestantism unconsciously acquired a set of cultural assumptions external to Christianity, which large elements of the population find unpalatable? How far has evangelization been an aspect, explicit or implicit, of Americanization? How far are the unchurched resisting, not the authority of God, but the paternalism of socially powerful classes institutionalized in the church?

Is it the major significance of the numerous bodies of remoter adherents to the church that they constitute a reservoir out of which the church may dip members, or rather that such adherents receive stimulus to help them make their own religious connections? Thus, during the decades which marked the turn of the century, the Sunday schools of several of the major denominations in cities were thronged by children from former constituents of non-English-speaking churches of denominations which had clung to their ancestral languages in public services. As soon as these churches came to conduct their public services in English and were partially liberalized, they increasingly regained their hold on their own children, and the Sunday schools of the first-mentioned denominations declined. Was this failure for them, or success? How much of the time is it possible directly to assimilate large numbers of non-adherent populations so that they come to furnish a new center of gravity for the existing church?

Again, what should one recognize as constituting a normal life-cycle for the individual in his connection with the church as an organized institution? Between the infant in the cradle and the bedridden old man circumstances obviously change. Adolescence is the age which yields the highest average number of connections with the church. Church activity, like all other activity, is correlated with energy and self-determination. May some part of the unchurched represent not persons with whom the church has failed, but persons with whom it has succeeded so that their lives are stabilized and their minds permanently fixed in a religious attachment after they have ceased to be active in the institution or in most of the other avenues of social life?

These considerations leave it quite open to assert the crucial religious significance, at some point in every human life, of a definite declaration of religious allegiance, and of loyal and vigorous participation in the church in the light of a quickened religious consciousness. Participation, the assumption of responsibility, regularity of attendance are obvious factors of strength in any social group, and persons who have such qualities will always constitute its effective nucleus at any given time.

May it not remain, however, the more or less normal expression of the Christianizing of the life of the nation that the church should thus permanently have its center and also its circumference? Certainly there must be leaven to leaven the lump and to turn a mere aggregate of religious groupings into an approximation of an organic whole. But may this organic quality be at least partially achieved by the interlacing of constituencies existing on different levels of adherence, whose proportions shift from time to time? And may it be that the going and coming of individual components from one level of adherence to another helps to constitute the unity of the social groupings and processes whose grand totality is the visible church?

# CHAPTER IV

## Community Roots and Adaptations

The typical church of colonial America was originally identified with a small, simple and well-defined community whose total religious life it expressed. The community occupied a tract of land with definite boundaries beyond which lay the next community, or more likely the unbroken wilderness. The territorial parish, often identified with a local political unit, reflected the land-basis of the group life, and the legally established church enjoyed a religious monopoly therein.

The heterogeneity of elements frequently imported into the simplest land-based communities early challenged the exclusive territorial parish. Competing churches with overlapping parishes soon occupied the same territory. It remained, however, for new community patterns developed during the present century to disturb the essential ties between the church and its contiguous area. Recently the increasing mobility of rural populations and their redistribution and more definite integrations about centers; the bulking of population and its complex relations in urban communities; and everywhere the multiplication of churches based upon race or class and not upon occupancy of the same area, have conspired to obscure and modify, if not almost to obliterate, the close identification of the church with a particular neighborhood or community.

Nowhere is the effect of these changes more strikingly seen than in the phenomenon of the parish. The church's attempts to meet them constitute one of the most fruitful clues to an understanding of its contemporary behavior.

Generally speaking, the shifting of the rural community from a neighborhood center to a town-centered basis (with increasingly close relations with urban sub-centers) and in urban communities the virtual disappearance of the neighborhood, in the sense of association based on contiguity of residence, as a principle of religious grouping together with the development of the latter as a system of huge metropolitan regions, furnish the necessary background for a re-study of the present community roots and adaptations of the church.

What, then, is the present relation of the church to the local community, of which formerly it was a well-marked religious center and for which

63

it appeared quite obviously, to the eye of faith, as the visible organ of the life of God?

The narrative and analysis of the particular changes which have affected the church's community relations must be told separately for urban and rural communities respectively.

### RURAL COMMUNITY ROOTS AND ADAPTATIONS

To a very considerable extent the rural church still reflects the community of which it is a part, as well as those larger characteristics of the region of which, in turn, the community is a part. This is so largely true that before discussing its implications for the church it is important to note the two chief exceptions.

The church of some racial or otherwise non-homogeneous minority group is less likely to be influenced by the community than would otherwise be the case. It uses a different language at its services; its people feel a sense of social isolation in the community, or at least are subject to different social pressures from those of the homogeneous majority. They turn to their church as to an island of security. It reflects their group and little else. Only in the process of years, as its children grow up and mingle with those of the majority, as intermarriage takes place, and the long course of events breaks down the barriers will such a church become less of the neighborhood and more of the community.

Again, denominations maintaining modes, traditions, or rituals, which are distinctly different from those of the majority will yield but slightly to the influences of the community that prove so powerful in other respects. A Protestant Episcopal church, for example, may be more or less ritualistic, but, no matter how simple the community, in its organized worship this church will always be marked as liturgical in contrast with the prevailing type.

In the main, however, the rural church is an institution, which, like other social institutions, is inevitably woven out of the warp and woof of the life of the community in which it is located.

REGIONAL DIFFERENCES

This is shown quite strikingly in differences which churches of the major denominations or denominational groups exhibit from one region to another[1]

---

[1] Space prohibits an adequate discussion of this whole matter of regionalism. From the point of view of the church see especially Morse and Brunner, *The Town and Country Church in the United States* (New York: Institute of Social and Religious Research, 1923), chapter i; and Brunner, Hughes and Patten, *American Agricultural Villages* (New York: Institute of Social and Religious Research, 1927), Appendix B. See also almost any rural study by the Institute of Social and Religious Research for statistical evidence of significant regional variations.

Climate and soil condition agriculture. The type of agriculture dictates something of the life its devotees shall follow. But more than this enters into the influences of a region. Historic factors loom large, especially the type of settlers or the migrations that have peopled a region; for each new group of people brings along its own traditions of race, religion, social organization and behavior which, interacting with the environmental forces, weave the texture of social life. Chapter xi returns to this theme and indicates some of the major regional differences.

ECONOMIC CONDITIONING

The regional conditioning of the work of the church by economic factors is so important as to require immediate mention.

It has been conclusively demonstrated by various Institute studies that contributions to the church correlate closely with the variations in farm values and only a little less with average farm incomes. This is true not only for open-country churches but for those in agricultural villages as well. The proportion of adult males in church-membership also tends to increase with wealth, though attendance is not affected. Per capita expenditures for benevolent purposes vary positively with wealth, as indeed do contributions for other church purposes. There is a curious disposition within the church to neglect some of the implications of this fact. Quotas are laid down by certain denominations on a per capita basis without regard to the average wealth of the churches in various regions. Some of the debt-burdened church buildings erected during the late 1910's and early 1920's give evidence of too great trust that faith would overcome the low price of wheat, cotton, corn or what not.

What is true of the church's economic conditioning in rural communities is true also of the size of libraries, the per capita circulation of books, teaching cost per pupil in the schools, per member contributions to social organization and other similar indices. The single exception from this rule is instructive. When the top categories of wealth are reached,[2] the ratio of contributions to the church drops off slightly. Apparently, in rural America the church program is such a highly standardized thing that in any average situation it does not know how to use resources beyond a certain point. Excess resources go instead into a variety of other social organizations, many of them exceedingly worthy in their purposes.

CHANGED PATTERN OF THE RURAL COMMUNITY

But the most significant influence of the rural community upon the church, sociologically speaking, is to be found in the changed pattern of the rural community since the beginning of the automobile age.

---

[2] Measured by average per household wealth of more than $6,000, and per capita retail sales in excess of $500 per year.

Since 1910 the focal point of rural America has shifted from the neighborhood to the village or town acting as a service station to outlying farming areas. This shows in many ways. These places have relatively more stores in them now than in 1910 or 1920, and a higher proportion of their population are engaged in merchandising. These facts indicate they are getting more farmer trade. Again the proportion of farm youth in town and village high schools has been growing by leaps and bounds, regardless of whether or not school districts have been consolidated. Village social organizations, such as the luncheon clubs, musical groups, parent-teacher associations, and many others, now freely welcome farmers and their wives as members. Indeed, more than one-third of the membership of such village groups is made up of open-country people. Ill-will and misunderstanding between village and country are far less in evidence today than in 1924 or even in 1929. Active and continuing coöperation is frequent. The rural community of today is a village- or town-centered one; in brief, a town-country community. Neighborhoods still exist, but they are assuming new and less important functions.

What has this meant for the church? Church-members have responded individually to these tendencies without waiting for institutional action. In 1920 less than one-fourth of the members of village churches, and barely one in twenty of those in towns of 2,500 to 10,000 population, came from the open country. By 1930 the proportion was well over one-third in the case of the village and nearly one in four in the town churches. In some counties more than half the members of village and even of town churches now come from farm homes.

This considerable but unregulated conformity by individual church-members as individuals to a general trend in the community has had a number of consequences. The shifting of the center of church interests on the part of so many rural people from open country or neighborhood to village or town has weakened the church in the country, and disproportionately so, because it is the wealthier members who incline to leave it for the church at the center. In a very real sense this has brought churches even of the same denomination into acute competition.

DYING COUNTRY CHURCHES

This is one of the reasons, along with shifts in population, poor leadership, and other causes, why between 2 and 4 per cent. of all country churches close their doors each year and why this mortality is higher within the social and trade areas of villages and towns than elsewhere.

Church administrators here confront a problem of first magnitude in which a mixture of attitudes, traditions and facts makes any workable solution difficult of achievement.

America was churched as she was settled, according to the principles of individualism. The traditions of the pioneer still have some weight. She was churched, too, in the days when automobiles and hard-surfaced roads were as unknown to men as to Adam and Eve, when churches had to be sufficiently close together to be reached after the morning's chores and returned to before dinner. Today the automobile has made it possible for villages to have areas of social and economic service averaging, according to the region, from fifty to 250 square miles, and with an upward range of several times the average. Inexorable social forces make it inevitable that the church shall be deeply affected by this change.

Common sense would seem to indicate an easy solution: center rural religion in the town and village, serve the countryside religiously as it is served educationally, financially, medically, and increasingly, socially. On the other hand, these little country churches are more than buildings or even institutions. They have been immortalized in souls and enshrined in the hearts of many who have had in them their deepest emotional experiences, some of which are typified by the tombstones in the churchyard. They still command the loyalty of many who would for some reason never be drawn and held by the village or town church. And finally, most denominational supervisors view any report of a church closed as a calamity, a serious blot on their records.

Yet country churches are closing at the rate of perhaps 1,000 to 1,500 a year. Under the present system of laissez-faire the areas formerly served by them become religious no-man's lands. The church at the center manages to serve its members from the more immediately outlying neighborhoods, but by no means to reach the active population whose local religious institution has been wiped out by the competition of the center.

Some attempt at adaptation to this condition has been made by the linking together of village or town-and-country churches in a so-called larger parish, designed to minister completely to all the people of the area. The larger parish idea is theoretically attractive and the term has come into considerable vogue. Unfortunately such parishes are few and the number that have been tried and failed is probably as large as the number of the survivors. Among the eight or ten principal causes of failure the chief seems to be utter disregard of patent sociological facts and conditions in the organization of these parishes. Nevertheless, where conditions have been suitable and intelligent planning has been employed, the larger parish has met with a considerable measure of success.

The influence of regional and community conditions, and of social and economic factors cannot be ignored by the rural church. They operate all too patently year after year. Ignoring them is becoming increasingly costly in terms of the human spirit as well as financially and is fraught with grave danger. This has been amply indicated in the present section and was implicit in the previously discussed evidence of the rural church's failure to hold its own in the proportion of adults in its membership.

## COMMUNITY ROOTS AND RELATIONSHIPS OF THE URBAN CHURCH

Exaggerating the tendency which is carrying more and more rural people away from their neighborhood of residence to attend church at a distance, the urban situation is one in which half or more of all church adherents attend church and find religious fellowship outside of the areas contiguous to their homes, where their smaller children go to school, where their wives patronize the corner grocery, and where their fellow citizens gather at the voting precinct. In the extreme case not more than 2 or 3 per cent. of a church's constituency may live within a mile of it. Most city churches, however, retain vestiges of territorial parishes; the majority of their adherents are somewhat clustered about them—though in such ways as seriously loosen community roots. Sunday-school and subsidiary constituencies are more often drawn from contiguous areas than general church-memberships. But different constituencies may not only come from different distances but from quite different directions, the Sunday school, say, from one sector of the city, the chief membership from another. The whole constitutes a most complex and perplexing situation, whose factors must be disentangled before it can be understood or in any way controlled.

### URBAN COMMUNITY STRUCTURE AND CHARACTERISTIC PROCESSES OF CHANGE

First to be considered is the physical structure of the urban community. Here sprawls the city over its land-area, bounded and limited perhaps by river or ocean and conforming to heights and hollows. It has a center and a periphery, with connecting paths—its major streets and arterial highways—along which sub-centers develop. Population fills in and is organized upon this skeleton; there is more crowding at the center, more room at the margins. Ever-moving physical devices for the transportation of people and goods from part to part bind the city together and make its essential physical qualities those of a vast machine.

Within this continuously moving framework, many diverse elements mingle day after day, and vigorous permanent siftings of population take place and persist. Each district of the city comes to have its peculiar use and every inhabited area comes to represent a distinct social and economic level of population. At the center lies the retail shopping district and the wholesale district; next come the industrial districts, with adjacent racial or foreign colonies and blighted areas or slums; farther out the workingman's and middle-class areas; finally the wealthy districts, urban and suburban. A mapping of any city according to the purchasing power of people in different areas or according to average social advantages and disadvantages of their environments shows how completely like is compelled to find place with like, and how vastly common fortunes vary between adjacent areas.

Upon such structures and according to such patterns cities grow; by territorial expansion at the circumference, by crowding and tall building at the center. Each element of urban activity competes with the others for room. The enlarged business and industrial areas crowd out residences. The generally poor and often foreign colonies clustered about these centers are consequently thrust out into contiguous residential territory of higher economic quality. This invasion drives before it the former inhabitants who scatter among the yet better areas, adding to them, deteriorating them and in turn evicting the previous populations, who ultimately take to the suburbs. Thus, a given area sees a succession of populations, perhaps also of nationalities and races. The palace of today is the slum of tomorrow. A Furnished Rooms for Rent sign ornaments the old Rockefeller homestead in Cleveland. Slum clearance and high-grade apartment-house developments set up a counter movement in a few areas. But until checked by zoning ordinances and stabilized by city planning, these successive waves of deterioration, initiated by displacements at the center and the obsolescence of the city's older housing and facilities, tend to roll on and on. The mass of these movements is, of course, determined by the size of the city, and their violence is proportionate to its rate of growth.

COMMUNITY RELATIONSHIPS AND MOBILITY OF CHURCHES

Scattered as they are over the face of the city, the majority of churches whose constituencies are localized take their characters from those of the populations which the processes of city-building have sifted out into their particular areas. In more stabilized areas of cities, on whatever economic level, they fairly and accurately reflect the quality of their immediate neighborhoods. But in all rapidly changing areas the situation is muddled by the presence, in addition to the characteristic population of the moment, of stranded elements of departing populations and by the advance guard of populations still to come. This is especially the case because population invasions take place along major transit routes, leaving eddies and pockets a little off their routes, where the life of former days persists. In brief, areas in transition cannot be truly homogeneous in spite of their average distinctly marked levels. Many of the churches of a given locality accordingly represent mere fragments of populations. They are churches of the stranded remnant or of the new and exceptional few rather than of the mass.[3]

In areas of rapid change, where old populations are being evicted, five

---

[3] See p. 255.

general alternatives are open to the existing churches: (1) to die because of the diminished number of nearby adherents of the sort which the church formerly reflected; (2) to survive as churches of stranded minorities, an alternative obviously open to but few; (3) to move along with the type of population for which it has established affinity; (4) to adapt itself to the incoming population and rebuild the old institution out of it as fresh material; or (5) to maintain its location and draw adherents of the old sort from a distance. The second, third and fourth choices enable a church to maintain a contiguous body of adherents, but only removal ordinarily permits a church to find a relatively homogeneous area in which it can reflect total community characteristics as the original parish church did; and here it will almost certainly have to divide the advantage with rival churches.

Each of these choices is actually taken by considerable numbers of churches, and the story of church fortunes under each is instructive. In typical cities, one-fourth of all Protestant churches which ever existed have died. Most of the stranded ones live on only at a "poor dying rate." Especially interesting and thrilling is the history in typical cities of removals and attempted adaptations to changed communities.

On the evidence of 1,000 cases, three out of every four city churches do not continue upon the original cornerstone. They have moved at least once in their histories. Colonies of churches—often the leaders of their respective denominations—have been neighbors and rivals in three or four different locations—each moving to the "best" new territory every time its old territory went bad. Many of these removals were institutionally for the better. Most of the abandoned church buildings were sold to churches of the incoming populations, some of which were themselves removing in order to follow the migrations of their adherents. All told, then, the urban Protestant church is very much on wheels and finds it most difficult to stay put while cities change.

The story of that minority of churches which stand and try to adapt themselves to the incoming populations is more appropriately told in its effect upon their internal organization, and as an aspect of the social-welfare efforts of organized religion; and will be returned to when these topics come under consideration. It is almost invariably associated with the ability, in part at least, to bring leadership and supporting adherents from outside of the neighborhood.

In contrast with those churches which seek to maintain primary roots in the local community is the essentially delocalized type, which sets its building on a central site, but is largely dissociated from the neighborhood life, and transports the bulk of its adherents from a distance.

All these types of adjustment may occur in combination with others, and few "pure" cases are actually found. The various solutions that they attempt of the churches' community relations invariably register in the experience of church-going adherents and in resulting parish arrangements. The story, therefore, remains to be told from these two viewpoints.

THE CHURCH-GOING ADHERENT

It one takes an entire metropolitan area, religion stands out as one of the more localized interests. Church-goers do not travel regularly from the suburbs in any such proportions as workers, shoppers and amusement seekers do in their daily commutation. Within the boundaries of the city proper, however, at least half of all church constituents travel more than one mile to church.

The largest available samplings on this point are those of 41,346 constituents in twenty-six churches of seven denominations located in thirteen cities of 100,000 population and over and of 6,086 member-families in thirty-two St. Louis churches (representing more than twice as many individuals). In these two samples the distances traveled by adherents in church-going were as follows:

| | Per Cent. | |
| Distance in Miles | 26 City Churches | 32 St. Louis Churches |
| --- | --- | --- |
| less than ½ | 31 | 31 |
| ½ to 1 | 18 | 19 |
| 1 " 2 | 15 | 21 |
| 2 " 3 | 11 | 13 |
| 3 " 4 | 10 | 9 |
| 4 " 5 | 8 | 4 |
| more than 5 | 7 | 3 |

In both samples just about one-half of adherents come from within the first mile of church, but in St. Louis a much larger proportion than in the composite sample came from the second mile. Obviously the total size of the city limits the per cent. coming from the greater distances. Smaller cities do not afford so great distances to be traversed; consequently their average adherent lives nearer his church. Of 17,445 members in Springfield, Mass., 68 per cent. had less than one mile to travel.

Considering some of the different constituencies described in chapter iii, it is highly significant for church policy that detached individuals cannot be drawn so far to church as adherent families; that full church-members live farther on the average than members of subsidiary organizations; that regular attendants live nearer than constituents in general; that nearer adherents give their church more hours of attendance per month than remote ones; but that pledged contributors show the same distance-distribution as constituents in general. Members of subsidiaries other than the Sunday school are most localized of all constituencies. Members of clubs, circles, recreational groups and adherents to various minor activities do not come so far as members of worship or instruction groups.

Adolescents are more localized in their church-going than children, presumably because the latter are more frequently brought by parents; but children generally do not come so far as adults. Downtown churches—generally, but not invariably—are notably deficient in children. All this is but to say that, under urban conditions, different age groups differ in mobility and in capacity to use transit facilities to overcome distance. Parents who go far to church are inclined to leave their children behind,

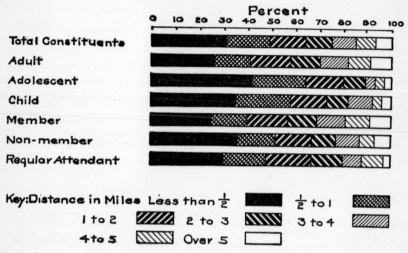

CHART VII—DISTANCE TRAVELED BY CHURCH-GOER, BY AGE AND TYPE OF ADHERENCE

perhaps in the nearby Sunday school, thus setting up religious dissociation in families.

On adherents with many attachments to the church, however, distance has almost no effect. One-connection adherents are but little more frequent within the first mile than beyond the fifth, while adherents with four or more connections are about equally distributed through the distance zones up to five miles. Space makes no difference with those who have many ties with the church.

CHURCH PARISHES

Retelling the same story from the standpoint of parishes, one finds indications that a large third of urban churches have scattered parishes, that is to say, those in which less than one-half of their members live within one mile, while about one-fourth have compact parishes, that is to say, those in which over 70 per cent. live within one mile. This generalization is based upon estimates from ministers of 813 churches in sixteen larger cities.

That scattered parishes are essentially a phenomenon of the less desirable areas (judged from the standpoint of social quality) is shown in Chart VIII.

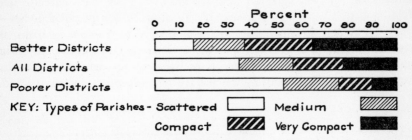

CHART VIII—TYPES OF PARISHES ACCORDING TO SOCIAL QUALITY OF URBAN TERRITORY

The territory of the 813 churches referred to above was carefully analyzed and compared by means of a battery of criteria.[4] The proportion of scattered parishes rose to 53 per cent. in poorer territory, and declined to 16 per cent. in better.

This, of course, merely registers the notorious fact that central churches which, by reason of strategic location and prestige, can draw on the whole

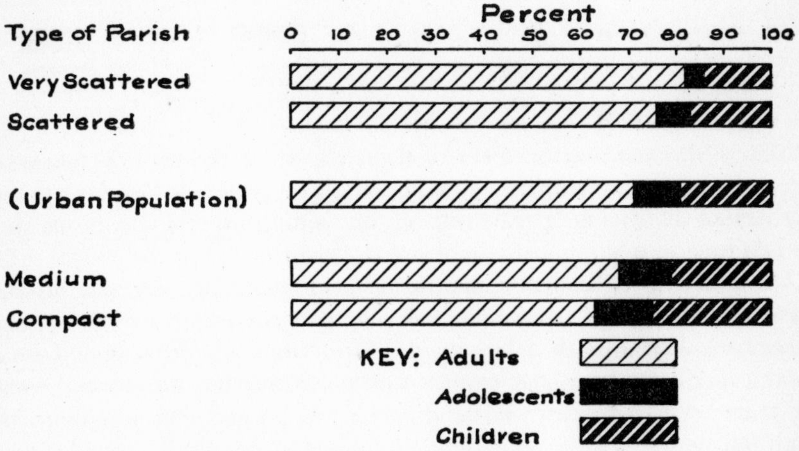

**Percent**

| Type of Parish | | | | | | | | | | |
|---|---|---|---|---|---|---|---|---|---|---|
| Very Scattered | | | | | | | | | | |
| Scattered | | | | | | | | | | |
| (Urban Population) | | | | | | | | | | |
| Medium | | | | | | | | | | |
| Compact | | | | | | | | | | |

KEY: Adults
Adolescents
Children

CHART IX—AGE DISTRIBUTION OF ADHERENTS, BY TYPES OF PARISHES

area of the city, are often surrounded by industrial, foreign and deteriorated districts which would make the church's location impossible if it depended upon the neighborhood for life and support.

---

[4] See p. 251.

It is not, however, the great city-wide churches alone that have scattered parishes. Churches of scattered minorities similarly find the city's center the most convenient place for their few sheep to flock together. So long, on the contrary, as such minorities live in racial colonies or Ghettos their churches are apt to be narrowly localized.

The unequal mobility of adherents according to age has already been noted. It is worked out for twenty-eight large city churches in terms of types of parishes in Chart IX. The per cent. of adults in the constituency declines and that of children increases as the parish becomes more compact —that is to say, as adherents on the average live nearer to the church.

LOPSIDED PARISHES

The average Protestant parish is distinctly a lopsided affair; first, because populations tend to scatter toward the less densely populated areas of cities. Institutions are conservative and do not move so quickly as people do. Hence the typical parish is described by a sector beyond the church building. Hour-glass parishes develop when a church removal to a half-way location leaves an old nucleus of adherents at the old site and a new one still beyond the new site. But churches in relatively stabilized communities also tend to draw very unequally from different directions. This is due, as has been noted, to the pockets and oases of stranded populations and the advance-drive of new ones along traffic lines. It is the rare church that does not draw selectively on its field. It picks and chooses according to affinity. It finds adherents to the north, not to the south, to the right not to the left. This may be seen in the case of a St. Louis church in Chart X.

Of three clustered churches on adjacent corners, one may virtually be the church of the north sector, the second the church of the south sector, while the third has no substantial relationship at all to any immediately surrounding territory. Obviously the three are not competitive; obviously too they can do little in making common cause in behalf of the whole locality. On the contrary, three central churches, none of which has any considerable body of adherents in the vicinity, may draw competitively from the same direction and exclusively from populations of the same social quality. Except in rare cases in especially homogeneous territory the symmetrical parish does not appear in cities. Physical barriers figure in many situations, but the chief reason is that city-building processes have already served to sort and isolate different types and levels of people, and the church reaches out in the particular direction in which its type is to be found.

ASSOCIATION BY SELECTIVE AFFINITY

All the phenomena reviewed in the foregoing paragraphs express and symbolize a set of conditions which compel urban people to find a different principle of human association from that which bound together the people of the rural neighborhood. The urban community is complicated and rap-

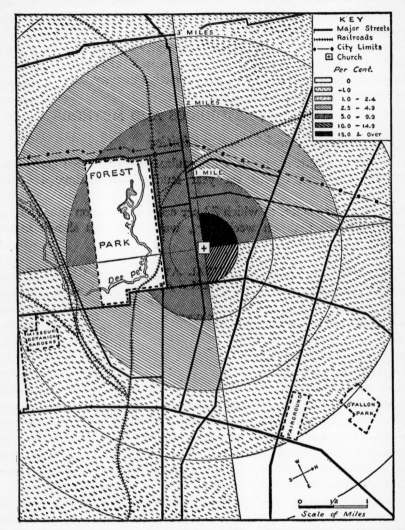

CHART X—PARISH OF A ST. LOUIS CHURCH SHOWING DISTRIBUTION OF CONSTITUENTS' HOMES BY ZONES AND SECTORS ACCORDING TO DISTANCE AND DIRECTION FROM CHURCH BUILDING

idly changing. Its changes very often result in the removal and relocation of churches. The pattern worn by the church-goer in traveling from his home to the church and back is exceedingly devious. The difference between the church's site and operating center and the church-goers' homes varies enormously both in distance and in direction.

To understand the significance of what has happened, one must consider that the relationships of the rural community concern the same people over and over again. There are regroupings, but the basic personnel of the community does not change. The back-door or barn-yard conversations and borrowings, meetings and passings on the street, trade in the shops, social functions and occasions, organized life in school, lodge and church, all concern the same human faces seen repeatedly in different connections. Marriage, occupation, economic opportunity and every-day working philosophy, all have to be achieved within the narrow range offered by the capacities of a few hundred people available for social relationships.

Full-blown urbanization, on the contrary, gives the adult city or suburban dweller a different set of fellows for every major relationship. The people near whom he lives are not those with whom he works, and when he plays it is with a still different group. Vocational and business specializations bring the individual into still other groupings, the trade, the profession, the group of fellow-workers. Special cultural interests or avocations place him in the literary, the artistic or the musical crowd. Recreation, sports and hobbies may each create an additional set of associations. All of these separate groups of associates are acquainted with the man in only a fragment of his life. Of the rest of him they remain ignorant. He has manifold ties in many directions, but all relatively superficial. These associations are based on selective affinity rather than on contiguity in a self-contained neighborhood or upon the deeper ties of the racial group or family clan which originally caused people to settle near together.

The fellowship of the urban church, as evidenced by the typically slender affiliation of its average adherents, tends to be reduced to merely one of the many ties which persons detached from locality, and, in great numbers detached from family, recognize with segments of their personalities, each expressing itself in a different setting and as a response to a different set of people and moral standards. This is conspicuously true of the relationships existing in many large downtown churches.

Needless to say, such complete urbanization has not been reached by all city people. Multitudes still live in colonies and Ghettos and are locality-bound by habit and ignorance. The hold-over of rural-mindedness keeps others to a narrow round of relationships. Clannishness is not abolished, only diluted. Even the scattered parish may represent people who used to live near together and were bound by ties of blood and race.

These same people, nevertheless, will be found shuttling hither and thither to make associations based on common interests in other directions. The church survives as the one grouping based on former contiguity, while others are increasingly based on selective affinity. The city, then, is dominated by a new inner principle of association very different from that which pertained when the same few men and women had all their companion roots in a particular community.

For better or worse the urban church must conform to this new principle. Even in the most homogeneous of residential neighborhoods, where social life within the contiguous group is most adequate, half of all church-goers will be found marching out from under the very eaves of local sanctuaries, including those of their own denominations, to find church fellowships at distant centers. In extreme cases almost the whole body of church-goers of a locality thus take themselves out of their immediate neighborhoods to get to church. Such wholesale mobility implies some real maladjustment between the churches of that locality and the neighboring population. However, for half of the people of a neighborhood to go elsewhere to church may fairly be charged merely to the free and perhaps proper exercise of selective choice under urban conditions.

### Consequences of the Changed Principle of Urban Association

Obviously all this has important consequences for the motivation of the individual and the determination of his conduct with respect to his church. The alternatives which confront him may perhaps best be summarized in the hypothetical case of Mr. A.

Trying to "do better by his family," Mr. A moves into the most attractive locality in which he can afford to pay the rent, his former place being immediately filled by another man from farther downtown also trying to better his condition.

Mr. A may now merely accept the fact that he has farther to go to church, exactly as he has farther to go to work. This is part of the price he pays for his other advantages, and he may pay it gladly.

Mr. A may, on the contrary, continue his membership in his old church, because he expects that the church will soon move out into the locality where he has gone along with other fellow-members. Agitation for such removal has doubtless already begun, as it is almost certain to do under such circumstances.

Mr. A may stay by his former church for loyalty's sake. Probably the area around it has begun to deteriorate. Yet he has less fortunate neighbors who have to stay there because they cannot afford to get away. Less loyal members have already withdrawn, thus reducing the church's financial support and working force. The church needs Mr. A.

Instinctively the church endeavors to maintain itself in the style to which it is accustomed. But this proves a barrier to the entrance of new-comers who have moved into the neighborhood. A household canvass proves the presence of an excessive proportion of the unchurched piling around the very doors of the church. Some of the new-comers do manage to get in. The difference between their cultural standards and those of the older members sets up a conflict. Mr. A is less happy and content than he was, and the ties of his loyalty are strained. To stay or not to stay becomes a vital question.

Mr. A may have become convinced that the solution of the church's problem is to be found in its radical adaptation so as to make it fully congruous with the standards and needs of the incoming population. He may decide to stay in order to help the church in this transformation. The motive of responsible membership and leadership in such enterprises always holds a few members.

If none of these things happen, Mr. A may decide to leave his old church, assuming that he will now select one of the churches in his own neighborhood as a church home. However, when he tries the experiment he may find to his surprise that it works out more naturally for him to become connected with some distant central church where many of the people with whom he works already go, or which he knows as an outstanding advocate of particular ideas which he cherishes.

In considering any of these alternatives, Mr. A will be affected by family considerations involving the unequal mobility of its various members. In this connection, he will have to face the fact that several of the numerous alternatives which he has considered are also open independently to his older children and perhaps even to his wife.

Actual chartings of the paths of the going and coming of urban church adherents by the tens of thousands, reveal the large number of alternatives between which choices have been made and the ultimately individual and essentially unfathomable considerations by which actual choices seem to have been dictated.

Whatever his choice, it may occur to Mr. A as an afterthought that he has a dual responsibility. Something at least he owes to the church of his neighborhood even though his private religious problem is most adequately solved by connection with the distant church. Community churches not infrequently allow a member to retain his previous connection at the same time that he enters into the new one. The complicated nature of urban social relations suggests the extension of some such practice.

CONSEQUENCES FOR CHURCH ADMINISTRATION

The more ultimate bearings of urban characteristics upon churchmanship are reserved for consideration in a later chapter. It should be obvious, however, that the attenuated community relationships of the urban church require the attention of ecclesiastical administrators and of all who are concerned for the fortunes of religion in modern cities. Among inferences which may fairly be drawn from the situation are these:

All kinds of relationships between churches and their localities are legitimate and necessary for the churching of cities. Extreme situations such as those in which only 2 per cent. of a church's adherents come from within a mile seem difficult to justify, but the primary responsibility of any central church is by no means to its locality. The city as a whole is the community of such a church, and the community relations which it expresses often have more authentic urban roots than those based on mere neighborhood.

When population declines absolutely or when population of the sort which the church can assimilate without radical transformation leaves, it may be better for the church to move where it can find people of its own sort.

This alternative is not open to all churches. Churches are not completely mobile any more than they are completely capable of re-adaptation. Those which can neither move nor change will have to die. The church is eternal, but to no individual church is institutional immortality guaranteed. It takes superb churchmanship and the ultimate measure of Christian grace to make the last days of a dwindling church its best, but it sometimes has been done.

Some churches should maintain themselves during the transitional period of a neighborhood, in order to serve its stranded population and to absorb the more assimilable elements of the new population. They may then be released to share in the second wave of removals.

Only a few churches probably are capable of such complete transformation as to insure permanence under the most radical of population changes.

In the main, each new wave of population must church itself. This has been true at least under a voluntary system of religious organization, and is in accord with the Protestant genius as it has expressed itself in the past. Most abandoned churches are sold to new churches, but not without the death of the old organization. Better management and less sectarianism might handle such transitions far better and sometimes secure continuity of organization as well as of physical plant.

The new areas of the expanding city must, of course, be churched either by removals of older churches following their former populations or by new churches. In either case the struggle to relocate and the need to acquire sufficient strength to carry on the normal work of a church constitutes a challenge to all church constituents resident in the neighborhood, since neither the location nor the prestige of these outlying churches can ordinarily give them city-wide appeal. Those responsible for locating or relocating churches, however, should understand in advance that they do not have the total population of the locality to draw upon, even as concerns people of their own faith and sect.  Perhaps one-half will and ought to be permanently churched elsewhere.

Since churches draw so selectively upon the population even of homogeneous areas, churches clustered at convenient centers should, if possible, become complementary to one another.  Each may have a very one-sided parish, but if it draws from a different direction it will not be competitive. On the other hand, it can appear as nothing less than a scandal when clustered churches draw competitively on the same sector and neglect or are unable to reach all the rest.

Non-adherents are to be evangelized on the same lines as those on which the adherents are to be churched, that is to say, in a considerable degree they are to be won to churches located at a distance from their homes, particularly through the central pulpits and the appeal of common interest groupings, which may take them out of their neighborhoods to find the best things of life, as other agencies sometimes take them to find the worst.

No scientific knowledge exists capable of working out an exact formula or equation showing how these often conflicting tendencies ought to work out in a given city.  But constant intensive study of the community roots of city churches and of the larger version of the urban community is gradually producing an art of churchmanship which greatly improves upon the largely uncomprehending methods of the past.

### COMMUNITY PROBLEMS COMMON TO RURAL AND URBAN CHURCHES

It remains to point out that some of the most basic problems of community roots and relationships are common to rural and urban churches.

For both, a new problem has been created by improvements in transit facilities permitting more alternatives to church adherents and a wider range of choice as to the location of their churches.

Such increased mobility is the condition and largely the cause of a new balance in functional relationships between the open-country and the rural village and between the outlying areas of cities and their centers.

Both environments show a corresponding shift of relationships between the central and the outlying churches, except that it is the outlying ones which are generally losing membership in the country, while it is the central ones in cities.

In both country and city the shift of community balance and relationships entails losses both institutional and personal.  Not all institutions can survive the transition, and the socially constructive relationships with many people are broken beyond replacement when institutions move or die.

Numerous churches, both rural and urban, are weakened by the removal of supporters to better located churches.  The rural are weakened when the better-to-do farmers transfer their memberships to the village, the urban when the more progressive downtown people move to suburban neighborhoods.

Under these circumstances many rural and urban churches alike die. Others move. These recourses, however, are much more frequently available to and characteristic of the city church. Considerable numbers, however, of new village churches are merely removals from the country seeking better locations with respect to their constituencies. Both the death and the removal of churches leaves stranded adherents in city and country not mobile enough to make new connections or to overcome the cultural gap between their old churches and the new ones to which they would have to go.

The unchurched remnant is disproportionately great both in city and in country where churches have died, removed or remained with dwindling strength.

Generally in the city, but also to a certain degree in the country, departing churches are succeeded by others on lower cultural levels, particularly those of the emotional sects.

Undoubtedly for both country and city people greater mobility and wider opportunity of choice means access to better churches institutionally speaking and possibly to more adequate religious satisfactions. In both cases, however, the more remote physical connection means somewhat reduced participation and probably a lessening average sense of personal responsibility for the church.

All this is to say that the problem of the church's uprooting from the community in its old phase and its reëstablishment in the enlarged community, whether or not involving the removal or radical change of any given institution, is accompanied by serious difficulties both in city and in country. On the whole there is relatively less conservatism in cities and greater capacity for meeting change; because city populations perforce are partially reëducated by urban experience. On the other hand, the new community in which the rural church has to establish its roots is still relatively simple, while the city's new states of mind have largely yet to be comprehended and conquered by religion. Particularly has the church found it difficult to incarnate the constructive purpose and idealism of the metropolitan city in its whole promise and vigor.

# CHAPTER V

*Church Organization and Life*

The church on the national or denominational level defines itself as a spiritual fellowship holding a common faith and ideals. This is the essential characteristic of the church universal—not a face-to-face group, but rather one bound together by some system of inter-communication; one in which assemblies of representatives act for the smaller territorial and ultimately for the local units, and chosen emissaries itinerate among them in an inspirational and supervisory capacity, keeping faith and ideals alive. These, with various forms of publication, constitute the chief vehicles of the church's larger group life.

The local church, on the contrary, in its most characteristic aspect is a congregating group which comes together frequently into direct face-to-face relationships. It gathers constituents to an habitual place of meeting, originally identified as the dwelling place of deity. The local church survives in the face of great vicissitudes by reason of the peculiar social vigor of such primary groups and the heightened efficiency of the religious life when stimulated by the common worship of congregations.

It is equally characteristic of the local church, though less obvious, that it follows its adherents back to their homes and secular businesses and goes out to recruit others. In brief, it also is a group which projects itself locally through means analogous to those which the church universal uses; namely, —through systems of communication and the pastoral and fraternal activities of itinerating representatives. This is the essentially individualizing phase of its group life as congregating is its collective phase.

The difference between the two phases is, of course, not absolute. The benediction follows the congregations to their homes and individualizing functions begin with the greeting of coming and going worshipers at the church door. Moreover, the church frequently fosters small and informal congregating groups, whose relations are highly individualized.

Both in its congregating and in its projecting aspects the group life of the local church has to be controlled and administered. Its local ordering and government is committed to officers, among whom ordained ministers usually have the most prominent place, but who always include laymen receiving authority, largely through democratic processes of selection, from the more or less self-determining group. Churches are voluntary associations, for the most part under paid leadership to which administrative functions are definitely assigned. In conjunction with lay officers, these paid leaders manage the church, coördinate its functions, and make its processes effective. Administration, then, constitutes the third major aspect of the local church's organized life.

These three aspects are exactly mirrored in the commonly distinguished functions of the ministry. The minister's priestly and prophetic offices are exercised in the administration of the sacraments and ritual, in preaching and teaching to the congregated group. The pastoral office is the essential expression of the projective aspect of the church, besides which the minister goes out in his representative capacity to share in many aspects of the constructive life of the community. Finally, as has already been noted, the minister is the church's chief administrator.

These characteristics fit most of the 250,000 local churches of the United States and determine the work of their almost 150,000 ministers. Obviously, however, their objective working out is largely determined by the size of the associating group. In the small rural church, with its infrequent meetings and its lack of resident paid leadership, organization is highly informal and one aspect merges almost indistinguishably into another. With the large church institutional structure becomes highly complicated, organization is formal and functions are specialized. The average American church, including all denominations, has 191 adult members; the rural church has 98; the small city church, 274, and the larger city church, 596. For cities of more than 300,000 population, the figure is 789 adult members per church. A careful estimate of the distribution of white Protestant churches urban and rural according to size is presented in Table II.

TABLE II — ESTIMATED DISTRIBUTION OF PROTESTANT WHITE CHURCHES ACCORDING TO THE NUMBER OF ADULT MEMBERS*

| Number of Adult Members | Total | Per Cent. Urban | Rural |
|---|---|---|---|
| 1,000 or over | 1.0 | 2.5 | 0.5 |
| 900–999 | 0.4 | 0.8 | 0.2 |
| 800–899 | 0.5 | 1.2 | 0.3 |
| 700–799 | 0.9 | 2.2 | 0.4 |
| 600–699 | 1.1 | 2.9 | 0.5 |
| 500–599 | 1.6 | 4.7 | 0.6 |
| 400–499 | 2.2 | 5.4 | 1.2 |
| 300–399 | 3.7 | 9.5 | 1.8 |
| 200–299 | 9.0 | 14.6 | 7.2 |
| 100–199 | 23.3 | 26.8 | 22.2 |
| 0–99 | 56.3 | 29.4 | 65.1 |
| | 100.0 | 100.0 | 100.0 |

* From May and Shuttleworth, *The Education of American Ministers* (New York: Institute of Social and Religious Research, 1934), Vol. IV, p. 54.

So wide a range of difference in the characteristic size of churches, urban and rural, involves differences in organizational problems. The congregating, projecting and administrative phases of the church thus have to be examined separately for the rural and the urban versions of the institution, and to a considerable extent separately for the smaller and the larger cities, after which certain common aspects may be recognized.

As already indicated, organization takes on a different aspect for the church in its super-local phases. The group of denominational churches, organized as a territorial association or district, the denominations in their still larger jurisdictions, as well as interchurch associations and agencies, all cohere by reason of the acts of elected representatives, by the goings and comings of itinerating representatives, and by intercommunication through publication.

Brief attention will be given to the organization of each of these more inclusive expressions of the church.

### ORGANIZATION AND LIFE OF THE RURAL CHURCH

Before the life, functions and organization of the rural church can be understood, it is necessary to recall something of the sort of institution it is.

In the American village the average Protestant church enrolls 149 members, though everywhere but in the West the figure stands at slightly over 160. About 120 of these persons are resident and active. In the last decade the church has had a slight growth, though not quite comparable to the gain in population. In the open country there will be seventy-seven enrolled members, with sixty more or less resident and active. As usual, these averages do not tell the whole story. One-fourth of the village and one-third of the country churches have fewer than fifty resident members; another fifth of the village and nearly two-fifths of the country churches fail to reach the one hundred mark. At the other extreme, one-fifth of the village churches and one in twenty-five of the country churches exceed 250 members. The units, therefore, are not large, and it is not surprising that such a high proportion, especially of the smaller churches, succumb to various adverse social forces and die, or that one-fifth of the village and nearly three-fourths of the open-country churches lack resident ministers.

In passing it is interesting to note that the deaths of rural and especially open-country churches in the trade areas of villages and towns exceed the births by three to two, and that almost all of the churches that succumb are small, many having fewer than twenty-five members and few more than fifty. These eliminations furnish one reason for the slight increase in the average membership of rural churches.

The chief function of the surviving rural churches is to unite the members and others interested in "divine worship," which to many means listening to preaching and prayer and the singing of a few hymns. Theoretically this assembling together is to take place regularly on the first day of the week. Actually, this is not what always happens in rural America. As noted, many churches have non-resident ministers, and such ministers frequently have "circuits" of more churches than can be reached on a given Sunday. Thus one-eighth of all village churches and more than three-fifths of all open-country churches are not open for "worship" or "preaching" on every Sunday. Usually these manage a service fortnightly, but in the South, where practically nine-tenths of the white and four-fifths of the Negro open-country churches do not have weekly services, many are open only once a month.

If one should assume for statistical purposes that only members attended church services, the total church attendance would equal the presence of each resident member at 3.5 services a month. In 1924 the figure was 4.0. There seems to have been in village and country alike a slight but definite slackening in the hold of the church on the people so far as this can be measured by attendance. Secular interests are crowding in; but there are also other influences, perhaps deeper and more significant. There are changes in attitude as to the purpose of the church and its services. There is dissatisfaction with the low intellectual caliber of the rural ministry. There are loss of confidence in the leadership of the church and criticism of interdenominational competition.

But the decline thus far is slight. The church still holds its active members fairly well. Beyond the activities of weekly worship, this membership arranges itself in various organizational patterns for carrying on the work of the congregation. These patterns follow rather natural lines of sex, age or even social status. Through them many of the social values of the church are realized and practically all of the activity in which the members may share takes place.

Most frequent of these subsidiary organizations is the Sunday school, which is often in session on more Sundays than the church itself. The importance in the religious-education program of the church is so great that special attention will be paid to it in chapter viii. Next comes a women's society of some sort, then a young people's organization of the familiar Christian Endeavor type, and finally, much less frequently, various boys', girls' and men's organizations. Each particular type of outstanding agency gets separate comment in chapter vii.

In all nearly nine-tenths of village churches and three-fifths of the open-country churches, equaling seven-tenths of all rural churches, have one or more organized groups of the types described. The average number of groups per church is 2.5, with the village church averaging more than three, and the country less than two.

In industrial villages each church averages 7.3 organized activities, with fourteen as a maximum. Agricultural villages nearly double both the average and the maximum, but open-country churches, of course, show far fewer.

Excluding the Sunday school and all of its organized classes, the churches of the average village-centered community show a total of about seventeen of these subsidiary organizations, or only four fewer than the number of secular social organizations in the same community. The membership of these church groups equals about two-thirds of the church-membership. Many people belong to more than one, and some belong who are not church-members. Even allowing for the 30 per cent. of the churches which lack all such agencies—churches usually numerically very small—it appears clear that not all adult members are brought into these societies. There may be many reasons for this, but the competition of many types of activities, secular and religious, for the leisure time of the average villager is acute and doubtless has some effect.

Certainly the aggregate membership of these secular groups is two and one-half times as large as that of the church organization. Indeed they exceed the membership in the churches themselves by one-third. They are, however, like the church, not keeping pace with the population, and changed fashions in social organization are quite evident in the rapid decline of some types, like lodges, and the rapid growth of others.

The congregational life of churches, however, is more than the sum of the routine activities and group organization thus far described. The church-members also represent a body of thinking that, in many a small community, is collectively a powerful instrument of social control. The face-to-face contacts of the rural community make public opinion in matters of personal conduct in such places highly efficacious. Within the church group, bound together as it is, in a measure, by allegiance to spiritual and moral ideals, this factor of social control becomes even more effective.

The records of many a rural church are filled with cases in which the church felt called upon to discipline one of its members for swearing, dancing, or joining a secret order, as well as for weightier matters. It is significant, however, that such cases are extremely rare save in a few small sects. The group controls are still strong, but the limits of control are narrower than they once were. There are two evidences of this. Outside of the South, Sunday evening movies were introduced in many places after 1924. Attempts to do this before that time had been snowed under. The final consummation in some communities was not seriously opposed. Again, the content of preaching seems to be changing. Certainly the old-time revival or protracted meeting, even in the South, is no longer as frequent nor as effective as in yesteryear. The younger clergy are showing more interest in the ethical and spiritual implications of every-day life than they did a few years ago. The programs themselves show a newer emphasis as compared to the days before the modern country church movement. That the future may show still more changes is indicated by many things, but quite significantly by the fact that rural churches in increasing numbers are surveying their communities and basing their programs of activities—both non-worshiping and preaching—on the information gathered. In 1930 more than one-fifth of the churches had made such a study within two years— nearly three times as many as in the years prior to 1924. This constitutes a new element in the parish program-planning and indicates a dissatisfaction with the traditional procedures from which much may possibly result in years to come.

## THE CITY CHURCH

The possibility of telling a single story for the church in the small city and in the large is due to the fact that the most frequent or modal church, even in the great city, is no larger than the average church of the small city. Indeed the most characteristic metropolitan church, that is to say, the church served by a single pastor without paid staff, is slightly smaller than the average church in the small city. Moreover, nine-tenths of these one-man churches belong to types which, as a later chapter will show, appear with almost no trace of special urban adaptation.

The real difference is not between the church in the small city and in the large, but between churches of different sizes; for larger churches everywhere strongly tend to have more complicated organization, to employ staffs of paid workers instead of the single pastor, and to undertake more varied programs.

It must, however, be recognized that the community setting of the church in the small city is less complicated and that its community roots are less often strained and tangled than those of the church in the large city. Otherwise its fortunes and those of the average church in the large city are much of a piece.

In attending, then, to difference between staffed and unstaffed churches— this difference ordinarily signifying a broader and a narrower range of functions—one may reach a generalization which will be typically true for cities of all sorts.[1]

---

[1] The objective data on which this generalization rests concern the virtually 100 per cent. surveys of Protestant churches in Springfield, Mass., and St. Louis; the 1,040 city churches in fifty-six cities, most of 100,000 population and over, reported in the author's *1,000 City Churches*; twenty-eight large city churches for which intensive case studies were made in *The Church in the Changing City*, and nearly 2,000 churches studied by Ross W. Sanderson and reported upon in *The Strategy of City Church Planning*. Data from numerous smaller surveys have been consulted.

URBAN CONGREGATIONS

The most characteristic aspect of the urban church, as of the rural, is that it brings adherents together in congregations.

The first aspect in which these congregating groups are to be examined concerns the types of occasion on which they gather. The most obvious distinctions are between the public religious services, the sessions of the Sunday school and the meetings of subsidiary organizations and other occasions of gathering.

How does the urban church divide attendance between these types of occasion? No general records exist on this point. The city Sunday school has a smaller average membership than the church of which it is a part, and, in general, it is natural to assume a smaller aggregate attendance. The rather slight available data covering church and also Sunday school and subsidiaries must, accordingly, be taken as indicating points at which the division of attendance between the three major types of occasion is significant for the urban church rather than as any evidence of what is a typical distribution.

Table III compares the percentage distribution of attendance for the twelve white Protestant churches of Tarrytown, a suburb of some 15,000 people, for twenty-eight large churches in great cities illustrating various degrees of adaptation to urban environment, and for the forty-five Protestant churches of Springfield, Mass.

TABLE III — DIVISION OF CHURCH ATTENDANCE ON MAJOR TYPES OF OCCASIONS

| | Attendance | | | (Hours Attendance) |
|---|---|---|---|---|
| | Tarrytown | 28 Large City Churches | | Springfield |
| Occasion | Per Cent. Distribution | Approximate Median | Range | Per Cent. Distribution |
| Public religious services......... | 57 | 52 | 15-75 | 48 |
| Sunday school.................. | 29 | 25 | 9-38 | 17 |
| Subsidiary and other............ | 14 | 23 | 9-51 | 35 |

The data presented by the table are significant at the following points:

Surveys of metropolitan areas by zones have shown that suburban churches are less developed than urban churches in any zone. This principle is evidenced by the Tarrytown churches which bring people together chiefly for church and Sunday school, their other occasions of congregation being mainly young people's societies of a conventional type. This is probably typical of churches on the metropolitan fringes which are under little distinctly urban pressure, and of churches generally in small cities.

The twenty-eight large city churches represent a body of more than 40,000 adherents. Their locations range from the most prosperous to the most deteriorated, and the churches reflect all degrees of economic pressure. The most significant aspect of the distribution of their attendance is the enormous range of difference, from as high as 75 per cent. of the total given to public services to as low as 15 per cent. Sunday-school and subsidiary attendance is similarly now a very small fraction of the total and again a very large one. The aggregate showing is that the city church is relatively less an affair of church and Sunday-school attendance and relatively more one of subsidiary gatherings than is the suburban church and probably than is the church in the smaller city. It has taken on a wide range of secular functions.

The Springfield data measure the distribution of attendance in another way, namely, by hours rather than by number of persons attending. That is to say, the average length of the occasion which brought the group together was considered as well as the number of persons present. The effect of this method of measuring is to reduce the percentage of attendance represented by the Sunday school, whose session is notoriously brief, and to increase that represented by the subsidiaries whose activities characteristically take more time.

Another way of showing how extraordinarily different one urban church is from another is to calculate the proportion of total attendance which falls on Sunday and on week days respectively. For twenty large city churches the Sunday ratio ranged from as high as 92 per cent. of the total to as low as 31 per cent., with an average of 73.

Obviously Sunday attendance is primarily attendance upon religious services, while week-day attendance is more largely social and recreational or cultural in the broader sense. The unequal extension of the church's organized life to command week-day time clearly evidences the fact that some churches have a distinctly broader range of ministries than others.

The extraordinary variety of subsidiary organizations in the modern city church and the increased aggregate proportion of time and attendance which they represent, entitle them to special study. The forty-five Springfield churches had an average of ten subsidiaries per church, the number ranging from two to twenty-four. Twenty large city churches had an average of eighteen and a range of from sixteen to sixty.

Table IV classifies the aggregate annual subsidiary attendance of these twenty churches (involving an attendance of 470,188 persons), as distributed between subsidiaries for the several age and sex groups and those differentiated neither as to age nor as to sex.

Chart XI summarizes the data of Table IV.

Differences in subsidiary organization are partly the effect of size, the smaller churches which maintain even a conventional program ordinarily having more subsidiaries relative to membership than larger churches with elaborate programs, and partly the consequence of theory depending upon

TABLE IV — DISTRIBUTION OF ANNUAL ATTENDANCE ON SUB-
SIDIARY ORGANIZATIONS AND STATED ACTIVITIES OF 20 CITY
CHURCHES

| Type of Organization | Per Cent. |
|---|---|
| Mixed adults | 5.5 |
| Adult men | 7.0 |
| Adult women | 9.8 |
| Mixed young people* | 13.3 |
| Young men | 4.1 |
| Young women | 3.5 |
| Mixed boys and girls | 13.3 |
| Boys | 9.3 |
| Girls | 9.1 |
| Mixed children | 8.3 |
| Classified by function rather than by sex or age | 16.8 |
| Total | 100.0 |

* Between 15 and 23 years of age.

whether or not a church deliberately undertakes to furnish a rounded program adapted to each age and sex group in its constituency.

Other differences are due to denominational usage, some denominations
being accustomed to organize the young people of the two sexes separately,

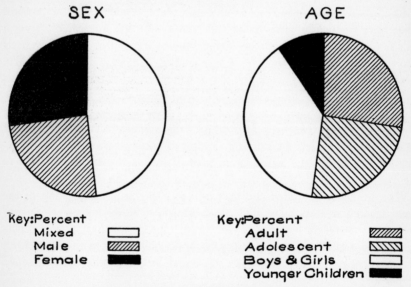

CHART XI—DISTRIBUTION OF ANNUAL ATTENDANCE ON SUBSIDIARY ORGANIZATIONS

while others mix them in traditional youth societies. The relative scarcity
of women's organizations in denominations of foreign antecedents reflects
the lesser degree to which these women have become emancipated and capable of self-expression.

Subsidiary organization also differs strikingly with respect to the relation of paid workers to it. The laity of the well-to-do city church are amply competent to manage their own subsidiaries, and the paid worker is merely a convenience like the expert in the country club, while in the church of poor and handicapped people the paid worker may be the director and virtual soul of the enterprise. The place of subsidiary organizations in the theory of the church's function, order and government involves still other differences which will have later consideration.

How far some churches have come from being Sunday congregations for strictly religious exercises and how numerous and complex are the groupings found necessary to organize their various constituencies have now been objectively demonstrated. The motives and pressures which have led to these organized forms and the ideas by means of which they are rationalized receive attention in subsequent chapters.

## THE PROJECTING AND INDIVIDUALIZING ASPECTS OF THE URBAN CHURCH

For the urban church in these aspects not even such scanty records exist as those which illustrated the story of its congregating aspect. Moreover, the functions themselves are less obtrusively expressed. They are widely diffused rather than massed as to time and place. Analyses of the pastoral office have frequently been made, and occasionally the number of pastoral calls is recorded, but a comprehensive picture of the church projecting itself into the community and the lives of its members has rarely been undertaken.

Records for a week's work by 153 urban ministers show, however, that pastoral work takes more time than any other single function of the ministry, absorbing about one-fourth of the total, or an average of fourteen and one-half hours per week according to this sample.[2] The proportion of total work-time which the minister devotes to pastoral work goes up appreciably when he has the assistance of a small staff, but goes down again in the case of large staffs which involve a maximum of administration.

With ministers of staffed churches calls absorb just about one-half of the time devoted to pastoral work. Calls obviously have a great variety of objectives. Some are intended to carry a message of personal religion, others have to do with church-membership or work, others deal with emergencies or with specific need, while others are social in the undifferentiated sense.

---

[2] These figures differ somewhat from those derived from May & Shuttleworth's 130 cases of ministers in large urban communities (*The Education of American Ministers*, Vol. IV, p. 180), on account of differences in classification. In making the present calculation, lectures and addresses on non-religious occasions where the minister is not presumed to speak with the authority of an ordained teacher of religion, are separated from the regular homiletical function. Otherwise, homiletics would be the minister's most time-consuming function, as is reported by May.

Even the most careful case records find it hard to unravel the mixture of motives involved in individual calls. The undifferentiated pastoral call is the one most often reported. Curiously also, formal religious conversation rarely dominates the pastoral call or interview. When not wholly formal its genius is essentially occasional; it concerns particular issues rather than abstract religious ones.

The next most frequent pastoral function is one of the several forms of pastoral sociability, opportunity for which urban ministers find most frequently in connection with church gatherings where the projecting and congregating aspects of the church meet. Contacts of this sort occupy about one-fourth of the time devoted to pastoral work. The remaining fourth of the time is divided between consultations in which people come to the minister, rather than wait for him to go to them, and various forms of long-range communication. These are proportionately more numerous in churches with large staffs where an office and office hours are maintained and where it becomes an accepted fact that the minister cannot be expected to "get around" as the minister of the smaller church can. There is economy in substituting the consultation for the call, and it is commonly agreed that consultation ordinarily is more definitely motivated and permits of the exercise of more expert pastoral relationships. In other words, it is even more highly individualized than the call.

Communication, as a method of projecting the church into the lives of its own constituents, also appears more frequently as a substitute for face-to-face relations, especially in the larger urban churches. Individual correspondence tends to be reserved for somewhat formal matters, while circularization and wholesale telephoning are habitual means of keeping in touch with the dispersed constituency; and publicity, through the secular press as well as through church bulletins and other organs, is increasingly relied upon.

Urban churches probably also tend more frequently to concentrate their projective activities by the house-to-house evangelistic canvasses and every-member canvasses for financial support. Into these projective and pastoral functions lay activity very largely enters. Large bodies of constituents are employed in the canvasses just mentioned, lay deacons and deaconesses share in the traditional oversight of the church's members and especially function on the side of charity.

The subsidiary organizations of the church cultivate their special constituencies along natural lines, in which calling, communication and publicity have large place. Exact studies of the chain of circumstances and influence which bring adherents into full church-membership, however, make it appear that the greatest single projective influence is that of individual members in their normal social relationships. Kinship, marriage, the gregarious habits of young people, and neighborliness are the most important influences. The organized effort of the church to project itself merely facilitates and supplements these.

A city church which desires to increase its projective power by the employment of a staff supplementing its ministry most frequently begins with a secretary. This generally means an appeal to communication as a substitute for face-to-face relationships. The next most frequent choice, however, will be an assistant minister, who will understudy the chief minister in several aspects and may or may not specialize on pastoral work. The third will be definitely a pastoral assistant. A study of the composition and work of staffs according to size, however, shows that the projective aspects are rarely increased as fast as the congregating ones as a result of additions to staff, while administrative functions increase most of all. In brief, staffs get people out to church more successfully than they get the church out to people.

Another channel for the projection of the church into the life of the community is the extra-homiletical addresses of the minister as a leader of public affairs and his attendance and participation as a quasi-representative of his church upon and in meetings and occasions of community importance. The *Middletown* study regarded such activity as the minister's attempt to compensate for his waning spiritual authority. Besides this, the church habitually gives publicity, advocacy and support to wide ranges of good causes. This function has further attention in the chapter on the church's social-service ministries.

While the representative city church feels that it never has lay workers enough and tends to be jealous of the calls of outside interests upon their time and energies, an occasional church systematically undertakes to project its members into community activities, such as memberships on the directing boards of social agencies and participation in general civic and social movements of the city. Others tend to specialize in the supra-parochial activities of their own denominations, or to project themselves into interchurch activities and the processes of the church at large.

Endless arguments have been indulged in as to the respective values of the congregating and the projective aspects of the church's life. Personal preference gives many ministers a distinct bias in one direction or the other, or else toward administration. The values at which pastoral work aims are largely personal and immediate, but by no theory are they consummated until they have been made permanent by participation in the larger life of the group as expressed in congregations, which in turn seems to many to be the condition of their largest projection into the ongoing stream of human relationships.

## ADMINISTRATION

While the processes of administration in the city church are colored by rival theories of the ministry and of the sources of religious authority as embodied in the polities of denominations, objective record shows that all work out in very similar fashion. The characteristic urban church is an evolving and as yet rather an incoherent organization by no means corresponding to the constitutional models originally projected for stable and homogeneous rural groups.

The city church is not a closely knit organization. "I have not the financial records of my Sunday school," replies a pastor, "and if I should ask for them I should be told it was none of my business." The numerous age and sex groupings of the typical church constitute a loose confederation of adherents in the name of many interests not always closely related to the central core of religion. They often appeal competitively to individuals of a given age and sex, or, as sometimes happens, some clique in the church assumes to be the bearer of the particular revelation once delivered to the saints and proceeds to control its own plans and purse with small regard to the church's central interest or its administrative unity. Such maverick subsidiaries are relatively frequent.

One inevitable result is that great gaps occur between the different interest and age groups. Continuity in religious culture and loyalty are not secured. The hold of a given organization on its following is often very brief.

All this reflects the Protestant church's plasticity and freedom for experimentation, but scarcely commends its mechanism. All theories of church organization are consequently outmoded by the necessity of securing greater unification through administration.

The natural coördinator of the church is its minister, and however averse individuals and types of ministers may be to undertaking administrative responsibility, it demands on the average only slightly less than one-fourth of the city minister's duty time on the basis of a sample of 153 cases. More explicitly stated, it takes the minister about eleven and one-half hours per week to make his church machinery go. Where the minister works alone or has only one assistant, pastoral and preaching functions take more time than administration. In staffs of from three to five workers pastoral and administrative work require about equal time, but with more than five workers administration is generally the dominant function. Furthermore, with the increase of staff, more and more of the time of subordinate ministers has also to go to administration.

Associated with the minister in administration are the church's constitutional lay officers, frequently divided between those whose concerns are primarily spiritual and those concerned with temporal affairs. On a sample of 22,000 constituents of large city churches, some 3 per cent. are found in various official positions in church and subsidiaries. Officers equalled 4 per cent. of the membership of forty-three Springfield churches.

About one-tenth of the time which the minister of a staffed church spends in administration has been devoted to meetings of such official groups. These constituted 18 per cent. of all subsidiary gatherings in the case of the Springfield churches. In addition to these, conferences with lay church officers find increasing prominence among the duties of the city minister.

Besides special committees assigned to temporary duties, the city church tends strongly to develop extra-constitutional machinery to secure some measure of coördination. When there are only moderate complexities to be overcome, this is apt to take the form of a church cabinet in which the heads of numerous subsidiaries are brought together to supplement the constitutional officers presumed to govern the church. When, however, organization becomes too complex and constituencies too distinct, this means of coördination tends to prove ineffective, and the church must be held together chiefly by the administration of a common staff.

In order to keep the staff itself united and permit it really to be the unifying machinery of the church, staff supervision becomes an increasing necessity. With about three-fifths of the staffed churches the tradition of a weekly staff conference has become established, though it is a tradition sometimes more honored in the breach than in the observance. Individual conferences with staff members take more and more time of the minister in the larger church. As executive of the church and with the authority of the lay boards which engage his associates, the minister assigns duties, judges work, and in most cases virtually determines employment and dismissals. Staff supervision, however, is generally informal. Less than one-half of subordinate staff members state that written reports of their work are required.

The supervision of loosely connected subsidiaries is naturally difficult. While the minister or some staff member has a certain unacknowledged responsibility for oversight of most subsidiaries, it is only to subsidiaries composed of the more dependent age groups that staff leadership is generally definitely assigned.

The more complicated the church organization, the larger the rôle occupied by records and accounting in its supervision. These means of impressive and objective control are increasingly in evidence; and in very large staffs more of the time of the joint force will be given to accountancy than to any other single function.

The necessity of unifying poorly integrated churches by means of administration results in a narrowing of the range of functions performed by the chief minister and the surrendering of the less imperative ones to others. In only a few cases has the experiment of turning over primary administrative responsibility to an executive secretary been successfully maintained over any long period of time. The chief minister must administer the church, as well as carry on the imperative priestly, prophetic and pastoral functions. There is a limit beyond which no type of function can be transferred to others. Within this limit, however, the minister of the highly organized church increasingly exercises a long-range control. The pressure of the situation cries loudly for simpler and more unified types of organization.

SUMMARY

Putting together the organized life of all the churches of a community into a single picture shows examples of churches of many sizes and types. The Census of Religious Bodies reports for each major city in terms of number of churches, membership, Sunday-school enrollment and total finances for each denomination. More varied aspects of organization and life are reported in typical surveys. One looks in vain, however, for a really comprehensive summary of the parochial life of any urban community covering most of the significant points involved in the foregoing interpretation. An illustration of the type of generalization which such a summary would yield is offered by the case of the New York suburb previously cited.

Week in and week out the organized life of white Protestantism in this suburb of 15,000 people amounts to this: that some 750 people, equaling 23 per cent. of the body of determinate adherents, gather for Sunday morning service. They represent only one-fourth of the population even potentially, but proceed to scatter in nine different directions to worship God in groups averaging seventy-five persons each. Half as many as go to church in the morning attend again in the evening. About 780, or 82 per cent. of the Protestant children and youths of five to twenty years of age break up into nine Sunday schools, with an average attendance of seventy. (A few pupils are actually under five and a few come from outside of the town.) Three hundred and seventy people, or a little more than 10 per cent. of the adherent body, attend one or another of some five dozen week-day meetings or stated activities (most of them occurring only monthly) maintained by the nine churches. The annual cost of these nine churches to the community, including all personal relationships and incidental ministries involved in church fellowship, is from $65,000 to $75,000.

Organized religion in the larger cities is not so terribly subdivided as this. The worshipping groups in a typical city average much larger than those of the suburb under discussion; but the aggregate size of the Sunday morning audience is only half that of the nominal membership and only one-half as many go to church Sunday night as go in the morning. About one-tenth of the number of Sunday church-goers attend a mid-week service, and the average Sunday school is slightly more than half as large as the average church, while there are nearly three subsidiary organizations for every one hundred members.

A community-wide review of parochial church organization thus yields a complicated pattern, partially justified by the great variety of the component elements making up the larger church constituencies and partially explained by their very unequal assimilation to the central core of religious interest. The church thus insinuates itself into life at many points, yet is so subdivided that its characteristic units are individually weak, while their aggregate is scarcely impressive relative to the size of population and the immense varieties of the community's concerns.

## SUPRA-PAROCHIAL ORGANIZATION

The church is, of course, more than the sum of the local churches. The local churches belong to wider ecclesiastical circles which have organization and a life of their own. These associations, presbyteries, and the like, are regarded by some denominations as creations of the local church group, while others think that valid authority is something handed down from above, through an ecclesiastical hierarchy. The territorial unit of such larger organizations is based in some denominations on areas substantially coterminous with the urban community; while in other cases, both city and rural churches are combined in larger district jurisdictions.

### DENOMINATIONAL ORGANIZATION

These more inclusive aspects of the organized church are expressed, first of all in denominational agencies and machinery. A denomination manifests itself as a system which unites a group of local churches, which supplements and directs their work, and which carries on specific activities in their joint behalf. Whatever the denomination's special form of polity, the following typical denominational phenomena tend to occur. The ministers of the denominational group meet statedly for fellowship and conference as to common problems. Organized machinery of denominational administration and extension develops. Its primary concerns are the founding of churches, the securing of ministers, aiding and directing weaker parishes through the many vicissitudes to which the church is heir. It will promote general denominational objectives, perhaps including the raising of money for the support of missions. In general it is designed to operate the church as a larger local unit. Churches whose government is decentralized leave their more local denominational organization in a rather shadowy state. Those with stronger policies attempt, not always successfully, to exercise genuine oversight and control.

In larger cities and with the stronger denominations, the original ecclesias-tical machinery set up by the church for general supervision of typically rural areas is supplemented by special extension agencies sometimes called city mission societies. The societies bring denominations to a more definite consciousness of the unity of the churches of a community and of the more distinctive religious needs of urban populations. Agencies of this type have taken varied yet rather similar forms in the various denominations. Their development has often been paralleled or combined with similar denomina-tional machinery for the administration and promotion of religious educa-tion. There is also likely to be a city-wide organization of the women's missionary interests of the denomination, some union or league of young people's societies, and possibly a city-wide organization of men. Finally there will be city-wide committees for the promotion of special movements like the devotional life, tithing, etc.

No sufficient data exist to warrant generalization as to the number of extra-parochial organizations in American cities. What the denomination amounts to organizationally may, however, be illustrated by the case of St. Louis. Thirteen major denominations in this city record a total of forty-nine such agencies as follows: thirteen ministers' meetings; seven city church extension societies; fourteen denominational city-wide women's organiza-tions; ten similar young people's organizations; together with a scattering group representing other interests.

Such denominational machinery, less elaborate in smaller cities, but still more elaborate in larger ones, is found throughout America.

Recently denominations have shown a considerable disposition to integrate some of these too manifold agencies. The strictly ecclesiastical and the special promotional functions are put under a single agency. The stronger city societies particularly incline to absorb the administration of religious education and the general promotion of denominational missions.

Another local type of denominational organization is represented by par-ticular institutions of education and philanthropy. These denominational schools and charities enable the parishes to do collectively what few of them could do alone. Most of these institutions bear distinctive labels so that an inventory is largely self-explanatory. Using St. Louis as an illustration again, one finds forty-five specialized denominational enterprises of this type, of which twenty-eight are children's, old people's and other homes, eight hospitals and nine schools of major rank. A few denominations in some cities make greater or less attempt to integrate all these agencies into a working whole. Largely, however, they are like the subsidiaries of the local churches, rather loosely related to the central denominational interests.

Limitations of space do not permit discussion to include the marginal fields of organization occupied by the church's extensions and allies, such as the Christian Associations and the non-sectarian philanthropies. Nor is there room for more than mention of constructive agencies like the Boy and Girl Scouts widely sponsored and housed by the churches.[3]

DENOMINATIONAL ORGANIZATION ON THE NATIONAL LEVEL

Internal integration in a still more inclusive phase has also been going on within denominations, particularly in the administrative sphere. Numerous specialized boards for missions, education and general promotion have grown up together with their regional and state agencies, and have become increasingly strong. Their diversity, and sometimes their rivalries, have hastened the organization of central councils or executive committees by which many denominations have sought to coördinate and control their over-complicated machinery.[4] In the more loosely organized denominations, which historically have been based upon the independence of the local congregation, this administrative centralization has involved considerable actual growth of central ecclesiastical authority. This has been true, for example, of the Congregational, Baptist, and Disciples churches. However much it has been denied that administrative centralization carries any ecclesiastical implication, and however much it has been attempted to limit the centralized administration to mere business matters, the fact is that social control within the denomination has been strengthened, and the subordinate divisions have been put under increasing group pressure. The true meaning of the process has been rightly discerned by reactionary movements in the Baptist and Disciples groups and has been met by opposition and revolt.

Like it or not, denominations have come to mean more than they used to. They exercise wider functions and their functioning is more necessary to the well-being of the local churches than ever before. Denominations increasingly supply the competent planning for their subordinate units and furnish the technical experts. The interdependence of parts and whole is ever increasing; and this is true in spite of movements for financial decentralization on the part of a number of mission boards.

INTERCHURCH ORGANIZATION

Interchurch organization and federation represent another type of supraparochial organization which has special attention in chapter xii. It is obvious that whether the problem be that of the relation of the loosely bound subsidiary to the local church, or of the church's affiliates and allies

---

[3] An organizational study of these agencies in rural fields was included in the series of Institute reports which this study summarizes. It shows that most of the essential problems of organization experienced by the church apply to these agencies as well. See Douglass, *How Shall Country Youth Be Served?* (Institute of Social and Religious Research).

[4] Brown, William Adams, *The Church in America* (New York: The Macmillan Company, 1922), pp. 250 ff.

with respect to the denominations, or of the total body of coöperating Protestantism, the matter of effective coördination takes central importance.

In federations, for example, the quasi-independent departments present a similar situation to that caused by the more loosely related subsidiaries of a local church.

As soon, however, as an organization ceases to be a face-to-face group the factor of representation begins to loom large. This begins with the officers of the local church and with the attempt to coördinate loosely affiliated groups by associating their leaders in a central church cabinet. When different and often competing denominations federate, equitable representation naturally becomes a central consideration. With most supra-parochial organizations the committee system reaches high development. Paid officials and offices multiply, involving the necessity of securing the unity of the larger group by means of communication and publicity. Special studies of the Institute have followed out these problems in detail in the denominational and coöperative organizations of representative American cities.[5] A specially difficult problem of coöperation is found in the fact that denominational units of administration so largely fail to cover identical territory.

### PROBLEMS OF ORGANIZATION COMMON TO RURAL AND URBAN CHURCHES

Many of the problems of organization are essentially the same with urban and with rural churches. The virtues of democratic control, active and loyal participation and creative thinking and decision are as important in the simple rural church as in the highly organized urban situation; and may be equally operative within the local parish and in the more inclusive ecclesiastical organizations. The difference between city and country in these points is not basic and can easily be exaggerated. However, the less definite attachment of the city church to a particular neighborhood, the dwindling influence of the urban parish as a definite area, to say nothing of the greater environmental pressure bearing upon the separate congregations, makes the organizational problem of the city more immediately acute. The human nature factors remain constant in either environment. Squabbles, scandals and schisms are equally fatal in city or in country.

### THEORIES OF ORGANIZATION

Among the common problems of organization the central one is the theory of organization itself. On what basis shall the various aspects and parts of the church be put together? The evolution of the church in the United States first added the Sunday school to the undifferentiated religious service, then a women's society, finally the young people's organization of the Christian Endeavor type. Beyond this traditional core organization has gone forward by accretion. Missions early established themselves as a

---

[5] See Bibliography to chapter xii.

specific and separately organized interest. This was followed in many churches by recreational or athletic activities and in some by specific social-service activities, each tending to be rated as a separate interest or department. As measured by the enlargement of city church staffs, this is still the predominant method by which the church develops its structure. A new type of worker is added to the old ones to facilitate whatever new set of interests the church's expanding life may come to include. This is the vertical method of organizing the church, a committee, "department" or paid worker being provided to care for each major interest.[6]

In many cases the new interests are quite unadjusted to the old; and although the constitutional structure of the church has become overlaid with these mushroom growths, there has been no overhauling of the whole fabric.

One consequence of the method of growth by accretion is that the church's interests appeal competitively to the same constituency. That is to say, the same person is solicited time and again, within his own age group, for interest, service and generally also for money. In the end, he is asked to belong to more things than he can or will attend to loyally or for any length of time. As already noted, such competitive appeal is largely fruitless, since constituents with a single connection with the church still remain the majority.

A contrary theory of organization has originated in the ordinary methods of religious education and now seeks to apply itself to the entire church. Starting with the graded Sunday school, it desires to gather up all the interests of each age and sex group into a single control. It would like to regard, for example, the organizations of the young people's society type as a freer but still an educational expression of the life of the same group in the Sunday school; and would attempt to attach worship, social and recreational activities to the same scheme of organization till a rounded program has been reached for people at every age level.

Missions and community service, which have often been organized as separate interests, are increasingly gathered up under this enlarged conception of religious education and conducted as a unified process rather than in a duplicatory and competitive way. This is the horizontal method of organizing the local church. Table VIII suggests the variety of subordinate staff workers who have been employed under one or the other of these schemes of local organization.

The theory of horizontal or graded organization of the church shows hopeful promise in cases where the church's constituency is relatively homogeneous. Even so, however, a resolution of the church's governing body that "the young people's organization shall hereafter be regarded as an expressional aspect of the young people's department of the Sunday school" may

---

[6] See Table VIII, p. 125.

result only in the discovery that the two organizations are dealing with two quite different groups of young people, and that not only are the members of the young people's society not in the Sunday school, but that they do not even live in the same part of town.

In the case of churches whose numerous constituencies are widely separated in the social scale, the notion of a horizontal organization, gathering everybody of a given age and sex into a common category and making all that the church does for persons on that level phases of a unified program, simply fails to appreciate the facts. It has already been noted that such a church is unified administratively, not by the constitutional machinery of the church nor even by the extra-constitutional cabinet, but essentially by the activities of a common staff.

Both theories of internal church organization consequently are justified— each in its place. Psychologically it is sound to regard the worship, instruction, expressional activities and social life of a group as phases of a single integrated process. Sociologically it is necessary to attach different constituencies to the church at different levels of interest and to recognize the necessary dangling character at any given time of many of these attachments.

FREQUENCY OF ORGANIZATIONS

Closely related to the question of method in organization is the question of quantity. What constitutes under-organization or over-organization? Obviously these are relative terms depending on the size of the constituency to be organized. One has found an average of ten subsidiary organizations per church in a city like Springfield (one for every forty members), and fifteen per church in a random sample from larger cities. The maximum is sixty subsidiaries in a single church. But even this is not necessarily over-organization. That comes, first of all, with the imitative traits of the over-small church and its effort to maintain a traditional pattern. Not infrequently this results in a subsidiary for every ten members and in the extremest case, a subsidiary for every three.

The over-large church, on the contrary, finds difficulty in supplying the normal number of relationships to the more numerous adherents. A possible solution, already noted, is to project the energies of some of these surplus adherents into the general life of the community and to count that as more important than their mere regimentation within the confines of parish life. Even so, the vast church finds it difficult to devise means of active participation for all its adherents, and fails to afford the culture which active participation alone brings.

DIFFERENTIATIONS AND SPECIALIZATIONS

Another major problem of organization is the effect of differentiation and specialization upon the church. The experience of the "larger parish" shows how serious this issue is in the case of the rural church. This highly significant effort to furnish country churches with the same variety of leadership that city churches have does not manage to work out quite according to theory when confronted by the closer-knit ties of the rural community group. The staffed and departmentalized city church, on the other hand, confronts populations for which the church has already become only one out of a large number of social groups involving different people. For such populations, consultation with experts may be more satisfactory than the closer personal ties and relationships of the more intimate group.

In the development of denominational structure beyond the local parish it is obvious that all the churches are increasingly dependent upon specialized talent, not because they need financial aid or lack ability to control themselves in normal relations, but because in such technical fields as religious education, social work, missions, and finances, only the group of churches collectively can afford the necessary specialists. In most denominations, even the stronger church has become more dependent than formerly upon the larger group life.

This review of the organizations and life of the modern church invites one to moralize upon some of the religionists' suspicions and fears of institutionalization as set forth in the opening chapter. It helps to explain why the church often appears like a factory shut down in order to undergo a process of reorganization. Why, ask pious souls, this loss of time in eternally tinkering with ecclesiastical machinery?

But with a broadening conception of what religion implies in human association and service and with improving organizational techniques, it can scarcely be otherwise than that the ecclesiastical machinery will need constant modification.

Organization, left to grow wild, does soon become external even to the immediate aims of a social group, and may ultimately block its normal institutional processes. Then, indeed, the suspicions and fears of the religionist will be amply justified. The whole institutional aspect of the church will be following its essential objectives "very far off."

Nevertheless the religionist's impulse to ignore or abandon organization in hope of serving the spiritual life immediately is quite obviously wrong with respect to the actual church which this chapter has described. The philosophical maxim, "mechanism everywhere present but everywhere subordinate," applies specifically to such a church. Organization is indeed to be suspected, and consequently to be controlled. It is at this point that the church's self-criticism needs to be most constant and relentless. On these terms organization may be used, modified, made as efficient and technically as perfect as possible, valued for what it is, but never confused with what it is not.

# CHAPTER VI

## *The Ministry*

Whether the minister is regarded as a priest and divinely appointed intermediary in the relations of God and man, or essentially as merely a gifted layman set apart as a religious specialist by the action of his church, the ministry, objectively considered, constitutes one of 572 gainful occupations engaged in by citizens of the United States and one of about thirty professions. It employs more men than any other profession except that of medicine.

### NUMBER OF MINISTERS

The 1930 Census figure gives the United States 148,848 ministers, about 98,000 of whom are white Protestants available for the service of the 163,538 white Protestant churches. There are thus about 600 ministers for each thousand of these churches.

Seven-tenths of village and open-country churches have only a fraction of a minister each. Two-thirds of the open-country churches have non-resident ministers. Village churches alone average about one-half of a minister per church. Two-thirds of town churches maintain their own full-time ministers. The typical city church has a full-time minister, while probably from one-fifth to one-fourth of all city churches have additional paid religious professionals in their employ. Considering the extremes, the country church has no minister, but nine times out of ten borrows a small fraction of his services from the village or town, while the city church has a full-time minister or more.

### CHARACTERISTICS OF THE PROFESSION

Besides inner qualifications for religious leadership, the ministry requires certain skills determined by the nature of the agency which it serves. As has already been shown, these directly relate to the congregating or projecting aspects of church life and to their administration. The main qualities, however, sought by employing churches are of a more generalized sort. An analysis of many letters of church committees, describing the sort of ministers they desire, shows that personal likeableness and such social qualities as are symbolized in the term "good mixer" are the first requirements. Second come those of pastoral aptitude, sincerity and tact; next, capacity to attract young people, and "adaptability," which apparently means capacity to get along with whatever conditions one finds. In a significant sampling, only one church in four puts chief stress on preaching ability, and one in six on executive capacity. What the churches want in a minister is essentially a successful salesman for their enterprise. A striking feature of the analysis of the ministerial qualifications desired, is the virtual absence from them of any doctrinal specifications. Still more significant is the fact that the actual demand for ministers virtually assumes the maintenance of the religious *status quo*. It is leadership in things as they are and adaptability to conditions as they stand, rather than innovative or prophetic leadership, that is demanded.[1]

VARIETY IN THE CHURCHES TO BE SERVED

The profession resulting from a demand of this sort finds enormous objective differences in the churches to be served. They differ in environment, in size, in the characteristics of their constituencies, in organization and program, in financial strength. Differences between the conditions confronted by the urban and the rural ministries respectively appear at almost every point. Although so few rural congregations have resident ministers, ministers are relatively much more frequent in the country than in the city, on account of the smaller average size of the country church; that is to say, there are more ministers per hundred thousand population in the country.

Some two-thirds of all ordained ministers are engaged in the parochial ministry; that is to say, in pastorates of local congregations. Many of the remainder are in the service of the overhead denominational agencies or of the religious extensions and allies of the church which earlier chapters have described. The present discussion, accordingly, while generalized in terms, applies primarily to the parochial minister. The chief topics covered are his recruiting and response; educational requirements; educational status; induction to the ministry; placement and supervision; tenure; the minister's actual task; his economic basis; and his reaction to his work. To these are added brief comments on the non-parochial ministry. Major differences between urban and rural conditions are discussed under each heading.

RECRUITING AND RESPONSE

The annual demand for new ministers for the white Protestant churches is estimated at 6.5 per cent. of the total number, or 6,400 recruits. Twice as many of these places, in a given year, will be filled by untrained ministers

---

[1] The above characterization is based chiefly on May, *The Education of American Ministers* (New York: Institute of Social and Religious Research, 1934), Vol. II, chapter vii.

as by trained ones. The present graduates of theological seminaries furnish only 21 per cent. of these necessary replacements, though, as will later be seen, even this fraction represents more men than can be employed at reasonable salaries. Relative to the need for recruits, the supply from seminaries has remained constant for fifty years.

RECRUITING METHODS

The recruiting methods by which the depleted ranks of the ministry are supplied belong more to the tradition of the church than to its organized machinery. As the chief influences in their decisions to enter this calling, ministers enumerate pastors and parents. The average minister expects to be on the lookout for choice prospects in order to fill up the future ranks of the vocation. Pious homes sometimes dedicate children to the ministry in infancy and all along direct their ambitions in the same direction. Systematic recruiting begins in the denominational colleges or summer assemblies of young people. Finally, the seminaries do their own competitive recruiting of students. Prominent alumni pass along promising candidates to their own schools, and canvassers go among the colleges seeking replacements.

ENVIRONMENTAL BIAS

In inquiring into the candidate's fitness for the ministry many churches formally interrogate him as to the consciousness of a divine call or sense of religious vocation, and half of the ministers interrogated testified to having experienced such a call. The responses show a very striking environmental bias. Returns from 1,800 pastors show that 12 per cent. were brought up in large cities, while 26 per cent. were from small cities, 14 per cent. from towns and villages and 48 per cent. from communities of less than 1,000 population. Of fully trained ministers, 44 per cent. came from the smaller rural communities. This is a very different distribution from that of population.

The number of rural churches furnishing recruits for professional religious service seems to be increasing and possibly the proportion of the total ministry secured from such sources is increasing as well. Between 1920 and 1925 at least one-sixth of about 1,000 village churches examined sent one or more persons into the ministry or into missionary service. Of some 1,200 open-country churches, one-twelfth similarly responded. Between 1925 and 1930 the proportions had increased respectively to one-fifth and one-tenth. On the average, whenever a rural church had produced one recruit, it secured another within a five-year period. Churches with trained and resident leadership made a considerably better record in this respect than others.

Only one-half of the parents of the 1,800 trained ministers cited above, and one-third of the parents of the untrained had had more than a grammar-school education. Rating their homes as to economic level, 4 per cent. reported their parents as well-to-do, 31 per cent. as poor or very poor. Of the fathers of these 1,800 ministers, 15 per cent. were skilled or unskilled laborers, and 53 per cent. farmers or small tradesmen. Ministers' homes provided twenty-five times their natural quota to the replenishment of the ministry.

When one considered still larger classes of population, native-born whites, either of native or of foreign and mixed parentage, furnish a smaller proportion of ministers than do foreign-born whites or Negroes. Constituting only 9.9 per cent. of the population, and furnishing but 3.7 per cent. of the professional population, the Negro race produces 15.4 per cent. of the ministers. In other words, responses to the call of the ministry are strongly skewed in favor of candidates from small communities, from relatively humble antecedents, both educationally and economically, and from the less well-established racial elements of the population.

### EDUCATIONAL REQUIREMENTS

The theoretic terms on which the modern churches recruit are that the candidate for the ministry shall undergo the necessary educational processes to fit him for his work, after which he shall be examined in all aspects of his suitability and if found satisfactory, inducted into office. But the controversy lying behind this theory, both as to the necessity of an educated ministry and as to the appropriateness of the particular educational requirements to be maintained, has been one of the profoundest and most far-reaching episodes in the history of the American church.

#### THE DECLINE OF THE EDUCATED MINISTRY

Very early in the colonial period sectarianism began to trace the gospel back to the "unlearned and ignorant" leaders of primitive Christianity. Baptist and Quaker exhorters challenged the religious monopoly of the parsons of the state church and became naughty intruders "within the bounds of other ministers." Revivalism exalted native religious gifts and decried education. Graduates of Presbyterian "log colleges" seceded from a presbytery which limited ordination to the graduates of New England and European colleges. Finally, beyond the Alleghanies, the triumph of the Jacksonian democracy marked the reckless entry of the nation upon the path of experiment. The characteristic frontier farmer-preacher of the period reflected the deep popular prejudice against either an educated or a salaried ministry. Hordes of Methodist lay exhorters were started out to "exercise their gifts" without formal preparation. Ultimately the frontier came to parade its contempt for culture and to glorify its own uncouthness. In order to open the possibilities of the "American dream" to the common man, it seemed necessary to dethrone the past. In James Truslow Adams' phrase, "America secedes from the Old World" and, as part of the process, largely abandons the ancient tradition of ministerial education.

While, through subsequent years, the nation has been slowly rebuilding its own authentic culture, it cannot honestly be said ever to have whole-heartedly returned to the tradition of higher education for the minister. Not only do traces of frontier attitudes survive over considerable territories, so that even now mountain preachers Sunday after Sunday compare their claims of immediate inspiration with the "factory-made preaching" of the educated type, but a very much more widespread religious folk tradition maintains itself which is not sure that learning hits the necessary spot in the minister's equipment. Considerable minorities in the larger denominations agree with this position. The laity are deeply convinced of the danger of professionalism and formality and, as already noted, are interested primarily in the minister's practical ability to make religious enterprises successful. In short, the country is not solidly "sold" on an educated ministry, and the assumption that the church should have such a ministry is not nearly so authentic as are the characteristics of Main Street.

It only adds to the seriousness of the situation to reflect that the school shares it with the church. "The American school," writes a well-known educational authority, "reflects the vices as well as the virtues of the American people. The low standards of scholarship, for example, which have commonly characterized educational practice in the United States, may be traced to the fact that ordinary men and women have controlled the school. And the American tradition of putting trust in the untrained teacher is to be understood in the same way. The relatively uncultured pioneers and farmers who have shaped the policies of the public school in the past have been quite content to identify learning with literacy and to rate a teacher as well-trained if he could read, write, and manipulate numbers with some degree of facility. To them an elaborate form of professional training has seemed entirely unnecessary and superfluous. Today, because the people themselves have reached a higher level of educational attainments and because new social classes are coming into power, they are beginning to demand teachers of higher qualification. But the point to be observed is that the school must inevitably exhibit the cultural limitations as well as the ideals and purposes of the forces in control."[2]

Evidence in behalf of this disturbing verdict is found in the fact that the level of ministerial education has continuously declined from the earliest

---

[2] Counts, *The American Road to Culture* (New York: The John Day Company, 1930), pp. 50-51.

colonial times to the present day. The rate of decline has been checked, but the downward trend has never been reversed. Commenting upon this sensational fact, one of the leading newspapers in America is merely moved to remark that "St. Peter was not the product of a seminary" and that the apostles had no salaries. Such attitudes partially explain why the proportion of college graduates in the ministry has been smaller in every decade since 1640, and the percentage of college graduates entering the ministry or other religious callings has sharply declined for fifty years.[3]

SCHOLASTIC REQUIREMENTS

Contemporary standards of ministerial education indicate official effort to make a stand against these tendencies. The majority of the great denominations do lip service to the notion that a minister should be a highly-educated man. Denominational standards, however, vary strikingly with the different theories of church government held by the denominations; both as to the terms of definition in which they are set forth, and with respect to the scholastic levels for entrance to the ministry which are required.

The centrally controlled denominations generally make explicit educational requirements. Some denominations, particularly those of the Presbyterian and Reformed families, define them in scholastic terms. They specify formally that a minister must be a college graduate with two years or more of additional theological training. The episcopally governed denominations, on the contrary, tend to define ministerial preparation in terms of an ecclesiastically required course of study rather than a scholastic one defined as to content. In the case of the Protestant Episcopal Church this course ordinarily presumes college standing, while the great churches of the Methodist family or of Methodistic antecedents habitually ordain a majority of non-college men. These they attempt subsequently to educate on the job through conference study courses.

In contrast with the centrally governed denominations, the congregationally organized group, by nature of their theories of church government, cannot maintain universal official standards. The educational level of their ministries is determined by the strength or weakness of favorable tradition and by advisory standards set up and recommended to the local ordaining bodies by the minor denominational units, such as state conferences. Some of the larger denominations of the congregational type have made some head against the frontier tradition of the uneducated ministry, others very little.

In spite of these variations in average level all major denominations provide for at least some completely trained ministers, by the maintenance of

[3] May, *op. cit.*, Vol. II, chapter iii.

theological seminaries and other training agencies of which denominational colleges also are important factors. The content of the education provided by these agencies will be discussed in the chapter on Religious Education. It is noteworthy that denominations whose training facilities are most ample get the largest proportion of well-trained men.

### EXCEPTIONS SUBMERGE THE RULE

The single common factor in denominational educational standards and requirements for the ministry is their provision for exceptions. In every case somebody is authorized to let down the bars in the case of men who, it is believed, will make useful ministers without the traditional training. The administration of the standards consequently becomes the crucial point in the situation. With few exceptions, relative to their theoretical policies, the administration of the denominations has been lax. The administrators have been governed by the pressure of popular demand, by the importance of supplying scattered populations with some kind of ministry, and by the inexorable need of manning feeble churches in order that they might not die. Wholesale transfer of ordained ministers from denominations of low educational standards to denominations with higher standards has diluted the educational quality of the more exacting. The result has been to give the nation a low-grade ministry with respect to its education.

### EDUCATIONAL STATUS OF THE MINISTRY

Of this fact the Census of Religious Bodies of 1926 brought convincing evidence based on statements by ministers as to their own education. These were tabulated for twenty-one denominations covering 74 per cent. of the churches of the United States. According to the raw returns, four out of ten white Protestant ministers were graduates neither of college nor of theological seminary. This figure is based upon the ministers' own say-so; and, in view of the wide discrepancy in the educational standards of so-called colleges and seminaries, is actually decidedly too low. An extensive sampling study defining college or seminary graduation as graduation from schools recognized by the standard educational associations (reported as "revised census data" in Table V) puts the percentage of untrained white ministers as high as 45.6 per cent. Eighty-five and two-tenths per cent. of Negro ministers are similarly untrained. On a sample from nineteen denominations untrained ministers appear to serve 50.4 per cent. of all white Protestant churches.[4]

The facts are more comprehensively stated in Table V.

---

[4] This, of course, does not mean that so high a proportion of ministers are untrained, since the average rural minister serves more than one church.

TABLE V — PROPORTIONS OF TRAINED MINISTERS (ORIGINAL AND REVISED, CENSUS DATA) AND PROPORTIONS OF CHURCHES SERVED BY THE FOUR CLASSES OF MINISTERS*

Per Cent.

|  | Both College and Seminary Graduates | College Only Graduates | Seminary Only Graduates | Neither College nor Seminary Graduates |
|---|---|---|---|---|
| In Twenty-three Denominations |  |  |  |  |
| Original census data............. | 33.1 | 12.2 | 11.2 | 43.4 |
| Revised census data............. | 22.3 | 16.1 | 12.2 | 49.4 |
| Churches served................. | 19.1 | 15.5 | 11.3 | 54.1 |
| In Nineteen White Protestant Denominations |  |  |  |  |
| Original census data............. | 35.1 | 14.7 | 11.0 | 39.2 |
| Revised census data............. | 23.6 | 18.6 | 12.2 | 45.6 |
| Churches served................. | 20.3 | 18.0 | 11.3 | 50.4 |

* From May, *op. cit.*, Vol. II, p. 14.

EDUCATION OF URBAN AND RURAL MINISTERS COMPARED

Urban and rural differences are also extreme. Most of the churches served by untrained ministers are small rural ones. Most of the vacant churches at any given time are those of less than fifty members. The percentage difference between the training of urban and rural ministers, according to the 1926 religious census returns, is shown in Table VI.

TABLE VI — TRAINING OF URBAN AND RURAL MINISTERS FOR 21 DENOMINATIONS, 1926*

Per Cent. Having Specified Degrees of Education

| Ministers | Total | Neither College nor Seminary | Both College and Seminary | College Only | Seminary Only |
|---|---|---|---|---|---|
| Total.................... | 100.0 | 44.9 | 31.7 | 12.6 | 10.8 |
| Urban................... | 100.0 | 24.2 | 49.5 | 12.6 | 13.7 |
| Rural................... | 100.0 | 56.3 | 21.9 | 12.6 | 9.2 |

* Fry, *The U. S. Looks at Its Churches* (New York; Institute of Social and Religious Research, 1930), pp. 152, 153.

One notes that the city has just about as many fully trained ministers as the country has untrained ones.

As with so many rural figures, the foregoing table seriously obscures the great differences between the village and open-country churches in the extent to which they enjoy trained ministers.

As against a census proportion of 21.9 per cent. of all rural ministers with college and seminary training, exactly 40 per cent. of village ministers were so trained. Only three-tenths of the village pastors had had neither college nor seminary. Moreover the larger the village the better the record, though even in places of less than 1,000 population more than one-third of the clergy were college and seminary graduates. Residence, too, was associated with training. The resident minister giving full time to a single village church was twice as likely to have had the full traditional training as a non-resident. Even more important was the question of the major region, but this is elsewhere discussed. All these things are again but an evidence of the economics of the situation stressed elsewhere in this chapter.

Classifying rural communities in greater detail, it is found that 40 per cent. of the white village and town ministers are graduates of both college and theological seminary; 20 per cent. more have attended some recognized college. It is in the open country that the record is very bad, only 17 per cent. holding both college and seminary diplomas, and 20 per cent. more college only. These figures, secured in 1930, show a decline for the total rural group from 35 to 31 per cent. in the proportion of college and seminary trained men, but an increase of from 20 to 22 per cent. in college graduates.

THE PROTESTANT AVERAGE: CATHOLIC AND DENOMINATIONAL DIFFERENCES

Averaging the trained ministers of all degrees together with the untrained, it appears that the American ministry has had two years of college work and 1.6 years of specific preparation in divinity. Eight years of schooling separate the untrained from the graduate of college and seminary.

The contrast with respect to education between the Protestant and the Roman Catholic ministries is terrific. Almost as striking is the range of difference as between the white Protestant denominations. This is shown for twenty-three denominations in Chart XII.

As causes of such amazing differences, comparison of denominations indicates the presence of two types that are deep-rooted. The first is tradition. Denominations which maintain the more churchly viewpoint in religion are apt to have a more exalted conception of the ministry. Questionnaires from large numbers of Protestants show clear traces of such a conception in Lutheran, Presbyterian and Reformed churches. Backed by such attitudes toward the ministry, a higher than average ratio of fully-trained ministers is secured by these denominations. The second cause is the presence or absence of frontierization in denominational history. Denominations which, by reason of their provincial or urban character, escaped the discipline of the frontier, or which represent migration to the United States after the peak of the frontier period had passed, have managed to retain higher educational standards than those which partook more completely of the break with inherited culture, that most authentic note in the evolution of American civilization.

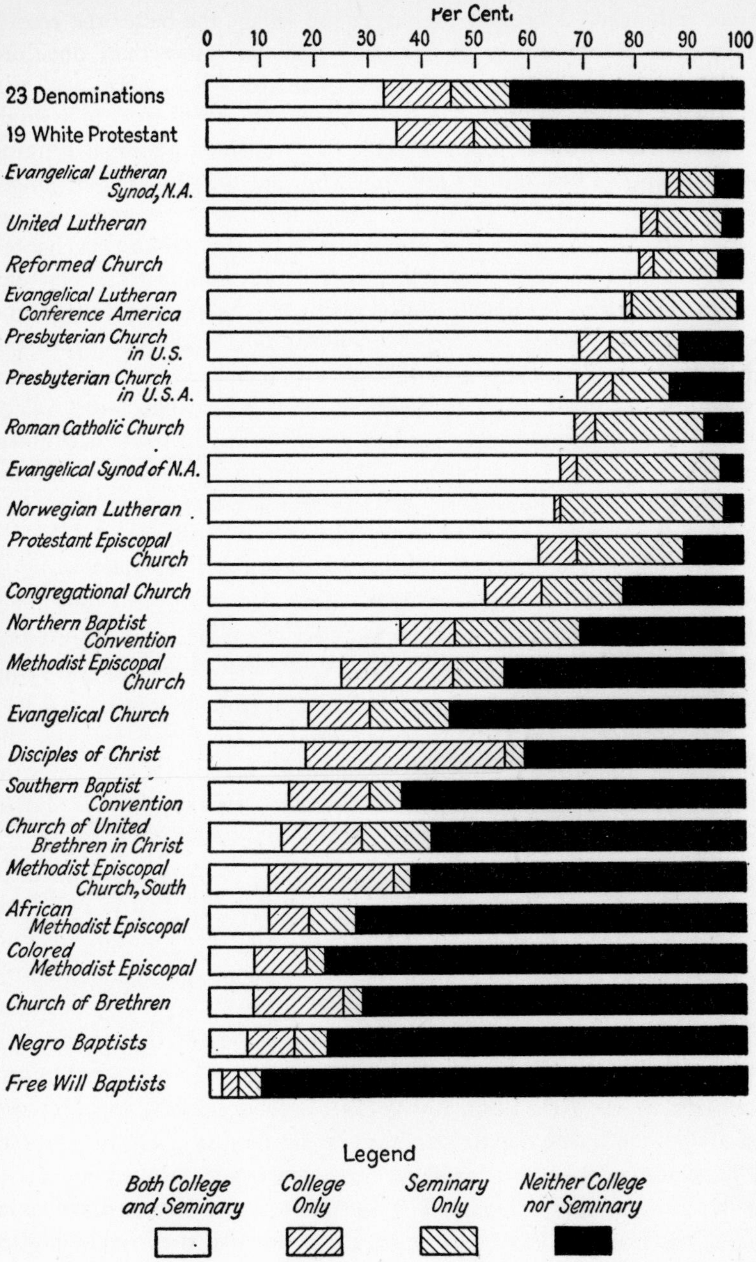

Per Cent.

0 10 20 30 40 50 60 70 80 90 100

23 Denominations

19 White Protestant

Evangelical Lutheran
Synod, N.A.

United Lutheran

Reformed Church

Evangelical Lutheran
Conference America

Presbyterian Church
in U.S.

Presbyterian Church
in U.S.A.

Roman Catholic Church

Evangelical Synod of N.A.

Norwegian Lutheran

Protestant Episcopal
Church

Congregational Church

Northern Baptist
Convention

Methodist Episcopal
Church

Evangelical Church

Disciples of Christ

Southern Baptist
Convention

Church of United
Brethren in Christ

Methodist Episcopal
Church, South

African
Methodist Episcopal

Colored
Methodist Episcopal

Church of Brethren

Negro Baptists

Free Will Baptists

### Legend

| Both College and Seminary | College Only | Seminary Only | Neither College nor Seminary |
|---|---|---|---|

CHART XII—TRAINING OF MINISTERS IN TWENTY-THREE DENOMINATIONS
CENSUS DATA, 1926

THE CHURCH'S ABILITY TO SUPPORT A FULLY TRAINED MINISTRY

Besides the influences of tradition, of historic evolution and of the limited educational outlook of the homes from which ministers chiefly come (as noted in an earlier paragraph), the most obvious factor explaining the total situation as to ministerial education in the United States is the present financial incapacity of a majority of local churches to support a fully trained ministry.

Two-thirds of the rural Protestant churches and almost 30 per cent. of the urban ones have less than one hundred members each.[5]  Some 84,000 of the 163,538 white Protestant churches do not have a full-time minister of any sort, and not one in six of the total has the full-time service of a fully trained man.[6]  The reason is clear when one notes that it takes a church of 350 members at the average current rate of expenditures to pay a salary of $3,000 and parsonage, which is estimated as the average remuneration of the completely trained man.  Only some 18,000 of the 163,538 white Protestant churches could afford the full-time services of a fully trained minister at this average rate of remuneration, even if they wanted to.

To redistribute members into churches large enough for each to employ a minister would be to abandon more than 100,000 of the present white churches; and no scientific prediction of future growth of population makes it likely that these 100,000 could ever be supported adequately.

Comparing denominations on this point, one finds differences for which full explanations are not easily discovered.  The Protestant Episcopal and Presbyterian, U. S. A., churches, together with the larger denominations of the congregational type, which have relatively high official requirements as to education, employ fewer fully trained ministers than the average membership-size and expenditures of their local units would lead one to expect. In some cases the dilution of the ministry by admission of ordained men from other denominations may offer a partial explanation.  Considering the Protestant denominations as a whole, Dr. Mark May guesses that 70 per cent. of the differences found are due to incapacity to support a ministry and 30 per cent. to all other factors.

POSSIBLE REMEDIES AND THEIR LIMITS

Obviously, even if the difficulty could be accurately located, it would not be solved.  In thinly populated areas and in the case of racial, cultural or theological minorities it is frequently impossible, within an area of practicable size, to get together enough constituents to form an effective church unit, and nowhere can this be done by a wave of the hand.  The problem involves the meaning of the separate parochial groups as social phenomena,

----

[5] Chapter v, p. 83.
[6] Fry, *op. cit.*, Table XL, p. 76.

the history and validity of the separate denominations, and the total problem of church unity. Some progress is being made by the practice of comity and the coöperative adjustment of competitive situations; more is being made by reason of the death of churches and the slowing up of the rate at which new ones are founded. The country is slowly getting fewer and larger churches.[7] Otherwise there is no solution and a generally educated ministry is economically impossible.

This verdict is the more shocking in view of the vast discrepancy between the church's record and the rapid improvement of American educational standards generally. There have been extraordinary gains in American culture measured, for example, in the proportion of young people going to high school and college. Yet, by reason of its present organization, the church is utterly inhibited from supporting a ministry corresponding with this progressive tendency. As has been shown, the focus of the difficulty is the rural church. Here the situation is doubly serious. The failure to improve the situation, moreover, is in sharp contrast with the improvement of the rural schools. In the villages, for instance, in 1924, barely two-fifths of the teachers were college graduates. By 1934 this figure had risen to between three-fifths and two-thirds. In the same period the teacher with less than normal school training had all but disappeared. Similar, though not so great, educational improvement had been made in the open country where the church situation is worst. This means that the poorest grade of religious service is being given where the most children live, where Protestantism is strongest, and where most of its new recruits for the ministry arise.

#### INDUCTION INTO THE MINISTRY, PLACEMENT AND SUPERVISION

Ministers are finally received into their office by action of some church authority which sets apart and ordains them. Some form of examination determines whether they have met the technical requirements, including education. Among these requirements, agreement with the theological position of the church and vows of subjection to its government frequently figure. The effect of ordination in all denominations is to give the minister life status. Ordination is frequently delayed until a licensed minister has a preliminary call to a parish or it may be conditioned upon his receiving a call, but ordination does not in itself settle the question of actual employment.

The average age of entrance upon the ministry is about thirty both for trained and for untrained ministers. This means that ministers are older than men of most other professions are when they enter upon their work.

---

[7] Fry, *op. cit.*, p. 46.

Trained ministers have already spent on the average 4.5 years in non-religious work and untrained 7.7 years, the average for the two groups being 5.3 years.

MINISTERIAL PLACEMENT IN THEORY AND IN PRACTICE

Ministers get churches and churches get ministers by a variety of means, a realistic account of which is hard to extract from the available data. The ministry is a highly competitive occupation. Efforts to get a representative sample of ministers to describe exactly the processes by which they obtained their present positions did not secure comparable data, but showed that types of influence not set forth in any theory of church government had much to do with the situation. In the theory of episcopally organized churches, ministerial placement is by the bishop. In the Presbyterian theory, the presbytery is the pastor of all vacant churches and initiates the settlement of the new pastor. With churches of the congregational type, and also with Lutheran churches, initiative and appointment is with the local church, as is also true with the Protestant Episcopal communion. In the latter case, however, approval by the bishop is required; while forms of recognition and confirmation of the local church's choice by the denomination are practised in some of the congregational bodies. In the cases of denominations in which appointment to the pastorate rests in the power of the local church, recommendation by denominational officials is nevertheless frequently influential. Numerous denominations have set up official bureaus for the registration and recommendation of ministers to churches desiring them. Aided churches in all denominations are naturally amenable to suggestions of denominational bodies from which they receive subsidies.

DENOMINATIONAL OVERSIGHT

After the minister is ordained and placed in a parish, denominational oversight of his work and relationships with his people vary according to the polity of his denomination. In the episcopally organized bodies, official visitation by bishops and superintendents belongs to the essence of the situation; and certain rites, such as that of confirmation in the Protestant Episcopal Church, are traditionally performed by these superiors. In churches of the presbyterian and congregational types, ecclesiastical officials do not intervene in parish affairs except as admitted by courtesy or upon invitation in the carrying on of common problems. Aided churches are naturally supervised by administrators who have to account for the moneys invested in them; and the increasing number of specialists and special services set up by modern denominations, involves numerous contacts and virtually a considerable degree of central supervision for churches of all types. Without admitted change of theory, the practice of the denominations is bringing most of them nearer together at this point.[8]

## TENURE

The average pastorate of the rural minister lasted 2.1 years in 1924, and 2.7 years in 1930; while that of the city minister averages four years. Tenure varies with denomination, but correlates most strongly with success. City ministers whose churches are more successful than the average of their respective neighborhoods stay twice as long as those whose churches are less successful than the average. Ministers also stay longer in the more highly developed types of churches; but at best tenure is relatively brief.

On the evidence of 8,680 cases drawn from four large denominations, seminary graduates remain in the ministry twenty-five years on the average. Non-graduates are less successful in the ministry than graduates, which may explain why their total tenure as well as tenure in the particular pastorate is briefer.[9] This fact raises problems for denominational pension systems. The poorer the man the sooner he tends to come on the pension list.

### THE MINISTER'S PROFESSIONAL LIFE-HISTORY

Generalizing 1,805 cases, May works out the service-sequence for trained ministers and untrained ministers as follows: After twenty years of educational preparation, 20 per cent. of trained ministers become assistant pastors, while 80 per cent. go first to rural or village churches. Ten years later only 25 per cent. of them will be left in rural and village churches. The rest will have gravitated to city pulpits where they will be serving churches averaging 370 members each, and receiving average salaries of $3,220 and parsonage.

Untrained ministers average thirteen instead of twenty years of training; but get no earlier start in the ministry on account of the longer period (seven and seven-tenths years on the average) spent in other occupations, chiefly farming, business or industry. Turning to the ministry after relatively so long secular experience suggests that they were not always very successful in their secular pursuits. Ninety per cent. of the untrained ministers begin in village or rural pastorates, and 40 per cent. will still be in such pastorates ten years later. Their churches will have 190 members on the average and they will be receiving $2,200 and parsonage as salary.

### LEAKAGE FROM THE MINISTRY

Not all who are trained for the ministry remain in that profession. Indeed a considerable number of seminary graduates never begin. The

---

[8] Chapter v, p. 99.
[9] May, *op. cit.*, Vol. IV, p. 66.

vocational disposition of 1,040 seminary graduates between 1900 and 1904 immediately following graduation, as compared with their vocational position twenty to twenty-five years later, is shown in the following tabulation:

| Vocation | Number of Cases | |
| --- | --- | --- |
| | Imme-diate | 20-25 Years Later |
| Pastorate.......................... | 891 | 735 |
| Non-pastoral religious callings........ | 76 | 98 |
| Non-religious callings............... | 73 | 207 |

These figures measure the very considerable leakage from the ministry. It is slightly mitigated by a relatively few graduates who started in non-religious callings (presumably because they did not immediately get pastorates) but came back later into the active ministry. The chief "secular" rival of the ministry is educational work, in which may be found many of the same opportunities to exercise constructive personal influence that the ministry affords. The most significant strand in this body of evidence is, however, that the leakage from the ministry has become greater with more recently graduated seminary classes. This seems to measure a growing restlessness in the profession.

## THE MINISTER AT WORK

The minister's headline functions, namely: (1) the conduct of worship and administration of the sacraments, (2) preaching, (3) pastoral ministries, and (4) the administration of the church, are so familiar as merely to require listing. They grow directly out of the nature of the institution which the minister serves, as earlier chapters have set it forth.

Minor ministerial functions, some habitual and others occasional, need more specific recognition. Briefly characterized, they are:

(5) *General Cultural Pursuits*—Time spent in serious study or attention to cultural interests which react immediately upon the quality of the worker's services.

(6) *Pedagogical*—Teaching or direction of study of classes or groups and direct preparation for the same. (This does not include educational administration which classifies under administration.)

(7) *Preparation and Delivery of Formal Discourse—other than homiletical,* e. g., lectures, papers, articles for publication, etc. In these the minister speaks as a competent man and community leader, but not as a religious authority nor officially in behalf of the church.

(8) *Civic*—Services performed by the minister especially for the welfare of the community or larger area, usually in coöperation with laymen and in movements under lay initiative and control.

(9) *Clerical*—Duties like those of the secretary, stenographer and general official worker, incident to homiletical, pastoral and administrative work.

(10) *Specific Professional Work of Technically Trained Specialist*—Functions performed by the minister in place of a trained specialist: e.g., those of athletic coach, choir director, moving-picture operator, etc.

(11) *Leadership of Systematized Group Activity*—Especially as directors and leaders of group work for boys and girls following a more or less set program other than that of the class or the school session: e.g., Scoutmasters.

(12) *Duties Involved in the Maintenance of Essential Tools or Facilities of the Job*—Such as the upkeep of an automobile used professionally, or incidental janitorial functions.

(13) *Attendance at Meetings*—On which attendance is expected of one in the worker's position, but which he does not conduct and for which he is not directly responsible.

(14) *Duties Involved in the Maintenance of Social Position*—Social life required by the minister's position. Courtesies, social entertainment and attendance on functions which the church expects and which thus become the worker's obligation.

Such are the fourteen points of the minister's professional life.

CONVENTIONALITY OF MINISTERIAL DUTIES

Strange to say, in spite of extraordinary environmental and organizational differences between the churches which they serve, rural and urban ministries show no substantial difference in the distribution of their time between the various classes of duties. This is shown in Table VII, which compresses the fourteen types of ministerial duties in seven categories.[10]

TABLE VII — DISTRIBUTION OF MINISTERIAL DUTY TIME BETWEEN SEVEN MAJOR TYPES OF DUTY

| Type of Duty | 687 Ministers | Hours per Week 130 Ministers in Industrial Communities | 247 Ministers in Farming Communities |
|---|---|---|---|
| Ministerial | 16.2 | 15.3 | 16.8 |
| Homiletical | 22.5 | 22.6 | 21.7 |
| Pastoral | 19.5 | 20.6 | 19.1 |
| Administrative | 8.9 | 9.7 | 8.1 |
| Educational | 4.2 | 4.0 | 3.8 |
| Civic | 4.0 | 3.3 | 4.1 |
| Mechanical | 3.1 | 2.6 | 0.0 |
| Total | 78.4 | 78.1 | 73.6 |

[10] Constructed from data in May, *op. cit.,* Vol. IV, p. 180. It is odd that rural ministers report no time spent in mechanical pursuits, considering that they must often have to tinker with their automobiles.

Furthermore, trained and untrained ministers use their time in about the same way. Considering not merely the major classes of duties, but the specific activities, urban and rural ministers are found performing about the same number under each major classification. Again, urban and rural ministers agree in the order of importance which they attach to the several types of duties and in the degree of difficulty which they ascribe to them. All this suggests an enormously conventionalized vocation.

This is not to say that the tasks ought not to differ nor that separate training is not needed. The habits, reactions and social organization of rural people manifestly differ from those of urban. It is thus quite possible that ministerial work is too standardized and that more attention in training to the differences between city and country and greater diversity in function might result in stronger churches for both types of community.

COMBINING OTHER VOCATIONS WITH THE MINISTRY

Manifestly the vocational aspects of their calling are greatly modified for one-fourth of all rural ministers, who are carrying on some other occupation at the same time. This proportion is much higher in the South, as respects both white and Negro ministers, and rises to five cases out of eight in the mountainous counties of the Southern Highlands.

Half of the ministers that have another calling are farmers. Students and teachers constitute the other largest groups.

The pattern of the rural ministry also gets important modification in another way. Tradition and economic necessity alike have, as previously noted, compelled thousands of rural churches to be content with the partial service of a minister and conversely have forced the minister to divide his time among the churches of several communities. This is the well-known circuit system. Slightly in excess of two-fifths of all village churches, but less than one-tenth of all open-country ones, however, command the whole time of one minister. Another three-tenths of the villages and one-seventh of the country churches are served by a resident minister who also goes elsewhere to minister to one other church. But seven-tenths of all open-country churches and about one-fifth of all village churches never see their pastor unless a service or other necessity brings him to them. This obtains especially in the South.

The result is that services cannot be held every Sunday in many churches, that the program is meager and frequently that the church dies. From the point of view of the survival of institutionalized religion in rural America, it is unfortunate, therefore, that while village and open-country churches average slightly larger than in 1924, in part because of the death of many small churches of less than fifty members, the proportion of churches with non-resident ministers increased sharply from 1924 to 1930 and seems to be even larger today.

## HOURS OF LABOR IN THE MINISTRY

The 687 ministers who estimated the time spent on duty for a week for Dr. May's investigation claimed an average of seventy-eight and four-tenths duty hours per week, or more than eleven hours per day for seven days. An editing of more exact work records in which 150 ministers in larger cities actually set down their use of time for a week and gave their own classifications of the type of duty involved, reduces the average duty time of the city minister to about nine hours per day. The reduction is primarily due to the editorial omission of such items as thinking over one's sermon while he is shaving, time spent in a Turkish bath, naps, "relaxation periods" and being subject to call when no call comes and the minister is actually following his private devices. The sample case cited by May in evidence of the minister's work included "playing nursemaid," "getting the children off to school," "helping the wife put them to bed" and a "short nap," as parts of the day's work. Urban ministers frequently claimed as duty time the hours spent in commuting from a distant home to the church, although no code would recognize this as counting as hours of labor and federal income tax regulations classify the cost as a purely personal expense.

However, the nine hours remaining after all deductions are quite long enough for any reasonable work day.

From the standpoint of the distribution of time between duties, not much difference appears in the reports of ministers of different denominations. On account of greater stress on the sacraments and the larger number of services traditionally held, Protestant Episcopal ministers and those of other liturgical churches spend somewhat more time on the average in priestly functions. That the difference is not more extreme is another evidence that the minister's task is essentially conventionalized. The amazing fact that all kinds of ministers of all denominations do substantially the same things throws some light upon the interchangeability of ministers and the possibility of church unity.

## TYPES OF MINISTERS

While the work of ministers, urban and rural, trained and untrained, and of all denominations, averages up in much the same way, rather wide variations in individual cases remain to be considered. Opposed to the traditional pressure for uniformity in the performance of the minister's task are the varied preferences and temperaments of the ministers themselves. Though all do what they must, so far as possible they magnify what they like to do and presumably what they can do best. Consequently, in the competition of duties different types of choices appear. One minister is revealed as predominantly a pastor, another as a pulpiteer, a third as an executive, a fourth, but more rarely, as a scholar. The characteristic vocational emphasis is thus to some extent "self-made." As many as 80 per cent. of city ministers contrive to stress some one major type of duty considerably beyond the average. In the long run, they tend to gravitate to churches where these particular emphases are needed or valued.

EFFECT OF STAFF RELATIONS UPON THE CHARACTERISTICS OF THE MINISTRY

Although, as has just been noted, the distribution of the work of urban and rural ministers among the various types of duty shows no substantial

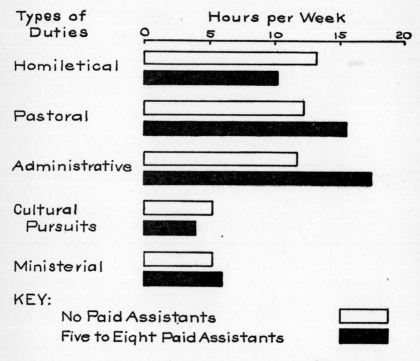

CHART XIII—TIME GIVEN TO MAJOR DUTIES OF URBAN MINISTERS IN STAFFED AND UNSTAFFED CHURCHES

difference (probably because most urban churches have only one minister), the job records of ministers of staffed churches begin to show distinct differences. With ministers with small staffs, homiletical duties, which take more time than any other type with the whole body of ministers, sink to second place; and to third place with ministers with large staffs; while administrative duties correspondingly rise. Of the major types of duty, the pastoral and ministerial are least affected by staff relationships. The minister of the staffed church, however, concentrates on fewer kinds of duties than are engaged in by the minister who works alone, and he gives relatively less time to such minor duties as clerical work, attending meetings for which he is not responsible and, regrettably, to cultural pursuits. On the contrary, he gives more time to civic duties.

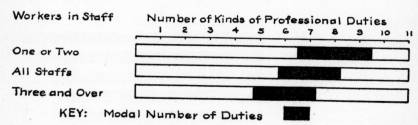

CHART XIV—INCREASED TENDENCY TO CONCENTRATION IN URBAN MINISTER'S WORK WITH INCREASED SIZE OF STAFF

### SUBORDINATE MINISTRY

The extensive staffing of urban churches introduces into the story of the ministry a whole set of new situations relating to secondary and subordinate paid workers. In contrast with the traditional ministry, which is composed almost entirely of ordained men, the subordinate ministry is chiefly made up of unordained women.

The occupational interrelations of the two groups gravely modify the vocational pattern. Priestly and prophetic functions are almost entirely reserved to the ordained group. Administration, pastoral and teaching functions are shared by both; while secretarial functions are mainly shifted from the principal to the subordinate ministry. Other technical specialties and the functions of specialized leadership of subsidiary groups generally appear for the first time with the coming of a subsidiary staff, only a trace of these functions being found in the work of ordained ministers. The few rural churches that employ staffs, usually the so-called "larger parishes," have relatively more directors of religious education and of community service and far fewer clerical or secretarial workers than do urban churches.

Putting the matter in another way, in a sample of 296 cases 59 per cent. of lay paid workers in city churches appear to represent the partial transfer from the principal to the subordinate ministry of kinds and methods of work already being carried out by the clergy, while 41 per cent. represent essentially new fields of vocational activity or such specialization in method as to define a new vocation.

FREQUENCY OF TYPES OF SUBORDINATE WORKERS

The most numerous class of paid subordinates are secretarial workers, including financial secretaries and bookkeepers. Second in number come workers definitely labeled as belonging to the pastoral visitor type. Women "pastor's or parish assistants" doing a little of many sorts of work, but often majoring on pastoral visitation, are also frequent. Third in number rank associate and assistant pastors as general understudies for the chief

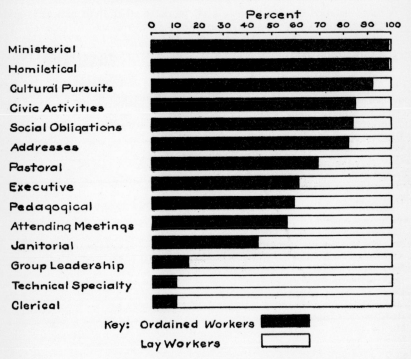

CHART XV—RELATIVE CONTRIBUTIONS OF ORDAINED AND LAY MINISTERS TO FOURTEEN TYPES OF DUTY IN STAFFED CITY CHURCHES

minister; and fourth, directors of religious education. It is characteristic, however, of most subordinate staff members of all sorts that their duties are ill-defined and that they may spend much time in kinds of work not at all suggested by their titles. Nevertheless, in 80 per cent. of the cases their employment seems to aim at some degree of specialization on the part of the church.

Less frequent classes of lay workers than those previously enumerated include occasional workers who have risen to essentially principal executive positions, though sometimes their rank is not formally recognized. These include a few male executive secretaries; but more often are capable women, who, though labeled merely as church secretaries, actually have a large place in running the church. A few pastoral assistants are actually social case workers of professional competence.

A classification of the 1,025 pastors and 1,059 other paid workers employed by 1,025 city churches studied in 1932 divides them between pastors and all other paid professionals, between lay and ordained, and between principal and subordinate workers in proportions shown in Chart XVI. The fourth diagram subdivides the subordinate ministers.

A more detailed classification of paid workers other than pastors is given in Table VIII.

TABLE VIII — CLASSIFICATION OF PAID WORKERS OTHER THAN PASTORS IN 1,025 CITY CHURCHES

| Types of Workers | | Number | Per Cent. |
|---|---|---|---|
| Other principal workers.................................. | | 242 | 25 |
|   Associate pastors....................................... | 59 | | |
|   Assistant pastors....................................... | 84 | | |
|   Directors of religious education......................... | 85 | | |
|   Other executives....................................... | 14 | | |
| Secretarial workers (other than financial).................. | | 205 | 19 |
| Financial secretaries and treasurers........................ | | 77 | 7 |
| Pastoral workers (deaconesses, visitors, "missionaries")...... | | 152 | 14 |
| Undifferentiated workers (in traditional lines chiefly pastoral-secretarial)......................................... | | 122 | 12 |
| Department specialists..................................... | | 162 | 15 |
|   Teachers (parochial schools, kindergartens, choir schools).. | 56 | | |
|   Religious educational subordinates....................... | 41 | | |
|   Athletic and recreational............................... | 20 | | |
|   Social service ("directors," nursery supts., etc.)............ | 19 | | |
|   Leaders of group activities............................. | 7 | | |
|   Heads of adjunct institutions (parish and neighborhood houses)............................................. | 7 | | |
|   Health workers (chiefly nurses)......................... | 7 | | |
|   Musical directors...................................... | 4 | | |
|   Dramatic director...................................... | 1 | | |
| Age- and Sex-Group specialists............................. | | 85 | 8 |
|   Men's................................................ | 2 | | |
|   Young people's........................................ | 25 | | |
|   Young women's and girls'............................... | 4 | | |
|   Boys' and girls'....................................... | 40 | | |
|   Boys'................................................ | 6 | | |
|   Girls'................................................ | 3 | | |
|   Children's............................................ | 5 | | |
| Other (miscellaneous classifications)....................... | | 14 | 0 |
| Total............................................ | | 1,059 | 100 |

This classification greatly over-simplifies the facts. Workers designated by two titles are very numerous. Secretarial workers subdivide into numerous specialists as different as accountants and telephone operators. Age and sex specialists include girls' and women's workers, boys' and men's workers, young people's and children's workers. Departmental specialists involve numerous types of recreational or social workers. Part-time workers are not adequately distinguished. Janitors and caretakers and paid musicians

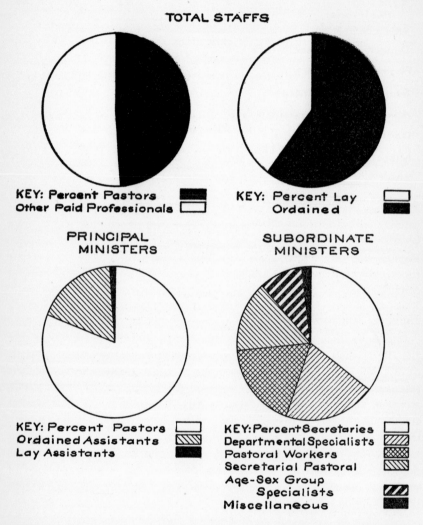

**TOTAL STAFFS**

KEY: Percent Pastors
Other Paid Professionals

KEY: Percent Lay
Ordained

PRINCIPAL
MINISTERS

SUBORDINATE
MINISTERS

KEY: Percent Pastors
Ordained Assistants
Lay Assistants

KEY: Percent Secretaries
Departmental Specialists
Pastoral Workers
Secretarial Pastoral
Age-Sex Group
Specialists
Miscellaneous

CHART XVI—DISTRIBUTION OF CHURCH STAFF IN CITY CHURCHES, BY PASTORS AND OTHERS, ORDAINED AND NON-ORDAINED, PRINCIPAL AND SUBORDINATE

(except in the very rare cases in which they give virtually full-time service and are responsibly related to the religious or social programs of the church) are omitted from this classification.

Chart XVII includes non-ordained principal workers in the total and shows the disposition of all non-ordained by types of vocation.

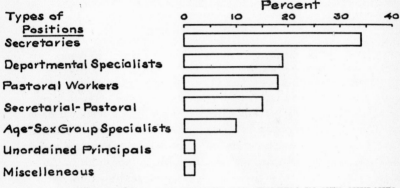

CHART XVII—DISTRIBUTION OF NON-ORDAINED PAID WORKERS IN CITY CHURCHES

All told then, it is clear that the church has several dozen types of subordinate ministries in the making. Potentially each one has its own vocational story; most of them have never been the subject of any adequate scientific and comparative study. And many of the subordinate workers are shockingly treated with respect to terms of employment and working conditions.

THE STAFF MINISTRY

Neither do there exist any competent studies of the ministry which take the church staff as a unit. Preliminary analyses by the writers, of staffs of different sizes, show, for example, that the most frequent three-members staff combination is that of pastor, assistant pastor and secretary, with pastor, secretary and visitor as a distant second; that most of the four-worker staffs limit themselves to pastor, assistant pastor, secretary and visitor, with director of religious education substituted either for secretary or for visitor in about one-fifth of the cases; and that the larger staffs begin to show the doubling up of assistant secretaries and visitors, etc., and the addition of more specialized social and clerical workers without any discoverable type of combination being dominant.

Twenty-seven thousand, eight hundred and sixty-nine hours of service performed by staffs of 203 city churches turned out to have consisted of the following elements in the following proportions:

Just as the individual minister may be essentially a pastor, a preacher or an executive, so the staff as a whole may show strong bias toward one or another type of ministry. This may be both cause and effect of the peculiar

| Type | Per Cent. |
|---|---|
| Total | 100.0 |
| Ministerial | 4.8 |
| Pastoral | 21.8 |
| Administrative | 22.1 |
| Homiletical | 9.4 |
| Pedagogical | 4.7 |
| Attendance on meetings | 5.6 |
| Secretarial | 19.2 |
| Seven other types | 12.4 |

balance of the individual church's program. Since, however, ministerial functions and preaching are not to any extent shared with the unordained group, the chief distinction is between churches in which the work of the staff as a whole stresses pastoral work much beyond the average and those in which the added staff functions are primarily administrative. As previous analysis would lead one to suspect,[11] in cases where the control of the church is much affected by methods of long-range communication, a third emphasis develops. Clerical work may become the chief type of activity on the part of the staff as a whole, record-keeping and absentee communication being substituted for ministerial functions relating to the church in its face-to-face or congregating phase, as well as for those pertaining to its pastoral outreach, or to its first-hand administration. This marks the completest stage of institutionalization.

SIGNIFICANCE OF THE SUBORDINATE MINISTRY

Summarizing the significance of the subordinate ministry, and of the staffing of urban churches, it is important to reiterate that one part of its effect is to supplement the previous work of ordained ministers, while another part is to enable the church to perform a wider range of functions, including some not to any great extent previously performed by ordained ministers.

The quality of the subordinate workers naturally varies with the financial ability of the church, but probably also with the definiteness with which it undertakes the broader functions which the subordinate worker implies. Chart XVIII shows the increased per cent. of college graduates among women workers in more highly developed types of churches.

Perhaps the most serious problem of the staffed church is the extent to which paid workers are made substitutes for lazy laymen in work which would be more wholesomely performed by the rank and file of the constituency under the necessary technical supervision. No standards exist to enable one to pass judgment upon this point; but in a sample of twenty-six large churches, there were found all the way from seven to fifty-two

---

[11] P. 95.

hours of paid staff labor per hundred persons in attendance upon church activities of all sorts, with a median of seventeen staff working hours per

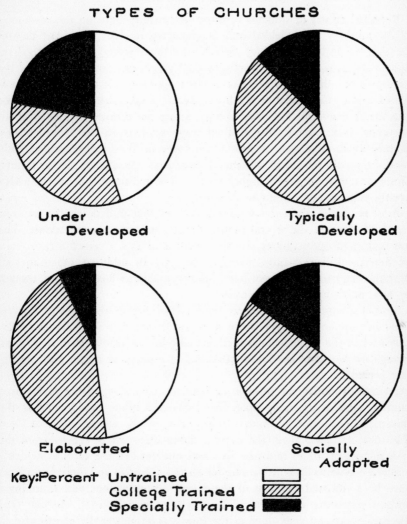

CHART XVIII—DEGREE OF EDUCATION OF PAID WOMEN WORKERS IN CITY CHURCHES
OF SPECIFIED TYPES

hundred persons in attendance. It would seem obvious that churches enjoying three times the median staff service—as, in extreme cases, they did—are overstaffed; while those enjoying less than half the median are presumably understaffed. The median range tentatively affords some index of a nominal proportion between the volume of the church's activities and its supply of paid workers.

### ECONOMIC BASIS OF THE MINISTRY

Repeated efforts of students to throw satisfactory light on the economics of the ministry have yielded only fragmentary results. The chief reasons are that the facts are lacking. Salaries are not reported by the federal religious census nor by most denominational year-books; and the value of the minister's perquisites has never been fairly appraised for any adequate sample of cases. Cash salaries are low. Recent studies have shown that for two major denominations they average $1,407 per minister, which is about the same as the annual wage of all wage workers in the United States, slightly lower than that of federal employes in Washington, and slightly higher than the wages of automobile workers. As already noted, trained ministers receive decidedly higher salaries than untrained, and averages vary greatly from denomination to denomination.

It is, of course, the rural ministers' salaries that pull down the average, especially those of the several thousands who have other occupations. The 477 pastors of open-country churches studied in 1930 received a cash wage of $1,062. Village pastors averaged $1,573. In addition practically all of these men had a house rent-free. Since 1930 salaries have declined, though by how much cannot be determined.

Studies attempting to interpret nominal salaries in the light of fluctuations in purchasing power make it appear likely that real salaries of the ministers in the United States were actually less in 1920-28 than in 1890-99, though the wages of employed workers as a group rose 25 per cent. during that period.[12]

As already noted, the most acute students have dodged the problem of putting a monetary value upon free rents and other emoluments of the ministerial profession. Limited studies made by the writers convince them that these factors add on the average about one-sixth to the value of the cash salaries of urban ministers in about one-third of the cases.

Pension systems designed to care for retired ministers and their dependents have been initiated by most of the major denominations and from these systems payments were received by 33,159 persons in 1933. In one type the employing churches alone or the ministers alone statedly contributed to the fund from which the pensions are drawn, while in the other type both contribute. This puts them partly upon an insurance basis. But in the last analysis specially secured denominational endowments and reserve funds have to supply approximately three-fourths of the capital fund. No comprehensive data are available as to the proportion of ministers receiving

---

[12] May, *op. cit.,* Vol. II, p. 107.

pensions of any given amount, but it is obvious that such deferred re-muneration is somewhat widespread, and will become more so in the future, and that it has to be considered in any estimate of the economic status of the minister.

It is well, finally, to recall that, while some measure of solution of the economic difficulties of the profession may be found in the circuit system or the doubling up of small churches under the pastorate of a single minister, and more in the carrying on by ministers of other occupations, multitudes of the existing churches are unable not merely to support a well-trained minister, but decently to support any minister at all. When such churches have adequate reason for being, the supplementing of their slender resources by denominational missionary funds is obviously indicated. When, however, they are competitive burdens upon communities, it is quite as well that they cannot support even the poorest minister.

### The Minister's Reaction to His Work

The testimony of behavior, notably the minister's relatively short term in particular pastorates, and the conspicuous permanent leakage from the ministry, seem to convict the profession of restlessness and instability. This evidence is partially overborne by the very large proportion of ministers' sons who enter the ministry, in spite of the fact that they must know the worst about it. A considerable body of evidence as to ministers' attitudes, secured by direct questionnaires in various studies, seems in the main not to have reached men on the lowest-paid and wholly uneducated level. It is, however, significant that, of some 1,800 replying, 61 per cent. of trained and 83 per cent. of untrained ministers said that they had never regretted their choice of profession.

It is noteworthy also that the body of available data as a whole registered no overshadowing stress upon economic problems. While ministers often explain that low salaries compel them to resort to unpleasant domestic makeshifts, salary is not paraded as the minister's chief worry. The reason may be that the profession furnishes a field of relatively free competition, that ministers are very frequently successful in the struggle for promotion, and that even for the untrained man the profession, as revealed by life histories, does not lead into a blind alley.

On the other hand, responses to questionnaires show that ministers regard their calling as high, holy and unique. Indeed, one-half bear witness to some personal experience which they accept as a divine call to the ministry. The majority profoundly believe in the ministry as it is. They are convinced that the conduct of worship, preaching and pastoral ministries are and of right ought to be their chief functions. They are but little disturbed by the possibility that there ought to be changes in its aspects and emphases; but are greatly concerned with the effort to do the conventional duties better. The minister's account of his problems and difficulties shows an extraordinary similarity in rural counties and in Chicago. Both emphasize a vocational outlook of the conventional type little modified by environmental conditions.[13]

The minister's self-esteem and morale are undoubtedly greatly sustained by the religious value which he puts on his vocation. In the sense of these values he finds refuge from external ills. Indeed, there are many signs that using the familiar trick of psychological transfer, he sets up conflicts in the inner realm of the spirit which are really transcriptions of more mundane problems. Comments and responses to vocational investigations show that ministers as a group are disinclined to face the objective realities of their callings or to think of themselves as employes and salary earners. They are highly sensitive to vocational criticism having to do with the outer forms of their work. When confronted by its seamy material aspects, they habitually make appeal to its inner significance, rather than turn to aggressive remedial efforts. They over-identify themselves with their institution. They are unable to tell when they are on and off duty. They claim longer working hours than their actual records justify. They feel continuously in a hurry. They have an uneasy consciousness of always being subject to call. They are habitually irritated by trifling interruptions. They are perplexed by competing duties. They are strongly individualistic in vocational attitudes. They dislike to judge the work of subordinates objectively, which makes them poor supervisors. All told, the minister is a bit too sensitive about himself as a holy man caught in very earthly situations. With large individual exceptions, the profession at large seems the victim of a mild vocational psychosis.

## NON-PAROCHIAL MINISTERS

Apparently about seven-eighths of active ministers are in the pastorate and one-eighth in the non-parochial service of the church and its allies. A few ordained men are directors of religious education; others are evangelists at large, and still others chaplains or executives of the church's philanthropic institutions. A few are Y. M. C. A. secretaries. The special vocational characteristics of directors of religious education and of Y. M. C. A. secretaries have been the subject of competent study; and something is known of the preparation and work of institutional chaplains.

On the whole, the most important group of non-parochial ministers are, however, the overhead officials of the denominations, their bishops, mission-board secretaries and other general and local superintendents, together with similarly employed men in interdenominational organizations.

---

[13] May, *op. cit.*, Vol. II, p. 186.

Some of the characteristics of the above class may be inferred from movements of the church to which they are vocationally attached,[14] but no competent objective studies of it exist. Bishops as a group have never yet been taken into the scientific dissecting room.

## SUMMARY

It is very difficult to summarize in any strict sense such varied data as those which the chapter now closing has presented about the ministry. If, however, it were required to give in briefest compass, answers to the five most pertinent questions about the ministry, the answers might run in about the following form:

What kind of a man is the minister? He is chiefly a man of rural origins, drawn from the humbler levels of society. He is only partially educated for his calling, averaging about two years of college and a year and a fraction of seminary training. He goes from parish to parish, having pastorates averaging not more than five or six years and a total ministerial activity of less than twenty-five years.

How does the American church condition the minister's job? The church has established so many and such feeble units that the vast majority cannot support a minister on the level of the theoretical preparation which it expects. The grouping of several churches under one minister, missionary subsidies, perquisites and pensions somewhat soften the economic difficulties of the profession. The churches are primarily interested in ministers possessing the qualities which make them successful. In the case of the more ill-advised and superfluous churches success is manifestly impossible.

Evidence to be adduced in a subsequent chapter tends to minimize the minister's power to control situations where social tendencies are highly favorable or unfavorable to the church as an institution. In borderland cases, however, the minister's capacity may make all the difference between the church's life and death. In view of this fact and the discovery that what the churches chiefly value in a minister is his ability as a go-getter, it is not strange that denominations depart greatly from the full strictness of their educational requirements in many cases in favor of the man of practical capacity.

What kind of a job is the minister's? It is a varied job divided among seven or eight frequent types of service, and much less concentrated on any one line than are those of the major types of subordinate staff members. But it is also a highly conventionalized job, occupying rather long hours a day for seven days a week, and taking about the same forms in country and in city. The exercise of the priestly office, preaching, pastoral work

---

[14] Chapter xiii.

and the administration of the church as an enterprise constitute the chief bloc of the minister's work. The most definite vocational differences arise from the presence of a subordinate staff in the larger city churches and the demands of the wider program which such a staff implies.

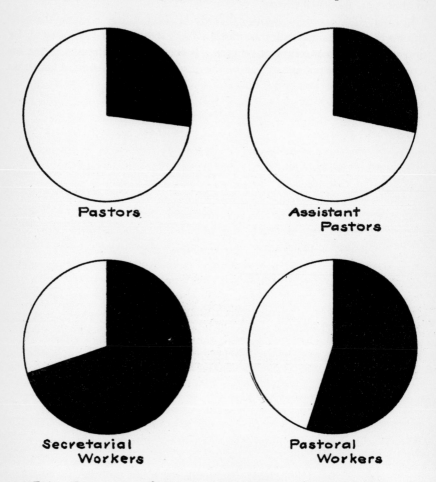

Pastors

Assistant
Pastors

Secretarial
Workers

Pastoral
Workers

KEY: Percent of total duty time given to the
Major Duty

CHART XIX—MINISTER'S VARIED JOB CONTRASTED WITH SUBORDINATE'S SPECIALIZATION

What special factors have the greatest bearing upon the ministry? The most conspicuous modifying factor is that of the degree of the minister's training. Fully educated ministers have larger churches, better pay, longer average tenure and greater average success as objectively measured.

How does the minister regard his own calling? The minister does not have more vocational regrets than other flesh is heir to. His dissatisfaction is not primarily economic. He believes strongly in the values of his job as it is. He is sustained and sensitized by the feeling of its inner values to almost an abnormal degree.

In brief, even a rigidly vocational study of the ministry leads to the conclusion that its characteristics are deeply dyed, if not indeed dominated, by the fact that it is a ministry of religion. It bears profound marks of the interest which it serves as well as of the institutionalized forms which this interest has taken.

# CHAPTER VII

*Activities and Program*

Chapter V has already discussed the major forms in which the organized life of the church expresses itself. To a considerable degree the naming and characterizing of these forms suggest the particular activities carried out under each of them, and their detail has been further disclosed by a study of the kinds of functions performed by ministers. In some cases, however, the form does not serve sufficiently to recall the range of activities associated with it; and the church has developed a good many novel activities not involved in its habitual forms. The practical operation of a church naturally involves techniques for the performance of activities in detail and for their organization into deliberate programs. Consequently, the organized activities of the church merit further consideration.

Three chapters are now to be given to church activities as they are combined into programs. The present chapter introduces the topic and deals with the more conventional and frequent activities, with some supplemental mention of novel ones. The two following chapters treat respectively of activities in the specialized fields of religious education and of social welfare.

## ACTIVITIES OF RURAL AND URBAN CHURCHES COMPARED

The church is the church whether in country or in city, but the things which the church does in the two environments show striking differences. A consistent series of changes from simplicity to complexity of program corresponds with the size of the community which the church serves. Thus, rural churches rarely go beyond activities represented by preaching, Sunday school, a women's organization and a young people's society. But only 42 per cent. of open-country churches have even a women's organization, and only 25 per cent. a young people's society.

These proportions are greatly reduced in more backward rural areas. Thus, in seventeen counties in the Southern Appalachian highlands women's societies are only a little more than one-third as frequent as in open-country areas generally and young people's societies one-fifth less frequent.[1]

---

[1] Hooker, *Religion in the Highlands* (New York: Home Missions Council), p. 165.

The village church, on the contrary, has some form of subsidiary organization in eight cases out of ten. Yet fewer than half of the village churches have even a Christian Endeavor society.

The town church, on the other hand, stands close to the church of the smaller cities with respect to frequency of subsidiary organizations, though it is distinctly below the average large city church in complexity of organization and program.

The distinction becomes most definite when one compares what may be regarded either as the highest form of rural church or as an intermediate type, namely, the church of the town. Compared with the average city church, the differences in frequency of organization are as shown in Table IX.

TABLE IX — FREQUENCY OF CERTAIN SUBSIDIARY CHURCH ORGANIZATIONS IN TOWN CHURCHES AND IN MODAL CHURCHES OF LARGE CITIES

| | Per Cent. Frequency | |
| Organization | Town Church | Modal City Church |
| --- | --- | --- |
| Some subsidiary organizations besides Sunday School | 93 | 100 |
| Women's organization | 87 | 99 |
| More than one women's organization | 44 | 81 |
| Mixed sex organizations (usually young people's) | 67 | 77 |
| More than one mixed sex organization | 37 | 8 |
| Men's organization | 10 | 53 |
| Boys' organization | 15 | 52 |
| Girls' organization | 20 | 34 |

In this table the only item on which the town church stands ahead of the city church is more than one mixed sex organization; but this is exactly what the city church is trying to get away from in favor of separate organizations for men and women, boys and girls. In brief, the city church in its average range of activities lies distinctly beyond the utmost point which the rural or intermediate town church has reached. Consequently separate stories must be told for the churches of the two contrasting environments.

### ACTIVITIES AND PROGRAMS OF RURAL CHURCHES

The preaching services and Sunday schools of the rural churches are noted in other connections.[2] Sunday schools operated by laymen frequently are held more often than public worship, since the frequency of the latter depends upon whether the preacher is resident or non-resident.

The next most frequent type of organization is that of the women, usually the Ladies Aid or missionary society. About two-thirds of all rural churches, and four-fifths of all in villages, have one or more such groups. They con-

---

[2] P. 85.

stitute an increasingly important factor in the organized life of rural churches; for while the total number of subsidiary organizations in rural churches declined slightly in the last decade, the number of women's groups made a small gain. They now constitute 55 per cent. of all the organized groups in rural churches. An ever-present help to the budget in time of trouble, their chief concern is the welfare of the local church as an institution.

Mixed young people's societies of the Christian Endeavor type are the next most numerous group of organizations. These are for both children and adolescents, but the average rural church, if it has such a group at all, has only one. The greater emphasis upon young people's work since 1920 is doubtless to be credited for the fact that while only one rural church in three had a young people's society in 1920, nearly one-half now have them.

Other types of special age or sex group activity were relatively infrequent. About one church in twenty had a special men's group, usually social in character, though occasionally through its forum offering a substitute for the cracker barrel senate of the village store. Even smaller proportions of the churches had organizations for boys and girls. These were usually of the Scout variety. The proportion of churches conducting such groups seems to be slowly declining. This may be because of the great expansion in the youth-serving program of the agricultural and extension service, with their 4-H Clubs, of which, on the average, there are two in each village-centered rural community. The smaller numbers of these last three types of organization may also be due to the expanded program of the Sunday school, with its drive for organized classes and week-day activities. This, however, has not stopped the organization of women's and young people's groups outside the church school.

There is a decided tendency for the functions of the subsidiary groups to broaden slightly as the years pass. Once they were designed chiefly to help the church indoctrinate its youth and to allow for a bit of social life. Lately these objectives have been combined with others, or at least projects of various sorts have been added to them, often fitting into the larger program of the denomination.

Of just what does this program consist, beyond the worship and preaching activities and those related to religious education?

The old-fashioned social events still hold first place. In the rural areas the Sunday-school picnic, the oyster or chicken and waffle suppers and the strawberry festivals are events hoary with tradition and of social value in that they include whole families and bring together entire neighborhoods. All the stronger churches have such general social events. More unexpected is it to discover that three-tenths of the village churches and one-twelfth of those in the country regularly include lectures and concerts of various sorts in their annual roster of activities. Nor do efforts at adult education stop there, especially in the villages; where one-seventh of the churches conduct classes of one sort or another. Indeed, in the Middle Atlantic and Middle Western regions this proportion is several times higher. Such classes are often held in coöperation with university or agricultural extension groups and concern women far more than men or mixed groups. Again, more than one-tenth of the village churches (but less than half as many of those in the open country) have groups devoting themselves to a wide variety of special interests, such as athletic teams, hiking clubs, camping, dramatics, and the like. Such activities are also included in the programs of other organizations whose major objectives differ from those of the churches. In many such cases it appears that groups of like-minded people with similar interests are simply using their connection with an alert church to afford the auspices for the organized expression of this interest. The community-minded church, on its side, is glad to furnish its facilities for activities deemed wholesome and worth while.

Looking upon community service as a high responsibility such churches conduct, in the aggregate, a tremendous variety of activities. Some of these are purely within the realm of social welfare and are touched on in chapter ix. Others have in them little more than entertainment and the vague social values that flow from such efforts. The very listing of these activities would take several pages. The Institute of Social and Religious Research has devoted two small volumes to their analysis and description as found in forty exceptionally progressive town-and-country churches in 1923.[3]

### URBAN CHURCHES: FREQUENCY OF ACTIVITIES

The virtually invariable functions of the city church are preaching associated with public worship and the Sunday school; but more than nine-tenths of them also number a women's organization of some type and a young people's society. A Sunday evening preaching service is also very frequent and the lack of it appears to have been definitely established as a mark of sub-modality.[4] Two more items, namely, regular parish social events and the chorus choir, are characteristic of from three-fourths to nearly nine-tenths of city churches. These represent urban embellishments of church activities rather than the introduction of any new principle.

Coming down to somewhat frequent activities, that is, those characteristic of from one-half to two-thirds of the city churches, one is able to discover two definitely urban trends; namely, the erection of a specific organization

[3] *Tested Methods of Town and Country Churches* and *Churches of Distinction.*
[4] Sanderson, *The Strategy of City Church Planning* (New York: Institute of Social and Religious Research, 1932), p. 211.

to serve each of the more important of the specialized interests in the church, and differentiation on lines of sex and age. The first is represented by organized mission-study classes, the second by men's and boys' organizations.

Descending to the somewhat infrequent activities of urban churches, defined as those carried on by from 20 to 40 per cent. of their number, one finds a group represented by libraries, orchestras, daily vacation Bible schools and Girl Scouts. Here are further special interests, cultural and

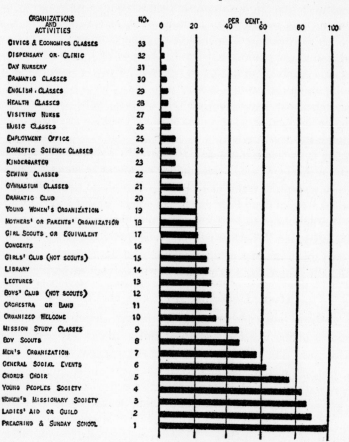

CHART XX—PER CENT. FREQUENCY OF CHURCH ORGANIZATIONS AND ACTIVITIES

recreational, finding expression in specific organization, and here is a still further extension of the principle of organization by age and sex.

Among the infrequent activities of city churches, namely, those characteristic of from 10 to 19 per cent. of their number, as shown in Chart XX, are gymnasiums, the daily opening of the church for devotions, young women's and parents' organizations. Here one notes further development of the recreational interest and provision for it by special forms and facilities, as well as the complete development of organization by age and sex.

The very infrequent activities of urban churches are those directly designed to meet the social needs of handicapped populations. They include kindergartens, dispensaries, day nurseries, visiting nurse service and employment offices. These occur in less than one-tenth of city churches.

Other novel activities fall into this low frequency group, such as the maintenance of church forums which are beginning to spring up in recent years. The frequencies cited are samples of a very much longer list of church activities whose presence or absence in city churches has been studied.

The above study of frequency of activities relates to the local church, not to the total organized religion of a city. Some of them are infrequent as local church activities just because they are so generally carried by specialized agencies of the church and its allies. Thus, if a group organizes for worship and preaching, it is almost sure to organize itself as a local church, though this is not invariable. If it wants to conduct religious education, it usually establishes itself as a Sunday school. When it comes, however, to ministering to the social life, it is about equally likely to do this through the local church or through some special agency like the Y.M.C.A. or Y.W.C.A. When it comes to recreation, there is more than an even chance that this will be done, if it is done at all under religious auspices, in a non-church agency rather than in a church. Finally, when social-welfare ministries, especially in their more technical forms, are contemplated, it is almost sure that they will be carried on through orphanages, hospitals, old people's homes and special chaplaincies and not through local churches. As activities of the church at large, such things are relatively frequent, as activities of the single parish, decidedly infrequent. Chapter ix returns to this point.

### Types of Urban Churches

The most illuminating method of classifying individual churches is according to the degree to which they confine themselves to invariable or frequent activities or to which, on the other hand, they indulge in adventurous novelties of program. Such a classification is far more illuminating than one by mere size of program, though the factor of size standing alone has some general significance. City churches have larger programs than rural churches, or than suburban ones, and on the average the larger churches have the more ample and varied programs.[5]

What is more important to notice is, however, that most churches do only

---

[5] Van Vleck, Joseph, Jr. (Director), *A Survey of Methodist Episcopal Churches in Manhattan, The Bronx and Westchester.* (New York, Methodist Episcopal Church City Planning Committee, 1931), p. 75.

what all the others do.  The infrequent activities necessarily belong to only a few churches.  From this standpoint five fairly distinct types of churches have been distinguished and elaborately compared.

## TYPICALLY DEVELOPED CHURCHES

The most frequent and characteristic church of the city derives its entire program from the frequent or invariable activities.  It exhibits a slight expansion of the rural church program.  Such churches are characteristic partly because of the strength of tradition.  The cities are increasingly populated by country people, which tends to limit their churches to what the church was accustomed to do rurally.  As has been noted, the great majority of city churches are small and unable to support a varied program.  Moreover, as has just been pointed out, numerous non-church agencies exist, maintained by larger ecclesiastical units, such as conferences and synods.  These serve to relieve the local church of the need of performing highly specialized functions.  These more traditional churches tend to have the more concentrated parishes distinguished in chapter iv, and all along the line to duplicate the essential spirit and pattern of the rural church in the city.

## UNDER-DEVELOPED AND FRAGMENTARY CHURCHES

Classified according to program, the second type of urban church is one which has an even narrower range of activities than the traditional one.  It makes no advance upon the country, and is distinctly sub-modal for the city.  It fails to do all that most churches do.  Its organizations are limited in number by its institutional weakness.  Here are found the abortive enterprises or very young ones, or else old and decrepit cases in which functions previously performed have been gradually lost, as an old man loses his faculties.  Careful studies have traced in detail the narrowing programs of churches that find it impossible to keep up with the general average of their neighborhoods.  However, in the case of these fragmentary churches the influence of especially narrow tradition has also to be recognized.  The ultra-reactionary spirit was first found in backward rural sections which are against Sunday schools, against missions, against organized social life;[6] but is less extreme in the city.  The same tendency, nevertheless, shows itself in churches whose extreme dogmatism and austerity of outlook keep their programs within the narrowest bounds.  Certain churches of foreign antecedents, moreover, do not give women the freedom to which they are accustomed in American life.  Consequently they fail to develop women's organizations.  It is noteworthy that these less-than-traditional or under-developed churches often have non-localized parishes.  Their limited pro-

---

[6] P. 27.

grams thus reflect in part the difficulty of drawing their scattered constituents to a narrow and unattractive version of a religious group life.

INTENSIVELY DEVELOPED OR ELABORATED CHURCHES

The third type of city church is one which consciously adds to its programs the cultural, social and recreational interests reflected in the infrequent activities previously discussed. It establishes, at least in outline, and tries to realize a complete and all-around program of activities fully differentiated as to age and sex. In its fullest development the many-sided constructive interests of life are organized around a religious core; and their expression is graded and adapted to each particular age group and to the peculiar needs of the two sexes.

SOCIALLY ADAPTED CHURCHES

As the list of highly infrequent activities has already indicated, a few churches definitely undertake to become agencies of social ministry to especially handicapped populations. They maintain the traditional activities of the church at the center of the enterprise, but add such health, recreational and economic aids as the especially needy types of population may require.

ERRATIC CHURCHES

A fifth type of city church puts the elements of its program together in such unusual fashion that it can be thought of only as erratic. Characteristically, it is a very weak church and frequently one of some special foreign or racial group. It may maintain only part of the traditional religious activities, but will associate with them some desperate expedient to meet desperate need. For example, a dozen Negro families in a northern city may undertake the maintenance of a dormitory for their members—an extremely novel enterprise for a parish church. To the erratic type also belong many home-mission enterprises such as Christian centers which deliberately minimize traditional religious functions and exalt social ministries in dealing with populations of non-Protestant antecedents.[7]

The most adequate examination ever made of a body of urban churches from the standpoint of classification by types of program yields the following numerical distribution of the types:

| Types | Per Cent. |
|---|---|
| Typically developed | 40 |
| Under-developed | 25 |
| Elaborated | 18 |
| Socially adapted | 4 |
| Erratic | 13 |

[7] Abel, *Protestant Home Missions to Catholic Immigrants* (New York: Institute of Social and Religious Research, 1933), pp. 12 f., and 58 ff.

This classification, based upon 1,044 cases, cannot be accepted as showing an exact distribution of urban churches by types, but pending more extensive data it is fair to think of about two-thirds of the city churches as traditional or fragmentary, somewhat less than one-fifth as having reached urban elaboration from the standpoint of normal populations, in that they have a broad scope of interests and a complete scheme of age and sex organization; while a scant fifth are socially adapted, either in the deliberate sense or in some one-sided erratic fashion.

Obviously the distinction between the types cannot be very clearcut. Transitional sub-types have to be distinguished. It should be clear, however, that a mere extension of program which chooses all of its increased activities from the traditional range is merely more of the same sort of thing and does not lift the church out of the traditional type. On the contrary, the recognition in specific organization and activity of novel interests begins to turn a church into another kind of institution, one performing an enlarged set of functions and supplying a wider range of values to a community.

The reliability of the classification of churches according to frequency of their program elements is greatly strengthened by the discovery that each type is marked by a fairly definite set of accompanying institutional characteristics. Churches with fragmentary programs are fragmentary all along the line, while the socially adapted churches have, all told, the strongest and the most highly developed institutional life. Thus, on the whole, the fragmentary churches are smaller than the traditional, while the elaborated are larger and the socially adapted the largest of all. The same order of distinction pertains to their average age. The elaborated and socially adapted are older; their programs reflect a longer period of evolution. Again, the most developed churches as to program have larger staffs which, as has already been shown, particularly reflect in their composition and functions, age and sex differentiations and social-service adaptations. Churches with more highly developed programs have more experienced and better-paid ministers, larger average church expenses and better facilities. The only institutional factor in which they are not superior is the relative size of the Sunday school. The fragmentary churches have larger Sunday schools relative to church-membership than any other type. This simply demonstrates that they are fragmentary and tend to be Sunday schools more than they are churches.

Perhaps the most important characteristic in which the church's variation according to type has been demonstrated is that of participation by its constituents. As the result of a study of a limited number of churches, it appears that typically developed churches get 7.5 hours participation per month from the average adherent, the under-developed 9.5 hours, the elaborated 8.9 hours, and the socially adjusted 14.6 hours. In this showing, two points are noteworthy. First, the small average membership of the under-developed church compels it to spend more hours per capita in operating a fragmentary program than other types do in operating a completed one. Participation thus becomes over-done in time considering how little there is to participate in. Second, the more highly developed types have not only more and more novel activities, but actually manage to attract the average adherents for a longer period.

DENOMINATIONAL FREQUENCY OF THE TYPES

The study of types of churches as determined by program reveals somewhat striking, but, on the whole, intelligible denominational differences as shown in Chart XXI. Traditional churches relatively uninfluenced by city

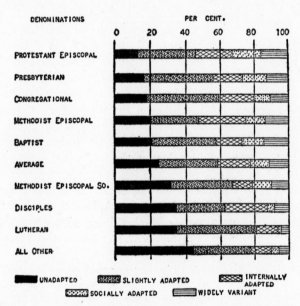

CHART XXI—PER CENT. DISTRIBUTION OF TYPES OF CHURCHES IN SPECIFIED DENOMINATIONS

environment are most frequent in the Lutheran denominations and least frequent in the Methodist Episcopal. In contrast with the large and well-established denominations, the largest proportion of fragmentary churches belong to those which get gathered up under the category of miscellaneous because their churches are too few for separate statistical tabulation. As already indicated, they reflect a narrow tradition and institutional feebleness. In contrast with this, the clear-cut Protestant Episcopal tradition of what a church should be, coupled with the inclinations of this denomination to locate in cities and its consequent lack of reactionary rural constituencies, gives this communion the smallest proportion of fragmentary churches. A higher proportion of Methodist Episcopal churches appear to have taken on all-around elaborated programs than have those of any other denominations, while socially adapted churches are most frequent with the Protestant Episcopal and Baptist communions. The Protestant Episcopal Church is notable for a high development of its social work all along the line, while the Baptist superiority at this point is partly due to deliberate missionary policy and partly to the large number of Baptist churches found in the poorer sections of cities where they are under environmental pressure to take on social-service functions.

RELATIONS OF THE TYPES TO TRADITIONAL CHURCH FUNCTIONS

Within the congregating, projecting and administering phases of organizations as set forth in chapter v, the various types of churches recognized in the foregoing analysis represent unequal expansions and elaborations of the traditional functions of the local church; namely, worship, instruction and humane service. Virtually every additional activity undertaken can be classified as an appendage to one of these phases of the church's traditional life.

Whether the present balance between the types of local churches is the right one for the present day depends in part, first, upon the sufficiently sensitive responsiveness of the church as an institution to particular local pressures which require modifications of the traditional program in one direction or the other; but also in part, as has been repeatedly noted, to differing convictions as to whether or not the church is at liberty to respond to such pressures. In other words, if the proper sphere of the church is defined by its traditional program some churches have evidently transgressed in going beyond that sphere. Further consideration of this issue is reserved for a later chapter.[8]

For the moment attention is to be concentrated upon the central and invariable activities of the local church; and, in contrast, upon certain exceptional ones which show the trend of evolution. These latter characterize the lines of the modern church's advance, though as a matter of fact they are confined largely to a relatively few churches of the especially elaborated or socially adapted types.

CENTRAL AND INVARIABLE ACTIVITIES

For three closely related reasons objective studies of the modern church have neither devoted much attention to its central and invariable activities nor thrown much light upon them. In the first place, these activities, centering as they do in worship, prayer and the sacraments, express the deeper

---

[8] P. 323.

mysteries of religion and are too profound for most attempts at objective examination. They reflect the projection of conduct into the super-social realm where it is not observable in its entirety as it is in the social realm.

Moreover these phenomena ultimately have to be evaluated subjectively rather than objectively. They celebrate religious experience; they belong to the world of art. Worthy praise or satisfying worship may indeed be appraised by competent experts in these realms, but not on scientific grounds. The critic who disagrees with any assumed sense of values has no objective basis upon which to argue. Science, in other words, is out of its depth in such matters.

Finally, the central and invariable activities of the church have presented less challenge to fresh study than others because they are so little changed. Where it is assumed that their permanent form has been fixed by authoritative revelations they cannot consistently change. In this respect, as observed by the Middletown study,[9] the assumptions of organized religion differ from those that govern all other phases of social interest, and the Middletown churches actually exhibited less change than any other type of institution in that community.

Observation, nevertheless, has recorded certain external changes in the central and invariable activities of the church, and, as a later chapter shows, their problems exhibit themselves to the modern mind in somewhat different ways from what they did formerly.

The immediately following paragraphs, consequently, deal briefly with the phenomena of worship and preaching as associated in public religious services, and take some account of evangelism as an intensified form of public religious activity and of minor devotional services as typical of its more informal aspect.

All these types of activity are attached to the congregating phase of the church's life. All, however, involve a valuable element of sociability, all minister to group morale, and all become the occasion of pastoral contacts. The most distinctive differences are those of mood and tempo, as traditionally exemplified, for example, between the morning and the evening services. The latter are often popularized and jazzed up so that, on grounds of taste, they become a distinctly different type of service. It is assumed that this involves purely accidental differences rather than essential ones.

WORSHIP

Public worship is accepted without question as a central and invariable activity of the local church, and its conduct has chief place in the minister's work. This reflects the church's deepest religious tradition.

A greater degree of conscious attention, however, has recently come to be

---

[9] Lynd, *op. cit.*, p. 103.

given to public worship as an art. The analysis of religious services according to dramatic and esthetic criteria has improved appreciation and received increasing interest, especially upon the part of non-liturgical churches. Numerous churches have created special commissions to study and report upon worship, and there have been important minor revisions of officially adopted rituals.

Interest in worship has progressively passed over into religious education. Most modern church school programs now attempt to give training in the devising of worship services. In striking contrast with the effort of the "Christian Endeavor" age to train young novices of the last century in the virtues of public testimony and extemporaneous prayer, the present age is more concerned with the dignity and fitness of formal elements of worship. While the great mass of Protestant church services is little changed, a considerable minority have exchanged the virtues of spontaneity for those of adequacy, balance and beauty through the greater use of liturgical forms.

Church music naturally has experienced a corresponding urban elaboration. Its technical aspects may safely be regarded as more or less of a side issue; but the improving of hymns and of the work of chorus choirs constitute a cultural tendency of great moment.

The architectural embellishment of the place of worship has also received large attention in connection with the enormous recent expenditures upon church plants discussed in chapter x. Thus the average church has secured a more effective and churchly setting for its central acts of traditional worship.

In view of their ancient place and authentic development within the church it ought not to seem strange that the theater arts—the processional, posturing, costuming and lighting—have received a modern reinstatement, and that all have been brought to bear to heighten the emotional effect of its services. All of these arts have also been used unconventionally, and possibly cheaply, in somewhat erratic hands—Aimee Semple MacPherson's Los Angeles Temple serving as an example.

Whatever the theory of the sacraments, their administration was already highly formalized, even in the so-called non-liturgical churches; and while these forms have suffered little change, the non-liturgical churches have given new attention to the integration of the sacraments into the total service.

Summarizing the worship of the more highly organized type of modern church, one must characterize it as less spontaneous and "folksy" than it was in the past, more self-conscious, restrained and consistent. The effort to "improve" rural churches along these lines has doubtless been greatly needed but has sometimes produced rather hybrid results. It is manifestly impossible in any scientific fashion to compare the values of the plain services of the old rural meeting house with those of the newer moods and observances, except to say that each serves best the people who like it.

When seasonality in the church's worship is considered later in this chapter the great elaboration and formal services at holiday, Lenten and Easter seasons will be a pertinent consideration.

PREACHING

In Protestant society preaching is commonly associated with public worship. Its absence from a service of ritual was formerly assumed by the more sectarian bodies to open the door to superstition and to substitute idolatrous emotions for an intelligent approach to religious matters.

The influence of public discourse has doubtless suffered a decline in recent decades relative to the influence of the printed page. With respect to its relative position in the church, preaching is involved in this decline, which is also obviously related to the weakening of the older forms of political democracy, and the increased educational emphasis of the church. The radio appears to be on the point of turning the scales again to public discourse as against the printed page. On the other hand, radio preaching directly militates against the congregating phase of the church's life and is a doubtful means of recovery to the pulpit generally.

Most ministers still cling to the sense of the supreme importance of the pulpit and give more time to preparation for its ministry than to any other phase of their work. All told, however, preaching appears to have stepped down a place relative to worship, on the one hand, and to the more active and practical phases of religious expression, on the other.

None of the objective studies of the church have developed a set of criteria useful for the study of preaching, either from the standpoint of its mere satisfactoriness or of its results on religious character. Collections of excerpts from sermons of Negro and mountaineer preachers add a colorful interpretive touch to descriptions of the churches of these groups, and notes on many hundreds of sermons in typical rural and urban churches enable one to classify them according to homiletical varieties and to point out the great vogue of catchy topics—many of them by no means justified by the body of the sermons. The present writers, however, are not in possession of any set of criteria which they believe to have scientific validity for the comparing or technical judging of sermons.

A certain decline of the dogmatic mood which formerly characterized preaching may be inferred from the more popular sermon topics in vogue and from frequent complaints that the old note of authority has gone from the pulpit. The tone of preaching has doubtless been modified by the growing conception of the co-authority of Scripture and religious experience, evidence for which is presented in chapter xv; by some sense of the immense complexity of the human mind and of the different levels of consciousness out of which experience and behavior come; as well as by enough experiments in dealing with contemporaneous problems to show how difficult they are and how many sides they present. All of this has produced a certain inclination in the pulpit to substitute the attitudes and technique of educational discussion for that of dogmatic pronouncement. These same moods, taken out of the pulpit, have produced the church forum which will be noted among recent novelties in a subsequent paragraph. While, relative to other activities, preaching has been somewhat deflated, a few ministers have glimpsed what they regard as high possibilities in the common thinking of small groups and are giving increasing attention to the cultivation of the neglected values of the so-called minor services of the church.

The newer interests which have pressed into organized expression in the church have naturally added additional range to pulpit discussion. Conservative efforts which have resisted these interests in other spheres have naturally resisted them also in preaching. It is significant, however, that highly traditional churches sometimes take on extraordinary functions under social pressure. Thus a rabidly pre-millenarian church, which regards all concern for the earthly comforts of humanity as purposely wrong, may nevertheless establish an employment service for those of its members that constitute a handicapped human group. This it does without any sense of incongruity. It is similarly interesting to note that, with the growth of industrial controversy in southern communities, the first to make social applications of Christianity to the labor crisis in a mill village was the untrained preacher of a reactionary religion, serving a congregation of operatives and perhaps himself employed in the mills.

### EVANGELISM

Comparative studies of the rural church show that reduced reliance is now being placed upon special evangelistic services as a means of winning adherents. Comparisons of questionnaires returned by trained and untrained preachers show that the latter group is more attached to the evangelistic method than the former. The Middletown study, however, and studies of the rural church generally show a wide survival of the method of holding special evangelistic services in the smaller cities and rural areas.

On the other hand, in common with the more urban types of city churches, many town and rural churches are making increasingly intensified use of the special seasons of the Christian year, such as Lent and Easter, which heighten and focus religious attention and gather large congregations. "Visitation evangelism," systematically undertaken from house to house over large territories, follows the method of projecting the church in pursuit of the people rather than that of congregating them in one place, and has often secured the reconnection to the church of many hundreds of its lapsed members.

MINOR DEVOTIONAL SERVICES

The gradual abandonment of the traditional mid-week services in the rural church seems established by the latest studies. Questionnaires from ministers, however, still report the conduct of such mid-week services as occurring in the average week of from 70 to 80 per cent. of them. Where such services survive in rural churches their earlier simplicity has gradually gone and they have become occasions of formal religious culture, of the discussion of current topics, or of the presentation of practical causes. The need for concentrating the varied interests of the modern urban church and of saving the time of adherents who come from long distances has somewhat frequently led to the development of the week-day "church night" in which the cultural, social, recreational and business activities of numerous groups are combined with worship, frequently in a common service, within a single evening intended to take care of most of the church's activities until the following Sunday.

The added activities of the elaborated and socially adapted churches, though generally reflecting a secularizing tendency in the church, usually manage to maintain some slight trace of devotional activities; and these frequently add considerably both to attendance upon and to the amount of time given to religious pursuits in the total program of the church.

SUMMARY

While this exceedingly slender review is believed to tell most of what can be recorded with respect to worship and preaching from the standpoint of objective observation, it should also be stated that techniques developed in the realm of character education, though much harder to apply to the results of worship and preaching, are applicable in principle, and may yield thoroughly objective results in the hands of future investigators. Something also might be done by recording the consensus of opinion of experts or of thoughtful participants as to values inherent in particular forms and occasions with respect to these central religious activities. These are among the many topics indicated in the preface which the Institute's investigations have never managed to reach.

SIGNIFICANT NOVELTIES IN URBAN CHURCH PROGRAMS

A comparison of the programs of considerable bodies of urban churches over a period of a decade indicates a distinct growth in certain infrequent church activities which may fairly be taken as indices of change. Churches are more frequently open on week-days for private devotion, and church office hours for consultation are more often maintained. This fits in with the greater anonymousness of urban church life and substitutes centralized routine for some of the church's outreaching pastoral ministry which formerly undertook to seek and to find men individually.

Again, separate children's congregations and means of organized adult education, frequently taking the form of church forums, are among the emerging activities. These reflect the more carefully graded organizations of the church and the substitution of educational for dogmatic attitudes, as noted in a previous paragraph.

The concentration of week-day church activities in a single "church night" is obviously an attempt to combat the unrelated development of separate interests and to tie them together in a common bond. Finally, radio broadcasting has appeared as an activity of individual churches. While for obvious reasons, of which keen competition for the air is the most compelling, the major tendency with respect to broadcasting assigns it to the larger units of the church and inclines to make it a coöperative venture, this enterprise of the local church in using this new instrument of human communication requires recording.

The emergence of this group of novel activities suggests some of the particular forces that work within the local church to elaborate and complicate its program. Some reflect environmental pressures; others, the moods of the age. That these novelties are not more widely expressed is partly due to their relative newness and partly to the resistance of tradition with its doubts as to whether they are the right things for the church to do.

## PERIODICITY IN ACTIVITIES

The congregating activities of the church and the life of its organized groups are more or less periodic, while the projecting and administering functions show somewhat concomitant variations. The tradition of the "Christian Year," attaching religion to the seasons and to historical anniversaries, is itself a highly significant mark of the institutionalization of the church. Besides these periodic occasions, the habitually recurrent activities of the modern church represented by its weekly or monthly gatherings for public services or for subsidiary activities, are increasingly seasonal. In the urban church the summer season is marked by relative inactivity and intensive programs are increasingly fitted so as to fall within the school year.

In addition to its recurrent and seasonal activities, a great part of the life of the modern church is bound up with novel occasions. Indeed, the quality of occasionality appears to be growing. This is particularly the case because publicity and news value attach to things which, at least ostensibly, are novel. Consequently the "special" service, the sermon series which claims special relevancy, whether or not it deserves it, the "topics of the day." Ministers go so far as to complain that all the Sundays of the year might be taken up by the celebration of anniversaries or advocacies of special interests. This tendency corresponds to the observance of saints' days in the Catholic church. Each of the newer emphases of the churches collectively—international peace, racial goodwill, economic justice and the like—has persevered until it has been able to appropriate some special Sunday of the year on which to dramatize its special virtues. Religion is thus coming increasingly to follow a fixed calendar in many churches.

## ACTIVITIES OF EXTRA-PAROCHIAL ORGANIZATION

Chapter v has followed the church out into its sphere of denominational organization above and beyond the local parish. Each of these higher levels —district, state and national—has evolved its corresponding group of activities and programs. The increasing complexity of the denominational structure of the modern church has been noted. Unfortunately objective studies have not dealt intensively with denominations as such, particularly because a denomination is the last ecclesiastical entity which is willing to subject itself to non-partisan study. In a few cases the administrative structure of national boards or denominational boards of missions or of education have been investigated and certain newer studies have set forth actual missionary processes, both in home and in foreign fields, in some detail.

### ACTIVITIES OF LESSER DENOMINATIONAL UNITS

As revealing the problems of extra-parochial organization, the most fruitful field of investigation has been found in the ecclesiastical units which rank immediately above the local churches. The intensive study of denominational city mission and extension societies, previously alluded to,[10] shows that the typical activities of these agencies fall under three major heads: (1) *incidentally* they serve as denominational headquarters performing services of information and expert assistance for the entire body or between churches in the fields of finance, programs, approach to a special public, and the use of facilities; (2) the *deliberate* programs of these agencies are departmentalized under the traditional heads of evangelism, religious education, social service, women, and young people's work, and occasionally recreation. Here are activities of churches grouped into larger denominational units, which correspond exactly to the wider programs of the more progressive local churches. (3) Finally, the *original and specific work* of this group of agencies, on to which the others have been grafted, is the aiding of needy churches in their maintenance and in the extension of their working facilities as set forth in Chapter III.

---

[10] Hallenbeck, *Urban Organization of Protestantism*, pp. 31 ff.

CHURCH FEDERATION ACTIVITIES

The field of interdenominational organization is well covered by intensive studies. Thus, the activities of church federations and councils, state and local, have been painstakingly exploited, as have those of councils of religious education in many American communities. Two-thirds of the large city federations departmentalize their work under the heads, evangelism, comity, religious education, social service, and international relations. Approximately one-half add interracial goodwill, law enforcement, finance, publicity, and women's departments. Less than one-third maintain departments or standing committees on young people's work, industrial relations, religious ministries in courts and hospitals, missions, radio broadcasting, rural affairs, moral reform, and sabbath observance.

Both the denominational and interdenominational organizations thus fall into three general types, namely, all-around agencies which carry on almost anything which the group as a whole does; agencies characterized by narrow and one-sided programs compared with the average, and a mediating or average type.

Thus, through observation of what is happening in the local church, one is able to trace the evolution and the elaboration of ecclesiastical activities on all levels. The traditional core of local church function, namely, public worship, preaching and teaching, and practical service is carried over as an almost invariable center of the denominational and interdenominational program. Next appearing, on all levels, is the separate organization and departmentalization of women's work. Peculiar to the denominational and interdenominational organizations is the issue of "comity," which governs the relationships of individual churches as determined by their overhead authorities. Meanwhile activities having to do with international relations, which received their first development in the interdenominational sphere, reverse the more customary direction of development and are working downward into the structure of the denominations and of the local churches. There is thus a movement from the top down as well as from the bottom up, which helps to explain the actual genesis and increasing variety of modern church programs.

CONCLUSION

Gathering up the more significant principles which have emerged in the foregoing review, one finds:

(1) The church's program of activities shows primarily the influence of tradition and of environmental pressure, somewhat modified by what a later chapter notes as the intellectual climate, that is to say, the set of special ideas which have vogue at a given time. Concern about international relationships is a good illustration of such ideas.

(2) Lack of homogeneity within the local church makes for variety in program. A set of distinct but unrelated constituencies, a lot of dangling subsidiaries, commonly reflect an adjacent population of varied antecedents, nationality and social status. This variety tends to express itself not only in a complicated church structure but in a wide range of functions, all more or less closely related to the traditional central activities of the church, but some greatly attenuating them and others registering them in highly novel ways.

(3) The invariability of the central core of activities reflects the conservatism of the church and the continuance of conventional religious evaluations as applied to activities. The church carries on many things for reasons determined in the past, whether or not they continue to be currently satisfactory. The reason for novelties, on the contrary, is generally carried on the face of the situation. They reflect a demand from some group or other in behalf of an interest believed worthy to be incorporated in the current life of the church. Novelties are first undertaken experimentally by a few churches. If they continue to "catch on" they spread by imitation.

(4) Different types of churches reflect the presence not of different situations but of what, on the whole, must be regarded as different cultural levels. Central values in one case are expressed through a more refined capacity for appreciation and on a superior esthetic level than in another. It needs, however, to be reiterated that whatever is most authentic for a particular population group is, for the moment at least, superior for the group, whatever else may be said about it.

(5) The review of the variety of church activities in terms of urban and rural churches has tended to substantiate the theory that the urban church is an evolved rural church. The traditional program, reflected not only in the less developed types of local urban churches but in the denominational and interdenominational fields as well, is essentially the present program of the rural church. Additions and elaborations supplied by the urban church and activities introduced by overhead agencies are novelties chiefly because the rural church as a whole has not yet reached this stage of specialization.

(6) It follows from the analysis of the church's structure that many activities listed as the church's activities are actually, in large measure, merely the activities of semi-independent constituencies: so that the programs ascribed on paper to a given church may have little reference to the program actually available to the individual adherent, or the one chosen by or participated in by a given constituency within the same church.

(7) Finally, since in the average case he belongs to the church in only one way out of a possible half dozen, dozen, or even score of ways, the individual adherent does not participate in many activities at best. His actual

religious culture through the church has a much narrower basis than the total range of activities which the church carries on. The broader program widens the church's appeal and the opportunity of the individual adherent. Participation is much more limited than the scope of the opportunities provided, and also much more crucial.

# CHAPTER VIII

## Educational Activities and Insights

The connection of religion and education has ever been close. Man's religious views have always been one of the strongest influences on his educational systems. Religion was closely identified with man's fears of natural phenomena, of famine and of death. He early developed devices designed to ward off the displeasure of spiritual beings more powerful than he. These devices in turn crystallized in behavior patterns and developed into ceremonials and rituals.

As these became more elaborate, as they passed beyond the family to the clan or tribe, there arose a twofold educational need. Men were required who could become learned in the mysteries and ceremonials of religion—i.e. priests. The populace, on the other hand, must be kept willing to play its part unquestioningly in the institutional structure that developed. From early times, then, there was a dual educational task—that of preparing the professional priest and that of indoctrinating the laity. The techniques employed on both levels, however, were designed to perpetuate an authoritative cultural tradition rather than to provide for the possibility of progress or innovation.

The mediaeval church took the religious beliefs of the early Christians, compounded them with the organizing skill of Rome and added such vestiges of Greek learning as could be adapted to its purposes. From these elements it developed an educational system which is still practised in a few countries and the influence of which lives on in many. Religious culture was its dominant aim even though secular learnings were employed as the means.

The Protestant churches carried over some of this ancient educational philosophy but made several significant contributions. The church no longer determined man's conduct. The Bible was substituted and made directly available to all. The individual came to have supreme importance. In order that all could have access to the Holy Writ, Protestantism soon came to stand for elementary education for all. But the primary motive for such education was to furnish a vehicle for religious indoctrination. This idea spread with the growth of Protestantism and was skilfully used for the perpetuation of its body of doctrine. The school followed the church; and where churches were planted in the New World the school soon followed. The clergy were often the schoolmasters. The parochial school of today, still found in certain of the liturgical bodies, was the outgrowth of this conviction. Though the Bible was supplemented as a textbook, the emphasis was the same, as witness the New England Primer. Here, then, was a highly significant fact in the history of the special psychology of Protestantism. Discarding the authoritativeness of the church, emphasizing as it did respect for personality, proclaiming the Bible as the guide to conduct and the individual's obligation to interpret it, Protestantism, none the less, by every known device, inculcated its concepts and doctrines as purposefully as ever did the mediaeval monk or the tribal priest.

Its basic, implicit philosophy, however, eventually overthrew its practice. Education became secularized, but Protestantism lost none of its interest in education. Especially was this true in North America. It early reared and still sustains an elaborate system. It pioneered in secondary (high-school) education with its academies. For long collegiate and university education was largely, at times almost exclusively, in its hands. It aimed to nurture the leaders of the learned professions throughout their whole period of preparation. It continued the age-long special preparation of "priests" in its divinity schools and theological seminaries. First in England and then in America, it attempted to bring some education and culture to the children of the poor in its Sunday schools. As the state took over education and made it a universal privilege, the church continued these Sunday schools as adjuncts to nearly every local church, to teach the Bible and its doctrines to all its children. Its missionaries duplicated this structure in all lands to which they went.

Inevitably, therefore, the methods used were the old ones of imitation and indoctrination; and inevitably, too, the Sunday schools (despite a change of name to Bible or church schools) were relatively untouched by the progress in educational theory and practice that has been made of recent years in secular education. True, better curriculum materials are used in some schools, some efforts have been made at grading; especially in cities the project method is to be found, though seldom removed from the indoctrinating philosophy. But the essence of John Dewey's contribution to secular education, the philosophy and most of the techniques of modern progressive education are not only foreign to the weekly procedures of the church schools, but are also opposed to its main objectives.

### INSTITUTIONAL ORGANIZATION AND RELIGIOUS EDUCATION

Other than the assembling of people for worship, the religious educational work of the local Protestant church in the United States is its greatest single enterprise. As such it deserves the most careful study. Four-fifths of all churches have such Sunday schools. The very bulk of the enterprise is most impressive. There are at least 185,000 Sunday schools in the nation, enrolling more than 21,000,000 persons, 95 per cent. of them Protestants, and served by more than 2,000,000 teachers and officers. Of these schools more than half are rural. The Sunday-school enrollment is only one-sixth below that of the public schools, though it includes, of course, many adults.

There is an officer or teacher for every nine rural pupils, compared with one for every eleven in cities. The vast majority of these teachers are unpaid, the majority untrained, so that Protestantism has initiated a far-flung teacher-training enterprise of a superficial sort.

The average enrollment of the rural school is seventy-six, only about one-third as large as that of the urban schools. Rural Sunday schools are, however, the more numerous and in rural America live more than half the children of the country, so that the rural schools will be first considered.

## RURAL RELIGIOUS EDUCATION

The rural Sunday school is relatively more important than the urban, for it is sometimes the only activity of the church other than the worship and preaching service, and on the average it receives a relatively greater amount of volunteer service from members. One-eighth of all rural church-members serve as teachers or officers of Sunday schools.

To a greater extent than elsewhere the rural Sunday school is a laymen's organization. Because of the fact that, especially in the open country, many churches do not have weekly services the school is the only religious educational activity of the congregation on a good many Sundays. At least two-fifths of the rural church schools on any given Sunday meet without the presence of the minister or other professional leader. Especially in such cases the success, even the survival, of the Sunday school is up to the untrained lay volunteer.

Partly because of the increased emphasis upon religious education, partly because many small rural churches, too small to operate a Sunday school, have died since 1920, the proportion of churches having schools has steadily increased.[1] In 1920, between one-fifth and one-fourth of all rural churches lacked schools. In 1924 the figure was one-fifth for the open country and less than one-tenth for the village churches. In 1930, only one-thirteenth of the village and about one-seventh of the country churches were without this characteristic adjunct to their programs. Average enrollment had also increased in the village, standing at 127 in 1930, but in the country it had

---

[1] This statement contradicts the findings of the 1926 U. S. Census of Religious Bodies, which reports a drop between 1916 and 1926 of 0.8 per cent. in the number of all churches operating schools. The contradiction is probably due to the Roman Catholic situation. This church reported parochial schools as Sunday schools in 1916, but did not do so in 1926. Between 1916 and 1926 Roman Catholic Sunday-school pupils declined 660,000, or one-third; parochial school enrollment increased 1,000,000.

remained almost stationary at sixty-six, as against sixty-seven in 1924. The increase was due in part to a gain in adult enrollment. About one-half the schools had one or more organized classes for adults. Enrollment in Sunday schools equaled three-fourths of the church-membership, but included less than one-fourth of the population. Attendance averaged less than two-thirds of the enrollment.

In equipment, either physical or pedagogical, rural Sunday schools, especially those in the open country, are seriously lacking. Two out of three meet in either one or two rooms. Where there is a second room it is usually and properly set aside for the primary department. Apart from this, except in many of the newer village church buildings, the Sunday school, like the old-fashioned little red schoolhouse, has all its classes in one room. It has, however, an advantage over the public school, in that two classes seldom have the same teacher; it is at a disadvantage in that it reaches its average pupil but thirty-four times a year. Less than nine-tenths of the Sunday schools are in session every Sunday.

Even when a school has more than two rooms, modern equipment is notably absent. Sand tables, stereopticons, maps, attractive interior decorations, proper pictures hung at proper heights, all these things and many other undisputed accessories of modern educational work are rarely found.

These handicaps are partly due to the limitations of building and finances described in chapter ix, and partly to the fact that the teachers are volunteers with no knowledge and little or no appreciation of modern educational techniques or equipment. In 1920, Dr. Walter Athearn found that the assets of the average Sunday-school teacher were a certain amount of loyalty to the church, piety, consecration and a lesson quarterly. This in turn has conditioned the type of curriculum materials. They have had to be quite simple. Curiously enough, however, they have seldom drawn on the rich rural settings of the Bible. Despite the large rural market, no special materials are issued for rural church schools. However, some series of lesson helps are now pointing out the rural implications of each lesson.

Rural churches have increasingly recognized these handicaps and have moved to meet them. In 1920, one church in eleven had a teacher-training class meeting from eight to twelve times a year. In 1930, the proportion had increased to one in six. Interestingly enough, the proportion was sharply higher in rural industrial communities than in distinctly agricultural ones.

This, with other facts to be noted later, shows that there is some progress in the field of rural religious education; but it is also clear that this progress has not kept pace with that which has taken place in the urban church. Expert leaders in religious education have been baffled by the small size of the rural school and the limited resources in facilities and personnel that are available. Their standardized plans involve considerably better equipment and larger numbers than are available in rural situations.

Thus it is that the rural Sunday school lags farther behind the public school than the urban. The adolescents of the average village-centered community go to one high school; they are distributed among eleven Sunday schools. Though the number of open-country schools and churches is about equal in the average community, the trend is toward reducing the number of the former. Thirty per cent. of the enrollment of village elementary schools comes from the open country. These children and all those of the village are taught in no more than two schools, usually in one. It is hard to see how there can be any considerable progress in rural religious education until, by planning or by surrender to slowly working social forces, there can be some consolidation of religious educational work comparable to what is going on among the public schools. This, of course, raises the whole involved problem of comity and the redistribution of churches which is discussed in a later chapter.

In the meantime in a few localities, especially those served by larger parishes, a temporizing device to meet this problem has been adopted, namely, the employment of a director of religious education for a group of churches. Significantly enough this has usually been done on an interdenominational basis. The director of religious education acts much as a supervisor of township schools. Because the local church school teacher is untrained, she holds training classes or conferences, attends teachers' meetings, conducts demonstration classes and the like.

Numerous other devices are employed to strengthen the rural educational situation. These include week-day religious instruction in coöperation with the public school, daily vacation Bible schools, classes for prospective church-members and schools of missions or classes for mission study. All of these have been taken over from urban church experience and only seldom can they be operated as efficiently in the country as in the city.

The first-named, week-day religious education, has had a set-back in recent years. One rural church in six was coöperating in such work in 1924. By 1930 the proportion was one in twelve. To much of this work public school credit was given. Classes met once a week, usually in the school building. A vast majority of the parents, over 99 per cent., approved the plan. Ministers usually conducted the classes, as urban college graduates could rarely qualify for teaching certificates for this subject. The 50 per cent. drop in the number of cases of such religious-education work is apparently due to changes in state laws or in regulations of state boards of education, to failure of ministers to coöperate in the work, and to the factor of ministerial turnover.

The daily vacation Bible school, conducted for from two to four weeks in summer, is another attempt to increase the amount of religious instruction. This movement was all but unknown in rural America in 1920, but in 1930, 18 per cent. of all churches in agricultural communities, and 33 per cent. of all those in rural industrial communities conducted such schools.

Classes to prepare for church-membership have also come more into vogue. They have long been part of the regular procedure of some bodies like the Episcopal, Lutheran, Reformed and Moravian, but the practice is growing with other communions. Nearly one-fourth of all rural churches, more than one-third of them located in villages, now conduct such classes. In 1920 the proportion was only one-sixth and the practice was largely confined to the denominations mentioned. The practice seems to be worth while. Rural churches with such classes gain proportionately more members and have a far lower proportion of inactives.

Finally, there are the mission-study classes conducted by a little more than one church in ten. The situation, history, program in one special field such as China, India or Africa, is considered in from six to eight meetings. A text-book is generally used. This seems like a superficial thing, but whether from this cause, or because only the stronger and richer churches have had mission study, per capita giving to missionary causes has been more than one-fourth higher in churches maintaining this educational feature than in others.

The facts here recorded in the mass and for the average rural situation vary according to the training of the minister and also according to his residence. The better trained the man and the larger the proportion of his time given to a given congregation, the better the religious educational program.

At best, however, in the rural church field there is much room for improvement in the educational procedures. This improvement seems to wait upon either the preparation of better materials and procedures for rural schools by religious educational experts, who have thus far largely neglected it, or the consolidation of church schools into units large enough to command the same leadership and facilities as are enjoyed by the urban church.

### Religious Education in Urban Churches

As was true in the rural church, formal religious education in the urban church is primarily focussed on the Sunday school. The average urban Sunday school in 1926 had 210 pupils. An extensive later sampling shows that some 45 per cent. of the total vary in size from 100 to 300, though more than one-quarter have from 300 to 500 pupils. In a more widely distributed sampling of 930 cases only thirty had enrollments beyond 1,000.

Confirming the evidence of census data that a slump has occurred in the Sunday school as an institution, a sampling of 1,881 urban Sunday schools compared with the churches to which they belonged showed striking differences in rates of growth for the decade 1919-1929, as follows:

| Per Cent. of Increase or Decrease in Enrollment | Per Cent. Distribution of Churches | Per Cent. Distribution of Sunday Schools |
|---|---|---|
| More than 5% decrease | 28 | 40 |
| Between 5% decrease and 5% increase | 10 | 9 |
| 5 to 25% increase | 16 | 15 |
| More than 25% increase | 46 | 36 |

The result shows substantially one-half of the Sunday schools stationary or declining as compared with only 38 per cent. of the churches.

Alongside of this evidence of failure to grow as generally as church-membership does must be put the fact that enrollment of urban Sunday schools only averages 63 per cent. of church-membership. As already shown,[2] Sunday-school attendance frequently does account for more than one-quarter of the total attendance at all church activities in urban churches. The Sunday school is relatively more of an institution in suburban samples available, and, as previously noted, bulked larger in the total religious life of the rural community.

It has also been noted that larger-than-average Sunday schools, relative to their parent churches, cannot always be taken as signs of health in urban situations. They chiefly occur where a church is just starting, or else where it is failing; and signify that as an institution it does not have the normal cross-sectional hold on all elements of the community. The average attendance in an urban Sunday school is about 60 per cent. of its enrollment. This is appreciably lower than the rural average.

Sunday-school age data are not included in most official statistics; but several rather extensive samplings warrant the rough generalization that about one-tenth of the enrollment of the average urban Sunday school consists of children under six, two-fifths of older children, one-fifth of adolescents between fifteen and twenty-one, and one-fourth of adults. Adult enrollment thus constitutes a very significant fraction of the total and implies corresponding problems of organization and methods of instruction. To a considerable extent adult classes represent the type of dangling adherence to which a good many subsidiary organizations are addicted; and they not infrequently compete directly with general church services for loyalty and attendance. In other words, they are organizations of separate constituencies loosely related to the church and not always reservoirs on which the church draws proportionately for its closer adherents. To some extent this also holds true for rural churches.

This tendency merely instances an extreme version of the problem of the

---

[2] P. 88.

integration of the Sunday school with other church activities which have educational significance. Obviously, preaching is an educational influence, as are many other forms of subsidiary church activities. This problem will have later attention.

Again, the urban church has developed numerous other formal enterprises in religious education to supplement the Sunday school. Among them are week-day classes, vacation schools, and various types of discussion groups. Many of these appear primarily outside of local parishes. Some of these also are discussed in the following sections.

### Denominational and Interdenominational Organizations for Religious Education

Historically speaking, organized religious education was essentially a lay movement under non-denominational auspices. Its piety and emotionalism were more noteworthy than its educational quality. The last two decades have increasingly brought the movement under denominational auspices and authority. This tendency is parallel with and doubtless largely due to the improvement of educational standards which a subsequent paragraph will present. Denominational machinery became the vehicle by means of which improved ideas sought to get authority. The process may be traced in the development of provisions for religious education in connection with local units of denominational structure, such as state and local conferences. Thus, of thirty-one denominational city extension societies studied in 1933 one-third had local departments of religious education, one-third came within the functioning of state departments, and only one-third had no departments.[3] Community programs of religious education have frequently experienced rather acute pressure to divert their activities into strictly denominational moulds.

While thus manifesting itself as an increasing tendency, denominational machinery for religious education has been particularly subject to ups and downs. In flush times denominations have set up their own departments and trained their own lay workers in schools preserving a distinct denominational emphasis. In times of depression they have seen that religious education was one of the things which "could best be done in common" by the Protestant churches and have carried the movement back into interchurch forms.

This uncertainty and impermanence in denominational action has left the chief responsibility for the organization of religious education beyond the local parish to local councils of religious education and church federations.

Interdenominational city Sunday-school associations, reflecting the lay tradition, established their roots deeply during the latter part of the last

---

[3] Hallenbeck, *op. cit.*, p. 60.

century and thus pioneered in the movement of Protestant coöperation more fully described in chapter xii. Somewhat later more comprehensive church federations were developed. These sought to establish all-round coöperative programs symbolizing the unity of the church and attempting whatever "could best be done in common" on all sides of the church's work. Federations undertook the work of religious education where it was not already represented by Sunday-school associations, developed novel phases which many of the older Sunday-school associations were too conservative to recognize, and by a great variety of affiliated devices sought to include the older movement as part of their own. The smaller cities usually undertook to maintain only one of these movements; but, in 1930, out of seventy-eight cities of 100,000 population and over, there was duplication or competition in twenty-seven between the two forms of interchurch organization. Duplication was also present in the field of religious education in a number of states.

Considering all forms of coöperative work having educational implications, careful studies made in representative cities in 1930 found that, "adding these to the loosely related organizations hanging over from the older era—such as the graded unions, and the adult Bible class leagues—and bringing in the newer organizations, it turned out to be not unusual for a city to show (1) a historic Sunday-school association, (2) a competing council of religious education, (3) an association for operating daily vacation Bible schools, (4) a committee for week-day religious education and (5) an association of young people's societies—all interdenominational and in addition to the increasing machinery of religious organizations within the denomination."[4]

While a considerable amount of chaos still remains in this "coöperative" field, recent developments recorded in chapter xii show a very large degree of progress in simplifying and integrating the situation. Thus, in April, 1934, the Executive Committee of the Federal Council of the Churches of Christ in America "approved the ideal that there should be but one coöperative interchurch organization in a state or local community representing all interests in which the churches desire to unite, this one organization maintaining the appropriate relationship with whatever agencies may be concerned in the several interests which it locally represents."

Similar recent action taken by the International Council of Religious Education marks the adoption, in principle, of a method which inserts religious education into the total program of the church's coöperative work, while at the same time it exposes the total program to a greatly needed educational impulse, and opens up the possibility of its radical reorganization.

---

[4] Douglass, *Protestant Cooperation in American Cities* (New York: Institute of Social and Religious Research, 1930), p. 165.

## EXTRA-PAROCHIAL RELIGIOUS EDUCATION: CHURCH SCHOOLS AND COLLEGES

"The churches today control almost a third of the colleges and universities of the country, own one-fourth of the properties involved, and furnish one-third of the endowment."[5]

The original primary purpose of all these institutions was to inculcate religion and train religious leaders; and all still officially endeavor to produce an educational climate favorable to religion. Most of them add also some direct teaching of religion.

### THE DISTRIBUTION OF INSTRUCTION IN RELIGION

"The distribution of the total number of semester hours taught in 100 denominational institutions in 1930-31, according to the different aspects of the field of religion, gives a concrete picture of what leaders consider necessary in higher religious instruction. The number of hours taught was 3,306; 546 hours (16.5 per cent.) were in New Testament, 373 hours (11.3 per cent.) were in Old Testament, and 242 hours (7.3 per cent.) in general biblical survey courses. Thus, 1,161 hours, approximately one-third of all instruction in religion, were Bible centered. About one-third of this work dealt with the Old Testament; 503 hours, 15.2 per cent. of the total, were given in religious education; 38 hours (1.1 per cent.), in character education; 89 hours (2.7 per cent.), in the psychology of religion. When these three groups are combined, they total only 630 hours, an amount scarcely more than half the hours devoted to biblical instruction. . . .

"Of the total, 328 hours (9.9 per cent.) were devoted to the history, philosophy, and problems of religion; 71 hours (2.1 per cent.), to comparative religion; 240 hours (7.2 per cent.) to ethics; and 155 hours (4.7 per cent.), to social ethics. Thus, the opportunity to study religion in its broadest international and interracial aspects, and to apply the principles of religion to problems of conduct, was extremely limited."[6]

This showing seems to indicate rather conventional emphases and methods and failure to keep abreast with contemporary interests. This is not very flattering to the educational progressiveness of the colleges.

### RELIGIOUS EDUCATION IN NON-DENOMINATIONAL INSTITUTIONS

The churches carry on religious education in many non-denominational institutions, both public and private. This stands in sharp contrast with the loss of the original distinctive religious quality in the denominational schools, and means an extension of the sphere of the church's influence and functioning.

---

[5] Hartshorne, Stearns and Uphaus, *Standards and Trends in Religious Education* (New Haven: Yale University Press, 1933), p. 217.

[6] *Ibid.*, p. 152.

"Ten denominations now employ 209 local university pastors and secretaries who give all their time to student work. The figures for individual denominations range from one to fifty-nine. The Disciples stress the teaching of religion instead of the work of the pastorate, having independent Bible chairs or representatives in coöperating schools of religion at ten different centers. Emphasizing relationship to local congregations, the United Lutherans have 201 local pastors who are serving Lutheran students through their parish ministry. One hundred and one Methodist ministers and secretaries, forty-one full time and sixty in local parishes, are connected with seventy Wesley Foundations. The Congregational church has thirty-four representatives in non-denominational institutions, and there are about 450 ministers and workers near colleges and universities having some kind of student constituency. The full-time workers are functioning through centers known variously as Pilgrim Houses, Societies, or Foundations. The Presbyterian church has student work established in fifty university centers, organized as Westminster Foundations or by other names, receiving the service of fifty-nine workers. . . .

"A real but intangible sort of service to students is attempted through local parishes where, in most instances, one minister must care for both the permanent constituents and the transient students. It is difficult to secure exact figures, but there are certainly more than a thousand such parishes."[7]

The resources of religious education summarized here and in the foregoing quotations do not appear entirely ample when distributed among the nearly one million American college and university students.

Moreover the trend in religious instruction in the colleges is such as to raise serious questions.

"The teaching of the Bible is falling off; interest in the contributions of psychology, philosophy, sociology, and ethics in religion is increasing. Is the Bible merely poorly taught? Are departmental requirements in other fields, the general enrichment of the curriculum, and pre-vocational interests crowding out the Bible? Should it hold a relatively smaller place in the religion education of youth? Is it well that youth are turning to contemporary experience and to an understanding of the whole of reality, as revealed by the social and physical sciences, to effect their religious adjustments?"[8]

What these questions seem to imply is that one must look to the total educational influence brought to bear upon youth rather than to a segregated block of instructions labeled as religious to judge how religion will fare in American intellectual circles tomorrow.

RELIGIOUS EDUCATION THROUGH MISSION SCHOOLS

The formal connection of the church and education is most completely maintained in systems of mission schools, chiefly of primary and secondary

[7] *Ibid.*, p. 199.
[8] *Ibid.*, p. 219.

grade, which certain denominations operate for handicapped races or localities. A comprehensive study of such schools in the Southern Appalachian area was included as one of the projects financed by the Institute,[9] and their number in the United States and distribution according to type of work have been noted in other connections.[10]

## COMMUNITY PROGRAMS FOR RELIGIOUS EDUCATION

The denominational and interdenominational structures with which the last section has dealt are only significant as the means of bringing a better type of religious educational privilege to communities than could be secured by the parochial churches working separately.

The growth of the conviction that religious education requires a community-wide program has been primarily due to experience. The training of efficient Sunday-school officials and teachers under the growing pressure of standard requirements, usually showed itself to be beyond the capacity of individual churches and frequently beyond that of the average denomination. Community training courses were clearly more economical; and these naturally afforded the most frequent aspect of the developing community program. Extensive provision for the preparation of teachers grew up in most of the cities and has operated with greater or less success.

A still more profound demand for a community type of religious education was discovered in the challenge of progressive public-school systems. Here, on the one hand, were the day schools commanding the pupil's time and attendance, their education marked by highly-trained professional teachers and elaborate modern equipment; here, on the other hand, was the Sunday school crowded into part of a single hour per week, taught by untrained volunteers and in the main without specially designed buildings or facilities.

These striking contrasts wrought deep dissatisfaction. An incipient system of week-day church schools has grown up in many cities in the effort to meet this challenge. In the main these schools have had to be projected upon an interdenominational basis because public authorities refused to deal with divisive sectarian schemes of education.

The essence of the week-day school project is that public-school systems surrender certain hours, usually falling within the school day, during which pupils are dismissed from the public school for religious instruction under church auspices. Where the matter lies within the legal discretion of public-school authorities, it has generally been possible to secure an arrangement by the development of sufficient community sentiment. In order that the public school may give its approval the work of the week-day religious

---

[9] Hooker, *Religion in the Highlands* (New York: Howe Missions Council, 1933).
[10] P. 196.

school obviously has to be of standard scholastic quality, and this has proven to be the crux of the experiment. When adequate supervision and suitable teachers and facilities are available, it has generally worked well, especially when the curriculum of the religious school attempts to connect with the "latent religious resources" of the public-school curriculum. This means, briefly, when the religious schools have attempted to give a religious interpretation and application to the experience which the public schools themselves are furnishing.

The week-day religious schools generally concern the children of the first six elementary grades, only occasionally reaching into the high school. In two independent recent investigations relative success and progress were discovered in a considerable majority of cities where the plan was in vogue.[11]

The chief complication involved in the scheme for week-day church schools lies in the divergent theories of Protestants, Catholics and Jews as to public education. The three faiths have been unable to agree upon any version of religious teaching which can be inserted within the public education system itself; and where their numbers are strikingly unequal have sometimes blocked one another's plans for securing released school time. Such inter-faith difficulties are reduced to a minimum where religious instruction is strictly parochial, each child going to its own individual church, and where the religious school is held after the school hours. Such an arrangement involves no official relationships with the public-school system. In New York City, for example, very excellent coöperation between the three faiths in fostering week-day instruction has now gone on with increasing satisfactoriness for a considerable number of years.

Most observers of the development of week-day schools are clear that, even when immediate problems of public policy and of inter-faith sensitiveness are solved, the movement goes only a small way in the direction of securing an adequate religious education for communities. It must be very much more than it is, both as to universality of adoption and methods of execution, or it is in danger of becoming less. And at any rate, for anything like its proper realization, a really adequate type of Protestant religious education demands a unification of Protestantism beyond anything yet reached.

### EDUCATION OF MINISTERS

Attention now turns to the second major phase of religious education in its institutional aspect, namely the education of the professional leaders of the church, whose characteristics and work were described in chapter vi.

---

[11] Hartshorne and Miller, *Community Organization in Religious Education* (New Haven: Yale University Press, 1932), p. 45.

While the majority of ministers are not trained in professional institutions, but get such religious education as they possess in non-degree courses or through reading or correspondence study, the official theory that the churches should be in position to provide for standard professional education for its leaders is partially realized for most denominations through the theological seminary. These institutions represent a wide variety of types and characteristics.

The habitual denominational requirements and pledges of loyalty to the historic standards of the church, exacted of the trustees and faculty of theological seminaries,[12] are evidences of a hold-over in the modern church of the strictly authoritarian mood in which priestly culture was transmitted in the primitive religions. These requirements are intended to put the custodians of religious truth and tradition under closely defined group control. Every effort is made to guard the guardians.

In summarizing the more external aspects of the theological seminaries it is necessary first to classify institutions represented under the term. Four groups are to be distinguished: (1) Seminary organizations independent of other educational institutions, (2) post-graduate departments of colleges and universities, (3) undergraduate departments of colleges and universities, (4) Bible schools of lower scholastic rank. Some seminaries are more localized in constituency or more strictly denominational than others. A few are definitely non-denominational. Some are exceptional in that they recognize and train for the differentiated ministries described in chapter vi.

Since the seminaries have the common object of educating ministers, little difference of objective meaning is to be found in the various denominational terminologies by which this aim is described. Its actual realization in the seminaries is modified, first, by the expansion and consequently the competition of the successively introduced elements of their curricula. Again, their intended denominational character is frequently diluted by the admission of students of other denominations. Still again, the seminary reflects, on the one hand, a demand for the carrying up of its studies to a higher educational level, and, on the other hand, a need for making them more elementary in order to match the level of poorly prepared candidates. In the long run it is the type of education demanded by available candidates that determines and dominates the quality of an institution.

The seminaries, as a whole, center the education of the ministers upon a historic common core of curricula, consisting of English Bible, biblical Hebrew and Greek, church history, systematic theology and practical theology. More recently added groups of studies include comparative re-

---

[12] See Kelly, *Theological Education in America* (New York: Institute of Social and Religious Research, 1924), pp. 35-41.

ligion (often associated with the study of missions), religious education, with its parallel psychology, and applied Christianity, involving sociology. The appearance of these newer disciplines reflects the rise of interests and movements in the church which have been narrated in other chapters.

The present distribution of the elements of curriculum, as exemplified by the courses of fifty-three typical seminaries, is shown in Table X and Chart XXII.

TABLE X — PER CENT. OF TOTAL HOURS OF INSTRUCTION IN 53 THEOLOGICAL SEMINARIES WHICH ARE OFFERED IN DEPARTMENTS LISTED AND PER CENT. OF OFFERED HOURS WHICH ARE REQUIRED FOR GRADUATION*

| Departments | Per Cent. of Total Hours Offered by Departments | Per Cent. of Offered Hours Which Are Required for Graduation |
|---|---|---|
| English Bible..................... | 20.9 | 35.0 |
| Bible, Greek and Hebrew........... | 17.2 | 20.0 |
| Practical Theology................. | 15.3 | 36.0 |
| Theology and Philosophy.......... | 12.5 | 30.0 |
| Church History.................... | 10.4 | 37.0 |
| Religious Education and Psychology. | 10.3 | 21.0 |
| Comparative Religion and Missions . | 6.7 | 13.0 |
| Christian Sociology................ | 6.7 | 13.0 |

* May, *The Education of American Ministers*, Vol. III, p. 49.

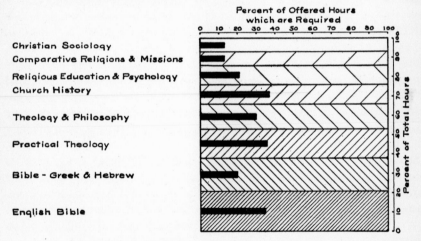

CHART XXII—DIVISION OF THEOLOGICAL CURRICULUM ACCORDING TO PER CENT. OF HOURS OFFERED BY SPECIFIED DEPARTMENTS, AND PER CENT. OF OFFERED HOURS WHICH ARE REQUIRED

In contrast with the rather rigidly traditional curriculum of the seminaries as this table reveals it, is their almost complete lack of common tendency in administrative standards. Except where seminaries are affiliated with colleges and universities, the widest variation prevails with respect to conditions of admission, promotion and graduation. More than three-fourths of the seminaries admit non-college graduates and with many of them the only fixed regulation is that the candidate shall have a high moral character.

Faculties average eight professors per school. The average professor is a rather mature man. One-half of them are reported as being beyond fifty years of age, with an average of sixteen years experience. Three-fourths have previously been pastors. The average duty-period is ten class-room hours per week.

Teaching methods vary widely with the subject taught. Theology and philosophy commonly use the lecture method, language teaching the recitation, while practical theology, religious education and Christian ethics incline to the discussion and project methods. Rather imperfect library facilities supply further means of instruction; but there is little coördination between libraries and other departments.

Three-fourths of seminary students have already begun some practice of their future vocation. Forty-five per cent. of these are serving as acting pastors, the others as church assistants in various capacities. The object of this "field work" is partly to enable the student to secure financial support during the period of his education and is partly itself educational. Field work is sometimes conceived of as laboratory practice, but on the whole is not well supervised; so that its educational values leave much to be desired.

As has already been seen, the minister is recruited chiefly from rural communities and derives from humble antecedents. Only one-third of all seminary students come from cities. The majority have attended small denominational colleges, 15 per cent. of which are not accredited by any recognized educational body, and 29 per cent. only by a sectional educational association.

On tests of mental ability, theological students rate below college students and also below candidates for law and medicine. Ninety per cent. of them are economically poor, requiring the assistance of free tuition, scholarship funds, room and board at cost, loans and outside employment.

Seminaries are well financed and equipped compared with other privately supported institutions of higher education. They are better endowed (endowment in the sample group yielding 54 per cent. of their total income in 1929), and pay better salaries. Their financial assets, however, did not increase as fast as those of the churches in general during the last census decade.

Naturally the seminaries attempt to minister to the personal religious lives of their students as well as to their professional preparation. The results, however, are not highly satisfactory to the student. In an extensively used questionnaire, the value of chapel service was rated at between 60 and 80 per cent. of its possibilities on a scale of 100; student devotional meetings at between 32 and 85 per cent., and the celebration of communion at between 40 and 93 per cent. Private devotions and small group discussions were felt to be the most fruitful means of cultivating the religious life.

The seminaries as a whole reveal themselves to careful examination as a conservative group of educational institutions. They have come into a certain instability of equilibrium as a result of a sort of jamming of their methods and processes, by reason of the introduction of one subject of instruction after another without fundamental reorganization, and by the introduction of the yeast of new ideas. The interpretation of the Institute's recent investigation of theological education on behalf of the Conference of Theological Seminaries, held that the primary purpose of theological education should be to furnish students "with a working philosophy of life" by introducing them to the "fundamental philosophical disciplines" and "to those historical studies which shed light upon the origin and development of Christianity and its present place among the religions of the world, the Bible holding central place with reference to its message to the present needs of men." "Most intelligent preachers," it is argued, "will acquire the practical skills necessary for the conduct of the church much more efficiently and quickly in the pastorate than in the seminary. The seminary, therefore, should not devote too much time to them unless it wishes to specialize in clinical work."[13]

A "broader view" is, however, recognized according to which a seminary is not so much a place where a student gets information as it is a place where he has educative experience. But this broader view is ". . . hard to carry out in practice" and it is insisted that vocational work should for the most part be deferred to the latter part of the course, while the earlier years are devoted to "laying a broad foundation on which all the latter study must rest."[14]

### THE MODERN RELIGIOUS EDUCATION MOVEMENT

Behind the growth of the institutional structure of religious education in the rural and urban churches, a vigorous movement of thought and endeavor has gone on during the last thirty years. The more common and outstanding currents of this movement have to be traced in order to understand the specific objectives and pre-suppositions of the agencies with which

---

[13] Brown, William Adams, *Ministerial Education in America: The Education of American Ministers*, Vol. I, pp. 190-191.
[14] *Ibid.*, pp. 122-124.

the chapter has thus far had to do. The nub of the situation is this: new concepts of general education accompanied by more varied and experimental types of pedagogy have seeped in upon the field of religious education as dominated by the traditional Sunday-school association. This field had been intellectually stagnant and organizationally routinized. Its established marks were the one hour a week Sunday school, under volunteer and chiefly untrained leadership, with its interests chiefly focussed on children under eighteen years of age. The Sunday school was financially independent of the church and little integrated with its total life. In many, perhaps most churches, it was virtually a separate institution.

Newer ideas have effected official improvements in pedagogy and have resulted in a mild reorganization of the traditional stereotype of the Sunday school. But they have had all too little general effect. Such modification as has been secured chiefly concerns certain technical standards of church school excellence. Beginning with 1895, the efforts of Sunday-school leaders have been continuously devoted to these matters. The standards have been repeatedly revised and improved upon. The process culminated in 1929 in the adoption of the A and B standards of the International Council of Religious Education, representing respectively the more and the less exacting versions of what a good school ought to be. With these standardizing efforts, which enlarged and refined the traditional pattern, have gone the accreditization of training schools for Sunday-school teachers and certification of teachers who follow certain specific courses of preparation.

The results of introducing these standards as norms of practical American religious education got their first comprehensive investigation in Dr. Hugh Hartshorne's study of 1933.[15] His examination of 746 more than average Sunday schools yielded the following generalization:

"Analysis of the internal organization of the 746 schools in the investigation reveals a traditional administrative pattern. Church schools are still administering largely to children. They are still chiefly *Sunday* schools with a one-hour session. Even for this brief session, the per cent. of attendance is low as compared with public schools. There is apparently little attempt to keep records of individual attendance that are permanently available for study as possible incentives to progress. The leaders are church members who volunteer their services. It is only rarely that they have had the educational background and training represented by college graduation or public school teaching experience. The minister gives a proportionately small amount of his time to educational work in his parish. Church schools still remain laymen's organizations. The church itself, beyond furnishing rooms and leaders, seems to regard the schools as sepa-

---

[15] Hartshorne, *Standards and Trends in Religious Education* (New Haven: Yale University Press, 1933).

rate institutions. No money for educational work is included in the majority of church budgets. The schools are supported by the small 'nickel a Sunday' contributions of the children, who frequently know very little about how their money is used. The gifts for benevolence are very small per pupil—roughly estimated at one cent or less each week for half the schools."[16]

On seven out of nine criteria of church school excellence the majority of these schools fall below the standard requirements. Valuable experimentation with standards continues, especially "as to their significance as measures of excellence and means of applying them." On the other hand, considerable rebellion has cropped up among field administrators of the movement as well as in local churches, against the alleged rigidity of the standard-makers at headquarters.

The very limited realization of the goals officially sought through the standardization movement is significant measured in terms of professional leadership. Six hundred and eighty-seven ministers interrogated in the study of theological education reported that they give only an average of 5 per cent. of their time to the educational work of the church or little more than they have to give to janitorial service. In the better-than-average schools of 746 churches, constituting Dr. Hartshorne's sample, the average time given by ministers to religious education reached 17 per cent. of the total. Out of 1,025 urban churches investigated by Dr. Sanderson only 9 per cent. employed directors of religious education, even including directors who combined these duties with those of assistant pastors. Very few directors are employed outside the cities and suburbs (except in college towns), and no appreciable number are employed outside of four or five denominations. Moreover, the prevailing attitude of the clergy toward the official agencies seeking to promote standardized religious education is none too enthusiastic.[17]

Meanwhile the so-called movement of progressive education within the secular schools has found its counterpart in the pioneering experimental efforts of small groups of religious educators. The ideals of this group are in basic conflict with formal standardization. They call for "creative" teaching, utilizing the real experience of the learner, such experience to be secured in connection with authentic "life situations," either those deliberately created within the church schools or set up as projects to be realized outside of the school and then made the subject of educational concern and assimilation.

---

[16] *Ibid.*, p. 63.

[17] Hartshorne and Miller, *Community Organization in Religious Education* (New Haven: Yale University Press, 1932), p. 106.

A typical set of criteria prepared by progressive educators for use in determining the excellence of religious education was elaborated into ten statements for use in Dr. Hartshorne's *Case Studies of Present-Day Religious Teaching*,[18] as follows:

1. The pupils show increasing respect for one another and for those with whom their activities bring them into real or imaginative contact.

2. The pupils are on real situations and are responding to the situations rather than to the teacher, for it is the function of the teacher to bring the pupils into vital relationship with these situations.

3. The situation, while continuous with out-of-school situations, is simplified so as to make possible the maximum freedom of the child without confusion or disaster.

4. The pupils view the situation objectively rather than through their prejudices and emotions.

5. Those phases of experience which are primarily acts of appreciation are so handled as to permit the children to make their own evaluations and to compare their judgments with those of others.

6. In facing new situations, the process of thought is such as to lead to valid conclusions. That is, the scientific method is used.

7. In facing new situations, the pupils make use of relevant past experience, so far as they can gain access to it.

8. Problem solving includes foresight of consequences of various possible procedures and a choice of one or the other in terms of their believed harmony with the general direction of the life unit or phase of which it is a part. When issues are critical such evaluation takes the form of worship, and is in terms of the value of persons.

9. The conclusion of a project is the occasion of measurement of progress in skill and appraisal of results in terms of objectives. This latter may involve worship when the results are of sufficient importance.

10. The pupils' responsibility includes the experiencing of the results of their experiments as well as the planning of them.

Applying these criteria to the 102 best "units" of progressive teaching which could be found, Dr. Hartshorne's studies ranked the group achievement as standing at 52 per cent. on a scale of 100.

The most conspicuous weakness of these best cases, when judged by the above criteria, was the relative failure of the teaching process to increase respect for personality in the case of remote groups or characters in history. As between teacher and pupil, pupil and teacher, or pupil and pupil, definite behavior-improvement could be traced; but prejudice against people of other nations and color, and stock judgments about historical personalities were very little revised under the best techniques yet available.

---

[18] Pp. 139-140.

EDUCATION AND CHARACTER

The notable character education studies of Hartshorne and May reached largely negative conclusions as to the ability of religious and formal education to effect directly the improvement of character. They showed that certain general ideals which are part of the social tradition are prepotent in any particularly moral situation, and that the general level of the intelligence and environment from which the school child comes affects his general character, defined as response to the approved traditions. On the other hand, the character education investigation showed that the teaching of general ideals through present methods does little good. Deliberate attempts to clothe them with emotional power and thus to enable them to direct conduct, do not work. From this point of view little successful moral education is now going on. The particular reason is that a moral characteristic, like honesty or dishonesty, is not actually a unified trait of character, but merely a name for a series of responses to numerous diverse situations involving conduct. When goodness is made sufficiently easy conduct is good; when it is made unduly difficult conduct is bad. There is no transfer of a particular tendency to conduct in one type of situation to the control of conduct in another situation unless there are prepotent factors common to both situations. External standards, such as formal codes, dominate conduct only when they validate themselves as belonging to a particular situation and not otherwise. Any complete integration of character, such as would cause the desired conduct to appear in all situations, is itself a specific achievement, and one not often reached through any of the present resources of the religious educator. What the whole educational effort of the church actually amounts to thus remains a very large question. Bartlett, for example, compared the Oak Park public-school children who attended week-day religious instruction under a federation of churches with those who did not. Those who attended knew more about the Bible but showed no higher degree of Christian motivation in situations involving conduct than did those who did not attend.[19]

SUMMARY

The story of the broadening movement of religious education obviously is that of a series of very unequal developments. One part of the movement creeps while the other leaps forward. The mass of religious education remains substantially within the traditional mould. The official pace has quickened, and commendable modifications have been secured in the better-than-average church schools; particularly to the forms of organization of classes, of courses dealing with specific ethical applications of Christianity,

---

[19] Bartlett, "Measurable Moral and Religious Results of Week-Day Religious Instruction." *Religious Education*, Volume XXIX, No. 1 (Jan. 1934), p. 35.

local social service, recreation activities and maintenance of week-day and vacation schools. About 57 per cent. of the churches of the sample had classes in preparation for church-membership.

The spear-head of the still more advanced movement represented by progressive religious education, is significant because it symbolizes an adventurous mood and has some capacity for testing its own weaknesses. When, however, one professor of religious education writes confidentially to another the story sometimes runs like this:

"You raise some problems that I often think about. (1) What does the field of religious education include? (2) What does the scientific attitude involve? (3) What are these modern progressive philosophies and how soon will we discard them for something more radical and perhaps less modern?"

In other words, modern religious education is not without its overtones of disillusion or reaction. It has not reached its final goal.

Proposed Institutional Reorganization of the Coöperative Movement Around Religious Reëducation

Chapter v, on the church's organization and life, has shown how the structure of the local church has grown chiefly by accretion, adding new machinery to implement each new interest which the church develops, without any thorough overhauling of the old structure. This tendency has increased the number of subsidiaries in the ordinary urban church to an average of from ten to fifteen. Ordinarily there is only one to every forty adherents, often one to ten, and sometimes one to every three. The result has been great competition of one part of the church with another, resulting in a diverting of interest on the part of constituents, who on the average yield but dangling adherence to the church at best.

Religious educational ideals have challenged this unreflective process. They have insisted, first, upon the adaptation and rationalization of many church activities so as to fit them more exactly to the needs of the different age and sex groups.

Since all the church's subsidiary organizations, as well as its traditional ones, assume to exert a character-forming influence on their adherents and ultimately to minister to the cultivation of their religious life, it was only natural that religious education should also have offered itself as furnishing a unifying principle by means of which the complexity could be reduced. The essence of its proposal was to conceive of all the different activities of the church as phases of religious education, some instructional, others "expressional."[20]

---

[20] See p. 90.

Earlier paragraphs, showing how essentially separate, socially and even geographically, are the constituencies which often constitute an urban church and how lacking they are in any face-to-face association, leave nothing further needed to demonstrate the futility of any effort to get these constituencies together by the magic of a simple formula. To regard different subsidiaries as different phases of religious education does not even assure that they are dealing with the same people. In Dr. Hartshorne's star case, a large proportion of the families of the Sunday-school children were not connected with the church.

In the highly homogeneous church, however, religious education has an important contribution to make to unity and simplicity of organization. The church could be a more important influence in the lives of its constituency if it could more definitely relate its organized activities to some primary principle and could continue to touch experience on many sides at once without disintegrating it.

On the other hand, if it is to dominate the field of local church organizations, religious education is in great need of unstiffening. The present multiplicity of organizations illustrates at least the virtues of free initiative and social authenticity. It would be a devastating prospect if, for example, the movement for forums and discussion groups now getting under way, should fall into the clutches of formal education.

PROPOSED EDUCATIONAL REORGANIZATION OF COUNCILS OF CHURCHES

Religious education has recently exhibited an ambition to reorganize the coöperative organization of the churches as well as the local churches. Councils of churches, like local churches, have departmentalized in vertical sections. Each new department has reflected a separate wave of interest in some aspect of religious life or service. The resulting forms of organizations have often been stupid, and slavish imitation has made matters worse. Now comes the definite claim: "Christian education is germane to the entire program of a council of churches. It cannot be segregated to a special department. It constitutes an indispensable function of every activity in which coöperating churches participate when seeking to effect desirable changes within the individual or his environment."[21]

In the application of this thesis, the claim has sometimes been modified so as to read that all departments of the church federation, *except that of comity*, might better be carried out under religious educational auspices.

The present majority opinion, however, holds that the coöperative administration and conduct of interchurch activities is one thing and coöperative education in religious ideals quite another. Not comity alone,

---

[21] Guild, Roy B. and Sanderson, Ross W., Editors, *Community Programs for Coöperating Churches* (New York: Association Press, 1933, p. 21).

but the conduct of institutional social service and of movements for civic betterment or moral reform, and the performance of most technical and service functions, fall into the category of doing rather than of teaching. So do all specific activities involved in publicity; so also does evangelism in the thought of most ministers. The traditional proclamation of the gospel through preaching and the celebration of the church's sacraments have obvious educational significance, but their conduct belongs primarily to a different order of activity, for which religious education as yet has offered no alternative acceptable to the rank and file of the church. Furthermore, whatever be the logic of the case, so long as women desire the control of their special organizations they are not likely to become unified under anybody's scheme.

It should be possible, on the other hand, to unify the entire group of departments of federation work which deal with the transmission and promulgation of religious and social ideals, including those relating to industry, race relations, and peace. Besides putting all those under the common category of religious education it would seem logical to commit to religious education all processes dealing with the training of the laity for service in evangelism and social service, as well as for service in religious education as such.

### PROBLEMS OF RELIGIOUS EDUCATION

The foregoing review has shown the many-sided significance of the church's educational insights and activities. It has served, however, not so much to advance one to certain conclusions, as to throw numerous remaining problems into relief.

These problems relate in part to particular institutional issues in the field of religious education. In part, however, they dip down into mooted questions of underlying educational philosophy and objectives; while from still another angle they relate to the most general problems of the diffusion of culture and the control of civilized society by the transmission of accepted values from the past.

#### INSTITUTIONAL STRENGTH AND WEAKNESS

One central problem is that of the serious decline of the Sunday school. This has been registered on a national scale and has appeared as a challenging urban phenomenon. The central issue is how to make a Sunday school better without making it smaller. Its numerical decline is partly counterbalanced, if not entirely outweighed, by the spectacular growth in recent decades of other forces of character-developing agencies and other means of the transmission of religious culture. Systems of supplementary week-day and religious schools have developed. The wide variety of character-building agencies for youth have also appeared. Beyond these there has also been a much more carefully graded approach to childhood and youth as expressed in children's congregations, and the more skilful preparation of children's materials in the fields of missions, peace, racial good-will and so forth. All told, then, there has been not merely a wider range of educational agencies at work but a further permeation of all agencies by the educational spirit. Yet, all together these forces leave too many of the nation's children and youth untouched.

INTEGRATION AND SIMPLIFICATION

A second major educational problem which emerges from the foregoing review relates to the piecemeal development of the educational agencies and processes just indicated, with the consequent crying need for their integration and simplification. This problem does not lie wholly on the doorstep of religious education but pertains to the church in all its manifestations. Nevertheless, it is particularly the more intelligent educational efforts that are blocked by reason of the chaotic internal evolution of the church.

On the one hand stands the oft-proved fact that the many social groups that make up the modern church have stubborn sociological traits and cannot be forced together arbitrarily. The dangling structures which extend so irritatingly at different angles from the main purpose of the church cannot be coerced without destroying them. In the flux of a mobile society numerous special-interest groups organize themselves according to a simple leader-follower pattern which proves more authentic than amenable to ecclesiastical or educational control. All this merely states the problem but provides no solution. Only a profound unstiffening of the methods of education, together with willingness to work through slow assimilative processes without attempting strong measures of unification, can absorb all this variety of social structure into the over-arching organization of the church. On the other hand, the challenging need of integration in order to avoid internal duplication, and the unrecognized but significant claims of the central values of the church to pre-eminence over the special interests of its subsidiaries, remain points of irritation until some valid solution can be worked out.

TECHNICAL PROGRESS

The third major problem concerns the rather slow rate at which technical improvement is winning its way over the vast traditionalism of the field of religious education. Though much qualitative advance has been evidenced, the official standards are far from being realized throughout the great body of the churches. More time for religious education, better training of teachers, more technical skill all around, more adequate evidence and equipment all constitute valid demands upon the modern church. The standards, although far from satisfactory, ought to be able to carry forward much farther than at present.

Turning now from problems of institutionalized religious education to larger matters of the transmission and restatement of Christian cultural values, one reaches more baffling areas of educational doubt and controversy.

### INDOCTRINATION VS. DEVELOPMENT OF ATTITUDES

Thus the need of a profounder clue to the underlying philosophy of education arises out of the contemporary controversy between the theory of education as indoctrination and that of education as the development of wholesome attitudes not committed to particular doctrines. The new education on its secular side has gone far toward abandoning any assumption of finality in what it teaches. Instead of attempting primarily to conserve traditions, it attempts rather to start each generation upon its own quest for truth; with such tentative light as the past can throw upon the present, but without attempting to make up the mind of any given generation as to what is ultimately that generation's own business. Education thus conceived has particularly to do with the forming of right attitudes toward problems, and with a technique for meeting and solving problems in a spirit of fair-mindedness and fair-play through the medium of group experience realized as far as possible under school conditions. This, roughly speaking, was the basis of the "progressive education" movement.

Its thesis was, however, scarcely more than formulated and its experiments were still in their incomplete stages when a revolt to a still more modern version of education occurred. There was a sudden reversion to the theory of indoctrination in behalf of a better social order. Greatly impressed by Russian, Italian, and, more recently, German experiments in re-educating nations, the newest radicals desired to get the child on the right side of the social struggle exactly in the spirit in which religion all along had tried to get the child on the right side of the moral struggle.[22]

Meanwhile, a new skepticism was arising as to the ability of education, either through deliberate indoctrination or through the training of attitudes, to get any large results in terms of the direct formation of character. Culture was obviously being transmitted and attitudes were being achieved; but schools of all types were in increasing uncertainty as to their exact contribution to this result. Education must see its own way more clearly before it can proceed with much confidence in the religious field.

---

[22] Cf. Counts, *"Dare the School Build A New Social Order";* (New York: John Day and Company, 1932).

RELIGIOUS EDUCATION AND SOCIAL CONTROL

The effort to secure more time for religious education by extending its activities beyond Sunday as the traditional day of religion to week days has brought the organized movement of religious education into sharp contact with the sphere of public education. Under the historic American theory of the relation of church to state, the state was to recognize and encourage voluntary religious organization; but beyond this the two great forces were each to go its own way in complete separation.

This tradition is now being challenged by new recognition that a civilization must seek specific ends, and that nations must plan their courses so as to reach definable goals. The consequent strict mobilizing of all cultural forces and their regimentation under the state has brought revolutionary change to many modern nations. Even when no restraint has been put upon voluntary groups, government has frequently attempted, through propaganda, to quicken their pace, and to sharpen their influence in behalf of state-determined goals.

As a supra-mundane society the church is necessarily at war with any attack upon the supremacy, for herself, of her own sources of authority. The universality of Christianity is essentially at war with aggressive or proscriptive nationalism. On the other hand, reality, applicability, and contemporariness in religion are largely bound up with its ability to identify itself with the actual aims and motives of living men in any generation. Religion, then, can by no means ignore the effort to secure the supreme social values of justice, security and happiness through the medium of the state. All such efforts of the democratic and liberal state find some of their chief backing in the church. Nevertheless, many aspects of the problems of relationship of church and state remain, and their ultimate adjustment in the field of religious education has not yet been reached.

# CHAPTER IX

## Social Welfare Functions and Agencies

The church's concern with social welfare is expressed not only within its local congregations and parishes in the partial care of their own poor, but particularly in the wide variety of specialized institutions and agencies which collectively rank the church among the important community forces for social welfare. Equally fundamental is the church's function in interpreting and teaching Christian social relationships. Not only does it enforce ethical obligations between individual men and social classes, but, going deeper, it has often undertaken to explore the ethical and religious implications of the systems of society with which it was associated, especially those which impose obscure and remote consequences of social conduct upon classes and individuals. While, in many of its institutional instincts, the church has usually been on the side of the *status quo*, nevertheless its thinking has always contained a critical strain and it has often come into sharp conflict with social conditions which produce and tolerate glaring inequalities in human fortunes.

The church also, to an appreciable extent, inspires and trains constituents for social welfare activities through non-church channels and develops a constructive community leadership much of which functions beyond its own agencies.

Finally, in numerous ways the churches directly back and support the non-church welfare agencies of their communities. All these aspects must be recognized in a review of the church's functioning in the welfare field.

SCOPE AND DIVISIONS OF THE SOCIAL WELFARE FIELD

Unlike the field of religion which the church traditionally dominates, the field of social welfare is shared by many agencies of which the church is only one, and a minor partner at best. The determination of the scope of the field, its technical divisions and classifications and its special standards are primarily settled by other agencies. The church has consequently to fit its work into such classifications and adjust itself to the larger realm which it does not primarily control.

It is accordingly important that the church's social welfare work should conceive the field as broadly as the best of general thinking in this field requires. Thus, many of the most important of the social-welfare forces of a community are non-institutional. They correspond to the projecting and individualizing phases of the church's life which reach out here and there in pastoral ministries rather than congregating people at a single time and place. A contrasting group of social-welfare agencies is highly institutionalized, as in the case of homes and asylums, which deal with groups of people permanently brought together under a common roof. Still other welfare agencies manifest both the congregating and the projecting phases of the church's group life; and all are related with and supplemented by other constructive agencies, such as church schools, which work to similar ends but in different ways.

Again, the significance and particular methods of welfare work in all phases are conditioned by the economic levels and social needs of the populations which they serve. Social-welfare work is not limited to the dependent classes of the community. Child-welfare activities, hospitals, recreation and education are expressions of community need whose benefits are shared in by the well-to-do and self-supporting as well as by the poor. Preventive social work applies to populations on all social levels. Social-welfare funds raised through community chests, etc., habitually include provisions for the maintenance of character-building agencies for average youth as well as those which have to do with some acute social maladjustments. The church is properly interested in normal people as well as in abnormal. Much of its pastoral insight has to be expended upon border-line cases. Remedial effort for the abnormal and maladjusted cannot, therefore, be segregated from preventative and border-line effort and should not be taken as the whole of welfare work either for the church or for the community.

This makes it necessary to conceive of the church as *per se* a social agency, in that its normal group life is one of the strongest and best of the character-building forces. Its charities for the poor and handicapped require separate attention; but they should not be separated in thinking from its total welfare mission.

Again, social-welfare activities of the churches are intimately interrelated with those of other agencies. Churches classify among the voluntary agencies in contrast with public agencies which, in times of acute depression, increasingly have to bear the financial burden of community welfare. Among the private agencies they are to be distinguished from the so-called secular ones, which are carried on by the initiative of people of goodwill without respect to church affiliation. Of the social agencies under definite religious auspices some, like the Y.M.C.A., represent allies and extensions of the church, while others are strictly ecclesiastical. Finally, of the ecclesiastical agencies the majority are denominational, though some are interdenominational or non-denominational.

A typical inventory of Protestant social-welfare work under religious auspices includes, in addition to the essential character-building and preventive ministries of the local church, considerable groups of churches which have turned themselves into social agencies in important aspects of their functioning;[1] and in addition, dozens, scores or even hundreds of community centers, settlements and the like, children's and old people's homes, hospitals and other forms of health service, hospices and other homes for transients, chaplaincies, and various types of pastoral work in public or other institutions, probation and other work in connection with the courts, a vast system of instrumentalities which secure and distribute necessary financial support to all these agencies, and financial processes which initiate social-welfare ideals and standards and pass them on through educational and promotional processes. Larger cities show a strong development of all the aspects of church social welfare which have been inventoried above.[2] The very largest cities function as religious capitals for the nation and are the headquarters of national denominational boards which gather and redistribute resources to the smaller communities and which promulgate and disseminate the authoritative social ideals.

Smaller communities have a share in many of the above-mentioned forms of welfare work supported by territorial units of the church. Thus, while the rural community rarely has a hospital or home of its own, many rural churches are supporting hospitals and children's and old people's home maintained by the synod, conference or state organization of the denomination to which they belong and which are generally located in a larger community. This makes the story of the church's welfare work in rural communities very different as to magnitude and variety from that characteristic of the cities, and compels the telling of the story in two parts.

## THE CHURCH AND RURAL SOCIAL WELFARE

Perhaps one of the greatest contrasts between urban and rural church work lies in the field of social-welfare functions and ideals. The social-welfare ideals of the churches, as represented in the social creeds and other pronouncements of the various protestant bodies, are little known in rural America. In part this is because of the conservatism of a majority of the clergy and their suspicion of any emphasis in religion upon anything except individual salvation. In part it is due to the lamentable lack of training on the part of large sections of the rural clergy in some of the denominations and in some sections of the United States. In part the cause is to be found in the ignorance of rural matters on the part of the agencies and movements, both denominational and interdenominational, concerned with the formulation and promulgation of social ideals.

---

[1] See p. 143.
[2] See p. 98.

Again, the absence until very recently of any statement of Christian social ideals in agricultural terms has militated against much emphasis upon the social ideals of the churches even among progressive rural churches. Something of an exception must be made in the case of internationalism. Among churches in rural industrial villages it was found that 30 per cent. stressed the social ideals of the churches on Labor Sunday. Here again the attitude of the clergy and their theological position was a determinative factor.

The social-welfare work of the rural church is likewise, professionally judged, almost non-existent. That, however, is not to say that there is none of a sort. Few are the rural churches that have not aided the poor or unfortunate among their own number. But the average rural church-member would be surprised to hear that having the Boy Scout take care of Widow Jones' fires or that sending garments to tenant Smith's children after they were burned out, classified as social-welfare work. Rural people are neighborly and they are chiefly neighborly within the social groupings to which they acknowledge allegiance. It is in such a way that a rural church moves to relieve distress when confronted with it.

The fact remains that there is much social-welfare work in rural America that needs to be done. A survey of seven counties in the mid-western states, selected from the few in which rural social-welfare work was then organized, showed 994 rural families on the records with fifty different classifications of disabilities. These included old age, disease, juvenile delinquency, broken homes, marital friction, unmarried mothers, poor housing, mental difficulties, in addition to difficulties because of poverty.

The need for social-welfare work in rural America is, then, considerable. An urban scale of professional organization for such work is economically impossible. The few social workers there are must, therefore, depend heavily upon such churches, or more accurately, upon such ministers as are ready to coöperate. This coöperation has resulted in a wide variety of interesting enterprises, though in no sense can it be said that these are numerous enough to characterize as an accepted or acceptable social-welfare program for rural churches. Each particular project is an opportunistic local response to some acute need. Thus one may find a few rural churches running employment bureaus, at least at harvest time, or more recently barter exchanges; others operate clinics of various sorts, others seek in case of need to secure adequate social service from nearby agencies; some have arranged to transport doctors to open-country patients to save high charges and insure better medical care. Some ministers have been appointed probation officers or have assumed other official welfare responsibilities. Especially in the neediest areas during the great depression, rural ministers have been active as local executives for the Red Cross or Federal Relief Administration. The more elaborate programs are to be found in areas of great permanent need when a body of local work is directly manned and supervised by a national mission board, as among the Southern Highlanders or the Indians.[3]

During the 1920's an increasing number of states set up various types of state welfare departments, some with county organizations and workers. It was generally recognized that the case work carried on by these county workers would have to be what in technical jargon is called "undifferentiated." There was not the possibility of financing the highly specialized urban program. There was also a growing recognition during this period that rural social work, if done, would have to be far more largely a public enterprise than in cities, where private agencies had preceded governmental ones.

If future development follows these lines the chief function of the rural church should be that of intelligent coöperation. With its small membership and limited resources no other course seems practicable, and even this would carry the average rural church beyond its present position over against the whole field of social welfare.

Such coöperation should include hospitals, dispensaries, clinics, health education and the varied programs usually found where neighborhood or community centers under special workers have been established. There are probably not more than 200 enterprises of all these kinds in rural America, and they are, practically without exception, specially financed.

As a phase of the coöperative enterprises of the national interdenominational agencies, a joint committee of the Home Missions Councils, Federal Council and International Council of Religious Educators maintains a secretary whose function it is to foster the integration of the work of the churches with that of the schools, agricultural extension agencies and welfare boards, especially in rural communities.

### URBAN ASPECTS OF PROTESTANT SOCIAL-WELFARE WORK

LOCAL CHURCHES

By far the most numerous of Protestant social-welfare agencies, either in country or in city, are the local churches themselves. Even the more conventional ones make important contributions to this field. Their pastoral and fraternal assistance to constituents has both a preventive and a remedial aspect. They render material aid, help in sickness, exercise vocational guidance and contribute to employment, all as a matter of course, without much consciousness that these are social ministries. The church's contribution to social morale is essentially beyond measurement. It is entirely demonstrable, however, that in the pre-depression era a full third of all the social-welfare funds, both public and private, expended in typical American cities were

[3] See p. 197.

expended for the support of leisure-time and character-building activities, entirely paralleling the normal activities of organized groups in the church often sponsored by churches and generally supported by church people. The share of the church in welfare work, as a by-product of its religious value, is accordingly enormous. Its more highly organized groups for women, young people, boys and girls, realize many, if not most, of the values found in the organizations undertaken for similar age groups in the name of social work.

Again, the majority of city churches report somewhat systematic relationships with community social agencies and the stronger churches are exceedingly important backers of these agencies, in finance, publicity and management. In extreme cases from forty to more than a hundred members of a single church have been found listed in the directorates of the community agencies of the city.

Obviously the local church's particular version of social welfare varies with the economic level of its constituency. It has been insisted above that normal group relations are among the strongest preventive agencies. The best social thinking lays even greater stress upon the social value of the contribution of the churches of the very poor and handicapped populations to their group strength. This is especially important with new and segregated groups whose churches are among the most important influences making for the conservation of old values and protection from demoralization incident to too rapid change. Apart, then, from the prevention of social ills through the maintenance of Christian standards and the tonic effect of fellowship, the total life of the church group constitutes a constructive use of leisure time, a direct exercise of the best social virtues, and a strengthening of social morale.

Churches whose ordinary group activities are merely of the conventional sort sometimes maintain welfare adjuncts such as children's and old people's homes, cemeteries and the like. Again, as will be shown later, the local churches support great chains of welfare activity in connection with their missions at home and abroad.

Certain limitations upon the impressiveness of these claims have immediately to be noted. First, the quality of the pastoral case work and of the social by-products of parish life of the average church are not always rated very highly from the standpoint of expert agencies.

Second, according to an extensive collection of work records, the average minister actually gives very little time to extra-parochial service of any sort. While a few gifted and influential ministers are much in evidence in these fields, they stand in striking contrast with the average.

Again, the direct material aid and relief rendered by the average church is not impressive. The Springfield, Mass., Protestant churches studied in

1926 were giving only about $150 worth of direct aid annually on the average; and an extensive Chicago survey at the peak of the depression demand in 1933 also showed an average of $150 per church in cash for direct relief, with an estimated value of second-hand clothing, etc., raising the estimate to $200 per church. The resulting total is infinitesimal within the total community expenditures for direct relief.

CHURCHES STRESSING SOCIAL WELFARE

Chapter vii has identified, as a special type, a group of socially adapted churches which have definitely undertaken the task of serving handicapped neighborhoods and populations, under the names institutional church, community center, Christian settlement and the like. Apart from social values which inhere as by-products in the life of the conventional churches, welfare work in the local parish form is highly concentrated in the churches of this type. Churches with all-around social programs ministering to health, education, recreation, culture and material necessities of their dependent populations are estimated as constituting not more than 4 per cent. of the urban total, while the more narrowly specialized enterprises of the Christian center type, carrying on with fragmentary rather than all-around welfare programs, may reach as high as 13 per cent.[4] Only about one church out of one hundred will be found operating a dispensary or clinic, and only three or four out of one hundred engaging in any other form of health ministry. In brief, the more specialized forms of welfare work are very infrequent in local Protestant churches and are generally carried out through specialized agencies. The conditions under which socially adapted churches develop will have further attention in the chapter on the environmental conditioning of the church.[5]

The fairly equal fidelity of the Protestant denominations to urban areas of especial need has been shown earlier, together with the somewhat greater emphasis of the Protestant Episcopal and Baptist denominations upon churches of this type. An abundant descriptive literature upon the more striking forms of church social-welfare work has developed in connection with the publicity of the various denominations, and some of the more acute problems, especially as related to the place of social-welfare work in connection with a religious program involving proselyting from other faiths, have been subject to periodic critical discussion.[6]

An obvious characteristic of the socially adapted and specialized churches is that of financial dependence. Since their constituents are unable to sup-

---

[4] See p. 143.
[5] See p. 251.
[6] See Abel, *Protestant Home Missions to Catholic Immigrants* (New York; Institute of Social and Religious Research, 1933), chapters iii and v; also Morse (ed.) *Home Missions Today and Tomorrow* (New York, Home Missions Council, 1934), chap. vi.

port them, they are particularly under the control of the fostering and standard-making agencies of their denominations, especially the local city mission societies or the denominational national boards. This frequently gives such enterprises a somewhat exotic character in a community. It is too much something set down from the outside and too little rooted in the local situation. Frequently their relationships with other constructive agencies of the community are poorly maintained. Particularly churches of competing faiths cannot easily share in constructive measures benefiting and uniting the community.

Though they result in churches classified as belonging to the same type, movements promoted from the outside are in striking contrast with the occasional highly novel efforts of handicapped people to do for themselves. These efforts frequently are ignorant and ill-advised yet their authenticity sometimes lends them greater social potency than better plans and measures paternalistically administered.

TRANSITIONAL TYPES

Between the conventional churches and those which have definitely made themselves into community social agencies in whole or in part, stand several transitional types. In one set of cases a traditional church develops a second constituency for which it does welfare work, either through a branch church in a separate locality, or in its own parish house. The second constituency is served by a common staff, but the original elements in the church have very little direct contact with it.

Again, traces of real social adaptation are to be recognized in churches of the type earlier distinguished as elaborated. The typical situation which produces these churches is that middle-class people living under urban conditions find themselves crowded into increasingly narrow living quarters. This reduces the possibilities of home life and leads them to seek group facilities for their social, recreational and cultural interests. As earlier indicated, many such churches develop what are virtually club-house facilities and programs and establish elaborate systems of group life reflecting a variety of interests in addition to the strictly religious one and affording carefully graded provision for every age and sex. For example, 30 per cent. of 994 urban churches recently studied offered some form of organized athletics to its younger adherents.

SOCIAL ETHICS AND ADVOCACY OF SOCIAL CAUSES

An aspect of the social-welfare functions of the local church, which presumably underlies the whole realm of overt action, is the church's teaching as to social ethics, justice and good-will and the ideals of human relationship behind which it puts religious sanctions. An extraordinarily rapid increase is traceable since the World War in the number of points at which a definite church conscience on social issues has been registered. The pulpit, formal religious education, discussion groups and forums and reinterpretations of the foreign missionary outlook have all conspired to lay new stress on the social implications of the gospel.[7]

## The Church's Specialized Welfare Agencies

In contrast with the above-enumerated ways in which the local church ministers to social welfare without abandoning its essential characteristics as a church, stands the wide variety of philanthropic and social agencies of specialized types which the church has created and which it maintains. Some of these fall into well-marked types, of which hospitals, children's homes and old people's homes are the most frequent. But there are numerous mixed types, as when a home takes both children and old people, also a large miscellaneous group difficult to classify.

### ENUMERATION AND AUSPICES

In spite of several efforts to gather comprehensive nation-wide statistics, no satisfactory listing of these institutions has been made. There appear to be from 275 to 350 Protestant hospitals and sanitariums, between 250 and 325 homes for the aged, and some 400 children's homes. A study of the U. S. Bureau of Labor Statistics in 1929 classifies 42 per cent. of all homes for the aged as being under religious auspices. A study published in the *Journal* of the American Medical Association in 1930 credits 15 per cent. of all hospitals to church institutions and 12 per cent. of all hospital beds. This study also declares that church-supported hospitals are increasing more rapidly than any other type.

The typical institutional equipment of the stronger denominations in American cities consists of a hospital, a children's home, a home for the aged, some type of temporary shelter for new-comers to the city and a group of community centers which may or may not have dissociated themselves from the church form. Weaker denominations cut this list to a minimum, but the stronger ones add still more specialized agencies, such as homes for convalescents or incurables. Conspicuous groups of such church-supported institutions occur in virtually all the cities of the nation.

The problem of understanding and tracing the relationships of these institutions is complicated by the fact that they are under the auspices and control of church bodies at different levels, some parochial, some representing local or district denominational units, while still others are under the control of national boards. A very few are interdenominational, while a considerable

---

[7] Johnson (ed.) *Social Work of the Churches* (New York: Federal Council of Churches, 1930), pp. 122 ff.

number—and they are especially difficult to classify—were founded through the private initiative of members of a given denomination and are named and chiefly operated as denominational agencies, yet without being under formal denominational control.

INVESTIGATION OF TYPES

Most of the types of church institutional philanthropy have been subjects of expert investigation, either in connection with community surveys, or as special denominational studies. A description of the peculiar technical problems of the various types carries one too far afield for the present purpose. Most of the investigations have found it necessary to be constructively critical. Children's homes, for example, are so limited in usefulness by denominational and age restriction, that a community frequently has numerous institutions with empty beds, and yet is unable to receive the needy children of a sister denomination. Striking differences also are found in other respects. Thus, in a study of representative children's homes of the Presbyterian Church, U. S. A., only 27 per cent. of the inmates were found to come from Presbyterian families. Few denominations have so liberal a policy.

Another greatly criticized aspect of child-welfare work is its tradition of institutionalization. Whereas modern child-welfare thinking generally believes that children should be placed in individual foster homes, a representative study of children under the care of a group of Protestant denominations found 80 per cent. still kept in institutions. In the children's homes of a great denomination crowding has had to be reported—of a sort not only detrimental to health but to sex habits. A few houses even mix normal and feeble-minded children!

Protestant hospitals frequently do not meet the standards necessary for full accreditization by the American Hospital Association, and frequently have to be criticized as too small for efficient and adequate specialization and lacking in social-extension facilities. A friendly appraisal of the staff workers of the children's homes of a typical denomination by a representative of the Child Welfare League of America has to point out that their executives frequently lack any special training for special service and that their house mothers are not always competent in child training. The staff workers are frequently overworked and salary scales and facilities are not always such as permit of the suitable carrying out of the weighty responsibility for the health, culture and character of child dependents.

Putting together these existing bits of scientific information and expert appraisal compels one to conclude that the viewpoint of the church charitable institutions is frequently not the most forward-looking and that rather numerous deficiencies exist in standards, equipment, support and the training and competency of workers.

## SOCIAL REFORM AGENCIES

In contrast with the distinctly philanthropic agencies of the church stands another important group of organizations devoted to social reform. These include the law-enforcement and similar organizations working in defense of public morals. Some of them have formal recognition by Protestant interdenominational bodies; most of them originated with Protestants and function as the more or less unofficial auxiliaries of the church in this phase of welfare. The reform agencies have frequently been criticized as being more concerned with the enforcement of somewhat rigid moral codes than with remedying underlying conditions of social injustice.

## CHURCH WELFARE WORK IN CONNECTION WITH NON-CHURCH AGENCIES

All the aspects of the church's welfare work hitherto enumerated are carried on under the church's own auspices in local parishes, specialized institutions or through denominational or affiliated agencies. An important aspect of church welfare work, however, is that done in connection with non-church agencies.

No inventory exists as to the number and kinds of activities of this sort, but comprehensive studies have been made in a considerable number of representative cities. Here the chief forms of work with non-church agencies are chaplaincies, visitation in prisons and hospitals and probation work in connection with the courts. Numerous denominational agencies promote work of these sorts. Their carrying on is a frequent function of local church federations.

Appreciative appraisals of the value of this work have, nevertheless, had to record some of the same shortcomings noted in connection with church institutions, namely, inadequate training of workers for the specialized types of ministry involved and insufficient resources to secure thorough work.

In still another aspect the churches have important relationships with non-church agencies of social welfare. They function very widely as the sponsors of character-building organizations, such as the Boy and Girl Scouts, and frequently lend their facilities for the use of constructive community agencies of a non-sectarian sort. All told, the churches make a very large contribution in these lines.

The helpful relations of the churches to the non-church agencies is seriously handicapped by the fact of denominationalism. This is very amply evidenced by the experience of church federations. Public institutions, like hospitals and prisons, cannot tolerate the presence of chaplains from a wide variety of denominations, all competing for time and facilities. The courts are glad to recognize a single representative as a valuable ally in probation work, but, they cannot bring themselves to deal separately with the multiplicity of Protestant sects. Consequently, the pressure and authority of the public agencies increasingly serve to force these functions into interdenominational forms. On the other hand, the state increasingly has to recognize religious bodies in the public administration of welfare. It commits its wards to children's homes and detention institutions according to the faith of the parents; and it frequently is critical of Protestantism because it lacks interdenominational agencies for dealing with such problems comparable with those furnished by the Roman Catholic and Jewish faiths.

OTHER RELATIONSHIPS WITH WELFARE AGENCIES

Beyond such supplementing of the work of secular agencies as the last paragraphs have described the church finds many contacts with social agencies in the attempt to deal with needy people in their own homes. Poverty, sickness, unemployment, domestic discord and delinquency frequently bring the same families both to the church and to the social agencies. Here, then, are not only common problems but common cases. The situation obviously demands the utmost of mutual information, counsel and cooperation. Difficulties arise, however, out of the conflicting philosophies of the two types of agencies and the disparity of their technical standards. Secular agencies commonly hold that the churches should refer to them exclusively all cases of people not definitely connected with the church in some way. They are sure that the church should report its cases to the central charity registry, so that there may be no duplication of aid or difference in counsel. Church social workers on the contrary sometimes want to get their hands on new cases in order to bring them under church influence and are gravely disinclined to expose the needs of the "church's own" to the unsympathetic secular agency. Returns, secured in 1934, chiefly from representative church social workers in the middle west, revealed that two-fifths would at least visit a "case" brought to their attention without prior conference with any other agency; and that an appreciative proportion would use their judgment as to any later conference. One-half might assume responsibility, after conference, for families not previously related to their institutions. A considerable majority would not agree in advance to report to a clearing agency all the facts discovered about a "case."[8]

This clash of standards turns up at nearly every point. The better secular agencies undoubtedly possess a more thorough appreciation of the technical problem of social need and remedy, and greater expertness. They stand

---

[8] Federal Council of Churches, *Information Service*, Vol. XIII, No. 12, March 24, 1934.

for adequacy of remedial measures to a degree that the church does not and frequently cannot command.

The problem is particularly complicated by the presence of the volunteer whose zeal is not according to knowledge. Christianity makes men want to help their unfortunate neighbors. The church often attempts to project its members into volunteer social work. The local church or church federation, for example, may inventory the community demand for volunteers and attempt to enlist people for such service. This, however, involves problems of fitness and standards of work which the church does not always value as a professional social worker does, and many an agency has to cry for protection from the dabbling religious volunteer.

In a relatively few cases church federations are beginning to provide for the competent training of volunteers through courses of study set up in connection with councils of social agencies or more rarely in training schools of religious education. This would seem to be one of the natural functions of coöperative organization and is most necessary if the volunteer religious social worker is to be competent and acceptable.

### Extra-Community Aspects of Church Welfare Work

The foregoing review of the church's welfare work has regarded it primarily from the standpoint of the local community. As already noted, many denominational philanthropies are supported by and serve the larger territorial units of the church; and consequently are not narrowly related to the communities in which they chance to be located.

Two additional aspects of extra-community welfare work require mention.

#### HOME AND FOREIGN MISSIONS

The vast work of missions in the United States and abroad includes a large body of welfare work in various aspects. An assembly of data from the majority of home-mission boards in 1933 enumerated 638 community-welfare enterprises employing 1,633 paid workers. These were operated in behalf of eight specially handicapped or racially dependent populations. The work included ninety-five medical enterprises employing 400 doctors and nurses. The rest are mainly divided among a variety of institutions, such as orphanages, homes, community centers, hospitals, dispensaries and special industrial projects, as well as many mission schools concerning industrial or agricultural training.[9]

In the field of foreign missions, both evangelism and education frequently come into direct conflict with social evils highly repugnant to Christianity

---

[9] Morse (ed.) op. cit., pp. 19-31.

but accepted in other societies. Of forms of deliberate welfare work, medical missions have the greatest expansion. They constitute an enormously expanded and highly popular endeavor. Agricultural and industrial missions in most cases are exceedingly secondary, but a new sense of their

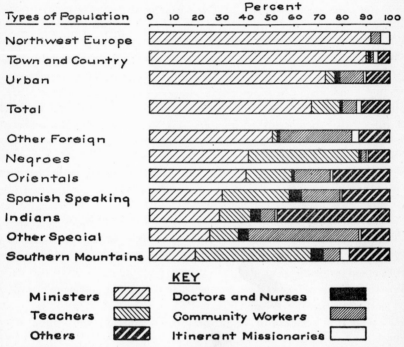

CHART XXIII—KINDS OF MISSIONARY WORKERS DISTRIBUTED ACCORDING TO TYPES OF POPULATION

importance has developed and many new experiments in their direction are under way or contemplated.

DEVELOPMENT OF NEW ETHICAL INSIGHTS AND IDEALS

When social ideals have achieved conventional acceptance, they naturally fall within the habitual teaching of the local church. Many of these ideals have ancient roots. They have impelled the church to build the vast army of organizations and to undertake the many welfare functions which have been reviewed. Yet many applications of social ideals are technically related to the problems of the industrial age and could not explicitly appear prior to our day. Chapter xiii will show how the development of new insights in this field have constituted a striking modification of the church's intellectual outlook. These ideals, first worked out by pioneers and prophets, have slowly percolated down into the local church, largely through modernly trained ministers and the pressure of non-local agencies. Many denominations have created departments of social service, and the formulation of social ideals and standards and their dissemination have always been a most important phase of coöperative Protestantism through church federations and the Federal Council of Churches.

## PROFESSIONAL LEADERSHIP OF PROTESTANT WELFARE WORK

While only a small fraction of churches are so characterized by social-welfare activities as to be labeled "institutional" churches, "community-serving" churches, "Christian social centers" and the like, most of the departmental specialists who make up 15 per cent. of the subordinate workers in city churches, many of the age- and sex-group specialists who constitute 8 per cent. of this total, and many of the pastoral workers, such as deaconesses and visitors who make up 14 per cent. of the total, are in fact engaged primarily in welfare work, and owe their positions to the needs of church constituencies whose living standards are below normal or whose racial or other handicaps are extreme.  A very considerable amount, also, of the demands put upon the secretarial workers in church offices arises out of the pressure of such social needs.  Consequently, though ordained ministers as a whole give relatively little time to social work, and although the information available does not fall strictly into the categories now being employed, it seems reasonable to guess that approximately one-third of the paid professional service of the staffed church in the city falls in this field.  This is in addition to the primary social values of wholesome group fellowship furnished by the total life of the church.

The variety of workers in social-welfare lines has already been suggested in the chapter on the ministry.  So far as specifically labeled they included directors of church and community houses with their staffs, family case workers, recreational and group leaders for men and women and boys and girls, kindergarteners and day nursery supervisors, other teachers, nurses and clinic assistants.  When the actual work of these persons comes to be examined in detail on the basis of weekly records one finds that the church inclines to use its employees in a great variety of duties, many of them little related to the work for which they are ostensibly employed.  This is in line with the mixed motives with which it undertakes social work.  It prevents competent specialization.  Almost no professional standards of work exist.  There is a deplorable lack of definiteness of status, highly uncertain tenure and most unsatisfactory pay.  In brief, the social welfare of the church's own parochial employees has been largely forgotten in connection with its efforts in this sphere.

MOVEMENTS FOR THE IMPROVEMENT OF PROTESTANT CHURCH SOCIAL WORK

Some progress in the professional organization and the development of standards is beginning to be made through the Church Conferences on Social Work fostered by the Federal Council. This organization meets annually in connection with the National Conference of Social Work and it is encouraging the voluntary organization of church social workers in the interests of professional ideals and group morale.

Besides this embryonic general movement for better standards, church federations in a considerable number of communities have attempted to meet the rather widespread and sometimes outspoken criticisms of the social workers in their communities by definite policies of coöperation, including training courses for volunteers such as were mentioned in the previous paragraph. They have also sometimes undertaken to educate the churches in newer phases of social work. A good many churches are just as conservative in social thinking as in theological. They are interested in and insist on giving money to discredited forms of social work and sometimes to discredited institutions. Church federations have a great responsibility for advice and leadership as well as for keeping alive the mood of continual self-criticism without which social work goes stale, just as do evangelism and all other aspects of the church's interest.

CURRENT MOVEMENT FOR THE CORRELATION OF PROTESTANT WELFARE WORK

One prime reason why Protestant welfare agencies do not coöperate with the general social-work movement of the community is that they are not themselves unified. The church federations have not made greater progress with them because they are not in the federations. Their origins were largely parochial or narrowly denominational, or else they grew up as independent institutions bearing a denominational name but not very amenable to denominational control. In many communities the financial pressure of the immediate present has driven these hitherto divided agencies to contemplate the advantage of strength through unity. An important conference of representatives from more than twenty cities met in New York in 1934 and initiated a movement looking to the general integration of these forces and their inclusion within the coöperative movement of Protestantism through its city and national federations.

PROBLEMS

As was the case with the review of religious education, this review of church social-welfare activities leads to a bristling array of problems rather than to any set of simple and easy solutions. The central problem of the church and state has already been noted. Upon analysis the remaining problems seem to fall into three categories: (1) those relating to the location and division of social-welfare responsibilities; (2) those dealing with the source and authority of ethical insight as related to social issues, that is, with social philosophy; (3) those dealing with the actual motivation of welfare work.

### DIVISION OF SOCIAL WELFARE RESPONSIBILITY: PUBLIC VS. PRIVATE AGENCIES

Beginning with the first group, one has to register the church's growing perplexity as to the division of responsibility for social welfare between public and voluntary private agencies.  Apart from any basic issue as between church and state, the state increasingly assumes its primary responsibility in certain fields such as the care of dependent children.  At numerous points it exercises a certain supervision of agencies which undertake welfare responsibilities.  The major problem in this field is, however, the decisive change of balance between public and private agencies incident to the depression.

The total bulk of voluntary philanthropic expenditure, both denominational and non-sectarian, is taking diminished place relative to the vastly increased expenditures of the state during this period.  Indeed, in spite of its hundreds of specialized institutions and scores of community-serving churches, the church's part in welfare service as such is so diminishing that the question is seriously raised whether the church will not cease to occupy any considerable place in this field with which historically its roots are so closely entwined.  It is partly for this reason that the essential character of the normal group life of the local parish as a welfare agency has been stressed in preceding paragraphs of this chapter, and that the social by-products of the ordinary on-going of the church have been magnified.  It seems likely, however, that the church's problem will increasingly be that of discovering the type of welfare work which it is permanently best fitted and most competent to do, in contrast with some of its present institutionalized charities for which the state is taking increased responsibility.  Very possibly it will prove that the church is most apt and competent in activities directly reflecting its pastoral function.  The church has already proved that there is room for it to exercise this function on a vast scale through its association with public institutions.  If, therefore, much of the work of the private institutions now in the hands of the church shall in the future pass over to the state, the church may still find large opportunities for service in directly spiritual ministries and in those which personalize and individualize welfare in terms of friendliness and insight, making for the restoration of morale and the rehabilitation of character.

Another vexing problem of the relationships of public and private welfare effort has been aggravated by the depression.  The insupportable burdens thrust upon private agencies have led to a new demand for state subsidies for their philanthropies by certain religious groups. The formal Protestant answer, rendered through the Federal Council in behalf of its constituent denominations, has reiterated the position that there should be no expenditure of public money except under public auspices. Particular exceptions have, however, involved further difficulties. For example, the state places a ward in a sectarian institution to its own advantage and for the ward's good. When this is done in quantity, payments for such services may become the main resource of such an institution. Consequently, what is quite permissible in the single case becomes a virtual subsidy when applied to many cases at once. In other words, there are numerous details with respect to which the problem is far from settled.

VOLUNTARY SECULAR VS. RELIGIOUS AGENCIES

A second major problem of the division of social-welfare responsibility concerns the voluntary secular agencies in contrast with those operated under religious auspices. Are these voluntary agencies proper vehicles for the philanthropic impulse of religious persons and groups, or must the church set up its own ecclesiastically controlled agencies?

Different theories relative to the proper balance between secular and religious agencies have been held traditionally in different sections of the country. Any proper comparison takes account of these different viewpoints. Thus the Springfield, Mass., church survey was able to credit only 5 per cent. of the annual operating costs of voluntary social-welfare agencies in that city to the Protestant churches and denominations as such, whereas the St. Louis church survey credited them with 37 per cent. of the total operating costs and 40 per cent. of the property investment. The difference reflects varying regional attitudes. Religious people in New England for a long time have expected and desired, in the main, to do their philanthropic work through non-sectarian agencies; while the denominations dominating in the South and Southwest are particularly given to denominational institutionalism. Comparisons between twelve denominations as to the care of dependent children show that southern denominations emphasize denominational agencies much more strongly than denominations of the similar families in the North. Southern denominational attitudes, in turn, reflect a serious lack of provision for child welfare in the southern states on the part of city, county and state governments.

Apart from these regional differences the Protestant Episcopal and Lutheran communions turn out to be the ones which are most insistent upon their own social-welfare institutions. On the other hand, most denominations in some sections of the country and some denominations in all sections incline away from the policy of multiplying denominational philanthropies and in favor of Christian support for non-sectarian agencies and the development of a state system of welfare work which shall be Christian in spirit.

At this point, again, a theoretical issue is complicated by actual conditions. Numerous communities are registering increasing concern as to whether church-supported philanthropies are getting a square deal in the making of recent social-welfare policy. Community chests representing secular leadership are suspected, not only of institutional partisanship, but also of ignoring the scientifically demonstrable place of religion as a contributor to morale and as a solvent of the moral problems which underlie social evils. The church often feels that it merits a more appreciative recognition upon the part of secular agencies, in return for its recognition of the duty of coöperation with them and of the superior standards which they demand of the church.

### PROTESTANT VS. ROMAN CATHOLIC AND JEWISH PHILANTHROPIES

Within the group of religious welfare agencies problems also arise as to the devision of responsibility and the practical relationship between those maintained by the Protestant church and those of the Catholic and Jewish churches. These problems are complicated by conflicting philosophies and policies with respect to welfare work and, in some instances, by actual competition for financial support.

The strict maintenance of the Jewish religious community is insisted upon among Jews as essential to race continuity. The Catholic church is regarded by its adherents as the organ of salvation. From both of these standpoints it is highly important that the church care philanthropically for its own people under its own auspices. In contrast, the dangling adherence of the majority of Protestants to their churches leaves the particular auspices of social-welfare work less important to them. Nevertheless, the Protestant instinct for social service under religious auspices is deep-seated and permanent. This gives Protestantism very vital sympathy with the welfare work of other communions in its competition for recognition as over against narrowly secular work. On the other hand, the greater stubbornness of the other communions with respect, for example, to the control of marital relations or the training of children, sometimes leads to Protestant suspicion that they are using undue influence in behalf of their clients in the matter of funds derived from public sources. From the standpoint of the state, the maintenance of sectarian systems of social welfare by the three major faiths (in addition to a system of voluntary secular welfare) greatly complicates the situation and adds to the difficulty of the national problem of providing for the dependent and unemployed.

ECCLESIASTICAL VS. VOLUNTARY PROTESTANT AGENCIES

Within the Protestant group itself a subsidiary issue arises between the ecclesiastical agencies and the non-denominational group whose antecedents are strongly Protestant but which are themselves auxiliaries to the church rather than ecclesiastical bodies. Thus it has frequently been a live question whether the Y. M. C. A. and Y. W. C. A. would make common cause with the declared agencies of the Protestant churches in policy making and in financial campaigns.

SEGREGATION AND SEPARATE ORGANIZATION OF PROTESTANT SOCIAL AGENCIES

All these problems focus upon the question whether a group of Protestant ecclesiastical welfare agencies is to be recognized as having common interests, as over against the state and secular agencies, the welfare agencies of the Jews and Catholics, and the non-denominational agencies for character-building of Protestant antecedents. Should this group segregate itself and separately organize in order to gain strength, raise standards, develop professional leadership, and compete in proper and honest ways with other agencies working in the common field? The findings of the 1934 Conference on the Correlation of Protestant Social Work, already alluded to, recommended that there should be formed, in every community, central coördinating agencies or welfare councils of Protestant agencies, to be affiliated with the church federations where such exist. The wide organization of such central community agencies would involve and require a more thoughtful and deliberate attack upon the problems just enumerated than is possible when they are made piecemeal by hundreds of unrelated agencies and scores of denominations.

PROBLEMS INVOLVING SOCIAL PHILOSOPHY

Coming now to problems involving differences in social philosophy, one has to note that issues as between the faiths involved in welfare work are sometimes theoretical at bottom. Thus, for example, birth control and sterilization, from the Roman Catholic and more conservative Protestant viewpoints, are matters to be weighed exclusively in the scales of eternal values. The short cuts which social expediency may wish to make are thought to contravene the will of God as understood by the church. While these diametrical oppositions of conviction continue, coöperation at such points is manifestly stopped.

MOTIVATION

Problems of motivation arise because the church's social welfare has always been based upon a variety of motives. The "spiritual" motive wants to put men into right social relations in a supra-mundane world. The narrower or philanthropic motive wants to overcome human evils and to release human beings from their bondage. To realize the first purpose, most religious people think that it is necessary to share a particular religious outlook with others. To raise funds, large numbers of Protestant philanthropic agencies have felt it necessary to declare explicitly that their ultimate objectives are evangelistic. This statement is written into thousands of records, yet it frequently causes resentment when pointed out by critics.

In its cruder version of the evangelistic motive, social work is little more than a bait to get recipients of charity to allow themselves to be exposed to religious propaganda. The writers' personal surveys have discovered great and distinguished churches which compelled attendance upon a devotional service as the price of participation in their recreational and social activities. A more refined version of the religious motive insists that the charitable person is fully warranted in desiring to share his supreme values with others and in testifying to them as to what these values are. In this field it is exceedingly difficult to do justice; but church people generally have undoubtedly lacked adequate sensitiveness to the viewpoints of the recipients of their social benefactions when these benefactions are closely bound up with religious aims. Both in the Near and in the Far East, whole nations have been willing to deprive their people of needed and valued services rather than have them submitted to foreign indoctrination in schools and hospitals. When direct religious propaganda is forbidden, one type of missionary inclines to drop social-welfare activities and confine himself to purely religious propaganda. Another type persists in welfare work, on the theory that the whole personality is involved in any serious contact between groups of men and that the profoundest values manage to communicate themselves in spite of limitations as to form and method. In view of the weakness of direct religious teaching in securing direct character results even in Protestant Sunday schools, it would seem safe largely to trust to good works to speak for themselves. This in very large measure has been the practice of the Protestant churches in spite of their proclaimed evangelistic theory, as witness the very many dangling subsidiaries, with their remotely religious programs, to which previous chapters have called attention.

Still more profound problems of social-welfare work are brought to light when it is discovered that such work often involves an implicit cultural conflict between an older and better established social group and latercomers who are the beneficiaries of the former. The older group is apt to assume that welfare is identical with some particular version of "normal American standards of life."

Social welfare, therefore, gets to be closely associated with Americanization. To be sure American cultural dogmas are not set up crudely for uniform acceptance nor violently forced upon minorities; but valuations of the results of the work usually refer to American standards as norms, and the work is not continued unless these standards are measurably satisfied. The unspoken assumption is that the cultural minorities are to be absorbed in the tradition of the major group. It is this assumption that creates the problem. An alternative assumption is called cultural pluralism. It looks not only with toleration but with appreciation upon a variety of social practices and standards, and conceives of the social unity of the nation as being permanently realized in diversity. Obviously, the perpetuation by minorities of old-world animosities in America and political agitation by emissaries subsidized from abroad remain utterly distasteful and not to be tolerated. On the other hand, most minorities are so clearly losing out in their frantic rear-guard resistance to the dominant culture that it seems scarcely necessary to press them too hard. Moreover, no nation more than America needs the humility which is willing to learn from the rest of the world.

Concluding this review of church social-welfare work, one naturally inclines to compare this field with those reviewed in previous chapters. The most striking difference is that here is a field in which extensive factual investigation has been conspicuously lacking. Slender data have had to be padded out with generalities. Particularly for this reason, the re-thinking of Protestant social-work problems has also been lacking. There are no data with respect to Protestant philanthropies such as the Federal government provides with respect to churches, or such as the churches themselves, in their annual statistics, report with respect to their conventional activities. An inventory which shall merely state the magnitude of the problem, classify the different types of service and show their relative size and importance, is greatly needed. Not less needed is the study of their quality and the applicability of current standards to their particular situations. Even more imperative is a study of changing conditions which have made many of the ancient charities of the churches not only uncouth but actually detrimental to a forward-looking program of social action. Finally, a long process of pondering upon contemporary currents of social thinking and experience is needed. After this, with an adequate body of facts in hand, patient and long-continued conferences ought to be able to adjust many of the present conflicts of the numerous and ill-adjusted forces. Welfare, as consisting of mutual understanding, good-will and co-operation between these agencies, is not less momentous than that which seeks to bring a "full dinner pail" to all the people of the nation.

# CHAPTER X

## *Finances and Facilities*

One inclined to moralize upon the vast expenditures of the American people on purely ephemeral or whimsical fashions, or, on the other hand upon the immense sums spent in "doing things right" according to some relatively meaningless social traditions may question, by the same token, how much or how little the financial transactions of the church fall under the same categories. Is the church supported because it has vogue or because it has a conventional place in civilization? Or, on the other hand, do church expenditures reflect the satisfaction of deep and abiding interests? The widespread critical mood of the age toward the church, the fact that in the United States its support is entirely on a voluntary basis, together with its extraordinary ability, on the whole, to weather depressions, makes the latter answer the more probable. Long-continued financial support by millions of people, through prosperity and adversity, is good sociological evidence of a genuine sense on their part of those inner values in the church which religious people so ardently assert. The church constituency is, moreover, a thoroughly representative cross-section of the nation, representing different levels of financial capacity as well as varying degrees of willingness to support religion. Church support is probably the most widely distributed form of voluntary cultural expenditure. It is indulged in by people who read no books and take no newspapers. These considerations combine to make church finances, including both current expenditures and investment in plant and facilities, a very pertinent and reliable index of the status of the church in the minds of the people.

### CHURCH FINANCES

Gross data dealing with church finances are fairly ample, though seriously out of date. The last nationwide figures, those of the 1926 Census of Religious Bodies, showed the combined expenditures by local churches of $840,000,000 annually. This approximated 1 per cent. of the national income. These expenditures were at the rate of $10.22 per inhabitant of over twelve years of age. For rural churches the average was $13.27 per adult member, for urban $21.50. Chart XXIV shows the same data for churches inside and outside the principal cities.

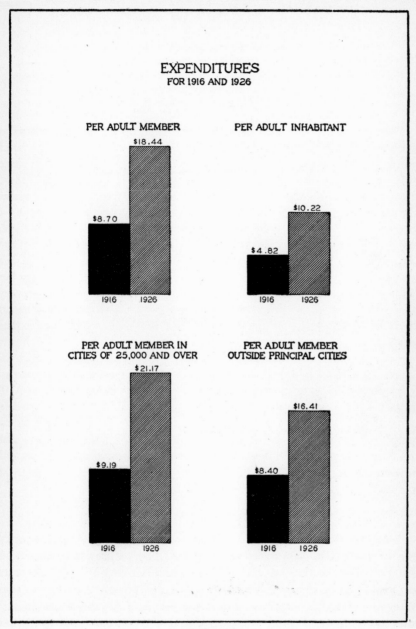

EXPENDITURES
FOR 1916 AND 1926

PER ADULT MEMBER

$18.44

$8.70

1916    1926

PER ADULT INHABITANT

$10.22

$4.82

1916    1926

PER ADULT MEMBER IN
CITIES OF 25,000 AND OVER

$21.17

$9.19

1916    1926

PER ADULT MEMBER
OUTSIDE PRINCIPAL CITIES

$16.41

$8.40

1916    1926

CHART XXIV

When one considers trends, the 1926 figure (shown in Chart XXV) registered, in dollars, an increase of 149 per cent. over church expenditures of 1916, a more than 50 per cent. gain even after adjustments taking account of differences in the purchasing power of money. Financial support of the churches gained one-third faster during this period than did the national income, though it is noteworthy that public-school expenditures increased still more rapidly. All types of church constituencies reflected the general tendency. Negro church expenditures, for example, shared in the national gain to a remarkable degree, though not fully keeping pace with white church expenditure.

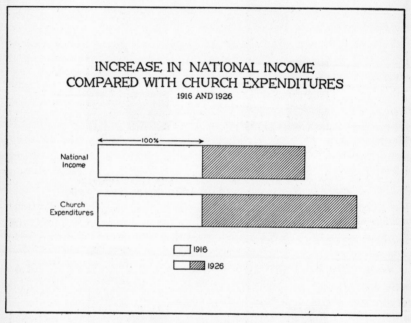

INCREASE IN NATIONAL INCOME
COMPARED WITH CHURCH EXPENDITURES
1916 AND 1926

National Income

Church Expenditures

1916
1926

CHART XXV

No exactly comparable data exist by which to measure the effect of the current financial depression upon church finances. Twenty out of thirty-five leading denominations compared in 1934 had reduced their total expenditures by from thirty to fifty per cent. and five over fifty per cent. Yet four had actually increased expenditures and it is fairly certain that the average income of the national benevolent boards of the major denominations has not been reduced as much as have the personal incomes of the American people, or their personal expenditures and savings.

Of the expenditures thus accounted for four-fifths were for local church maintenance and one-fifth for philanthropy and missions. Substantially the same ratio held in 1932.

Different sections of the country naturally registered different rates of gain, the greatest increase being shown in the most rapidly growing states; but with the great majority of states the increase for the decade exceeded 100 per cent.

Of course not every local church shared in the general prosperity of the "boom" period; very many churches took themselves out of the picture by dying. No separate data exist for rural churches, but for urban churches it appears that, in piping times of prosperity, to survive at all means to increase expenditures. Of 1,821 churches in sixteen cities whose financial expenditures were compared for the decade 1920-1930, only 10 per cent. decreased expenditures, while 42 per cent. increased them up to 100 per cent. and 48 per cent. more than 100 per cent. Of the sixteen cities the one with the poorest record showed 80 per cent. of its churches gaining financially, while for the best city the per cent. was 95.

ACCOUNTING DIFFICULTIES

Such data gathered on a nation-wide scale partly average out difficulties brought to light by more intimate studies of church finances for limited groups or areas. On the other hand, the national generalization obscures, if indeed it does not entirely falsify, some of the facts. Thus, the study of many churches, one by one, shows a tendency to an understatement of total financial expenditures. This is largely due to lack of reporting of finances of the loosely related affiliates described in chapter v. When these do report finances to their local churches they are apt to present net figures rather than gross.

On the other hand, the study of denominationally gathered financial reports for city or district areas involves a constant danger of duplicate accounting. Some of the funds spent within such areas originate internally, while others are brought in from outside in the shape of denominational or missionary subsidies and are merely redistributed within the area.

Still again, the important distinction made in an immediately preceding paragraph, between expenditures for support of local parishes (commonly called "home expenditures") and expenditures for missionary and benevolent purposes is much less clear-cut in actual accounting than the census distinction would suggest. This is largely due to uncertainty as to how local benevolence is treated in accounting.

Another special accounting problem relates to the "overhead" expense of running denominational and missionary enterprises; that is to say the costs beyond those directly relating to the operation of parishes and local institutions. Much interest attaches to this problem, and church constituencies are extremely sensitive over expenditures for the maintenance of what they suspect of being ecclesiastical bureaucracies. But no generally accepted agreement as to what constitutes overhead charges has been reached.

In view of such intricacies of fact, and with no uniform systems of accounting as between different denominations and types of religious institution, any high degree of accuracy in financial statement is out of the question.[1] One can nevertheless give certain generalized figures illustrating the factors involved and raising the major problems of financial support for the church as an institution.

In the following paragraphs local church finances will be discussed first, their rural and urban phases being separately treated, after which typical aspects of extra-parochial financing, denominational and interdenominational, will be presented.

### LOCAL CHURCH FINANCES: RURAL

The 1926 census gives the average expenses of rural congregations as $1,400, or $13.27 for each member. This figure not only varies by region from $7.54 in the East South Central states to $21.94 in the Middle Atlantic, but also again conceals significant differences between village and open-country churches. Congregational expenses for rural Protestants increased about 25 per cent. throughout the 1920's, though most of this increase occurred prior to 1925. The average village church operated on an income for current expenses of about $2,300; open-country churches got along with $750. Interestingly enough, open-country churches located on the fringes or outside of the community areas of villages and towns spent well over $100 a year more than those within these areas. This is another indication of the effect of the competition noted previously of village and town churches with those of the open country. Churches in towns of from 2,500 to 10,000 population spent about $4,000 a year. Total expenditure figures thus increased with the population, but per member gifts varied little in communities of more than 1,000 population.

The increases in budgets between 1920 and 1930 came not so much from increased giving by members, at least after 1925, as from an increase in the number of persons giving. Between 1924 and 1930 per member gifts varied little and stood in the latter year at $16.38 for village church-members and at $8.57 for those in country churches. In the South and Middle West per capita giving had definitely receded by 1930 from the 1924-25 levels. It has undoubtedly declined further since that time.

As a general principle, the smaller the church the greater the cost to the individual belonging. Churches with fewer than twenty-five members, con-

---

[1] See Morse (Ed.), *Home Missions Today and Tomorrow* (New York: Home Missions Council, 1934), p. 13.

stituting about one-sixth of all rural churches, often pay more per member, to sustain their meager programs of a fortnightly or monthly preaching service and to keep their one-room church in repair, than it costs the average member of a village or town church to enjoy the services of a resident minister, the facilities of a reasonably adequate building, and to share in a program of religious education, recreation and community service. In areas of low population density very small churches are inevitable. Elsewhere they exact a disproportionate price in return for the privilege of individualism in religion. The price is high because there is obviously a point below which the program and activities of a church cannot fall if the church as an organization is to continue. If there are only a few to pay for this minimum each one's share is large.

Similarly, as already noted, there appears to be a maximum program beyond which the average rural church does not go. With such a program the more members a church has the lighter the individual burden. This is clearly shown when rural Protestant and Roman Catholic churches are compared. The latter have twice the membership of the former. Their budgets are one-third to two-fifths higher but per member contributions are 25 per cent. less.

The influence of the wealth of the community on per member giving was noted in the discussion of the effect of community conditions upon church fortunes.

Information as to the proportion of their funds allotted to benevolent enterprises by rural churches prior to 1910 is rather meager. It seems safe to estimate that in the 1880's and 1890's between one-tenth and one-eighth of each dollar collected went to such purposes. By 1910 this had risen to between one-seventh and one-sixth. With the 1910's the study of rural churches by modern survey methods began in earnest, and there are many evidences that the proportion of the income spent for missionary and allied purposes was steadily increasing. By 1920 rural churches were spending thirty cents of every dollar received for benevolences, with little difference between village and country. Village ministers were getting forty and country ministers forty-seven cents of each dollar and the remainder went for other general expenses. By 1924-25 the peak seems to have been reached. Benevolences were getting 32 per cent. in village and country alike. Ministers had also advanced a point or two. By 1929-30 a decided shift had taken place. Ministers' salaries absorbed half the income, benevolent causes dropped to about one-fifth and general expenses rose to three-tenths.[2] In

---

[2] The 1926 census of religious bodies gives 20 per cent. as the proportion given to benevolences by rural churches. This is much lower than the 1924-25 figures obtained through nation-wide field surveys of white Protestant churches. Part of the difference is doubtless due to the census' inclusion of the Roman Catholic figures. The rural churches of this

terms of money the reduction in missionary giving, despite an almost unchanged total per member gift, declined from $5.64 to $3.54 per member per year in the village churches and from $3.28 to $2.15 in the country churches. This small loss in per member giving probably made a difference of over $20,000,000 in the income of denominational benevolent boards and agencies in 1929 as compared to 1924-25. The trends noted obtained in all regions and among all denominations, though the proportion that various denominations allot to benevolences varies widely,[3] and there is a slight variation among the regions and between churches served by a resident or a nonresident pastor.

There are many possible explanations for this falling off in the proportion of total income that rural churches spend on benevolences. Some attempted to remedy the economic handicaps of their ministers by increasing salaries. Many discovered that their fixed charges increased because of the interest on mortgages that had been taken out on new buildings. A few were finding that an expanded program of service was costing more. Undoubtedly, too, loss of interest in certain types of missionary enterprise and a growing doubt as to the value or efficiency of some of the work were contributing causes. The older motives for missionary giving were also losing their force.[4] As the agricultural depression deepened and it became more and more impossible to increase the total contributions to religious agencies, the first group of causes to suffer were the benevolent. There are some evidences that the position of such enterprises is relatively worse now than in 1929-30. For instance, a study of so-called larger parishes in 1933 revealed that these highly publicized rural church projects were giving only one-eighth of their receipts to benevolences.

### URBAN CHURCH FINANCES

Chapter vii has shown that the characteristic urban church merely represents slight embellishments of the traditional rural church pattern. The financial expression of this embellishment is found, for example, in the more frequent payment of janitors and musicians whose services in the country church are often contributed. As already noted, the average urban annual expenditures of $10,000 per local church means $12.50 per capita for adult members, compared with the rural average of $8.70.

---

large body spend a far smaller proportion on benevolences than do those of the Protestants. The Negro denominations, which were not proportionately represented in the sample surveyed, and which devote only about one-seventh of their income to missionary causes, also help to account for the difference. Another factor is the difference in what are considered benevolences by the various denominations. The field surveys made corrections to reduce all results to a comparable basis, while the census did not.

[3] For instance, some churches have an unpaid ministry. One of these, the Seventh Day Adventist, gives away four-fifths of its congregational income.

[4] See chapter xiii.

But the average misrepresents the most frequent case—nearly two-thirds of all urban Protestant churches spent less than $10,000 in 1926, and over 40 per cent. less than $5,000.

While numerically less frequent, the more highly developed types of urban churches distinguished in chapter vii represent religious organization on a more definitely urban scale. The operations of these larger and more complex institutions involve new problems of finance. They get income from more varied sources and have a wider range of expenditure.

The only data throwing intimate light upon finances of urban churches are derived from a limited number of case studies from which no final generalization can be drawn. They serve, however, to show how financial matters work out in the more characteristically urban churches, especially those of the consciously adapted types.

CASE STUDIES OF CHURCHES—INCOME

If we consider first the sources of support drawn upon by local churches, a distribution according to source for twenty-three city churches of more than average size, with distinctively adapted programs, and an aggregate constituency of nearly 500,000 persons, yields the following results:

| Source | Per Cent. |
| --- | --- |
| Individual pledges | 49 |
| Special gifts | 14 |
| Plate collections | 11 |
| Subsidies | 8 |
| Commercial transactions | 6 |
| All others | 12 |

This showing serves rather to reveal the nature of the situation than to furnish evidence as to a typical distribution of income according to source. Extraordinary deviations occur which make bare averages of little significance. Thus, in the twenty-three cases the proportion of support derived from individual pledges ranges from 9 to 83 per cent. So high a degree of variation is made possible because pew rentals are substituted for individual pledges by a few churches as a chief source of support, while a few others depend very heavily upon loose plate collections. This enables nearly a third of the churches to reduce their individual pledges to less than one-fourth of the total budget.

Loose collections, in turn, furnish from 1 to 28 per cent. of the total income in the twenty-three cases. Ten churches got less than 10 per cent. of their total income from this source, and ten others from 10 to 20 per cent., leaving only three which supported themselves by talking money out of their various congregations from Sunday to Sunday. In these few extraordinary cases financing was mainly done by a skilfully reiterated begging from the pulpit. The financial appeal came out at three or four points in every service, including very pointed reference in prayer to financial needs.

Only a third of the twenty-three churches derived any income from pew rentals. Half of these used rented pews merely as a supplemental source, while the other half made them a major source of income, reaching in one case as high as 68 per cent. of the total.

Next to pledges, the most uniform financial resource was found in special gifts often secured from the congregation at Easter or other set time, or else representing the bounty of one or more individual financial angels whose gifts supplemented those of the general congregation. In extreme cases of churches carrying large social-welfare programs some of these special gifts came from community funds or from donors in other churches.

About three-fifths of the sample churches made some use of commercial transactions as means of support. In the majority of these cases such transactions consisted merely in a few entertainments or sales yielding at the outside 4 or 5 per cent. of the total income. In one case, however, a week's annual bazaar constituted a major resource, as was true of income from rented property in another case.

Several of these churches included in this sample represented major projects of city extension boards or national boards of missions. These churches got from 16 to 71 per cent. of their total income from denominational treasuries. Such cases reflect the necessity for large outside aid in the more radical experiments in the adaptation of churches to urban communities in extreme need. In one of these cases three denominations combined in subsidizing a federated church.

About a third of the sample cases reported appreciable receipts budgeted as coming from subsidiary organizations. In the main, however, the income of these organizations is so trivial as not to be separately accounted for. It is generally derived from the special memberships or constituencies of the subsidiaries concerned.

The above generalization leaves 12 per cent. of the average budget to be accounted for as coming from miscellaneous sources. In two-fifths of the cases this included income from small fees or dues received in connection with the operation of such special facilities as classes, gymnasiums and health facilities. But in no case was a church found which secured any such proportion of its resources from fees and dues as does the typical Y.M.C.A. and Y.W.C.A.

In the main the above data as to income represent a wide variety of factors in different combinations instead of any distinct set of trends. They simply serve to show the highly diverse sources from which money for the support of the urban church comes.

INCOME FROM CAPITAL FUNDS

No general data exist as to the extent to which urban churches are supported by endowments. A well-distributed sample of nearly 1,000 churches in large cities, representing more than forty denominations, indicates that in 1930 somewhat more than one-fifth were endowed. Half of this number, however, had endowments of less than $20,000, while those of less than $5,000 were most characteristic. In other words, most of the endowments would not yield 10 per cent. of the average church budget. The other half of the endowments were widely distributed over amounts ranging from $25,000 to more than a million, one-tenth falling between $100,000 and $150,000. Four churches of the sample had endowments of more than a million dollars.

CURRENT EXPENSES

The distribution of city church expenditures between the main items also shows great variation, and the number of cases is not sufficient to establish any common trend. Omitting payments to capital account, and limiting the statement to strictly current expenses, the following distribution is found:

| | Per Cent. | |
|---|---|---|
| Object of Expenditure | Approximate Average | Range |
| Salaries | 40 | 25–66 |
| General operating expenses and upkeep | 22 | 10–45 |
| Music | 12 | 3–18 |
| Administration, office and communication expenses | 6 | 1–12 |
| Departmental expenditures | 6 | 1–24 |
| Publicity | 4 | ... |
| Ecclesiastical overhead expenses | 2 | ... |
| Miscellaneous | 8 | ... |

As will be noted, the range of difference for salaries is smaller than the range for other items. Operating expenses and upkeep should obviously vary with the character of the property and the variety of the program. The small per cent. of expenditures departmentally budgeted corresponds to the limited income from these sources already noted. Generally the costs of the more habitual departments such as the Sunday school are covered with the general church budget. However, five churches out of the twenty-three which maintained separate parish or community house organizations devoted approximately one-fifth of their expenditures to their maintenance, apart from salaries.

It should be said again that the above figures have value as suggesting variety in the distribution of expenditure rather than as presenting normal averages. They are, however, somewhat strengthened by an extensive sampling of Negro urban church budgets which also devote about 40 per cent. of expenditure to salaries and 25 per cent. to general operation and upkeep.

UNIT AND PER CAPITA COSTS

The resources secured and expended in the variety of ways just indicated are in the last resort expenditures of particular churches and come out of the pockets of individual supporters. Financially speaking, urban churches range from the poverty-stricken groups spending a few hundred dollars to the vast institutional enterprises with more than fifty employes and annual

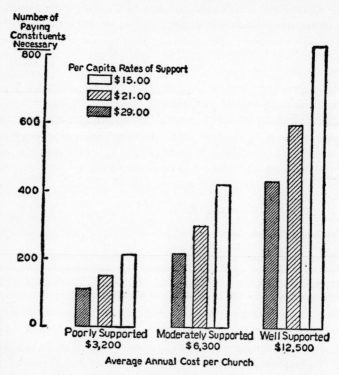

CHART XXVI—NUMBER OF PAYING CONSTITUENTS NECESSARY TO SUPPORT CHURCHES OF TYPICAL COST GROUPS AT PREVAILING PER CAPITA RATES OF CONTRIBUTION

budgets which reach as high as $75,000 or $100,000. The average cost per urban Protestant church approximates $10,000 per year. The per capita cost per adult member is $21.50, and somewhat less in the very largest cities.

It takes approximately 470 members to support an average Protestant city church at the average per capita cost. But the average Protestant city church has only about 300 members and the most frequent size is not over 200. The majority of churches, then, would have to double their member-

ships to have average resources. In other words, the average is a very poor
measure, since it is pulled up by the relatively few wealthier churches.

The small churches cannot support the average program and enjoy the
average facilities without paying much more than the average rate. But
nearly every city has made recent economic surveys. These invariably have
proved that the people of one area differ tremendously in wealth from those
of another. Many parts of the city cannot possibly reach the average per
capita rate of support for their institution, let alone exceed it. These areas,
then, are doomed to have sub-standard churches unless they are financially
aided from the outside. But such aid becomes ruinously expensive if it
has to be disbursed to small sectarian churches. In the city as well as in
the country Roman Catholic churches are in striking contrast with Protestant
on this point. They manage to provide fairly high-grade services to their
poor constituencies by the device of gathering them up into large congregations. City surveys have shown the most elaborately equipped and staffed
churches, and churches with the broadest range of program, costing no
more per capita and often less than poor sub-standard churches, because the
former distribute the cost among large numbers of supporters, while the
others must impose it upon their few supporters.

The same phenomenon appears in the recent study of urban Negro
churches where those with fewer than 500 members cost, on the average,
$12.27 per capita, the rate decreasing with the increasing size of the church
until it is only $5.41 per capita for churches with more than 3,000 members.

Here, then, is a point at which the objective study of the church definitely
challenges the righteousness of costs which so largely originate in a divisive
and non-strategic form of parochial organization.

### URBAN-RURAL, REGIONAL AND DENOMINATIONAL COMPARISONS

A few comparisons between the financing of urban and rural churches
will serve to bring together the two lines of evidence previously offered.
Compared with the average city church whose maintenance costs $10,000
annually is the $1,400 which has to support the average rural church. Com-
pared with the urban per capita rate of $21.50 per adult member is the rural
rate of $13.27.

The per capita costs of church support increased faster during the last
decade in cities than they did in the country. This reflects the tendency of
wealth to concentrate in cities and of the cities to splurge in material expenditures.

Average and per capita church expenditures vary regionally as well as
between city and country. The results of the regional data clearly reflect
differences in wealth and in the average size of the church, among other
factors. But at many points they are confusing rather than illuminating.

Denominational comparisons also appear to reflect a wide variety of factors, not all of which have been isolated and measured. Per capita costs vary greatly from denomination to denomination. On the whole it is a fair generalization that they reflect unequal wealth rather than unequal devotion to the church. This appears as the result of regional analysis. Denominations concentrated in the poorer states spend relatively less upon the church than those characteristically urban or identified with wealthier territory. Other factors obviously entering into the situation are national and racial antecedents and the time the denominational constituency has lived in the United States. Thus churches of non-English-speaking origins and Negro churches show lower rates of financial support than those of the older national stock.[5]

All told, then, when the vast sum of money spent in support of the church is spread over the entire area of the nation, divided between the many denominations and the more than one-quarter-million of local churches, it produces exceedingly feeble units financially speaking. An actual majority of rural churches are sub-standard in the sense that they are unable to support a fully trained minister according to their own theories of suitable training; while the typical city church is not an institution projected on an urban scale nor distinctly adapted to an urban environment.

The direct use of many of the foregoing comparisons based upon periods of time is precluded by changes in the purchasing power of money. As already noted, the more than doubling of the per capita contributions of all church-members in the United States between 1916 and 1926, when measured by purchasing power, actually amounted to an increase of only 50 per cent.

This whole subject of the purchasing power of money as related to church finances has been too little studied, in part because of the technical difficulties involved in determining what index or indices to use; but it is likely to become a matter of increasing importance to religious, educational and other social institutions. The one rural church study dealing with this point is an intensive investigation of a single county divided into twenty-eight rural communities or neighborhoods and with twice as many churches. The study covered the years 1886 to 1920 and showed that, though gifts in dollars had increased 82 per cent. in this period, the purchasing power of these dollars decreased 29 per cent. Considering 1910-20 alone, the period of the World War inflation, the dollar increase was 70 per cent., the purchasing power decline 13 per cent. If the efforts of the present federal administration to restore the 1926 price level are successful, it is probable that the purchasing power of the church will for a time lag behind any increase in its money contributions.

[5] See Fry, *The U. S. Looks at Its Churches*, p. 91.

## EXTRA-PAROCHIAL FINANCING

Beyond the costs of maintaining local churches, financial support has to be found for the varied supra-parochial agencies described in chapter v. These include local ecclesiastical and administrative organizations for each denomination, together with a variety of specialized local agencies; also local interchurch agencies like federations; and, ranking above these, state and areal agencies like dioceses and synods. In order to be adequate, financial support must be sufficient to include the authorized expenditures of the national denominational missionary and service agencies, such as mission boards and departments of church building, Sunday-school missions, and church-supported schools and colleges.

These demand very extensive financing, not only by reason of their bulk and complexity but because the kinds of centrally performed functions and services are increasing. Thus the constitutional administration of many denominations is based on the requirements of an era of expansion, now largely past. Here is a clamorous demand in important denominations that expenditures on this account should be decreased. On the contrary important new interests of the present church have added various forms of specialized administration and service, not only for weaker churches which are receiving denominational financial assistance, but for all of the churches. In brief, a denomination does many more sorts of things and attempts to mean more to its local churches than formerly. Consequently the financial demands of the "functional" ministry may be legitimately increasing. Financial aid, however, in the support of local churches still remains the chief item in extra-parochial expenditures.

The relations of the many elements of supra-parochial financing are hard to untangle. The more general denominational supervisory systems, represented by bishops, district superintendents, etc., are usually financed by direct quotas or by per capita charges against local churches; but specialized administration is largely attached, somewhat parasitically, to agencies originally designated to carry on more limited phases of benevolent work, and its cost is largely covered-in under "benevolent" administration.

No total accounting for all these factors of extra-parochial finances has ever been made for the American church at large, but the data at hand throw a certain light on typical aspects.

ASPECTS OF DENOMINATIONAL FINANCING

The chief urban spending agencies of the denominations are the city mission and extension societies. Thirty of these societies, well-distributed geographically and denominationally, have recently been studied. Their average expenditure in 1932 was approximately $80,000, or the cost of about eight average local churches. This figure was an increase of 162 per cent. over that of 1912, but a decrease of 36 per cent. over 1927.

The distribution of the combined expenditures of the thirty societies was as follows:

| Distribution of Expenditures | Per Cent. |
|---|---|
| Administration and Overhead | 24.5 |
| Home Mission Aid | 52.8 |
| Building Grants and Loans | 24.6 |
| Repayment of Loans and Mortgages | 6.1 |
| Transfer to Capital Account | 5.5 |
| Miscellaneous | 0.2 |

As compared with 1922, this distribution shows an increased proportion of the total going to administration and overhead, because reduced transactions represented by the smaller resources cannot immediately bring corresponding decreases in administration and because (as noted above) of added service functions charged to this account. Repayment of loans and mortgages have also increased, indicating the partial liquidation of debts after a building splurge. Building grants and loans have relatively decreased, while home-mission aid has remained most nearly stationary.

Where did the average city society get the $80,000 which it spent on its budget? An analysis of income shows the following division.

| Distribution of Income | Per Cent. |
|---|---|
| From denominational treasuries | 13.0 |
| From local churches | 37.2 |
| From individuals | 12.9 |
| From invested funds | 27.2 |
| From current bequests | 9.7 |

It will be noted that current receipts from local churches and individuals account for just about one-half of the total. Receipts from denominational treasuries have declined since 1922, while those from invested funds and bequests have considerably increased. These increases, however, were largely concentrated in one or two cities and denominations. Gifts from individuals have relatively declined; but this is quite intelligible in the light of the history of the city societies. Many of them were founded on individual initiative, in advance of denominational sentiment, and were at first carried on almost entirely by contributions from individual sources.

On the average, contributions to the maintenance of a denominational city society from all regular denominational sources equal 4.75 per cent. of the combined parochial expenditures of the churches of the denomination concerned, while total receipts, including income from outside of the local group, equal 8.50 per cent. of combined expenditures. When it is considered that a very appreciable part of the cost of administration and overhead goes into services directly benefiting the contributing churches, the extent to which they "share" resources with needier sister churches of the same denomination is scarcely conspicuous.

FINANCING LOCAL PROTESTANT PHILANTHROPIES

Almost complete ignorance exists as to the total cost of Protestant philanthropies, such as children's and old people's homes, hospitals and various other institutions. With most denominations, philanthropies of this kind are under no central system of supervision or accounting. As the last two chapters showed, the colossal present demands for material relief, coupled with sharp reductions in support, have greatly embarrassed the Protestant institutions, while the increasing of the part of the total philanthropic burden assumed by the state is greatly reducing the relative importance of the churches' part.

FINANCING THE NATIONAL DENOMINATIONAL AGENCIES

Much the largest proportion of denominational financial requirements on the national scale are for the support of vast systems of church expansion and maintenance which gather funds into central treasuries and disperse them to points of greatest need. Data covering the national home-mission societies of the denominations carrying the greater bulk of such work in the denomination have been analyzed for 1931-32. They account for expenditures of beyond twenty-seven million dollars. Slightly more than 10 per cent. of this went to church building loans, which will be repaid. The balance was used in current operations of some 30,000 missionary enterprises employing 27,000 paid workers.

The expenditure of this impressive total is divided as follows:

| Expenditures | | Per Cent. |
|---|---|---|
| Local home missionary enterprises................ | | 69 |
| Building loans.................................. | | 13 |
| Field services and supervisors................... | | 8.4 |
| Overhead: | | 9.6 |
| *Administration*...................... | *4.1* | |
| *Promotion*........................... | *4.3* | |
| *General*.............................. | *1.2* | |

The terms in which this account is rendered doubtless reflect the sensitiveness of donors concerning overhead costs. They isolate the item for field service and supervision, which is sometimes combined with overhead. This item stands for the costs of the intermediary supervisory agencies required by the state and regional organizations of the denominations, and for particular services rendered in local institutions by persons attached to central offices. Eighty-two per cent. of the total expenditure of these national agencies, however, goes directly to local enterprises, for their maintenance and for the salaries of resident workers.[6]

FINANCING BENEVOLENCE: SUBSIDIES TO LOCAL CHURCHES

Local church financing ordinarily distinguishes sharply between the cost of operating the local activities of the congregation and benevolent funds. The same distinction is carried out in the financial tables of the United States Census of Religious Bodies, which show approximately twenty cents of each dollar of Protestant receipts spent for benevolences and eighty cents for home expenses. Benevolences, in turn, are chiefly divided between home and foreign missions. As already noted, the chief object of the church's benevolent expenditure in the United States is assistance of the weak denominational church which is unable to support itself financially. This phase of financing requires special attention.

The exact number of subsidized churches in the United States is not known. From one-eighth to one-third of the churches of representative denominations of the strong and well-established type receive home-mission aid, the average being approximately 30 per cent., but multitudes of poor immigrant and Negro churches enjoy no such resources; neither do many churches of the newer and less well-established denominational groups. Consequently this ratio does not apply to the total. Important information has, however, been gathered concerning subsidies to rural and urban churches respectively, and this is now to be presented.

SUBSIDIES TO RURAL CHURCHES

One-fifth of the rural churches in 1930 benefited, at least indirectly, through the payment of a portion of the minister's salary by agencies of the denomination, either state, district or national. Such home-mission aid enables denominational churches to be kept open and operating that would otherwise have to be closed. In theory this money goes chiefly to work for economically disadvantaged communities or groups, such as the Eskimo, the Indian, the West Indian, the immigrant or the mountaineer. In practice much of it goes to the support of work in quite average open-country and village communities. Thus the matter of so-called home-mission aid enters into the comity relationships among Protestant denominations. That aspect will be discussed later in this chapter. Suffice it to say here that the decade from 1920 to 1930, and especially the period after 1924, saw an increase in the average grant per village church until it reached nearly $400; also an increase in the proportion of open-country churches aided, but a decline in the grant per church to $153. Taking all rural churches together the average

[6] Morse (Ed.), *op. cit.*, p. 19.

grant in 1930 was $275. The size of the grant and the proportion of churches aided varied, of course, from denomination to denomination, and according to the amount of competition in the community, from region to region. In all, Protestantism spent, in 1930, not less than $20,000,000 in such aid and quite probably as much as $25,000,000.

## SUBSIDIES TO URBAN CHURCHES

A recent study of nearly 1,000 urban churches found 15 per cent. of them receiving home-mission aid. The type of enterprises thus subsidized by denominational benevolences in cities and the outcome of such aid in terms of self-support are discovered by a study, in 1933, of the 1,404 projects aided by thirty-three mission and extension societies during the previous fifteen years. The results of this study are summarized in Table XI.

TABLE XI — DISTRIBUTION OF 1,404 AIDED PROJECTS OF 33 CITY EXTENSION SOCIETIES

| Types | Per Cent. Distribution 15-Year Period | Present | Per Cent. Still Receiving Aid |
|---|---|---|---|
| New churches, traditional type | 19 | 21 | 54 |
| Established churches unable to support themselves | 43 | 32 | 48 |
| Rehabilitation and adaptation | 5 | | |
| Foreign and racial enterprises | 22 | | |
|    Traditional churches..... *19* | | | |
|    Community centers, etc. ..... *3* | | 39 | 60 |
| New start to unsuccessful churches | 4 | | |
| Special departments or projects of otherwise self-supporting churches | 2 | | |
| Institutions, neighborhood houses, etc. | 5 | 8 | 85 |
| Total | 100 | 100 | 51 |

The types of enterprises represented by subsidized projects vary greatly from denomination to denomination and from city to city; but the composite picture as presented by this table brings out numerous points of general significance. While aid to new enterprises and established churches of conventional type has accounted for nearly two-thirds of the projects during the last fifteen years, the proportion of aided enterprises of these types at present is considerably reduced; that is to say, aid is being shifted from the support of merely weak churches to types of enterprises which give special attention to the needs of peculiar populations, or else to new types of projects. In short, expansion is diminishing and adaptation increasing.

The last column of the table shows what percentage of each type of enterprise aided during the fifteen years is still receiving aid at the end of the period. As would be expected, the largest proportion of continued dependency is found among the adapted and institutional churches. In the main, these lack natural supporting constituencies, and their maintenance is more or less a permanent responsibility of the denominational group. Churches of foreign antecedents also show relatively little progress toward self-support.

At worst, however, aid has been discontinued to 49 per cent. of the projects which required aid during the last fifteen years. In 63 per cent. of the cases of such discontinuance the financing of the work was undertaken locally, though often on a sub-standard level of expenditure. Eight per cent. of the time self-support was achieved through the merger of the aided churches with some other church. That is to say, an enterprise which, standing alone, was financially dependent became independent through a more effective combination of forces. Twenty-five per cent. of the previously aided enterprises died, and 2 per cent. were transferred to other denominations, which may or may not have continued aid.

This whole study of the subsidizing of urban churches mirrors the instability and flux of the local church in great cities, the wide-spread need of denominational aid, the very limited success in bringing subsidized churches to self-support, the accumulating burdens of denominations as they undertake more specialized forms of work, the need of highly critical scrutiny of the whole problem of subsidy, and the importance of a clear-cut interdenominational strategy such as may avoid duplicatory spending.[7]

NATIONAL HOME MISSIONS

Transferring attention from local denominational missions to those conducted by the national mission boards, it is important to note that church work of the conventional rural and urban type accounts for more than two-thirds of the 30,000 subsidized enterprises centrally accounted for, and that "mission" work of this type takes more than three-fourths of the money. The average grant in the pre-depression era was approximately $400. Such aid went chiefly to churches with fewer than 100 enterprises. Comparing rural and urban churches, four-fifths of all aided enterprises were rural and the average cost of the urban projects was more than two-fifths greater.

Schools, philanthropic institutions and community work are the most expensive types of missions, relatively speaking, since they require disproportionate numbers of paid workers as shown by Chart XXVII.

The more variant types of population in the United States, especially those racially separated from the major population, largely account for the remainder of the enterprises subsidized by national mission boards. These include Negroes, Indians, Orientals, Spanish-speaking populations both in the Caribbean area and in the continental southwest, Southern

---

[7] Hallenbeck, *Urban Organization of Protestantism* (New York: Harper and Brothers, 1934).

Mountaineers, together with work in Alaska and Hawaii. To a smaller degree the missions for urban populations of non-Protestant antecedents are also under national direction. The remoter a race is from American antecedents and from the Christian tradition, the more recent its immigration to this country and the more scattered it is, the more costly is mission service on its behalf. Thus the per capita cost of work for Indians is more than twice the average cost, while that for Orientals and Spanish-speaking populations is much beyond the average even of the entire handicapped group. On the other hand, per capita cost is very low for Negroes because they so largely do for themselves religiously. Among European immigrants,

CHART XXVII—DISTRIBUTION OF HOME MISSION ENTERPRISES BY TYPES, AND BY PAID
PERSONNEL

the evangelization of people of Roman Catholic antecedents is much more expensive than the evangelization of former Protestants. In representative denominations such work costs four times as much as the average aid required by the white American church.

GRANTS TO COMPETITIVE CHURCHES

On a large sampling of the churches of representative denominations subsidies were just about as frequent to communities where there are two or three or four other churches as to those where a denomination had the field to itself. Thus, of 1,245 aided churches investigated in Dr. Fry's study of Home Mission Aid, 220 were in two-church communities; 132 in three-church communities; and 200 in communities with four or more churches, that is 44 per cent. belonged to communities with more or less competitive situations. Of 343 in smaller villages of less than 1,000 population, 99 were in one-church communities; 202 in two-church communities and 106 in villages with three or more churches each. That is to say, three out of five of these aided churches in smaller communities were located where there was at least one other Protestant church in a diminutive community.

Of 137 aided churches investigated in a later village study, only seventeen were located where there were less than two churches per 1,000 inhabitants. Villages present the extreme situation; but it is conservatively calculated that from fourteen to eighteen million dollars annually is spent in competitive church situations. No sane person would argue that this expenditure is all in vain, or that denominational, parochial or institutional inefficiency can be abolished instantly. It is nevertheless important to count the cost of such doubtful luxuries if they are to be continued.

FINANCING FOREIGN MISSIONS

Nearly thirty million dollars were spent in 1929 in financing 12,485 Protestant foreign missionaries and their institutions in other countries. These figures recorded a four-fold increase in foreign-mission expenditures in twenty years. They were made possible only by an amazing post-war inflation of foreign-mission enterprises. The very drastic reduction of recent years, generally associated with the depression, may also in considerable degree be ascribed to a shifting viewpoint with respect to foreign missions. It is noteworthy, however, that the total reduction has not yet cut the support of foreign missions to a figure lower than would have been reached by a steady proportionate rise in financial support since the beginning of the present century. In brief, if the inflationary phase of the enterprise is ignored, the present basis of support is relatively normal.

FINANCING INTERDENOMINATIONAL WORK

The story of the financing of interdenominational work can be made exceedingly brief. Very little money goes into it. Church spending is usually and jealously confined to denominational hands. The average cost of a city church federation is only that of a single somewhat more than average church in a city. The predepression cost of the Federal Council of Churches was about $300,000 annually. The depression has halved this amount and has left only 14 per cent. of the support of this agency of all the churches coming from the central treasuries of the constituent denominations which compose the Council. The rest comes chiefly from interested individuals. However representative, therefore, the Council may be in the ecclesiastical sense, it is obviously not financially representative of the denominations which nominally coöperate in its support. All-told, the cost of interdenominational work constitutes a scarcely visible item within the local and national totals of religious spending.

FINANCIAL METHODS

In the last analysis local churches and their members have to support the vast fabric of extra-parochial enterprise just discussed as well as their own organizations and ministry. One of the most significant of recent changes in method is that this is increasingly done as the result of a single process of financial solicitation. Benevolence budgets are attached to local budgets and raised at the same time by means of an annual canvass. In a recent sampling of nearly 2,000 city churches, 78 per cent. reported the use of such an every-member canvass in their basic financial method. For rural churches in 1924-25 the per cent. was 67. Pledged subscribers under such method do not exceed 42 per cent. of the average urban church's adherents.

Within local churches considerable traces remain of the traditional distinction between "spiritual" and "worldly" or financial affairs. Different sets of officials frequently preside over the two interests. Again, within the realm of finance, women's agencies undertake the support of important special projects with somewhat jealously guarded budgets. Religious education is still chiefly financed by the pennies of Sunday-school children. In spite of attempted unification, competitive financial appeals within the same churches frequently result from the characteristically loose organizations depicted in chapter iii. Obviously, under a voluntary system of church support every separate item of the complicated structure and function of the more elaborate church of the present age involves its own costs; and these often have to be directly provided by the limited constituencies sharing any given interest.

The specialized boards of the church at large have their elaborate machinery of financial promotion and appeal; but increasingly denominations are centralizing the financial cultivations of their constituencies through systems of apportionment and assessment to local churches intended to cover the grand total of authorized projects in all fields of missions and philanthropy.

## Church Facilities

Churches have to have buildings to house the congregating activities which are the essential expression of their group-life, and under urban conditions to serve as centers of administration for their projective activities. The problem of providing facilities is complicated by the many and small local units into which the church is divided. Protestant attitudes of mind also influence the case. It is only one of the church's functions to be a shrine for the worship of God. For the rest it must house a variety of interests and so far as possible provide each with a modern equipment for convenience, safety and efficiency.

### CHURCH PLANTS

Before the deflation of real-estate values the combined values of the property of American churches was estimated at $7,000,000,000. The changed purchasing power of money and general financial uncertainty make any present valuation impossible; but it is still pertinent to note that the 1926 total, as reported by the Religious Census, was three times that of 1906 and twice that of 1916. At worst the American church is a great property owner. Local church buildings account for only a little more than half of the total valuations; parsonages, educational institutions, and philanthropies for most of the remainder.

In boom times church buildings afforded one of the most important lines for the construction trades. The gains reported by the Census were very little effected by rise in land values. In the main they represented cash investments. The amounts thus invested naturally varied considerably with the wealth of the community or region to which the church belonged, but had reached an average of $86.63 per church member.

The little white church of the rural village or prairies stands in striking contrast to the towering cathedral of the great cities. The latter costs far beyond the average city church plant. Nevertheless, the city average in 1926 was eight and one-half times the rural, and this difference is sufficiently striking to require separate tellings of the story for urban and rural churches.

## RURAL CHURCH PLANTS

The rural church has come a long way since the days when its pulpit was in the stern end of a prairie schooner or when, as in the days of the Hoosier Schoolmaster, the neighbors gathered in some more than usually commodious kitchen to listen to an itinerant circuit rider expound the Word.

The next step was the one-room building, usually of frame construction, designed for little else than the function of preaching. It was the counterpart of the one-room school and as ubiquitous. But it, too, is passing slowly. Barely one-fifth of the surviving rural churches, as against nearly one-third in 1920, are devoid of all other rooms but the auditorium; and most of these are in the South.

The church building, of course, represents both the architectural and denominational tradition of the congregation, and its ideas as to the functions of the church and the facilities that should be provided for performing these functions. The first three decades of the present century saw remarkable activity in church building, urban and rural. The investment in church edifices in places of less than 25,000 population practically doubled between 1916 and 1926, at which later date it stood at $72.07 per adult member. The strictly rural figure was $55.77. The boom in church building was nation-wide. The per member investment increased sharply in every state between 1916 and 1926, in thirty-seven states by more than

75 per cent. and in seventeen of these, twelve of them Southern, by more than 100 per cent. Between 1925 and 1930 there was a further increase of 20 per cent. in the value of rural church buildings. The per member valuation of about 1,000 village structures in the latter year was $94.80. Village churches on the average represented the considerable investment of $14,126. The regional averages were as high as $21,327 in the Middle Atlantic states. The country churches, excluding those for Negroes, averaged $4,603, or nearly $60 per member.

This burst of church building parallels a similar period of activity in school building, especially in villages. It is the more remarkable because, during the last ten years of the period between 1916 and 1930, gross farm income was lower than in the first five years; and the ratio of prices received by the farmer to those paid averaged 15 per cent. below the pre-war parity, instead of 5 per cent. above as it had in the five years prior to 1921. Then, too, the 1920's were a period when taxes doubled and when more than 6,000 rural banks failed, inconveniencing some 7,000,000 depositors.

The explanation of this phenomenon is not easy. Pride, denominational pressure, enthusiastic salesmanship by ministers, played their part. But basically perhaps the reason for plant-expansions was that rural America had developed new ideas about the facilities a church should have. The improvement in educational methods and especially in school buildings revealed how inadequate were the provisions for religious education. The greater emphasis on beauty in worship accentuated the barrenness of the crude, single-cell country church. The pressure for community service facilities was a natural outgrowth of the assumption of responsibility for such service by many churches. Moreover, rural people traveled more and saw buildings such as they envied in the towns and cities. The new buildings, therefore, seldom had less than five rooms and, especially in towns and villages, often possessed as many as a score.

The results were not always financially happy. Indebtedness considerably more than tripled, and while the total rural per member debt of $3.43, or the combined city and country debt of $6.38, in 1926, does not appear appalling, it may not only have been underestimated, but it had certainly increased by 1930. Communities have been surveyed where the church debt per *inhabitant* was in excess of $100 and in many places the debt exceeded $50 for each adult church-member.

URBAN CHURCH PLANTS

The average urban church building in 1926 was worth $53,000. This average overstates the really characteristic value. The more fragmentary type, described in chapter vii, ran some 25 per cent. below the average, while the highly and socially adapted type had buildings worth three or four times as much as the average.  The average city church seats 450 to 500 worshippers.  Forty-one per cent. have from five to nine rooms.  Over 15 per cent. have fewer than five and nearly 10 per cent. more than thirty rooms each.  These naturally include the highly developed and socially adapted churches with numerous Sunday-school classes and clubs, the variety of whose interests and activities makes extensive space demands.

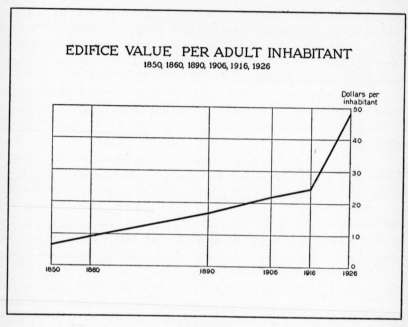

EDIFICE VALUE  PER ADULT INHABITANT
1850, 1860, 1890, 1906, 1916, 1926

CHART XXVIII

This means, of course, that church buildings have to be evaluated according to the extent and type of activity they house.  Aesthetic evaluation cannot be reduced to laws.  The church must fittingly symbolize the religious values for which it stands.  On the other hand, in such matters as construction and proper equipment with reference to safety, proper equipment as to light, heat and ventilation, and general adequacy and convenience, legal requirements for public buildings and score-card methods developed by students of public-school architecture furnish directly applicable standards.  The well-known Malden survey of church buildings showed how terribly deficient with reference to these standards were most of the churches in a representative middle-class suburb.[8]  The buildings

[8] Athearn, *Malden Survey* (Inter-church World Movement).

of some two dozen large city churches, with aggregate constituencies approximating 50,000, scored on the average less than 50 per cent. on the standard scale. Instead of these technical methods of evaluation other surveys have merely used common-sense observation. These indicate, for example, that a large fourth of the buildings of Negro city churches are in a definitely disreputable condition.

It must be recalled that the churches represent a very important type of public building. Recent improvements in lighting, ventilation and service systems are rapidly incorporated into public buildings of other types. Many of the churches are carrying on types of activities for which the original structures were never intended. New ideals of the requirements of religious education make demands upon older church plants which many otherwise expensive structures cannot meet. All told, a vast number of church plants need to be modernized in order to keep the church abreast with its own progress and that of the age. Unfortunately, many serious difficulties with plants cannot be remedied without additional land and without the erection of secondary structures in harmony with the rather exacting architectural line of the originals.

Data already presented have shown a vast recent increase in church expenditures. With this, as has been noted, went a building boom in the flush times ending with 1929. The receding wave has left many churches with building debts. The results of a recent questionnaire covering nearly 1,000 city churches shows that the burden of debt is much more frequently reported as a handicap than is lack of facilities. This judgment may represent the headache that comes after a spree.

No up-to-date figures as to debt are available. That of 1926, however, was relatively three times that of 1906, and nearly twice that of 1916, reaching an amount of $6.38 per member in cities of 25,000 population and over. The study of 1,000 city churches, mentioned above, showed that eighty-four had had building grants from their denominations during the last ten years and 142 building loans. About two-thirds of the grants were for over $10,000 each and of these more than two-thirds were over $5,000. The most frequent loan was also less than $5,000 although loans of from $5,000 to $10,000 were almost as frequent. The rate of debt increase was, however, less in the large cities than in towns and rural communities.

These figures throw no light upon the number of churches whose debt is represented exclusively by commercial loans, but many denominational treasuries have been seriously embarrassed by the failure of churches to repay loans counted upon to restore revolving funds. In fact the church property situation is a very fair reflection of the general property situation of the nation.

Probably the situation is worst of all with Negro churches. In 1926 they had an average property value of only about one-third as much as the churches generally. Negro investments in urban churches had reached the relatively high figure of $5 per member according to studies in 1930. This involved a debt load considerably above that suffered by any other group of churches.

Sixty-three per cent. of the churches studied were in debt, compared with 22 per cent. of churches in the nation at large; and the debt load had reached $18.66 per member. Debt covered 33 per cent. of the value of the average Negro church property compared with only 11 per cent. for the country at large. The extraordinary exigence of this situation was registered in the fact that debt service, including payments on interest and principle, absorbed nearly one-fourth of the current resources of these churches and that they had an average prospect of thirteen years of heavy financial bondage ahead of them before they could hope to free their properties from debt. No similar group of churches have ever faced such a staggering financial handicap.

RURAL AND URBAN WORKING FACILITIES

The facilities of the rural church are mostly in the rural church building. They have somewhat improved with its improvement.

A multitude of rural churches, nevertheless, have virtually no facilities beyond the parlor organ and a few Sunday-school papers. The only office equipment is such as the minister himself supplies, and thousands of non-resident ministers carry their office around under their hats. The occasional rural minister gets some allowance for automobile maintenance.

The equipment of the more complex and larger institutions, such as the average urban church represents, naturally involves more facilities. On a standard list of twenty-eight facilities, however, from five to ten was the number most frequently possessed by 500 city churches sampled. The typical church thus had only from a fifth to a third of the tools and arrangements presumed to constitute an efficient modern equipment. Larger and more highly developed churches characteristically enjoyed three or four times as varied a range of facilities as the average. This is simply to say that the physical equipment of the broader ministries undertaken by highly developed urban churches has to be more extensive to match their more numerous staffs and greater operating expenditures.

The most recent study of urban churches' equipment shows, for example, 68 per cent. of the churches reporting outside bulletin boards, 63 per cent. weekly calendars or bulletins of church events, 37 per cent. mimeographs.

Churches which centralize their projective functions, that is to say which increasingly bring people to them for pastoral ministries rather than going out to find the people, must have facilities for reception and consultation.

Again, churches which maintain elaborate departmental organizations have to have facilities to go with their specialized projects of recreation and social service.

The facilities even of large city churches do not always supply reasonable conditions of labor to employed workers. Church architecture, which expresses the worship tradition, is distinctly at war with modern working facilities. One can find a good many $10,000 ministers using offices whose lighting, heating and ventilating arrangements would not be imposed by secular industry upon a $15 a week clerk.

### FINANCIAL PROBLEMS

This review of church finances and facilities throws into relief a number of problems which dovetail closely into other issues of the church's life.

Most general of all is the problem of how to get the church supported under a voluntary system. The effort at religious motivation has generally taken form under some sort of doctrine of "stewardship," in which a religious man's money is recognized as belonging to God. God has the first claim upon wealth as well as upon life. Something is, nevertheless, lacking in ethical insight when one passes from this concept to the assumption that the church is a preferred creditor among the constructive and idealistic objectives of expenditure. As in all other ethical realms, goods are competitive: and, for any given time or situation, decision as to the greatest good, as it relates to wealth, has all the inherent difficulty of any other concrete ethical decision.

Another problem concerns the importance of finances and facilities in making the church successful. As chapter xi will show, the success of a given church as an institution varies pretty exactly with the wealth of its constituency. One of the great reasons why churches fail and die is that they cannot get money enough to support them. On the other hand, an artificial supplying of money to a church which lacks other factors of vitality is not generally effective, and as already noted, churches more often complain of being embarrassed by debt than by lack of facilities. At worst however debts on church property equal only eleven per cent. of its reported value in 1933. Suppose this value was twice too high—church property would still be far more nearly in the clear than American farms or American homes.

Financial efficiency, like all functional efficiency of the churches in its more basic aspects, is greatly affected by the size of the unit of organization. Larger churches would be less expensive as well as more effective.

When the future support of the organized Christian enterprise is considered it is fair to ask to what extent a juster social order would reduce the church's financial burden, particularly in the field of philanthropy.

For the state, however, to have the means of doing justice, it is increasingly recognized as a question whether churches should continue to be exempt from taxation. Besides possibly being more equitable, might not their taxation make for efficiency, in that it would reduce the number of over-small churches?

There is a perennial conflict between the method of church financing which consists in "putting over" a high-pressure campaign and that which creates and cultivates permanent interest in the values of the church. The former can be but a makeshift; while the latter, relative to the wealth of the constituency, assures the church as much support as it can prove itself to be worth.

The question, "What is money for?" is answered differently in every generation. The re-thinking of church finances is consequently a continual challenge to its supporters, as a phase of the continuous re-appraisal of the significance of the church as a vehicle of human aspiration and purpose.

PART THREE

CONDITIONING FACTORS

# CHAPTER XI

## *Environmental Conditioning of the Church*

This chapter marks the transition from studies of the church's institutional aspects and processes to three chapters that deal with factors of the larger situation which conspicuously condition the church's life as an institution. Constituencies, organization, leadership and finance—all these aspects of religious societies have been successively described as though the institution stood by itself. But every one of these aspects is dependent upon the church's relationship to those larger conditioning factors whose power determines whether or not the church's institutional labors shall be in vain. Three of these factors are to be considered.

The first is the concrete social situation which immediately surrounds the local church as an individual unit of religious organization. The quality and changes of this environment are almost inevitably communicated to the church. Differences in human fortunes suffered by the church's immediate constituencies and changes in these fortunes due to changes in the environment largely control the institutional destinies of each particular church. Where the environment is prosperous and progressive the church can scarcely fail to "succeed." Where it is miserable and deteriorating the church can scarcely avoid failure.

The church is conditioned, in the second place, by the fact of its division into denominations and sects, and by the alternations of divisive or integrative tendencies from epoch to epoch. It is only when integrative tendencies are uppermost that it is strictly justifiable to speak of the church as a unit. Otherwise the story is one of competitive churches pulling in opposite directions. The significance for civilization both of the denominational groups and of the local units (each in its environmental setting) is very different when they pull together from what it is when they pull apart, especially when they incline to get together in permanent units.

The church is also conditioned in important ways by the intellectual and religious climate of an age. Its institutional outlook ebbs and flows with fluctuations in the depth of meanings read into its forms and behaviors. If these meanings are profound the church is borne up on wings of faith; when they fail or decline it is correspondingly depressed. The sense of values behind the church creates the climate of its organized life. When there is reality and self-validating power within, the institution fares well;

when motivation fades it fares poorly. The church is now to be observed in the grip of these dominant forces. The present chapter concerns its environmental conditioning.

## ENVIRONMENTAL CONDITIONING

All institutions are ultimately interdependent and are affected by basic conditions arising in their common social environment, defined as the sum of the outward influences which directly affect group life.

Throughout previous chapters environmental differences between urban and rural types of civilization have been observed as they concern the church. In a very profound sense the characteristic mode of life and the means of livelihood employed by a population registers itself in any cultural institution which such a population develops. Usually the effects of these differences as between urban and rural communities have been objectively demonstrable.

More refined environmental differences appear as a result of regional comparisons, some of which were suggested in chapter iv. The different sections of the nation have had different historic backgrounds and characteristic ways of making livings. They differ considerably in wealth, and largely in biological and racial inheritance. Within the larger unity of the nation's mind, they show noteworthy varieties in their outlooks upon life. At only a few points do the data exist for measuring differences of this sort. Some of these are briefly noted in the following paragraphs—first regionally and as bearing upon the churches, then separately, for rural and for urban churches respectively.

Obviously the determinative power of environment lies largely in the degree and rapidity of its changes. The most crucial of environmental facts is that modern social changes are so many and so great and that they come so fast as to put unparalleled stress upon the church today. Consequently the following paragraphs will emphasize the results of social change as well as pointing out correspondences between present churches and their present environments.

## REGIONALISM

In order show the environmental effect upon local churches of the section of the country in which they are located, it is necessary to define and identify the regions. In order to have sociological validity the divisions adopted should indicate areas in which common social characteristics are found in contrast with those of other areas.

The regions thus identified will obviously vary according to the principle of classification adopted. Thus, for example, the United States Department of Agriculture divides the country into twelve so-called crop areas. The

Federal Reserve System and other credit institutions recognize twelve somewhat different financial districts. A more recent sociological development offers the concept of "metropolitan regionalism." "The larger cities of the country are becoming regionally conscious," and increasingly seek to delimit and understand their relationship to adjacent territory both in terms of function and of proximity.[1] Regionalism of this type is important and furnishes numerous fresh and valid insights into the relations of environment and institutions.

The most extensive data bearing on the church, however, is available only in terms of counties, states and larger census divisions. Consequently in building up the regional comparisons of the Institute's studies these have chiefly been used.[2] Combinations of census divisions, as for example, of the East and West North Central areas to constitute the "Middle West," have often been resorted to. On the other hand, the Institute has also frequently sub-divided regions and built up its understanding of smaller areas in terms of county data irrespective of state divisions. It was thus able to identify 250 counties in the Southern Appalachians as constituting a "mountain" province for the purpose of separate local studies.

All such broad classifications have validity for special purposes and are useful in the breaking up of national averages and trends into more exact terms. Their long-term importance is further demonstrated by the persistence of regional traits in American history. It is, for example, self-evident that New England, settled as it was and by whom it was, none too blest with good soil nor by a soft and kindly climate, would develop a different social organization from that of the South, with its far longer and warmer growing season, its agriculture which almost from the first struggled for a place in the world market, its huge land holdings, and hence its advantage from Negro labor. Soil, natural resources, topography, climate, vary fundamentally among the regions and greatly condition them. Agricultural, industrial and general economic trends play their part. Historical factors of major importance enter in and finally merge into the social temper of the sections. These last two include the influences of such crucial episodes as give character to social development. They may include war, as in the case of the South. But they are more concerned with the streams of migration which leave their cultural deposits, with racial groups and the composition of population, with dominant political alignments or religions.

---

[1] McKenzie, chapter ix of *Recent Social Trends* (New York: McGraw-Hill Company, 1933), pp. 451-461.

[2] The census divisions are as follows: New England, Middle Atlantic, East North Central, West North Central, South Atlantic, East South Central, West South Central, Mountain, Pacific.

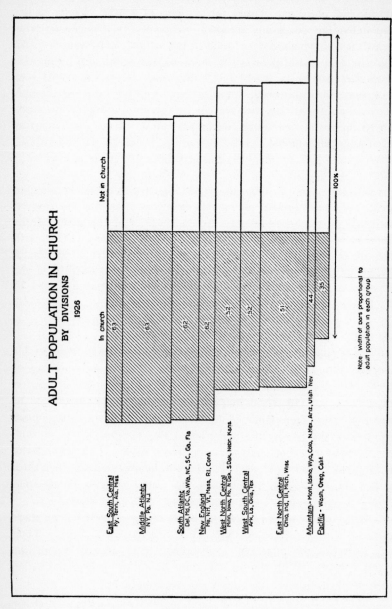

CHART XXIX—ADULT POPULATION IN CHURCH, BY DIVISIONS, 1926

## Particular Regional Comparisons

It is impossible, of course, within the confines of a brief chapter to describe and defend in detail any comparative set of regional characterizaions, even those for which data is found in the United States census. The proofs must be discovered in the census volumes themselves and in libraries of volumes that deal with regional characteristics. It is impossible also o indicate with these limits of space the many ways in which church phenomena vary significantly with regions or divisions. Only a few illustrations, with here and there suggested interpretation of such variations as are noted, can be attempted.

### PROPORTION OF POPULATION AFFILIATED WITH THE CHURCHES

Of first importance is the way the proportion of population enrolled in he church varies according to region. In this particular the area covered by the original thirteen colonies rates highest, with more than three-fifths of its adults as church-members. The middle-western states come next, with about one-half of the adults counted as in the church. The proportion in the far-western regions is sharply lower, with only about two-fifths of the adult population in church. These differences are shown graphically in Chart XXIX.

### EFFECT OF GROWTH AND MOBILITY OF POPULATION

Viewed from this angle the most determinative factors demonstrable from existing census data, are those of rate of increase and mobility of population. The more mobile the population the smaller the proportion of church-members. The seven states reporting the largest proportion of adult population in affiliation with the church had increased their populations but 39.27 per cent. between 1900 and 1920, and only 12.5 per cent. of their inhabitants in 1920 was born in other states. The seven states with the smallest proportion of the population in the church had grown three times as fast and received proportionately four times as many people from other states. These tendencies are revealed graphically in Chart XXX.[3]

This showing tends to take the mystery out of the fact that some states and regions of the nation are distinctly more religious than others. Their inequality proves to be primarily a phenomenon of unequal population growth and stability. With the more rapidly changing parts of the nation the church as an institution has simply not yet caught up.

On the other hand, with the more stable populations of the eastern seaboard, traditional loyalty to the church, like other social traditions, has

---

[3] May, *The Education of American Ministers*, Vol. II, p. 231.

been relatively little disturbed.   In the states of the northern Atlantic seaboard the influx of Catholic immigrants has also helped to swell total
church enrollment.   In the newer areas, with low population density, mere
survival was at first the primary consideration.   Their early settlements,

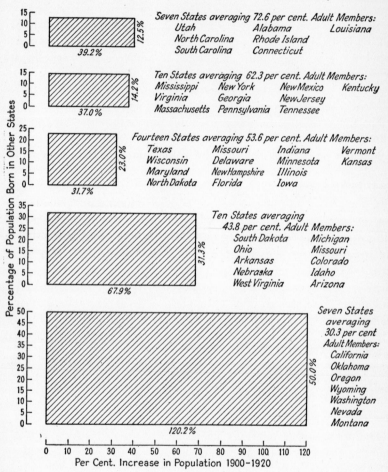

Seven States averaging 72.6 per cent. Adult Members:
Utah            Alabama         Louisiana
North Carolina  Rhode Island
South Carolina  Connecticut

Ten States averaging 62.3 per cent. Adult Members:
Mississippi   New York      New Mexico   Kentucky
Virginia      Georgia       New Jersey
Massachusetts Pennsylvania  Tennessee

Fourteen States averaging 53.6 per cent. Adult Members:
Texas         Missouri      Indiana      Vermont
Wisconsin     Delaware      Minnesota    Kansas
Maryland      New Hampshire Illinois
North Dakota  Florida       Iowa

Ten States averaging
43.8 per cent. Adult Members:
South Dakota   Michigan
Ohio           Missouri
Arkansas       Colorado
Nebraska       Idaho
West Virginia  Arizona

Seven States
averaging
30.3 per cent
Adult Members:
California
Oklahoma
Oregon
Wyoming
Washington
Nevada
Montana

Percentage of Population Born in Other States

Per Cent. Increase in Population 1900–1920

CHART XXX—INFLUENCE OF MOBILITY OF POPULATION ON MEMBERSHIP IN THE
STATES

unlike those of New England, involved no religious motive.   The break
with the ways of older communities was consequently extreme.   It took
time to build social institutions, including churches.

In addition, in the new and sparsely settled areas of the Farther West,
the low density of population made it difficult to find sufficiently large
groups of people, living near enough to a common center, to furnish either

the funds or the time necessary for carrying religious life through organized churches. Thus, where population density is less than two to the square mile the ratio of church-membership to total population is barely one-fourth. With between two and six persons to the square mile the church-membership ratio rises to nearly one-third, and so on. Within regions, moreover, sections or areas handicapped by poor soil, lack of rainfall, or other disadvantages that compel a lower than average density of population and a below average income, almost invariably make for a lower than average enrollment in the churches.

SEX RATIOS IN CHURCH AFFILIATION

The proportion of the sexes in church similarly varies by regions, with adult females always showing more loyalty to the church than males. This is equally true of rural and urban areas within a region.

INACTIVE MEMBERS

In the matter of the proportion of church-members who are inactive, that is, who no longer attend or contribute to the church, but who are still carried on its books, the regional differences so far as the rural churches are concerned are sharp. The regions follow conspicuously different patterns. The South carries almost twice as high a proportion of inactive members (30 per cent.) on its rural church rolls as do the other regions, and three times the proportion found in the Middle West. The South leads also in the proportion of non-resident members, as noted in chapter iii. This may be caused by the lower proportion of trained ministers in the South, the larger number of churches served per minister, the greater reliance upon emotionalism to procure members, and the consequent relative minimizing of education for church-membership.

EDUCATION OF MINISTERS

The proportion of ministers who have had the full college and seminary training varies also with the various regions, as Chart XXXI shows.

Some of the reasons for these differences have already been indicated in chapter vi. The situation is rooted in the tradition, both of the population and of the principal denominations, in unequal ability to support trained ministers, and in unequal degrees of supervision and staffing by national denominational boards of missions. The last-named influence shows up especially in the far-western regions; the first three particularly affect the New England and Middle Atlantic areas. Denominational tradition helps the Middle West, where the Lutheran bodies, especially strong in some rural sections, hold to a high level of educational requirements

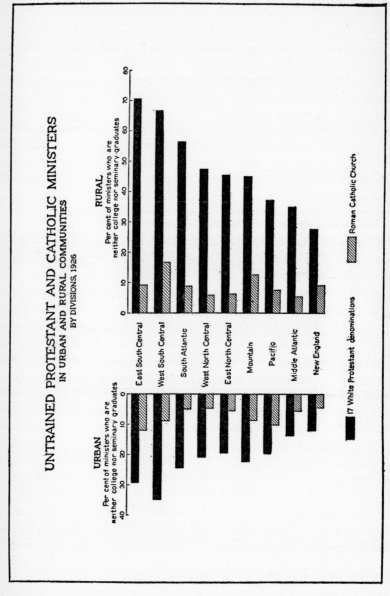

UNTRAINED PROTESTANT AND CATHOLIC MINISTERS
IN URBAN AND RURAL COMMUNITIES
BY DIVISIONS, 1926

RURAL

Per cent of ministers who are
neither college nor seminary graduates

URBAN

Per cent of ministers who are
neither college nor seminary graduates

East South Central
West South Central
South Atlantic
West North Central
East North Central
Mountain
Pacific
Middle Atlantic
New England

17 White Protestant denominations        Roman Catholic Church

CHART XXXI

for their ministers, and perhaps enforce them better than do some other denominations.

CHURCH SUPPORT

The problem of the support of a trained ministry raises the question of per capita giving. Here regional differences are much sharper in rural than in urban territory and are directly related, as shown elsewhere, to the level of income. Chart XXXII summarizes the situation.

The problem of supporting trained ministers, acute everywhere, as shown in chapter vi, is clearly most difficult in the South. Here, especially in rural areas, average salaries are lower than elsewhere and resident ministers fewer. Here, too, ministers supplement their incomes by engaging in other occupations. In the Far West, where the second lowest average salaries are paid, the second highest proportion of rural ministers with other occupations is found.

RATIO OF CHURCH ORGANIZATIONS TO POPULATION

It is interesting to note, however, that though the South ranks the lowest in per member contributions and average salaries, its rural areas indulge in more churches for every 1,000 people than any other region. This is partly because Negroes and whites maintain separate churches; partly because of the emphasis on denominational differences, and the consequent relative lack of coöperation; partly because roads are poorer and the proportion of rural families owning automobiles lower than in other regions. Town and country differences are also more noticeable in this region.

On the other hand, in the middle- and far-western regions, where town-and-country relations are relatively well-developed, where rural social life is centering more and more in the villages and towns, and where roads are good, the proportion of village and town church-membership coming from the open-country hinterlands of such centers is higher than in any other region.

Enough evidence has now been presented to show the inaccuracy of generalizations about church life and procedures when drawn exclusively on a national scale. The regional view corrects this picture and adds to its understanding many important items.

ENVIRONMENTAL CONDITIONING OF LOCAL CHURCHES

Many surveys have brought conclusive evidence of the effects of immediate environmental conditions upon various aspects of the local church. The most significant of these conditionings is perhaps found in the nature

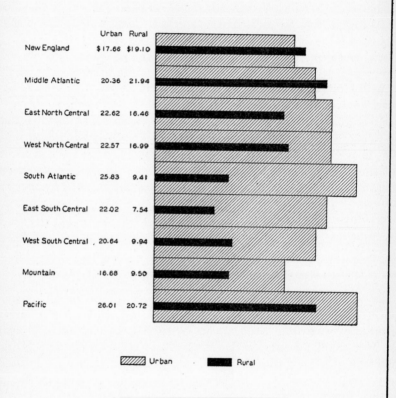

URBAN AND RURAL CHURCH EXPENDITURES
PER ADULT MEMBER BY DIVISIONS
1926

| | Urban | Rural |
|---|---|---|
| New England | $17.66 | $19.10 |
| Middle Atlantic | 20.36 | 21.94 |
| East North Central | 22.62 | 16.46 |
| West North Central | 22.57 | 16.99 |
| South Atlantic | 25.83 | 9.41 |
| East South Central | 22.02 | 7.54 |
| West South Central | 20.64 | 9.94 |
| Mountain | 16.68 | 9.50 |
| Pacific | 26.01 | 20.72 |

Urban    Rural

CHART XXXII

of the adjacent population. May[4] concludes that this is the most important single factor in the determination of the life or death of the city church. Homes owned free of debt also correlate with the church's organizational strength. The church, in other words, prospers most where the population is anchored to the locality by a stake in the land. Composition of population is also a factor of importance. The higher the ratio of men to women in cities or villages, the lower the proportion of the population attached to the church. Not all factors affect the church equally. Illiteracy seems quite positively to go with church-membership in city and state units; but a literate population makes for a church of greater financial strength than an illiterate one. Mobility of population, too, while detrimental to the church, affects membership far more adversely than it does finances, and is not an important factor in villages.

It is, moreover, not safe to conclude that the church is affected to the same degree as other institutions by all environmental factors. For example, a number of items that measure school prosperity fail to show significant correlations with church strength, among the reasons probably being the fact that, through state educational board requirements and state financial aid to local districts, the school has become a far more standardized institution than the church. Educational opportunity, while still unequally distributed among communities, and responsive to some environmental influences, is at least more democratically distributed than religious opportunity. On the other hand, the church is somewhat less affected by especially adverse environmental conditions than is the case with the vast variety of local social organizations; such as lodges, chambers of commerce, community clubs and the like.

### Environmental Conditioning of Rural Churches

Just as social institutions respond in different degrees to environmental influences, so the rural churches, village and open-country, are often affected in different ways from city churches by similar environmental conditions. Dr. May found, for instance, that the factor of home ownership is far more important to the city than to the village church, though many rural studies have shown that so far as the open-country church is concerned the proportion of farms operated by owners is a factor of great importance. The higher this percentage the more stable is the church.

The influence of environment on institutionalized religion is a fascinating and an important study, too little pursued by denominational administrators. Failure to take such influences into account explains in part, for

---

[4] Throughout this chapter references to May's study concern his *The Education of American Ministers* (New York: Institute of Social and Religious Research, 1934), Vol. II, chapter x and Vol. IV, Appendix B, Tables 28-49.

248 *The Protestant Church as a Social Institution*

instance, why so many larger parishes have failed, why city churches often move locations or perish where their neighborhoods change, why churches of equal numerical strength respond unequally to quotas or stereotyped programs.

The Institute from its inception has explored this field of inquiry, especially in the rural areas. It has shown the high correlation between farm values and per capita giving, between household wealth and benevolence offerings, and other similar relationships. Dr. May's low correlation between assessed valuations and various indices of church strength merely proves that the untoward conditions of the depression have destroyed the value of this particular index. This is shown by the following summary of a study made at the same time as May's, in which village retail sales, as determined by the 1930 U. S. Census of Distribution, were taken as the index. It is selected here, from a considerable mass of data, as the simplest and briefest illustration of environmental influences on one factor of church strength, namely giving.

Where the per capita retail sales in the village amounted to less than $200 a year the average per-member contributions to the churches were only $9.84. The remaining data followed in tabular form:

| Sales | Contributions |
|---|---|
| $200 to $300 | $13.05 |
| $300 to $400 | 14.48 |
| $400 to $500 | 18.38 |
| Over $500 | 16.92 |

The decline when sales passed $500 per person checks with many other similar results obtained by using different measuring rods. It is probably an index of the highly stereotyped program of the rural church. It is an institution that does not know how to exist without at least the fractional time of a minister and a place to meet. When, however, it has achieved a dignified and well-equipped edifice, a full-time minister, with perhaps an assistant, and a better than average program measured in terms of what churches are known usually to do, it has no item that calls for more money, save benevolences. Churches are larger in wealthier communities. The per capita cost consequently declines. It is in such areas that the surplus available for benevolences goes into county-wide social and socio-religious agencies with paid executives. Unless they are subsidized from the outside, it is only in such wealthier areas that such agencies are found.

URBAN ENVIRONMENTAL CONDITIONING

National social planning now contemplates wholesale removals of population from vast areas of non-productive and marginal land and its relocation in larger units of settlements accessible to all the resources of modern civilization. At present people are scattered in very uneconomic fashion over the territory of the nation, without reasonable chance to make a livelihood and with many of the advantages of life inaccessible to them. So long as the present conditions continue there must be churches for scattered people; but they will be condemned to share the ill-fortune of those whom they serve. Even on good land and with rural population of average density, strong traditional attachment to the denominational neighborhood church makes an efficient planning of rural religious organization difficult.

The case of the city church is different. Cities have already brought a higher proportion of their populations into church affiliation than the country has and have developed a more adequate type of institution. Current ideals of city planning are immediately applicable to the urban church's situation. There are enough people and resources to provide all urban populations with good churches of their own sort, made easily accessible by use of transit facilities. In other words, it is entirely possible to reach on paper a solution of the problem of churching the city. Consequently, it is all the more urgent that the church understand cities and their changes, and know how to meet them.

A STUDY OF URBAN ENVIRONMENTAL CHANGES

An elaborate study of the effect of urban environmental changes upon the church was published by the Institute in 1932. It was based upon information concerning nearly 2,000 churches of forty-seven denominations located in typical sectors of sixteen cities with over 100,000 population each. The sector method was used in order to secure a complete cross-sectional sample of population and institutions without studying entire cities. Starting with the city center it reached through all concentric urban zones to the suburban outskirts.[5]

MEASUREMENT OF CHURCH PROGRESS

The progress over the previous decade of some 2,000 churches of the sixteen cities was then studied and measured in terms of three familiar and available institutional criteria; namely, church-membership, Sunday-school enrollment, and financial expenditures. Rates of increase or decrease on these three points were calculated for each church.

The results of these studies have already been presented under the topics to which they related.[6] Their results for the total body of churches studied are summarized in Charts XXXIII and XXXIV. About two-thirds of the

---

[5] The cities studied were as follows: New York, Chicago, Philadelphia, Detroit, Los Angeles, Cleveland, St. Louis, Pittsburgh, Washington, Minneapolis, Cincinnati, Indianapolis, Rochester, Springfield, Mass., Albany, N. Y., and Wichita, Kansas. Three of the smaller ones were studied as wholes instead of by sectors.

[6] See pp. 53 and 209.

churches increased in membership, most of them by more than 25 per cent. for the decade; but on the other hand only one-half of the Sunday schools

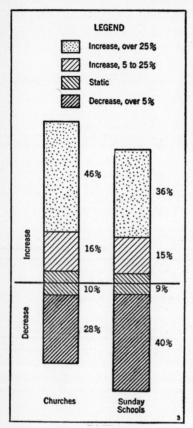
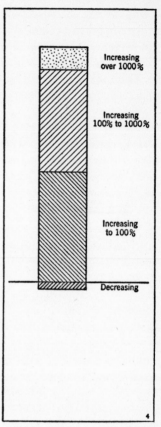

CHART XXXIII—PERCENTAGE OF CHURCHES AND SUNDAY SCHOOLS INCREASING OR DECREASING AT CERTAIN SPECIFIED RATES DURING THE DECADE STUDIED

CHART XXXIV — PERCENTAGE OF CHURCHES INCREASING OR DECREASING IN TOTAL EXPENDITURES AT CERTAIN SPECIFIED RATES DURING THE DECADE STUDIED

increased and at a slower rate. On the contrary, nearly all churches increased financially if they managed to live at all.

RELATION OF CHURCH FORTUNES TO ENVIRONMENT

Had environment anything to do with these varying rates of growth or decline? In the common-sense understanding of the case, obviously yes. This was confirmed by direct testimony taken from nearly 1,000 of the 2,000 churches. Typical stories of churches' failure run thus: "Our people are moving away. Jews and Negroes are moving in. Our property values are declining. Our financial support is diminishing." The contrasting stories of prosperity are not so spontaneously told because a church likes to believe that its own virtues are responsible for its successes rather than its environment. However, as the story of success is deduced from questionnaires, it runs: "There is a rapid growth of population in our vicinity of people of our sort. Our area is restricted by social standards and zoning laws against undesirable elements. Our financial support is increasing."

MEASUREMENT OF ENVIRONMENTAL TRENDS

At the risk, then, of merely proving the obvious the Institute's study next went on to an actual measurement of the trends of environmental change in the areas occupied by the 2,000 churches. From the sixteen city-sectors, 317 homogeneous survey districts were carved out. Proof of social homogeneity in the case of any particular urban area was made possible by the fact that the Federal Census gathers information in terms of small census tracts of a few blocks each and that many cities have gathered supplemental social data in terms of the same areas. As a result, it is now possible to demonstrate the degree of social similarity within any given group of census tracts on a considerable number of points and to measure their difference from adjoining or remote areas.

In the study in question, 317 survey districts in the sixteen cities were painstakingly compared according to eight factors of social change, namely: (1) population—increase or decrease; (2) elements likely to affiliate with white Protestant churches—increase or decrease; (3) economic status of population—improvement or deterioration; (4) desirability of residence—increase or decrease; (5) the transient elements of population—increase or decrease; (7) juvenile delinquency—increase or decrease; (8) health conditions—improvement or deterioration.

Each of the above factors considered by itself alone showed important bearing upon the fortunes of the churches whose people are affected by it. The distinctive method of the study was, however, to combine all eight factors into a single criterion of social tendency and to classify the 317 survey districts accordingly into four groups, namely, those showing respectively (1) the best, (2) above average, (3) below average and (4) most social trends.

CORRELATION OF CHURCH GROWTH WITH ENVIRONMENTAL TRENDS

The three criteria of church progress were similarly combined into a single test and churches grouped in five classes as: (1) most progressive, (2) progressive, (3) stationary, (4) declining, and (5) rapidly declining. When the five rates of progress indicated by these terms were calculated for the churches located in each type of territory as measured by its social trends, overwhelming evidence of correlation between church fortunes and environment appeared. Thus, in the best territory, socially speaking, 83 per cent. of churches gained in membership—in the worst only 52 per cent. In the best territory 67 per cent. gained at a much more than average rate, in the

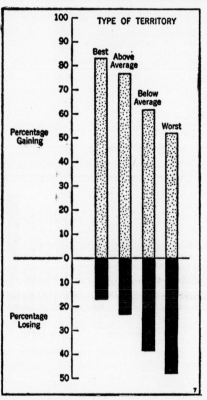

CHART XXXV—PERCENTAGE OF CHURCHES GAINING AND LOSING IN CHURCH-MEMBER-
SHIP IN EACH TYPE OF TERRITORY

worst only 21 per cent. These contrasts are shown graphically in Chart XXXV. Chart XXXVI shows in greater detail how many churches experienced each given rate of growth or decline in each type of territory.

The conclusion was clear and categorical: where one church is failing nearly all others are, because subjected to the downward pull of the common environment. On the contrary, where one church is gaining nearly all others are, because the common environment is on the side of all.

EXCEPTIONS

While approximately two-thirds of all the churches studied followed this rule, one-third did not. Close examination of these cases revealed, first, that many churches are not closely identified with their immediate localities. As shown in chapter iv, large populations will go almost indefinite distances to find churches to their liking, and these city-wide churches are not dependent upon the particular type of population immediately surrounding them for their constituencies or support.

The second explanation of exceptions is found in the spotty character of the so-called homogeneous areas. A number of contiguous city blocks

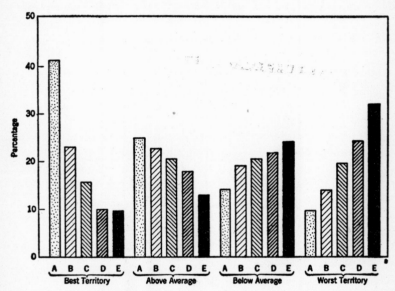

CHART XXXVI—DISTRIBUTION OF CHURCHES SHOWING FIVE DEGREES OF PROGRESS (A TO E) ACCORDING TO TYPES OF TERRITORY

constituting a recognized district and occupied by people of about the same type and economic level may, nevertheless, contain an island of low-grade population suffering from conspicuous deterioration; or, on the contrary, may perhaps include an oasis of surviving population of higher grade than the average. As shown in chapter iv, churches draw on their immediate areas selectively. Consequently a few churches which cater to exceptional types within a general homogeneous area follow the fortunes of the exceptions rather than of the area as a whole.

Still again, deterioration and disadvantage for one type of population and its churches may mean advantage for another. Thus, out of 188 Negro churches recently studied in five Northern cities 54 per cent. had secured their church property from departing white congregations while only 46 per cent. built new property. The decline of these neighborhoods from the standpoint of white population had created opportunities for another race.

When such exceptions to the exceptions are accounted for very few remain to challenge the rule. Whenever a church is closely identified with a locality, its success or failure is almost uniformly conditioned by the social fortunes of the locality.

REAL EXCEPTIONS

Such real exceptions as remain need nevertheless to be understood. Chart XXXVI shows that not all churches are growing in the best territory nor all declining in the worst. Why do some rise above the control of circumstances while others conspicuously fall below their opportunities? This question received specific investigation. Two hundred and forty-seven churches representing rather extreme exceptions—about 13 per cent. of the total—were somewhat intensively examined in order, if possible, to discover why they failed to follow the rule.

Case studies of these churches show that those which failed to reach the average growth of others in the same environment were apt to be too small, to lack a normal amount and quality of lay leadership, to suffer from relatively inadequate ministries, short pastoral terms, inadequate finances, frequent competition with neighborhood churches, weak programs, frequent and excessive debts, and failure in morale; and also that they were cursed by numerous squabbles, scandals, and schisms. In general they were lacking in adaptability to their environment.

In the effort to save these sub-modal churches leadership was frequently imported from outside. Resources were added to by subsidy. As a result these churches were not under-staffed. For one or another of the above reasons they simply failed to measure up to a situation in which most of the churches were succeeding. The most noteworthy discovery of this phase of the study was that, at best, it takes a combination of favorable circumstances to raise a church above the average opportunity. On the contrary, a single untoward circumstance, such as a church quarrel, is sufficient to cause failure.

Churches which had risen above their environments and succeeded where most others had failed, showed virtues contrasting with the weaknesses of the sub-modal group. They displayed exceptional leadership, unusual resources, extraordinary group solidarity, and they showed flexibility in adapting themselves to a changing environment.

All told, then, the conclusion "like environment; like church" is abundantly demonstrated. "As goes the neighborhood so goes the church," except when the church is not identified with the neighborhood but draws selectively upon exceptional populations or enjoys a city-wide constituency; or also, in relatively rare cases, where the church falls below or rises above its environmental conditioning by virtue of peculiar inner weaknesses or strength.

### SIGNIFICANCE OF ENVIRONMENTAL CONDITIONING

The significance of environment for the local unit of the church has obvious bearing upon the art of churchmanship.

Urban churches in the past have habitually bowed to environmental changes. When environment begins to turn against them they have moved to some other locality where environment was again on their side. It is true that, where evironmental pressure was only slightly adverse they have sometimes continued for a while, drawing selectively upon contiguous populations but not assimilating those of unaccustomed types. This policy of avoidance of difficulties has had a large measure of success. Many of the most prosperous churches of the present are those which found themselves beginning to go backward environmentally, but which made a favorable move in time.

Obviously such a policy creates acute transitional problems. What happens to the areas from which churches migrate? Is institutional success as significant for religion as the fortunes of the people who are left behind? On this point time cures many deficiencies. As previously noted, the removal of churches of one type creates opportunities for churches of another. When populations of one grade go, populations of another grade come in, with resources corresponding to their own standards of living. The incoming churches are usually feeble enough institutionally; but socially they are highly authentic. As shown in chapter iii, they reflect specific types of immigrant populations.

Moreover, these populations themselves are not static. They will succeed in their turn and develop a better type of institution—still keeping it in their own images.

The attempt to equalize opportunities by recourse to philanthropic and missionary subsidies may mitigate the difficulty of the transitional stage but cannot wholly remedy it. Imported leadership and resources, and direction from outside, almost invariably yield one-sided success. The assimilation of foreign populations to the American type has proceeded unequally, and has already worked cultural disruption upon many families. Children will be reached by the "adapted" churches but not adults; women but not men. One or more dangling constituencies of the sort described in chapter iii may be developed; but only a long lapse of time can ordinarily bring about the genuine assimilation of a new population, or secure for an "adapted" church the kind of success represented by a cross-sectional indigenous institution, ministering in due proportion to all elements of the population, as a normally constituted church with original community roots can do.[7]

The study of the environmental conditioning of the churches as a social institution thus yields, in one aspect, a somewhat disillusionizing conclusion. The church must needs summon all her best moral qualities to meet many of the situations revealed. If, however, it is possible for an individual to make his last days his best, it ought not to be impossible that a failing and dwindling institution should achieve both courage and cheerfulness as its strength decays.

The difficulty and only partially successful missionary effort to deal with transitional situations is, nevertheless, abundantly worth making. Environmental changes, moreover, are on the church's side somewhat more often than they are against the church. On the one hand then, the church certainly gets no warrant of institutional immortality at the hands of environment; and the many churches which are appointed to die must meet the prospect with the same resources of religious faith and tranquillity that serve in the individual cases. On the other hand, the churches' outward fortunes may safely rest their cause upon the progress and prosperity of the American people with whom they are identified. Unless good fortune has failed America for all time even average churches with average virtues are sure in the long run to get their share of it and perhaps more.

---

[7] See p. 79.

# CHAPTER XII

*Coöperation and Integration of the Churches*

This chapter has to present the second of the major conditioning factors which surround the church in America; namely a tendency at nearly all points toward an integration of the organized forces of Protestantism and toward their coöperative functioning, in contrast with their sectarian isolation, if not active competition, in the past.

Though, as shown in chapter ii, some tendency to integrate has been present in all eras of the life of the American church, it has frequently been subordinated and obscured by temporary divisive tendencies. This was particularly true during the frontier period. The present urban age still witnesses the backwash of sectarianism in certain quarters, especially in the less prosperous and more backward sections of the nation; but on the whole, the age is distinctly dominated by integrative forces.

Before presenting evidence in support of this general statement, it is desirable to point out certain distinctions within this total process of religious integration. Integrative tendencies take two forms. They manifest themselves, first, in the integrative behavior of Christians, either individually and in families; or in voluntary groups, such as the various temporary laymen's movements.

The virtually interchangeable use of denominations by vast numbers of Christians has already been noted in chapter iii. Passing back and forth with exceeding freedom between denominations, they have found that they can satisfy the needs for religious life and fellowship in more than one church. These transitions are, of course, not made without some difficulty and loss, but there is evidence that multitudes take it pretty comfortably as among the familiar experiences of a mobile, restless civilization.

Here is a man who testifies that he was born a Methodist. He married a Presbyterian wife. They joined the Presbyterian church. They had nine children. Meanwhile they had moved South and all had joined the Southern Presbyterian Church. All nine children are now married and scattered and the family represents six different denominations. The grandfather writes: "In eight cases the young people upon marriage agreed that the husband and wife should join the same church. There are twenty grandchildren and the single family in which the husband and wife did not go into the same church is the only one in which the grandchildren are not church-members."

Transitions like this may be going on in a million American families. And it is not the laity only who use the churches interchangeably. "Like people, like priest." To a very considerable extent clergymen pass freely from one denominational affiliation to another. In 1929 the Congregational denomination ordained ninety-six men, but imported ninety-two more from other denominations. The General Council of the Presbyterian Church in the U. S. A. reported, in 1926, an infiltration of ministers from other denominations to the extent of 38.1 per cent. of all accessions to the ministry, and of 38.5 per cent. during the previous five years.[1] On the "active list file" kept in a central Presbyterian office and listing 25 per cent. of the total ministers of the denomination, 20 per cent. of those entered came from other than Reformed denominations, that is to say, not only from outside the denomination but from outside the denominational family to which Presbyterians belong.[2]

In one of the smaller and strongly urban denominations a canvass of representative churches indicates that considerably less than half of the ministers had been trained under the church's own auspices.[3] Such ministerial transfers from denomination to denomination are of long standing and occur so frequently that they have ceased to be news in most denominations.

Beyond the behavior of individuals and families, integration is also increasingly realized through definitely ecclesiastical movements in which church bodies officially engage in their corporate capacities. These may go so far as the union of churches or they may stop short of union. The present chapter limits itself to those which do not go so far as union, but take on various forms of coöperation or federation.

Coöperation means more or less habitual co-action by denominational units which have not entered into any permanent ecclesiastical alliances or agreements. Federation, on the contrary, means formal ecclesiastical action which is binding within its terms and agreements, and thus "organic" so far as it goes, though it often does not go very far. Federating churches, however, may and do coöperate far beyond the literal terms of their federal agreements.

The effect of these movements is to modify the present denominational system; changing its spirit and methods of functioning without essentially changing its structural form. They are moving forward in a unitive direction, overcoming the acknowledged evils of the church's division, but with-

---

[1] Weber, Statistics of the Presbyterian Church in the U. S. A., General Council, 1926.
[2] May, The Education of American Ministers, Vol. II, pp. 99 f.
[3] Report of Fact-Finding Commission, Reformed Church in America, 1929, p. 154.

out pre-determining the further distance to be gone nor envisaging a definite goal to be reached.

Obviously coöperation and federation may have significance beyond the formal stage now reached and the conscious purposes professed. They may represent a stage of evolution in the denominational system which shall ultimately lift it out of itself. The participants may be building better than they know. On the other hand, it is conceivable that coöperation and federation are superficial movements which do not even have the values that appear on the surface. However, such questions as to the larger significance of the movement must be postponed until the facts have been laid before the reader. The present chapter, accordingly, proceeds with an objective report and exposition of current coöperation and federation in the American churches.

## THE LOW LEVEL OF RELIGIOUS PREJUDICE BETWEEN MANY DENOMINATIONS

An obvious underlying ground for coöperation and federation is found in the decline of religious prejudice, which now stands at a low level with respect to a majority of American denominations.

Most of them do not feel divided by any of the matters involved in the daily practical associations of fellow-members in a church. Direct data measuring feelings of religious nearness or distance were recently secured by means of a widely circulated questionnaire on church unity, in which 13,827 persons, chiefly Protestants, indicated the degree of difficulty which they felt in associating with members of other faiths and denominations in a set of twelve relationships regarded as normal and habitual within one's own denomination.

The relationships were as follows: (1) Sending a child to their Sunday school; (2) Habitually receiving communion from their minister; (3) Associating with them in the social life of the local church; (4) Feeling satisfied with a marriage ceremony performed by one of their ministers; (5) Supporting their local benevolent work; (6) Uniting in observing their Holy Days or other special celebrations; (7) Marrying a member of that church; (8) Reciting the Lord's Prayer with them in public worship; (9) Having a child baptized by one of their ministers; (10) Having a burial service conducted according to their rites; (11) Acknowledging their church as a genuine church of Christ; (12) Contributing to the support of their foreign missions knowing that they teach a form of creed and of worship different from yours.

Some of the relationships just enumerated were clearly more intimate and significant than others; some more apt than others to involve doubt or scruple as to the legitimacy or potency of the religious usages of other religious groups. Together they were regarded as constituting a simple yet

TABLE XII — INDEX OF RELIGIOUS DISTANCE, BY DENOMINATIONS AND GROUPS

| Rank | Denomination (A) | Number Persons Scoring | Average Score per Person | Rank, A, B, and C Lists Combined |
|---|---|---|---|---|
| 1 | Reformed Church in U. S. ................... | 141 | 5.76 | 1 |
| 2 | Congregational-Christian.................... | 1,273 | 6.69 | 2 |
| 3 | Presbyterian, U. S. A. ....................... | 1,189 | 7.06 | 4 |
| 4 | United Brethren............................ | 188 | 7.19 | 5 |
| 5 | Methodist Protestant........................ | 75 | 7.64 | 6 |
| 6 | Methodist Episcopal, South................. | 750 | 8.71 | 7 |
| | | | | |
| 7 | Moravian.................................. | 159 | 8.84 | 8 |
| 8 | Negro Methodist............................ | 221 | 8.90 | 9 |
| 9 | United Presbyterian........................ | 149 | 8.93 | 10 |
| 10 | Methodist Episcopal........................ | 3,206 | 9.09 | 11 |
| 11 | Evangelical Synod of N. A. .................. | 74 | 9.31 | 12 |
| 12 | Reformed Church in America................. | 203 | 9.39 | 13 |
| | | | | |
| 13 | Universalist............................... | 65 | 10.20 | 14 |
| | | | | |
| 14 | Evangelical Church......................... | 420 | 11.53 | 16 |
| 15 | Negro Baptist.............................. | 183 | 11.70 | 17 |
| 16 | Presbyterian, U. S. ......................... | 728 | 11.98 | 18 |
| 17 | Disciples of Christ.......................... | 648 | 12.02 | 19 |
| 18 | Baptist (Northern Convention)............... | 1,075 | 13.56 | 20 |
| 19 | Protestant Episcopal........................ | 853 | 14.33 | 21 |
| | | | | |
| 20 | Baptist (Southern Convention)............... | 400 | 14.81 | 22 |
| 21 | Friends.................................... | 345 | 19.20 | 24 |
| 22 | Lutheran (All)............................. | 629 | 22.28 | 26 |
| 23 | Church of the Brethren (Dunkers)........... | 171 | 23.57 | 27 |
| 24 | Unitarian.................................. | 281 | 23.87 | 28 |
| 25 | Holiness-Pentecostal bodies................. | 72 | 24.00 | 29 |
| | Sub-total.............................. | 13,498 | 11.53 | .. |

Denomination (B)*

| 1 | Christian Scientist.......................... | 28 | 21.18 | 25 |
|---|---|---|---|---|
| 2 | Latter Day Saints (Mormon)................. | 83 | 50.22 | 33 |
| 3 | Roman Catholic............................ | 59 | 50.97 | 34 |
| 4 | Jewish..................................... | 159 | 66.09 | 35 |
| | Total................................. | 13,827 | | |

Sub-Divisions and Group (C), Duplicate†

| 1 | Federated and Community Church............ | (150) | 6.84 | 3 |
|---|---|---|---|---|
| 2 | Minor denominational officials............... | ( 80) | 10.65 | 15 |
| 3 | United Lutheran........................... | (366) | 15.00 | 23 |
| 4 | Fundamentalist............................. | ( 84) | 26.80 | 31 |
| 5 | High-church Episcopal...................... | ( 37) | 29.89 | 32 |
| 6 | Missouri Synod Lutheran................... | ( 72) | 75.68 | 36 |
| | | | | |
| 7 | "No denominations"........................ | 98 | 26.60 | 30 |

\* B Sampling too small to be statistically representative.
† C Included in denominational counts in List A.

genuine index to feelings associated with customary behaviors involving other religious groups in contrast with one's own.

When every case of difficulty, on any of the above points with respect to members of another denomination, was counted for the nearly 14,000 persons replying ("hesitancy" to enter a relation scoring 1, "refusal" 2) the returns were tabulated and an average "distance score" per individual was calculated. The denominations were found to rank as shown in Table XII.

The following are among the outstanding points on which light is thrown by the table.

(1) The average distance or prejudice score for the regular Protestant denominations (shown in Group A) is small compared with the average for Group B.

(2) Denominations ranking in the upper quartile of the A section of the table only show from one-half to two-thirds as much discrimination against others as the A group as a whole has, while those ranking in the lower quartile show from one-half more to two-and-a-half times as much.

(3) Several denominations in the B section show from five to seven-and-a-half times as much discrimination as the average of the A group.

(4) People belonging to "no denomination" are more prejudiced than any "regular" Protestant group, except Missouri Synod Lutherans.

(5) Of larger denominations (those enrolling over 700,000 members each), the Congregational-Christian, Presbyterian, U. S. A., and Methodist Episcopal, South, rank in the upper quartile of the A scale; Methodist Episcopal in the second quartile; Disciples, Negro Baptist (Northern and Southern), and Protestant Episcopal in the third; and Lutheran, United and Missouri Synod, in the lower quartile.

What the table records is simply what nearly 14,000 American Christians say about their own feelings toward others. Representatives of denominations appearing at the top of this list state that they would find less difficulty in entering into the twelve habitual relationships of church life and usage with members of the other denominations named; denominations at the bottom of the list say that they would have more difficulty. Here, then, are actual differences in feeling toward other denominations objectively ascertained. For most denominations they are not great. Such as they are, they obviously condition the practical relations of denominations one toward another.

Chart XXXVII gives the results of a religious distance test from a somewhat different constituency with respect to willingness to marry a member of other specified denominations and to vote for him for President.

The most serious aspect of "distance" feeling between denominations is that, as shown by Chart XXXVIII, it is generally mutual.

The proof of the actual slightness of the prejudice professed by the ma-

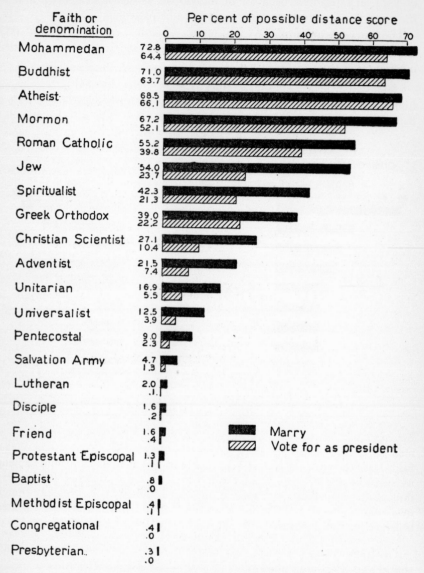

Faith or denomination | Per cent of possible distance score

| Faith or denomination | Marry | Vote for as president |
|---|---|---|
| Mohammedan | 72.8 | 64.4 |
| Buddhist | 71.0 | 63.7 |
| Atheist | 68.5 | 66.1 |
| Mormon | 67.2 | 52.1 |
| Roman Catholic | 55.2 | 39.8 |
| Jew | 54.0 | 23.7 |
| Spiritualist | 42.3 | 21.3 |
| Greek Orthodox | 39.0 | 22.2 |
| Christian Scientist | 27.1 | 10.4 |
| Adventist | 21.5 | 7.4 |
| Unitarian | 16.9 | 5.5 |
| Universalist | 12.5 | 3.9 |
| Pentecostal | 9.0 | 2.3 |
| Salvation Army | 4.7 | 1.3 |
| Lutheran | 2.0 | .1 |
| Disciple | 1.6 | .2 |
| Friend | 1.6 | .4 |
| Protestant Episcopal | 1.3 | .1 |
| Baptist | .8 | .0 |
| Methodist Episcopal | .4 | .1 |
| Congregational | .4 | .0 |
| Presbyterian | .3 | .0 |

Marry
Vote for as president

CHART XXXVII—INDEX OF RELIGIOUS "DISTANCE" FELT BY PROTESTANT CONSTITUENTS OF CHURCH FEDERATIONS TOWARD MEMBERS OF SPECIFIED FAITHS OR DENOMINATIONS WITH RESPECT TO MARRIAGE AND THE PRESIDENCY jority of those submitting to these distance tests, must be found in the widespread integrative behavior of individuals as earlier evidenced, and in the strength of movements for unity still to be presented.

The attitudes and situations which they disclose were supported by very numerous personal testimonies attached to questionnaires. Thus, a Methodist minister from Missouri writes:

"While pastor of a union congregation (not organized as a church) I prepared from among the young people in the congregation some who united with a Baptist church, one who united with a Congregational, one with a Methodist

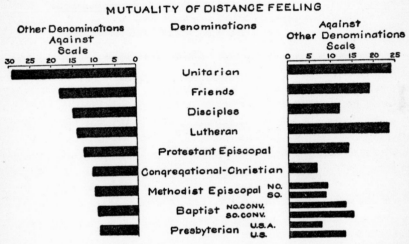

CHART XXXVIII—DISTANCE FEELING OF NINE DENOMINATIONS AGAINST OTHERS COMPARED WITH OTHERS' DISTANCE FEELING AGAINST THEM

Episcopal, and one with the Universalist church. They were prepared in a common group, and all pastors concerned approved my work. This was in Wakefield, Massachusetts. At present I am pastor of a church which includes among its members people whose backgrounds vary from the semi-formal Presbyterian through the fundamentalist Baptist to the near-Pentecostal. As the only church in a community of 1,000 it finds problems of creed and ritual subordinated to larger practical problems."

The fragmentary evidences which have now been presented reveal a widespread and deep-lying phenomenon.

Denominational differences have not meant so much to millions of people, either clergy or laity, that they could not make religious realignments and probably on the whole comfortable ones. Whatever the losses experienced, the difficulties were not insurmountable.

Many denominations are emotionally near and akin to one another.

At the same time it is not fair to ignore serious differences. Other denominations remain far apart. That these differences affect the prospects of uniting them is all too manifest. The division of the American population into religious types and groups has been and remains a major fact of the social history of the nation—so much so, that up to the present moment an adherent of only one type of religion can be elected President of the United States. The integrative tendency has conspicuous limits.

There remains, however, the massive fact of widespread integrative behavior and lack of sundering prejudice which underly and explain organized integrative movements.

### Coöperative and Federative Movements

The integrative agencies of the American churches mostly date from the last third of the nineteenth century. Within this period they included such voluntary associations of Christians of all denominations as the Y.M.C.A.; such federative movements of denominations as the Evangelical Alliance; and such proposals for organic union as the Lambeth Quadrilateral. All types and degrees of integration have thus been under way for half a century. Among the most specific fields covered by these movements were those of missions, as exemplified by the Foreign Missions Conferences and the Student Volunteer Movement; of religious education, as historically expressed in the Sunday School Union; and of moral reform, as in the W.C.T.U. and Anti-Saloon League. The Christian Endeavor Movement attempted to unify work for young people, and continues to a considerable degree on an interdenominational basis.

Along with these interchurch movements had gone a strong tendency toward intra-denominational integrations, illustrated by the organization of world alliance of several families of churches. Finally, the first stages of the movement eventuating in the Federal Council of Churches were already under way.

Passing over into the twentieth century with increasing power, organized coöperation went forward in the realm of religious education, through the interdenominational organization of the Sunday School Editorial Association in 1901, the Sunday School Council of Evangelical Denominations in 1910, the movement culminating in the International Council of Religious Education in 1922. The new century marks integration in the realms of foreign missions by the Laymen's Foreign Missions movement, and the organization of the Committee of Reference and Counsel, 1907. The Councils of Home Missions developed in 1908, and the Missionary Education Movement, serving both home and foreign missions, appeared from 1902 on. Special coöperative interests of men were expressed in the Men and Religion Forward Movement, 1912, as well as the Laymen's Foreign Missions Movement already noted. Coöperative movements among women included the Federation of Women's Boards of Foreign Missions (1913), and the development of Councils of Women's Federations from 1928 forward, culminating in the present National Commission of Protestant Church Women (1930).

The period of the World War saw a great intensification of contemporary coöperative agencies focused in the War-Time Commission of the Churches. It was followed by the ill-starred Interchurch World Movement, which perished with the reaction from war psychology.

The post-war period has chiefly been characterized by the consolidation of previous gains and the coördination of existing agencies.

While the movements suggested by this catalogue were projected nationally, nearly all were intended to work down through regional, state and local organizations.

Functionally, the movements represented a wide variety of aspects. Some, like the Federal Council of Churches, were strictly ecclesiastical; others, like the Home Missions Councils, administrative in general fields; others, subsidiary and limited as dealing with narrowly defined interests or special constituencies.

Ecclesiastical agencies of the types just mentioned are to be distinguished from non-denominational agencies voluntarily constituted by individuals as familiarly instanced by the Y.M.C.A.

### Current Protestant Coöperation

The system of Protestant coöperation in America increasingly heads up in the Federal Council of the Churches of Christ, with its surrounding group of affiliated and coöperating bodies. These bodies are becoming knit together more and more closely. The more important of them foster parallel state and local movements. More than three-fourths of all the Protestants in the United States are in denominations constituent to the total movement.

The more outstanding of the coöperative agencies require brief special mention.

#### THE HOME MISSIONS COUNCIL AND COUNCIL OF WOMEN FOR HOME MISSIONS

In contrast with the Federal Council, which is a formal alliance of denominations as such, the Home Missions Councils are federations of the denominations' specialized mission boards. These boards are the national administrative agencies of church extension, both urban and rural. They establish and aid in supporting churches, particularly on the frontier and in the more sparsely settled areas of the nation; in the changing cities and rapidly growing suburbs, principally among poor and foreign people. They carry on varied forms of religious and social ministries for the more radically variant racial groups throughout the nation, such as Negroes, Indians,

Orientals, and Mexicans. The financial aspects of their work were briefly touched upon in chapter x.

About thirty constituent boards of twenty-five denominations are now associated in the Home Missions Council, and some twenty women's boards of twelve denominations in the parallel Council of Women for Home Missions. Their combined activities, in 1933, employed more than 21,000 paid workers in nearly 30,000 separate enterprises, at a cost of approximately $25,000,000.

The possibility is just now being canvassed of extending the actual joint administration of missions enterprises by the Councils so as to cover all types of activity which is "non-productive from a denominational point of view." Work for American Indians, missions to lumber camps, missions to Alaska and in Mormon areas, work in isolated rural communities, Sunday-school missions, foreign-language colportage work, and missions for immigrant people are under discussion as possible fields for joint work. Other suitable areas for inter-board operation have also been proposed: in the field of promotion, a joint publicity bureau; more interdenominational summer schools for rural pastors; a service bureau for church architecture; a bureau for the placement of candidates; departments for research and survey; and for technical information on phases of rural and urban church work. Precedents should permit the rapid extension of inter-board coöperation to many such phases of work which carry but slight ecclesiastical implications.

STATE HOME MISSIONS COUNCILS

The national Home Missions Council recognizes twenty-three affiliated state home missions councils, four of which are also listed by the Federal Council as state federations. These councils are voluntary associations of ecclesiastical and board representatives rather than formal affiliations of the churches as such. Most of them deal exclusively with the field of church comity and the adjustment of local overlapping and friction. None of them enjoys the services of a paid professional leader, but a number are showing an inclination to develop into full-fledged councils of churches.

COMITY

Of the many forms which these coöperations and federations have taken, one of the most significant is the practice of comity in the establishment and maintenance of churches. Comity in practice simply means that denominations agree not to duplicate work or place a church without regard to the equities of religious forces already occupying the field. Specific agreements and codes of practice governing this field have developed over wide areas; so that they now cover most of the territory in which missionary extension work is chiefly found, and most of the important cities. Beginning with the purpose of keeping out of each other's way and avoiding the scandal of open competition, comity has evolved into a more positive phase. It now looks forward to the joint planning of religious institutions and begins to stress the possibility of a planned religious economy covering the major religious forces of the entire nation, as economic planning attempts to do in its field.

Unquestionably the coöperative practices of home-mission boards constitute a distinct modification of the old denominational system. The boards have limited functions, but exercise great powers within the area of these functions. Particularly do they control the functions of appointment and appropriation. Accordingly, their coöperation is of a highly concrete and effective sort, in contrast with the merely symbolic or verbal coöperation characteristic of the ecclesiastical bodies as such.

Moreover, the coöperation of these agencies of administration is fortunate in not conflicting with the sensitive scruples attaching to the action of strictly ecclesiastical bodies. They operate at points of little resistance; their agreements are entered into with almost no popular discussion, and may go far without awakening objection.

Coöperative undertakings and such comity measures as the withdrawal of a denomination from one field in exchange for another do, however, imply the substantial equality of churches. As a working assumption this is naturally unpalatable to extremists who think that their churches alone possess the truth. To them even coöperation is disloyalty; and failure to carry out competitive rivalries in any field which can be entered is lack of fidelity in the preaching of the gospel.

Moreover, even at best such administrative coöperation as has been outlined actually covers very limited areas. Comity itself largely amounts to a system of bargain and exchange whereby brotherly surrender of advantage at one point is compensated for by corresponding advantage at some other; or else, as has been seen, it is limited to the sphere of "non-profitable work"; that is to say, to the more radical problems of missions for unprivileged peoples which require relatively great financial outgo and relatively small denominational results. At these points, it is difficult to finance denominational zeal and the value of coöperative agencies becomes the more obvious.

INTERNATIONAL COUNCIL OF RELIGIOUS EDUCATION

From its beginnings in the 1820's, the prevailing system of Sunday-school promotion and instruction in the United States had been organized on nondenominational lines and was conducted primarily by laymen. Previous to 1922 its organization was of the voluntary rather than the ecclesiastical type. Meanwhile, a parallel association of church Boards of Religious Education had been growing up representing the strengthening of denominational ties and functions described in a previous paragraph. The two movements merged in 1922 into the International Council of Religious Education. This Council includes nearly all the denominations related to the Federal Council, with a considerable number of additional ones. Its control is divided equally between representatives of the coöperating denominations and of the territorial Sunday-school councils or associations.

The International Council creates the materials, the types of organizations and the standard methods for a system of religious education currently used by the great majority of Protestants in the United States.

The chief significance of the integrative process as thus organized in the field of religious education is the demonstration that voluntary coöperation along non-denominational lines can no longer hold the field in America. Coöperation, in order to be effective, must affiliate the existing ecclesiastical units. The parallel territorial units, which the International Council of Religious Education still attempts to maintain, constitute a factor of dwindling importance in its organizations.

OTHER NATIONAL COÖPERATIVE AGENCIES OF THE CHURCHES

Limitations of space allow only bare mention of still other major agencies. The Council of Church Boards of Education now affiliates nineteen boards concerned with denominational colleges and secondary schools, and with religious work in universities. The major foreign-mission boards are associated in the Foreign Missions' Conference and parallel women's organizations. Important single areas of missionary operation have their own coöperative agencies, like the Committee on Coöperation in Latin America. Joint publication and promotion of missionary literature are provided for the coöperating mission boards through the Missionary Education Movement.

COÖRDINATION OF AGENCIES

All told, then, in half a dozen major lines and with local organizations of some sort in more than three-fourths of the states of the nation, the majority of the Protestant forces are coöperatively organized, and function, at least nominally, in relation to one or more aspects of a national system. The closing months of 1933 were signalized by highly important conferences between the chief national interchurch organizations (since formally approved) in the interest of closer relations. This constitutes a partial response to those who have kept asking, "When will the coöperators themselves begin to coöperate?"

THE FEDERAL COUNCIL OF CHURCHES

Virtually all the agencies so far discussed are in definitely or regularly coöperative relation with the Federal Council, and with groups of subordinate interchurch councils or federations, state and local. All of them together constitute the Protestant coöperative system in its broader expression.

The Federal Council affiliates twenty-five denominations, representing a total constituency of about 22,000,000 members. "It exists to express the fellowship and the Catholic unity of the Christian church, and to bring the Christian bodies of America into united service for Christ and the world." It has no control over the constituent bodies, and no authority to draw up a common creed or form of government or worship. Its positive scope is indeterminate. It seeks "to do what can better be done in union than in separation."

During the more than two decades of Federal Council history, increasing content has been read into its charter. A fair summary of its major emphases during the quarter-century of its history was attached to an official appraisal of its work in 1932:

"1. Promoting the spirit of unity through the provision of constant opportunities for contact and fellowship between representatives of the different communions, both on a national scale and in the local and state areas, and also during recent years in the international field.

"2. Facilitating the coördination of denominational programs and the practice of coöperation in various fields of activity, especially in evangelism, social service and efforts for international understanding and peace.

"3. Providing a voice through which the common convictions of the churches may be brought to bear more unitedly and effectively in molding public opinion on contemporary issues in which Christian moral principles are at stake.

"4. Gathering and interpreting the relevant data which must underlie and justify any pronouncements of the Council so that they may be in conformity with the facts.

"5. Serving as an administrative agent of the churches in certain task for which no other agency is available. In some cases, the Council has erected special agencies, like the Central Bureau for Relief of the Evangelical Churches of Europe; or had a large share in setting them up, as in the case of China Famine Relief. In certain cases (for example, the responsibility for the churches in the Canal Zone) it has assumed direct administrative responsibility."[4]

In the conduct of the Federal Council's work initiation of action rests primarily with the Commissions, which are made up of representative persons chosen from the coöperating denominations, supplemented by technical experts. Though reporting to the central Executive Committee, the Commissions have inclined to considerable independence; and they are largely self-financing. Previous to a recent reorganization which combined certain types of work without discontinuing any functions, the following were

---

[4] "Major Emphases in Present Functions," from the Report of the Committee on Function and Structure; Official Handbook for the Quadrennial Meeting, Federal Council of the Churches of Christ in America, pp. 10-11.

rated as commissions: Commission on the Church and Social Service; International Justice and Goodwill; Evangelism and Life Service; Relations with Churches Abroad; Motion Pictures; Committee on Goodwill between Jews and Christians; Department of Research and Education. Standing committees are maintained on Mercy and Relief; Army and Navy Chaplains; Financial and Fiduciary Matters; Religious Work on the Canal Zone; Extension of State and Local Federations; Religious Radio; Editorial Council of the Religious Press.

DIFFICULTIES AND POINTS OF CONTROVERSY

The Council's attempt to unify the many agencies of fragmentary Protestant coöperation, to coördinate the plans of its extremely diverse component denominations, and sometimes to speak for them, has naturally been fraught with certain difficulties. The points of most controversy have concerned the Council's attempt to exercise effective leadership with respect to the moral and social problems of the age. Thus, the Council's advocacy of world peace and international coöperation, along with some of its more advanced economic positions, have undoubtedly been in advance of sentiment in certain sections of the church, and have been attacked as unpatriotic and subversive.

In a few cases reports of the Federal Council Commissions on matters involving changing ethical views or standards, notably a report which included a consideration of birth control, have also been vigorously criticized.

Other controversies have related to the Council's own constituents. The body of affiliated state and city federations gives the movements most of the actuality that it has in concrete situations, and conducts the coöperative life of the churches in its effective and authentic phase, namely, in local communities. Obviously the ideals and plans of a national body can be carried out only through such local agencies. About fifty church federations are permanently organized under professional leadership in large American cities and their suburbs. They exist in virtually all cities of 300,000 population and over, but become progressively less numerous in the smaller cities, until they are found in 5 per cent. of those of between 50,000 and 100,000 population. They enjoy a large measure of theoretical approval on the part of the majority of their constituents. This is evidenced by Chart XXXIX.

The latest revision of the Federal Council's constitution, however, denies the local federations any structural relationship to itself and gives them no representation. The local federations are left independent and bound to the Council merely by the strength of informal dangling ties.

Another issue relates to federated agencies covering limited interests of the church, such as that of religious education. The major organizations of this type have already been characterized. The Federal Council seeks to integrate them more closely into a single system.

Very recent agreements of the more important national interdenominational agencies have established the principle that state and local federations should henceforth be regarded as auxiliary to the whole group of national

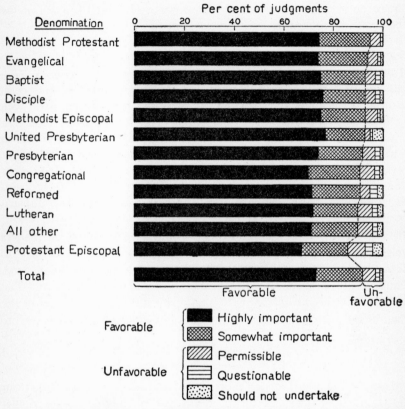

CHART XXXIX—DISTRIBUTION OF JUDGMENTS OF CONSTITUENTS WITH RESPECT TO THE IMPORTANCE AND APPROPRIATENESS OF CURRENT CHURCH FEDERATION PROGRAMS —12 DENOMINATIONS

agencies and should undertake all-inclusive programs of work in behalf of the entire Protestant constituency.

The 1932 revision of the Federal Council constitution guarded denominational initiative most strictly. It narrowed the concept of representativeness and gave it a legalistic interpretation. It attempted to limit the functions of the Council to areas of definitely delegated authority and to lines restricted by the formal expression of views by constituent bodies.

Moreover, the Federal Council has shown great timidity as to the possible implications of the coöperative movement and unwillingness to confess any interest in church union except in the most general and innocuous religious terms. It thus remains wholly equivocal as to the outcome of the movement which it purports to lead.

### OBJECTIVE SIGNIFICANCE OF COÖPERATION AND FEDERATION

Irrespective, however, of any ultimate appraisal of coöperation and federation in the light of the theory of the church's unity, one has at length to ask how much these movements have already come to as objective instruments and expressions of the integrative movement of the church. Altogether, it appears, they have genuinely modified the temper as well as the operation of the denominational system, and have remedied some of its more flagrant practical abuses.

Generalizing more specifically, it is significant (1) that the movement of interchurch coöperation, both as nationally organized and in the major American cities, has succeeded remarkably in gathering up the other coöperative religious agencies into a sort of loose unity.

This does not always mean that they have been merged into one organization. One who notes only the bitter exceptions, misses altogether the total trend. But if he will consider the facts locally, city by city, he will be convinced that federation does very largely federate.

(2) Coöperation in its stricter interchurch form is greatly enlarged and supplemented by the relating to the integrative movement of the church of the chief voluntary agencies of Protestant antecedents, such as the Y.M.C.A. and Y.W.C.A. These important allies and extensions of the church are increasingly being tied up with its organized coöperative movement. These and similar organizations have constitutional representation of a limited sort both in the Federal Council and often in the city Councils.

Here, then, is growing coördination; generally a loose organizational unity; a type of unity which often strains at the seams, but which does on the whole tend to make the churches hang together rather than fall apart. Here is something worlds away from the uncorrelated integration which set churches to unite in limited fields, but left the interchurch agencies in these fields to separate and sometimes competitive action.

(3) In terms of organized activities, coöperation has come to mean the habit of committing some responsibility, at least, to interchurch federations in such traditional areas as comity, evangelism, religious education, social service, etc. This works powerfully for coördination of plans and toward the emergence of a typical program of united Protestant effort.

(4) The federations are beginning to generalize their combined experience. Certain methods and techniques have proved themselves normally

successful. The result is the emergence of a proved body of practices, standardized in the sense that the local federations, meeting essentially similar situations over and over again and learning from one another, are at length able to put on paper a set of working principles generalized from experience for use as a fresh point of departure for their local practices. These inevitably serve as a check upon the more aggressive impulses of denominationalism and assure an instrument of common service in the major American communities.

## LOCAL CHURCH UNION

The increasing integration of the church, as expressed in the increasing coöperation of denominations through national, state and local agencies, necessarily involves many changes of situation in local communities. In point of fact, the effecting of such local adjustments has been one of the main objects of the coöperative movement through its comity processes. Comity is essentially a device for clearing up local competitive situations.

In contrast with movements working for this end but from the top down, consideration now turns to an equally significant movement working from the ground up, namely the movement for local church union. It is essentially an indigenous effort of American communities to adjust their local church situations. To this practically motivated movement a secondary body of convictions and effort has attached itself which directly seeks to promote local unions of churches on the theoretical grounds that this is the right way for religion to express itself in communities.

From the outset one has to recognize a variety of integrative tendencies converging upon the local community and standing at different angles to the larger integrative movement. Some regard local unions as the only form of integration worth concern; others regard local unions as supplemental to the larger integrative movement; the local phase of it is important but not primary.

A third attitude looks upon the local movement as promising to redirect the entire effort for church union. Movements from the top ought to be subordinated to the truly vital movement from the ground up.

The present section undertakes to place and describe the objective phenomena concerned in local church unions, considering them at first as an undifferentiated whole, and secondly, in connection with the major forms in which they have appeared.

### DESCRIPTION AND EXPOSITION

Beginning with local church union in its most general aspects, two main roots are discovered by the evidence. The first is the experience of the acute evils of religious division in small communities; the second, the tendency of certain urbanized groups to disregard denominational lines and to organize religiously on the basis of community groupings.

RELIGIOUS DIVISION IN THE SMALL COMMUNITY

The burden of the multiplicity of denominations upon small communities has been all too clearly established in earlier chapters. Quite apart from its denominational rivalries, the church throughout the nation was projected on too small an average scale and in too many separate units. The majority of rural communities have lost population and the larger percentage of villages have stationary or declining populations. Declining population or changes in the character of population left a smaller number of people than formerly to support the multitude of Protestant churches. Quickened competition inevitably resulted and soon became intolerable. The composite picture is that of the village of 300 or 400 population with three or more Protestant churches, all struggling for existence.

In a vast body of volunteered opinion gathered by recent studies, the practical motive for local church union is the one almost exclusively voiced. Promotional literature, on the contrary, is generally inspired by more or less theoretical ideals of the superior beauty and morality of unity. In order to understand this discrepancy, the present study made a fresh, intensive, first-hand examination of forty cases, probing very carefully to discover the original motivation of the union and its subsequent rationalization.

In the majority of cases the persons concerned had to be teased into any sort of profession of theoretical attitude with respect to sectarianism, the unification of the community, Christian unity or the wrongness of denominational divisions. No very pronounced theory of any sort and no common attitude on these matters could be discerned. Exclusively practical considerations had determined the particular local union in the great majority of cases.

Frequent judgments, for example, limited their approval of local church union movements to small communities. "I believe in church union in the smaller towns where they are all weak, but in large cities I believe the denominations will do more good separately. . . ." "You really should have had two sets of questions. One applicable to small communities without population or financial resources to support several churches, and one to larger cities. . . . I read one set of questions from the point of view of the small town, where I once lived, and another set from the point of view of the city, where I now live."

Still other replies specified mission fields, foreign and home, as areas where local union should be practiced, while not desiring to apply it to larger communities.

This reveals the movement for local union as based on the pressure of circumstances rather than upon ideal motives. It is not very much given to alleging ideal motives even as an afterthought. This characterizes the main stream of the movement.

## URBAN BASIS OF LOCAL UNION

The movement for local church union finds a secondary source in certain phases of the urban situation. A previous chapter has noted an extraordinary willingness of certain urban populations to make little of denominational ties and to use denominations interchangeably in their personal religious affiliations. Such people find little relish in the denominational struggle. A considerable number of suburban populations, accordingly, have refused to enter into this conflict and have set up for themselves various forms of local union in order to obviate it.

Thus, in cases of 994 urban and suburban churches in sixteen representative cities circularized by Dr. Ross W. Sanderson in 1932, 165 said that they called themselves community churches. Of this number, all but 6 per cent. said that the announced purpose to function as a community church had proved advantageous, while 16 per cent. claimed to be recognized as community churches by interdenominational agreement. Sixteen Methodist Episcopal churches in the Greater New York area covered by the survey of 1932 said that they had dropped the designation "Methodist" in their local advertisements and promotion. Further analysis showed that this phenomenon was particularly frequent in the more desirable suburbs.

The most difficult place to realize the community version of religion is the metropolitan center. Here the community character has almost departed from the social group, and community expression through the church is inclined to reduce itself to a commanding pulpit in which the comprehensive type of religious outlook is maintained. However, the downtown sections of cities show an unusual number of non-denominational organizations laboring in behalf of the depressed populations. The Salvation Army and Volunteers of America, both originally non-sectarian movements, are familiar illustrations.

## ATMOSPHERE AND ORGANIZATION

The movement for local unity is thus rooted in characteristic tendencies and circumstances both of urban and rural society. It finds stimulus in changed atmospheric conditions accompanying and resulting from the broader integrative trends of the present century. It has chiefly been an indigenous movement.

The movement, however, has recently found more articulate leadership in the Community Church Workers of the U. S. A., a voluntary organization, whose leaders are now attempting to formulate its widely diffused underlying ideas and to produce a philosophy for it. Negatively, they say, it is opposed to the denominational system; positively, it proposes the community instead of the church as the unit of religious organization. The community functioning at its best, whatever particular thing it does, is functioning religiously. The community itself is the potential church, the distinction between the sacred and the secular disappearing. At present the greater part of religion exists outside of the church. The churches ought to possess themselves of this great fund of religion by sharing in and serving the life of the community. "To such churches nothing human is alien. . . . If enterprises outside the church organization itself are carrying on well, they are backed up. If the church organization itself can furnish facilities which otherwise the town would lack, that is done. The one ideal is generous usefulness."[5]

According to this version of the situation, any church, whether nominally denominational or not, is a community church if it shares this ideal. And while, as previously maintained, no such definiteness of motivation can actually be found either in the origin or in the subsequent rationalizations of the majority of local united churches, nevertheless the emergence of such ideas definitely reinforces the movement and tends to furnish it with new point and power.

SITUATIONS CONGENIAL TO LOCAL UNION

In contrast with all such rationalizations, the principle of environmental conditioning, which chapter xi explored, leads one to an examination of certain highly specific situations out of which local unions have tended to grow. These furnish the most significant explanations of such unions in a large number of cases.

(1) Many local unions represent a temporary pre-denominational phase of religious development in the community. From time immemorial new religious projects have found it natural to start as non-sectarian Sunday schools or unorganized "union" projects. Their local leaders have no idea of establishing a permanently non-denominational church, but merely to secure religious privileges for their community pending such time as the enterprise will take what is to them a natural course, namely, graduation into a denominational status. It is explained with complete naïveté that this anticipated denominationalism is not stressed so that "everybody will join at first." This method is widespread and time-honored. But it does not necessarily add permanently to the number of union local churches.

(2) Many local unions represent religious organizations stranded in their non-denominational phase. The anticipated growth of the community in which they are located simply failed to come. A high proportion of specu-

---

[5] Weist, Carl, *"Philosophy of the Community Church Movement,"* address at the Biennial Conference of the Community Church Workers of the U. S. A., 1932.

lative real-estate ventures fail. Such half-developed communities may never become profitable, denominationally speaking. Their temporary union church, which would have become denominational if the community venture had succeeded, becomes stranded along with the people.

(3) Another situation favorable to local church union is that of the fluctuating community, represented by the average summer resort. Reduced to skeleton proportions in the winter, though having population by thousands in the summer, the small permanent population finds it difficult to maintain the church. The summer people are of many denominations. What more natural, then, than to develop a non-denominational church which shall appeal to everybody during the summer and serve the skeleton community the year round?

(4) Still again, local church unions are likely to arise in communities which are under the control of exceptional unifying forces. Frequently these forces are industrial, particularly as illustrated in the mill town dominated by a single factory. Under these circumstances the industry frequently fosters and largely maintains a single church, while it is unwilling to finance or encourage a variety of competitive ones. Sometimes the unifying force is a prison or an asylum. Government will afford religious facilities for a single organization of each major faith, but not for competitive denominations within the institutional walls. More recently planned community developments by real-estate interests have sometimes taken the position that denominational competition is a disadvantage to a community and have insisted upon a single church. This has sometimes caused bitter resentment on the part of the denominations as an unholy effort of business to control religion. Finally, certain major cases of local church union occur in school communities attached to great public institutions. Here again, the attitude of the educational authorities is against sectarianism, particularly in the approach of religious forces to student populations. Good examples of this type of local union are found in the college church at the Connecticut Agricultural College at Storrs, and the People's Church adjoining the Michigan Agricultural College at East Lansing. The merit for establishing such unions appears to belong to secular environment rather than to the initiative of the churches.

(5) Another type of local union represents local response in anticipation of denominational mergers. The Federated Presbyterian Church of Meridian, Miss., for example, recites, in its articles of federation, that it is established in anticipation of organic union between the northern and southern branches of the Presbyterian Church and that it shall belong to both denominations until such union has been effected. Complete mergers, such as that of the Congregational and Christian denominations naturally raise the

question of local mergers in every community where both are represented. Accordingly a considerable fraction of local unions are simply adjustments to conform to something which has already been settled at the top. That settlement at the top may leave a long and thorny pathway for the movement of local union to pursue is shown by the experience of the United Church of Canada.[6]

(6) Union churches in foreign capitals and commercial centers where Americans are few are a familiar phenomenon. These are repeated under the American flag at such points as the Canal Zone and San Juan, Porto Rico. Such churches furnish rallying centers for Americans away from home where they are not numerous enough to maintain denominational separation.

(7) Finally, certain conspicuous cases of attempts to create ideal communities have challenged coöperation to such an extent that local church union has been instituted under joint denominational auspices from the beginning. This is illustrated by the modern town of Radburn, N. J., a project of the City Housing Corporation, illustrating the most advanced ideas of community planning, and by the industrial community adjoining the great irrigation project at Boulder Dam.

The wide variety of special situations favorable to the establishment of local unions accounts for nearly all of the cases intensively examined. They have resulted in a considerable number of types of union churches. They are not generally marked by any particular kind of church program nor do they reflect any specific community emphasis. In the main, they are traditional churches.

Piper describes the churches claimed by the Community Church Workers as 82 per cent. rural.[7] Miss Hooker found five-sixths of her churches in places of less than a thousand population.[8] The 1926 United States Religious Census located 83 per cent. of its independent churches in rural communities. It is believed that the urban phase is developing more rapidly than the rural, but so far it remains numerically small.

The majority of local church unions are composed of denominational churches under various forms of evolution. As would be expected, the denominations most often concerned in them are at the same time the chief supporters of coöperation and federation from the top down. Even these denominations, however, differ. Some, with equal liberality of attitude, are embarrassed by historic politics which make participation more difficult than for others.

---

[6] Silcox, *Church Union in Canada* (New York: Institute of Social and Religious Research, 1933), chapter xi.

[7] *Community Churches* (Chicago: Willett, Clark & Colby, 1928).

[8] *United Churches* (New York: Institute of Social and Religious Research, 1926).

Of the Federated churches reported by the United States Religious Census,[9] the denominations most frequently involved were:

| Denomination | Times Federated |
| --- | --- |
| Congregational............................ | 225 |
| Methodist Episcopal...................... | 195 |
| Baptist (Northern Convention)............ | 105 |
| Presbyterian, U. S. A. ................... | 98 |
| 19 other denominations................... | 176 |

What has been portrayed in the above paragraphs is manifestly a group of rather heterogeneous phenomena, all resulting in local church unions of various forms but difficult to understand or appraise as a whole. These unions are sometimes deliberate, but frequently accidental. They are sometimes undertaken in a strongly anti-denominational spirit; again, they are sometimes merely the denominational churches of tomorrow. Some are theologically liberal, and, in the main, a degree of liberalism is generally involved in the willingness to break away from the accepted denominational system. The non-denominational church, however, is also a congenial medium for the expression of separatist tendencies under ultra-conservative teaching. Thus a correspondent in the *Christian Standard* informs his readers:[10]

"Many of the 'Community churches' in that Eastern area differ decidedly from those in the West in the one vital point that they are conservative in doctrine while the Western ones are liberal. They are composed of men and women that have left the denominational churches because of their disgust at the liberalism that dominates them. These churches are, therefore, on the way to the position of the churches of Christ who are set to reproduce New Testament Christianity."

The majority of community churches have entered into their various unions with no distinctive doctrinal tendency. A few are conscious of a new type of community religion and fellowship. The preaching of the majority presents a traditional religious message with conventional applications. In their publicity the majority make no special appeal to community aspects of religion, though a few definitely play up to a certain community quality in the church's outlook and life. Finally, some of the locally united churches are recognized as such by denominational authority or usage, while others are not.

In a field of such fluctuating boundaries, exact enumeration is impossible. No one knows exactly how many local church unions exist in the United States. The Community Church Workers mention some 2,000, but are quite cautious as to exact criteria on which the list is compiled. The Home Missions Council, as the result of extensive correspondence, has attempted a

---

[9] *Religious Bodies* (1926), Vol. II, p. 596.
[10] March 19, 1932.

revision of its list in 1933, and reports a good many abortive or lapsed cases. The present study accepts these approximations. One sees that, relative to the quarter of a million local churches in the United States, local church unions are infrequent. One sees that they embrace a variety of phenomena. How different are the entities thus locally produced by the integrative movement, and how impossible it is to define and enumerate exactly, becomes especially apparent as one comes to a study of the types of local unions.

### TYPES OF LOCAL UNIONS

From the objective viewpoint the really important consideration with respect to local unions is that they are being accomplished in a variety of ways. From the viewpoint of denominationally organized Christianity, on the contrary, analysis and discussion has been concerned chiefly with the question of how these different ways affect ecclesiastical relationships. Accordingly, the current definition of types follows ecclesiastical lines. It is customary to recognize three chief kinds: the non-denominational church, the federated church combining churches of two or more denominations, and the denominational community church.

#### NON-DENOMINATIONAL CHURCHES

Attitudes toward the non-denominational church naturally vary according to the prior assumptions held. Anti-denominationalists regard it as the natural means of realizing local church union and accuse denominationalists of thwarting this, the spontaneous community movement, by the devices of federation and denominational parceling out of fields. Denominationalists, on the contrary, condemn the non-denominational church. A typical expression of this view comes from a report of the Committee on Interdenominational Comity of the Connecticut Federation of Churches: "The establishment of non-denominational churches we consider an utterly mistaken policy. As a rule, a non-denominational church fails to develop a vigorous and complete Christian life."

In spite of such unfavorable opinions some of the better residential sections and a considerable number of desirable suburbs of nearly all the major cities have developed highly successful churches of this type which, for size and resources, leadership and breadth of outlook, rank well up with the average church of the denominations.

#### FEDERATED CHURCHES

Federated churches are local combinations of congregations of two or more denominations into a single functional organization without severance of the previous denominational ties of the combining units. Only 10 per cent. of the federations, however, concern more than two denominations.

Rural federated churches average more than one-half larger than the average denominational churches of the bodies generally participating in them, while urban federated churches surpass the average city church in size. Churches federate, in the main, only under great pressure of adverse circumstances; so that for them to survive at all is to be counted as ordinary success even without numerical growth.

The usual agreement for a federation of churches creates a unifying organ of local government, frequently called a joint committee. The members of the federating churches retain connection with their original denominations but new members are frequently admitted into the federated church as such, that is to say, as persons that have no particular denominational membership. Naturally federation occurs only when doctrinal differences are assumed to be negligible and when some traditional form of worship, sometimes with minor differences as to the observance of the sacraments, is accepted by all. Frequently provision is made that ministers of such a church must belong to one of the federating denominations and frequently rotation in the choice of ministers is practiced. Local finances are generally unified and the use of property is put under unified control, though titles to property may or may not be transferred to the federated church. It is customary to divide benevolences between the participating denominations. A frequent and highly unsatisfactory phenomenon of the federated church is the unfederated subsidiary. Minor organizations, most frequently denominational women's societies, insist on perpetuating themselves. Within a supposedly united group, this does not make for great success.

Long-continued successful federation, however, frequently though not universally, weakens desire to maintain separate denominations. A solution for such a condition is sometimes found in a bi-denominational relationship. The church becomes legally one; but is recognized by both denominations to which its members previously belonged. This has proven an acceptable solution in the case of the more liberal of the congregationally organized bodies.

Otherwise the federated church which desires local consolidation may ultimately become non-denominational or may go over to the denomination which has the strongest surviving elements. The latter course invites the charge that the church has been "gobbled" by that denomination.

This so-called instability of the federated church has occasioned its chief criticism by denominationalists. When, however, it is considered that denominational churches have died like flies in the areas and under the circumstances for which the federated churches are attempting a solution, this charge from denominational sources lacks a certain cogency. Moreover, as already shown, many of these churches are motivated by convenience only and assume that federation is a temporary device; so that their reversion to some other type is by no means surprising and no evidence of failure.

### DENOMINATIONAL COMMUNITY CHURCHES

As defined by the present study, a denominational community church is one formally recognized as such by other denominations. A group of coöperating denominations agrees to accord an exclusive field to the church of one of their members, usually upon condition that it broadens the terms of membership and maintains a definite community outlook, with or without an equivalent exchange of fields. This method remedies past division and prevents future competition. According to this definition, a community may unify itself on its own authority through the non-denominational church, but only ecclesiastical authority can establish conditions under which a genuine denominational community church is to be recognized.

The act by which a denominational church merely widens the terms of its membership so as to admit members of all denominations without condition, such as assent to a particular creed or re-baptism, is not accepted by the writers as a true criterion of the type. This has always been the theory of the more liberal churches of the congregational type, and has been the actual practice of multitudes of others, as proved by the interchangeable use of denominational churches by large populations as set forth earlier in this chapter. Whenever such an enlargement of the terms of membership on the part of a denominational church actually signalizes a radical departure in point of view that fact is of course highly significant, but it does not make the church a community church in the technical sense.

Denominational churches which have community aspirations and ideals but which have no authorization to represent a coöperating group of denominations, and have done nothing to change their ecclesiastical status, fall entirely outside of the definition of local church unions adopted by this study. They do not affect any ecclesiastical remedy for the religious division of communities, and their efforts are often so unconvincing as not to be demonstrable to anyone outside their own numbers. Considerable correspondence with churches of this sort has taken place in connection with the present study. Thus, in answer to the question how the "First Community Church" of a Kansas city differs from the Congregational church which preceded it, or from any Congregational church of the more liberal type which stresses the independence of the local congregation, the pastor is able to mention only the dropping of the denominational label and the admission of a few people who were previously in the parish but who would never join until the church became an outright community enterprise. The pastor hopes that the move will bring about a real change in spirit and outlook.

One needs to recognize the realities behind even so attenuated a version of the community church. It testifies to the softening of denominational asperities and to an atmosphere favorable to integration. Such churches should be differentiated from purely spurious cases where the label "community church" has been adopted for promotional purposes only. But this does not make them examples of local church union.

With respect to the churches of all the types enumerated above, a realistic viewpoint is far more important than a discussion of changes of formal ecclesiastical status. In the main they accomplish only partial local union of two or at most three denominations. Other denominational churches generally remain in the same communities. Moreover, even after the remedial adjustments have been made and the broader outlook and constituency secured, these churches sometimes fail to make a really positive demonstration of unity in community religion, perhaps in about the same proportion in which other churches fail in their more conventional ideals.

A very real challenge is found in the judgment of an experienced witness, who writes: "A community church is not really an inclusive church. Its invitation is inclusive but the very prejudice and traditions of the people, ranging from true conservatives to modern liberals, so work as to make the membership of a community church a selective one." The ideal of really making a single church the religious organ of the entire community is, to say the least, an exacting one.

### DENOMINATIONAL ATTITUDES TOWARD COMMUNITY CHURCHES

In the matter of official recognition of local church unions, a distinct change is to be recorded from the first adverse attitudes of denominations and the oft-repeated charge that here was merely another denomination in the making. The present official inclination is to take the community church movement under the wing of the movement of interdenominational coöperation. The Community Church Workers' organization has come into recognized affiliations with the Federal and Home Mission Councils. Community churches are often directly affiliated with state or local agencies of federated movements. Thus, state federations of churches in Massachusetts and Ohio have actively promoted local unions with respect to which they have served as overhead agencies of advice and administration. Fellowship and technical guidance is thus afforded to what would otherwise be a movement without a head. This tends to supply the lack of connectional resources so often complained of and to give the movement a world outlook.

Opposition on the part of denominationalists nevertheless continues. This tends to explain the vehemence of the findings of the Ohio Pastors' Convention in 1930: "District, state and national officials of the church are implored to give constructive leadership in securing by the proper consolidation relief from the intolerable conditions of overchurching and underchurching in their respective territories. The best interests of the community and of the Kingdom as a whole are to be held supreme in planning and carrying out any consolidation."

Incidental statistical evidence of the attitudes of a great denomination on local church union was secured by means of a questionnaire circulated among Methodist Episcopal constituents by the *Northwestern Christian Advocate*. The questionnaire included the question, "Should rural churches be federated on community lines?" Four thousand, two hundred and forty-eight replies were received, preachers and laymen voting in about equal numbers. Seventy-eight per cent. of the preachers and 81 per cent. of the laymen said "Yes."

All told, and within its limitations, the local church union movement turns out to be a valuable supplement to the larger movement of integration. It has authentic, indigenous roots. The varied forms fit many situations. It works with reasonable success. Its motives and objectives have been satisfactorily rationalized from the standpoint of those who participate in it. Some of the more valid criticisms against it are in process of being met by evolution within the movement itself.

## DIFFICULTIES AND LIMITATIONS OF INTEGRATION

The story of coöperation and integration as thus far told holds true for a strong majority of Protestant churches and constituencies. Most of them have little marked prejudice toward their churches. Most of them join organized movements of coöperation and federation. Most of them on occasion foster local church unions, especially in their federated and denominational forms. But some coöperate only partially, and some not at all. To complete the story, the difficulties and limitations created by these exceptions must be noted.

Difficulties stretch out along the line from unwillingness to take the next step in coöperation to new schisms actually involving a further rending to pieces of the present churches.

First there is a very considerable body of sentiment which applauds integration as far as it has gone, but refuses to go farther. Thus, at the end of a quarter century of history, after four years' study of the possibilities and after favorable preliminary action, the last quadrennial meeting of the Federal Council finally refused to broaden its base or widen its responsibilities. This decision was contrary to the mood and desire of the rank and file of church-members constituent to the denominations making up the Council, as ascertained by widely distributed questionnaires, and constitutes a real brake upon the natural evolution of the federation movement. The official majority, nevertheless, felt that integration had gone far enough, at least for the moment.

Others have always thought that it has gone ahead too far. Important denominations only partially coöperate in organized movements which the chapter has described. There are carefully defined points beyond which they will not go. Those who have most fully explained themselves, as is the case with the United Lutheran Church, base their refusal to coöperate more fully upon the feeling that interchurch enterprises are continually entering fields that are not the proper province of the churches, and also that they have omitted to base their attempt at coöperation upon a complete declaration of the common faith in strictly creedal terms. Their first difficulty is an excess seen in some of the coöperating churches' attempts to deal with moral problems involving political and social actions. Their second difficulty is a defect, the lack of a creedal basis being held to be a suppression of the church's full testimony to the truth.

From somewhat different angles the Protestant Episcopal communion has also felt it necessary to limit its coöperation. To some extent it accounts for this action by the conviction that non-episcopal bodies do not have full standing as churches, and to some extent by the fear that zeal for immediate coöperation will divert attention from the real point, namely, reunion of the separate churches into one organic body.

Controversies already noted in connection with the Federal Council have occasionally resulted in the withdrawal of a denomination from membership. The most important recent case was that of the Southern Presbyterian body. It is significant, however, that the General Assembly of this church almost immediately set up a committee charged with canvassing the possibility of re-entrance to membership.

A still more stubborn difficulty is found in the fact that certain denominations have never been associated with the national interchurch agencies described in an earlier section. A few of them belong to some of these agencies but not to others. In the main, however, those who stand outside of the zone of coöperation have not felt it possible to enter by any gate at any time. To this group belong several Lutheran bodies and the Southern Baptists.

Testimony shows that only a negligible minority of churches would refuse occasional coöperation as a gesture testifying to the spiritual unity of the churches. The Lausanne Conference on Faith and Order indicated coöperation in evangelical and good work as a minimum to which even non-Protestant bodies, except the Roman Catholic, might give assent. Nevertheless, a small number of extremists are doubtful about even so casual a form of unity.

A final limitation upon integration is that relatively small bodies of Christians are neither content to move forward nor yet to stand still; but even in recent times have insisted on breaking away from their own denominations and forming new churches. The communions chiefly affected by this tendency have been Southern Baptists and Disciples of Christ in the Southwest.

In responses to questionnaires, as well as in public utterances, Fundamentalists in various churches have often threatened schism. But probably the most significant aspect of this cleavage is that the threatened schisms do not eventuate. In no previous generation of American church history would the opposing wings of denominations have stuck together under such extreme provocation. This is high testimony to the power of the integrating trend.

SUMMARY

This chapter has brought evidence of a dominant integrative tendency expressing itself through a great mass of Protestant interchurch machinery, including agencies both of the ecclesiastical and of the administrative types, national, state and local, operating both from the top down and from the bottom up, extending in many directions, and breaking forth into new forms in many quarters.

Compared with a state of complete separation and especially compared with a state of competition, denominationalism, under stress of these forces, has suffered a transforming change. It results, at least, in something practically very different from the denominationalism in vogue previous to the last two decades.

How much change in actual behavior constitutes a change in principle and ushers in a new order may be a subject for speculative discussion. Men are now even debating whether the New Deal is a revolution or only the prelude to one. Similarly, it may be questioned whether or not the cooperative development and activity, which the chapter records, constitutes all told a basic modification of the denominational order. What is objectively established is that, in many and very important respects, the spirit of sectarian rivalry and its expressions in competitive attitudes and actions have given way to the habitual exercise of a different spirit, to the use of a different technique, and to very different practical outcomes.

# CHAPTER XIII

*Intellectual and Religious Climate*

A third great factor which conditions the life of the church as an institution is the intellectual and religious character and quality of the age to which it belongs. The church is inevitably made or marred by presence or absence of health and vigor in its religious interests at any given time and by the way in which its constituents take their religion. Ideally perhaps religion ought always to be a vital energy, dominating every age. Actually it ebbs and flows. Subjective factors, like fervor, sincerity, sense of reality and relevance, depth of motivation, now rise and now fall. Social psychology takes account of the various quantities and qualities of the energies and drives that work within social groups and institutions. Certain objective studies, such as this book reports, have given some shadowy account of these factors as they affect the church.

The prevailing way in which its constituents take religion in any given period constitutes a religious climate for that church at that time. For example, the rank and file of religious people today are deeply concerned for what they sense as the "vital" quality in religion in contrast with formal institutional adjustments. Popular religion doubtless ascribes a sort of magic to its own wishful thinking. It would like to be carried forward by resistless emotions and is sometimes more concerned with such an "induement with power from on high" than with painstakingly creating the entirely intelligible conditions of group morale. Nevertheless, popular thought is quite right in its main insistence upon vitality as a climatic characteristic able to make or mar institutional results.

Obviously the religious climate reflects the still more general intellectual and moral currents of the age. The historic creed-makers and prophets were all influenced by the dominant world views of their generations, which they largely took for granted. Similarly, the present religious climate is strongly influenced by prevailing philosophies and their correlative doctrinal or practical moods.

Of course, a religious and intellectual climate needs to be distinguished from local storms. Climates do change and whole civilizations have become extinct because the amount of rainfall shifted. Yet such changes do not occur overnight. Violent disturbances may be expected to occur when a super-heated prophet comes into conflict with an extra-chilled ecclesiastic.

It is easy, however, to overstate the significance of such a disturbance from the standpoint of permanent climate. Thus, for example, when popular interest is measured by five-year intervals over the last two or three decades, philosophy and pure science have both shared with religion in exhibiting periods of waxing and of waning. But probably no one imagines that, because these interests are tempered down, they are in danger of going permanently out of the human picture. Even automobiles and radios were more talked about when they were a novelty than now that they have become part of the social inheritance. Actual revolution in intellectual and religious climate must, therefore, be determined by long-time trends. Discussing the "requirements of social realities as determining the treatment of current social issues in education," Charles A. Beard has recently reminded the schools "that the living questions of the hour may be but ashes tomorrow, and that their formulation is certain to omit pressing issues already obscurely felt but not yet publicized."[1] World-shaking discoveries frequently ought logically to make more difference than they do and the popular ability to combine inconsistent ideas is apparently almost without limit. Nevertheless, the religious climate has changed and a church which has not changed correspondingly cannot be an authentic expression of religion today.

Objective data for the study of changes of religious climate are limited. Some changes are felt rather than understood. Their manifestations are subtle rather than specific. Certain studies of changes of religious attitudes, however, furnish limited data, and various measures of the amount and direction of shifts of religious interests have been attempted. Thus, it appears to be established that, when religion is talked about, it is more often in unfavorable terms than formerly. This is evidence of the growth of critical attitudes.[2]

OTHER INDICES OF CHANGED RELIGIOUS CLIMATE

A somewhat lagging but highly authentic proof of changes of religious climate is the appearance or disappearance of different organized structures in the church closely matching the flowing and ebbing of specific religious interests. Objective evidence is found, for example, in the ratio of religious books to the total number of books published, the ratio of articles dealing with religion to the total output of representative periodicals and the ratio of circulation of specific religious periodicals to the total magazine circulation. In all these aspects there has been some apparent relative decline of

---

[1] Beard, Charles A., *A Charter for the Social Sciences* (New York: Charles Scribner's Sons, 1932), p. 42.

[2] Hart, Hornell, "Changing Social Attitudes and Interests", *Recent Social Trends* (New York: McGraw-Hill Book Co., 1933), Vol. I, p. 402.

religious interest since the beginning of the century. For example, the 1931-32 ratio of articles on religion per 1,000 circulated copies of twenty-one American magazines was 24 per cent. less than at any period since 1905. In religious books, on the contrary, there has been a very strong recovery over the low figures of the immediate post-war period. A higher proportion of Christian ministers than ever before are included in *Who's Who*. This suggests a growing influence of the profession in the intellectual life of the age.

Perhaps an even more important index of religious climate is the increased recognition, on the part of religious authorities, of the possibility of change and their provisions of means and agencies for recording and regularizing it. Thus, the essential aim even of the doctrine of papal infallibility was to establish a regular means whereby new implications of religion might have authoritative recognition. The contrasting ideal of institutional self-criticism set forth in chapter i is incompletely, yet probably permanently, naturalized in Protestantism. This is simply an alternative to the Roman Catholic method—though a very different way of providing for the discovery and recognition of religious change.

The group of special studies upon which this book is primarily founded was chiefly devoted to successive aspects of the church as an institution and throws relatively little light upon phenomena concerned with religious climate. At certain points, however, they contain considerable illuminating data. Among the aspects thus illuminated are (1) the shifts of conventional ideas and practices particularly as related to overt religious observances; (2) the characteristic mental processes whereby the rank and file of religious constituencies adjust themselves to religious change; (3) changing specific attitudes toward (a) doctrine, (b) science and religion, (c) the church, (d) the Bible, (e) social applications of religion, (f) the uniqueness of Christianity; (4) modifications of conventional ethics; (5) the appearance of a new structure and changed institutional functions in the church; besides (6) limited data relating to inner apprehension of religious values and to (7) prophetic outlooks and expectations concerning the future of the church. Data relating to each of these topics will now have brief presentation.

### Shifting Tradition and Present Distribution of Religious Emphasis

The fact that the religious tradition has somewhat shifted its inner bases and that religious emphasis is distributed differently than in the past can be readily illustrated from available objective studies, though it cannot be strictly measured.

American church history reveals the development of a generalized Protestant religious tradition out of diverse sectarian versions. The fusing of experience on the new continent brought the most diverse denominations to a likeness of mood and method from which many of them later revolted.[3]

This homogeneous tradition was crudely and strongly Americanized in the school of the frontier. It became stabilized during the farm and village era of the nation's life. Though disturbed by the later migration of populations bringing different traditions, its homogeneity has been reasserting itself in recent years through the strong integrative movement discussed in the last chapter. The result is that, when one directly consults the religious habits of a typical urban church drawing constituents from many sources, very few persons will be found who have not at some time during their lives become habituated to a rather long list of common religious observances and practices. In other words, there is a great fund of essentially identical religious behavior which Americans bring with them, no matter where they come from. Indeed, it is possible to raise the question whether the common element is not too great already, whether religious practices are not over-standardized and too little individualized.

Differences in religious emphasis register their presence in terms of religious parties bearing theological labels. Although these terms of description are doctrinal, what they more truly express is a variety of attitudes toward religious change. Positions with respect to the church and to ethical practice are quite as much involved as dogmas. Nobody knows how many religious people adhere to any given party. Walter Lippmann's curiosity on this point led him to quote the remark of a Fundamentalist leader that nine-tenths of the vested wealth of the church had come from Fundamentalist sources.[4] Evidence presented in other chapters shows the extraordinarily rapid growth of church wealth and indicates that most of it was acquired within the last two decades during which "modernism" has had its chief vogue.[5] This suggests the probability that the Fundamentalist's claim is greatly exaggerated.

The most adequate evidence of the current distribution of religious parties is fragmentary. In 1932, however, Sanderson secured a theological self-classification of about 1,000 urban churches in answer to a questionnaire. Sixteen per cent. returned themselves as fundamentalist, 48 per cent. as conservative, 34 per cent. as liberal, and 2 per cent. as radical. No definitions were attached to these terms, so that the results do not constitute a scale in any exact sense. Roughly speaking, however, nearly two-thirds stood on the

[3] Chapter ii, p. 9.
[4] Lippmann, Walter, *A Preface to Morals* (New York: The Macmillan Company, 1929), p. 31.
[5] P. 208.

more conservative and one-third on the more radical side of an assumed middle. Fifty per cent. more fundamentalist churches and about 25 per cent. fewer liberal churches were found in "poor" territories as determined by careful social and economic ratings explained in chapter xi. This may mean that the less privileged and "disinherited" populations tend to find an escape in other-worldliness. The well-known Middletown study found conventional religion more effective among wage-earners than among other classes.

Why should one think that the distribution of religious viewpoints in terms of churches shows any evidence of their distribution among people? The New York and vicinity Methodist study of 1931 showed that, in four-fifths of the cases reported, a strong majority of members in a given church agrees with the theological emphasis which characterizes the church as a whole. In only one-fifth of the churches studied was a particular church somewhat equally divided between theological liberals and conservatives; and such divisions did not make for local peace.

SHIFTING EMPHASIS BETWEEN AGE AND YOUTH

A number of studies have attempted to differentiate religious attitudes in terms of age. They agree in showing that young people are generally more liberal theologically than their elders, though they may be more conservative about issues which have never been presented to them. Thus youth turns out to be more conservative than age in such matters as church unity and race relations. The temperamental radicalism of youth does not appear in connection with unfamiliar issues. On such issues youth is more inclined to accept the status quo than people of middle age are.

More clear-cut results appear when age differences are measured in terms of a homogeneous professional group. Thus Betts' notable comparison of the beliefs of seven hundred ministers in and near Chicago with those of two hundred theological students in the same area showed that the future ministers had shifted much farther in a liberal direction than their elders.[6]

What all this evidence proves is that the cultural complex traditionally identified with Christianity, including as it does a miscellany of customs, beliefs and moral convictions, is shifting as a result of inner conflicts. This is an obvious commonplace. The cloistered conservative may deny that any change has happened. The cloistered radical thinks things are settling in his favor and that it is all over but the shouting. The conclusion justified by objective evidence is that no extreme shift in the center of gravity has yet occurred. Thus Counts notes that, over most of the area of the United States, religion is virtually assumed as the basis for public-school instruction,

---

[6] Betts, *Beliefs of 700 Ministers* (New York: 1929).

and that the virtues which the nation attempts to inculcate through its schools are conceived of in conventional Protestant terms.[7]  The Middletown survey found that being a church-member ranked third in the order of specifications for a "good father" in the minds of high-school pupils, exactly as it does in the fastnesses of the Tennessee mountains.

Such a conclusion constitutes a very irritating discovery for religious radicals.  "I suppose," said Paul Hutchinson, in a Chicago address, "every one of us here this afternoon has spoken superciliously of the fact that enormous crowds will still turn out in this city to hear Mr. Darrow denounce religious ideas that went into the ash-can fifty years ago. But that shows how prone we are to fool ourselves.  The fact we should face is that, to a large part of the population of the city of Chicago, the ideas that Mr. Darrow *says* represent the religious outlook are still taken to represent the religious outlook.  We haven't much more than begun to deal with this issue in terms of the total public.  If one claims that Mr. Darrow is fooling the public, he has only to ask them to turn on the radio and find out!  And when you get outside a northern industrial city such as this and sample the religious ideas that still hold the field—and at the same time realize how inevitably the same ideas that have caused such changes in the restricted circles of which we are a part are going to penetrate within the next few decades into every nook of the country—well, when you once really begin to face all that you find yourself wondering whether these acids of modernity have really begun to work yet, let alone whether their destructive properties have been brought under control."[8]

What Mr. Hutchinson points out is that there are regional, and generally rural lags in the shifting of religious tradition.  There is, consequently, the need to break up any statement of the average into terms of smaller units, exactly as the statistical results of earlier chapters were broken up by states and regions.  Denominations concentrated in rural states, especially those including large backward populations such as the people of the Southern Mountains and plantation Negroes, have experienced least change of religious and intellectual climate.  There is this much truth in H. L. Mencken's ungracious reference to the "Bible belt."  Liberalism and Fundamentalism in many respects are phases of urban-rural conflict.  Studies of urban psychology have brought out how rarely in human history has any total population been dominated by scientific trends of thought.  Such a condition has been found only in the most highly urbanized groups subjected to intensive means of communicating ideas.  Upon the urban side the relationship between conservatism and poverty has already been noted.  Immigrants, experi-

---

[7] Counts, George S., *American Road to Culture* (New York: John Day Company, 1930).
[8] Hutchinson, Paul, "Revolution and Religion", *Chicago Theological Seminary Record*, March, 1934, p. 5.

encing a conservative revulsion in a new country and seeking refuge rather than readjustment, gravitate toward fundamentalist sects. Meanwhile, the continual replenishment of urban churches by rural immigrants keeps more distinctly urban attitudes continuously diluted.

It is clear, then, that the religious and intellectual climate has changed more in some parts of the nation than in others, but that no real general revolution has yet occurred. The slowness of progressive ideas to take effect has consequently driven many radicals to adopt the notion of a religious aristocracy. They doubt whether the "high religion" of the Masters will ever become acceptable to the masses.[9] This is obviously to abandon the expectation of a general change in the religious climate.

It is not necessary for an objectively-minded person to take sides in this controversy. Whether or not he is disappointed with the situation, the fact is that the nation as a whole remains essentially conservative in its religious attitude, although the growing power of cities and the spread of urban-mindedness (though checked by the depression) may make the situation different tomorrow.

### PARTICULAR CHANGES: RELIGIOUS PRACTICES AND OBSERVANCES

A previous chapter showed that church-membership is not declining in the United States. But are the practices of the church as well kept up and the observance of religion as frequent as they used to be? Dividing practices and observances into public, domestic and private, and taking church attendance as the most significant of the public practices, a piecing together of fragmentary evidences tells the story not wholly favorable to the churches. Thus a painstaking study of Windsor Co., Vermont, showed that church attendance had declined over a fifty-year period. A recent sampling study of general rural social trends indicated that attendance had decreased from 4.5 to 4.1 times per month per member between 1924 and 1930.[10]

The Middletown study of a small urban community found that church attendance on the average Sunday represented only eleven white males and eighteen white females out of 100 population and testified that attendance was somewhat declining. Although seven out of ten New York Methodists declared that Sunday church-going increased their effectiveness and happiness during the following week "very much," yet one-half testified that they now attend church less frequently than in the past and only one-sixth that they attend it more.[11] These phenomena are commonly connected with

[9] Lippmann, Walter, *op. cit.,* pp. 192-3.
[10] Brunner and Kolb, *Rural Social Trends* (New York: McGraw-Hill Book Co., 1933), p. 221.
[11] Van Vleck, Joseph, Jr., Survey Director, *A Survey of Methodist Episcopal Churches in Manhattan, The Bronx and Westchester* (New York: Methodist Episcopal Church City Planning Committee, 1931), p. 86.

changed habits as to "sabbath observance," legalizing of Sunday movies, ignoring of Blue Laws and their somewhat wholesale repeal as a result of a wave of candor following the repeal of the Eighteenth Amendment. On the other hand, much wider observance of special religious seasons, such as Lent, by the non-ritualistic majority of Protestant churches is to be recalled; and the total use of churches by their constituencies is doubtless considerably increased with churches of the elaborate and socially adapted types.

A similar decline of the week-day devotional services represented by the traditional prayer meeting is widely recognized.[12]

With respect to domestic religious practices little objective data exist. Two-thirds of the families of Hartshorne's "best" Sunday school maintained at least one domestic religious rite. Very limited sampling by means of schedules nevertheless substantiates the widespread belief that the practices of family prayers and of offering grace before meals have declined. In the sample quoted these were rated as of low value, and were among the few practices which an appreciable number of younger church adherents had never known anything about in their own families. On the contrary, discussion of religious subjects in the home was reported as increasing. This may register a transfer of religion from an atmosphere of formality to a freer and more realistic approach.

Of private practices the same limited sampling indicated a decline in devotional Bible reading and "personal work" in the sense of direct soliciting of others to become Christians. Prayer, however, was reported to be equally frequent or more frequent than in the past by three-fifths of those replying; while meditation, the support of benevolent causes, and humanitarian service were reported as increasing practices.

On a total battery of seventeen religious practices, 34 per cent. of those replying indicated an increasing frequency, while 45 per cent. reported them equally frequent and only 21 per cent. less frequent than in the past. It is perhaps significant that the largest proportion, both of increases and of decreases, were found in the group whose ages fell between twenty and thirty years. Here was a generation facing both ways. The sheer omission of formerly standard practices was most frequent with the youngest people, those less than twenty years of age. All told, however, the data appeared to show that, while some of the overt practices of religion were going, others were coming, and that the change was more of fashion than of fact.

### Popular Assimilation of New Elements of Intellectual Climate

Deep-seated traits of the American mind, its intellectual folk-ways, subject all new and challenging ideas to the test of practicability. The traits of the

---

[12] P. 151.

national mental type have often been indicated. Saying that the American is practical implies that he is characteristically non-intellectual. He is an "activist," who goes ahead uncritically on the basis of rather superficial traditional formulae of rationalization. This explains the all too general adoption of money as a measure of success. A curiously interesting commentary on the tendency is the fact that the profounder Calvinistic tradition of many of the older denominations turned into a practical Arminianism on the frontier and joined with sanguine and motor-minded Methodism in the conquest of the national though religious enterprise.

These dominant characteristics of the mind of the rank and file of American religious people act as a set of filters through which all intellectual novelties have to pass. In a recent study some thousands of marginal comments and separate notes attached to questionnaires were analyzed for evidences of mood as well as with reference to content.[13] These fresh samplings of raw sentiment prove that American religious emphasis is very largely determined by emotional attitudes. Novel issues very quickly get entangled in religious feeling. Thus, that all-time best seller, Sheldon's *What Would Jesus Do?*, was a highly successful attempt to bring a religious interpretation to modern social problems. It met with instantaneous and astounding success. It is equally easy to arouse religious fears against an unskilfully presented novelty. The American religious public has something of the caution of the backwoodsman scouting in a hostile forest.

Again, a re-examination of the data of naïve religious expression shows how generously the American mind reacts against specific wrongs, especially when they are spectacularly discussed. Reforming zeal is quickly started against any evil which is not too subtle.

Still again, in dealing with religious matters the American argues freely from direct personal experience. He continually applies the test of practicability rather than of authority. For this reason he finds himself in continuous conflict as between the ideal and the practical. His hasty reactions are not balanced by an adequate philosophy. The effect of his repeated perplexity is very amply documented from responses to questionnaires. In spite of his self-confidence the American repeatedly has to confess: "I do not know what to think." But the dilemma is quickly forgotten in an emotional response to the next call to action.

Of other working formulae which the rank and file of Americans apply to religious matters the most important has already been noted. It is the distinction between the vital and the formal in religion, that is to say, between what would stir an emotional response and what would fail to do so. The next most frequent formula is the distinction between essentials and non-essentials. Popular American thought has thoroughly adopted this

---

[13] Douglass, *Church Unity Movements*, chapter iv.

ancient instrument for evading sharp alternatives. Non-essentials are many and are always subject to accommodation. Essentials are few: and although most Americans try to preserve the "evangelical" distinction, that is to say to demand a version of the gospel based upon the concept of the divinity of Christ, yet the view that the church is the sum of the denominations makes it easy to regard non-evangelicism as in some sense embraced within its wider borders.

Finally, Americans generally believe in religious progress by stages. They do not want to go all the way at once and are not greatly concerned about goals so long as they retain the comforting sense that they are faced in the right direction.

The reverse of these habitually characteristic moods is widespread distrust of the validity of theological issues as they are sharply drawn by intellectuals. When the intellectual declares that two ideas are antithetical and that only one alternative is possible,[14] the common man feels within himself that differences between abstract notions are largely artificial. He has actually little patience with the "last stands" which hair-splitting theologians make on the grounds of intellectual integrity of conscience. There is no issue he believes, or almost none, that practical man cannot compromise. Differences that look big to doctrinaire minds have repeatedly been compromised and popular intelligence is not able to discover which part of them should not be.

The generalizations just stated are based upon the study of fresh data representing spontaneous expression of religious attitudes on the part of some thousands of Americans of various denominations and scattered in all parts of the nation. The religious life of the country is ruled by people who think after this fashion. In spite, then, of variations as to moisture and heat, which one properly recognizes as climatic changes, the mountain ranges and the seas are just where they always have been.

### REGISTRATION OF CHANGED ATTITUDES ON SPECIFIC POINTS

The essential religious conservatism of the American people and the sieve of practicability through which it compels all innovating ideas to pass, cannot, however, prevent ultimate changes in intellectual and religious climate. They only make them less certain and clear-cut, and slower in arriving than they logically ought to be.

Specific objective evidence of very considerable changes at numerous points is at hand and will have next consideration.

The introduction and persistence of a critical attitude within the church and its use of scientific means of investigation and control have been pointed out in chapter i.

---

[14] Lippmann, Walter, *op. cit.*, p. 143.

While the traditional doctrines continue to be held and newer ideas are added to them without adequate sense of incongruity, definite ways are apparent in which traditional Christianity has shifted. The study of *Recent Social Trends* showed, for example, that while approving references to traditional Christianity still outnumber disapproving ones nearly two to one in American periodicals, the ratio of approval has declined since the beginning of the century. The "intellectual" magazines now disapprove 50 per cent. more often than they approve; but "mass circulation" and women's magazines approve twice as often as they disapprove. It is, however, the sensational magazines that are most approving. In proportion as a magazine is unworthy to exist at all it supports religion! In brief, the masses are most conventional and the more low-brow the approach to their minds the more unaltered is the concept of religion which appeals to them.

Reference to specific points seems to prove that there is more mention of God in periodical literature than formerly, but more skepticism about Him; and that a less personal conception of deity is in vogue than formerly. Interest in life after death appears to have declined, though 70 per cent. of New York Methodists still assert that they believe in it "strongly." The Middletown study, however, found scarcely one-half of upper high-school pupils affirming the truth of the proposition "The purpose of religion is to prepare people for the hereafter," though this group had proved highly conservative on most religious tests.

On the contrary, attitudes toward what *Recent Social Trends* called "open-minded religion" have grown more favorable since the beginning of the century as judged by references in periodical literature. Two-thirds of references in intellectual magazines approve of religion of this liberal type and the favorable ratio in other magazines was as high as four and a quarter to one.

With respect to science and religion, American periodical literature registers increased approval of science as an ally in the religious quest rather than as an enemy of religion. This has gone with decreased reverence for creed, dogma and authority. A wide circularization of religious leaders and popular constituencies justifies the generalization that, while it is thought desirable to retain historic creeds as useful summaries of Christian conviction, they are recognized as having been strongly affected by the philosophies of the generations in which they were written, and are considered inadequate in scope as expressions of the faith of the present day. They are to be subjected to present-day interpretation, with wide latitude for individual freedom of understanding, and assent to them is not to be required as the formal basis of membership in the church.

With respect to the church itself, this entire book is evidence of considerable shifting in the Protestant understanding of the implications of institutional religion.  Not with enthusiasm, but sometimes with acquiescence and sometimes willy-nilly, the church has been subjected to objective scrutiny. Attacks upon the church have been shown to be largely elaborations of an historical anti-institutionalist attitude which Protestantism has always maintained in the interests of personal religion, and which has permitted a certain critical attitude toward the church to persist.  Other critical appraisers mix antagonism to institutionalism as such with attacks upon the church's shortcomings as an institution in modern society.  Sociological insight on the whole defends the institutional organization of religion as inherently necessary and effective, but joins with religion in pointing out its dangers and calling for continuous self-criticism on the basis of scientific studies.[15]

Attitudes toward the Bible as the traditional Protestant source of religious authority have undoubtedly suffered a shift of emphasis.  In periodical publications the Bible is now getting only half the attention it had twenty years ago.  This finding is subject to qualifications by the fact that biblical scholarship, once the subject of heated controversy has now become an acceptable commonplace of all the colleges.  The Bible was most discussed in the heat of the Bryan-Darrow controversy.  It now shares the fate of the automobile and radio in not being so much discussed as when it was a sensation.  Wide circularization of representative Protestant constituencies shows that the Bible is now regarded as the authoritative source of Christian faith and practices only in connection with and because confirmed by the historic experience of religious people in the church and by the contemporary experience of religious people today.  It does not stand alone, nor in its older antithesis to the church; nor is it final in the sense of repressing the quest for new truths.

Still again, the sense in which Christianity is regarded as a unique religion has clearly suffered a modification.  The Middletown study found 83 per cent. of public-school boys and 92 per cent. of girls affirming the truth of the proposition "Christianity is the one true religion."  Nevertheless, a widespread change in the conception of Christian missions was evidenced by the pressure and demand which led to the recent Laymen's Foreign Missions Inquiry; and the idea of substituting Christianity for inferior religions by any process of "conquest" has undoubtedly dwindled.  This change, like all the others mentioned, has not spread to all regions nor to all classes of religious people.  Hutchinson thinks that "when even 50 per cent. of the church-members of the United States grasp the significance of the substitution of 'Christianity as a faith' for 'Christianity as *the* faith' . . . religion in this country will be shaken from center to circumference."[16]

Perhaps, however, the religious masses will assimilate the new notion to

---

[15] See chapter i.
[16] Hutchinson, Paul, *loc. cit.*

their older belief without seeing the inconsistency, as they have already done on other issues times without number.

## Modification of Conventional Ethics

Very significant changes in the religious and intellectual climate have brought changes to the church in the field of conventional ethics. One of the most outstanding is the supplementing (perhaps logically the supplanting) of a strongly individualistic version of religion aiming primarily at personal salvation, by new ethical interests and agreements, largely in fields previously regarded as secular. These new interests are expressed in terms of problems of the present age.

The vehicle employed to effect this shift of interests and values was originally termed a social "creed," because churches are addicted to that word. In reality it consisted of codes of ethical pronouncements somewhat analogous to and, in its ideals, foreshadowing, newer business and professional codes now developed by many voluntary groups in America.[17]

Beginning with a set of judgments upon industrial relationships, the scope of these pronouncements has greatly increased during the last twenty-five years, by taking in agricultural and rural problems, on the one hand, and the more intimate problems of the family, on the other. So innovating a set of highly specific ethical definitions could not expect to find acceptance in so traditional a constituency as that of the churches without controversy—illustrated, for example, by the sharp schism in the Protestant churches over birth control. Nevertheless, the social morality of the churches has been increasingly modified in recent years and its novelties have extended their prestige through processes of rational discussion and education rather than through appeal to specific divine authority in behalf of the new positions reached.

Perhaps the most profound of recent modifications of the conventional ethical outlooks within the church are those having to do with family and sex ethics. For example, the report on Revised Ideals presented to the Federal Council in 1932, in the form in which it was adopted by the Commission on the Church and Social Service, declared for "a constructive approach to the problem of sex and marriage." The report went on to affirm, "In this area of experience where old customs are changing in response to changing conditions of life, care should be taken not to discard past social experiences merely because they come from the past, and equal care must be taken to protect an emerging experience which gives promise of enriching our common life and which may some day be institution-

---

[17] For historical statements and data showing the evolution of the Social Creeds see Federal Council of Churches of Christ, *Official Handbook for the Quadrennial Meeting*, 1932, p. 42.

alized."[18]   While declaring that "any form of marriage which from the start contemplates divorce is incompatible with the Christian idea and with the clearest lessons of human experience," the report continued, "divorce or separation may be preferable to the enforced continuance of a relation which has no true basis in mutual respect and affection; but it is evidence of failure, always to be deplored, and to be avoided if by any means success can be achieved even over what may appear insurmountable obstacles."[19]

The essential conservatism of the church was evidenced by the fact that the Federal Council declined to adopt these statements in the form submitted.  Nevertheless, the amazingly significant thing was that they should have been officially presented at all and have won the support of a large minority in the year 1932.

An earlier report of a Federal Council commission regarding birth control had been repudiated by the Council as a whole.  Nevertheless the issue would not down.  So many "troubled consciences" had appealed to them for counsel that the bishops of the Anglican communions in world assembly at Lambeth, in 1930, had felt constrained to speak "frankly and openly" upon the matter.  While, in their Encyclical Letter, the bishops as a body had appealed to self-denial as the ideal solution of difficulties in sex relations, the special report of the Conference, under the head of birth control, denied that the strong Catholic tradition against the use of deliberate methods of preventing conception was necessarily final; and, with great caution and in deference to medical and scientific findings, declared, ". . . if there is good moral reason why the way of abstinence should not be followed, we cannot condemn the use of scientific methods to prevent conception, which are thoughtfully and conscientiously adopted."[20]   Conservatism again voiced itself in the dissent of many bishops from the findings of the majority.  The significant thing, however, is the recognition, by the highest ecclesiastical authorities, of the need of a modification of traditional wholesale ethical prohibitions in the light of modern facts and conditions.

### INSTITUTIONAL EVIDENCE OF CHANGED RELIGIOUS CLIMATE

The most objective and solidly demonstrable evidence of a change of religious climate is registered in the appearance of new institutional structures in the church and its taking on of additional functions to match new aspects of thought.  Of this again the entire present book is witness.  It is seen in the broadened programs of the local churches and denominations, in their development of new types of religious professionals, and in the

---

[18] *Ibid*, p. 53.
[19] *Ibid*, p. 54.
[20] The Lambeth Conference, New York, 1930, p. 91.

supply of specialized facilities and equipment to carry out the expanding concept of the church's ministry.

Virtually all the leading denominations have developed departments of social justice and interracial good-will, while the interests of marriage and the home, and of peace movements have secured implementing machinery in the church and in interchurch organizations. Religious education has brought schemes of reorganization both to local churches and to the life of the church at large, together with new types of workers and new technical standards.

Finally, the whole organized movement and machinery of federation and coöperation, the development in many denominations of commissions on church union, and the actual mergers of numerous churches, constitute the strongest objective evidence of new thinking in the realms of interchurch relations.

CHANGES IN INNER APPREHENSION AND APPRECIATION OF RELIGIOUS VALUES

No data exist which one is warranted in regarding as representative with respect to changes in the inner apprehension and appreciation of religious values. A trace of processes which are actually going on may nevertheless be found by dipping into the facts at any point.

This section reports the direct testimony of a small group of persons of widely varying religious antecedents, who had been thoroughly exposed to a changed religious climate through present membership in a progressive church. In response to a questionnaire these persons indicated their present sense of the value of thirty-nine factors of the religious life, classified as practices, interests and appreciations. Data as to the practices have already been presented.[21] The fourteen items listed as "interests" were distinguished from the practices as being more inward, and were registered as indicators of the objects and ideals of personal life. Of these interests humane service and the ethical aspect of religion, represented, for example, in concern for social justice, together with the "spiritual life," were most frequently rated high in importance and identified as among the increasing interests, measured either quantitatively, according to the time or emphasis accorded them in experience, or qualitatively by the degree of satisfaction which they brought. "God" and "Jesus Christ" were also rated as interests of high value, but less frequently of growing value.

On the contrary, the future life, doctrines, the aesthetic aspect of religion, and revivals and evangelism were rated low in value, and recorded as interests of decreasing power.

The eight "appreciations" differed from the "interests" only in being more explicitly determined by their emotional color. In the current evaluation of the group in question, the appreciation of the religious worth and meaning of life and the sense of inter-relatedness or solidarity of God and man were most often ranked highest and stood first and second respectively in the list of increasing experiences. The sense of the divine presence, comfort and security was also given high rating, but less often appeared an increasing factor in personal life.

On the contrary, the experiences of struggle with temptation, of sense of guilt after wrong-doing, and of forgiveness were given low value and were rarely declared to be increasing factors in the inner life.

All told, progress in the terms of the interests and appreciations of religion as a whole was noted by more than one-half of the persons replying, while one-third more felt they had at least not lost ground.

One person in five also testified to experience of "a revolutionary renewal of value" with respect to one or more practices, interests or appreciations. The thing took hold of him at a profounder level than previously. This seems to mean that religion continues to perform inner miracles for a few of its adherents even in a modern liberal church. These cases of creative religious discovery were most frequently found among the younger group of adherents and were doubtless a modified version of old-time conversion experience. Such radical renewals of meaning occasionally referred to practices such as church attendance and activities or to private prayer; but most often concerned the apprehension of spiritual quality of life and its religious meaning and value.

So far as such slender data may be symptomatic of what is taking place in the more liberal churches, they indicate, what the studies of religious social trends and literature have already demonstrated on a national scale, namely, a swing toward the humanitarian and ethical aspects of religion as compared to the doctrinal ones, together with a certain obscuring of the more personal characteristics of deity. They, nevertheless, reveal the conservative heart of contemporary experience in that it still clings to the older symbols. It honors with a high theoretical rating values which it cannot honestly profess as having increasing power to command inner loyalty or to give satisfaction.

At worst, these data show a religion that somewhat more than holds its own for religious people. Quantitatively and qualitatively it is going ahead; with more frequency of progress on the side of interests and appreciations than on the side of external practices. A generalized sense of the religious values and meanings of life has become dominant over more precisely defined religious transactions for the adjustment of relations with God or for securing salvation.

If the church is regarded as the institutional shell built around inner happenings like these, sometimes facilitating and sometimes handicapping them, it seems clear that the quality of inner happenings as symbolized in the cases cited need by no means result in a feeble church. Climatic changes have altered the complexion of inner experience; but even in a type of church most subject to these changes there is no sign that religious life is exhausted or incapacitated as to either inner meaning or institutional expression. A church which is commensurate with the unquestionable persistence and vigor of current religion will be a church to reckon with still.

# PART FOUR

# FORESHADOWINGS

# CHAPTER XIV

## Prospects and Policies

At the end of a prolonged examination of the church in its several aspects, such as the previous thirteen chapters have reported, have any conclusive results been reached as to its essential lineaments and proportions? In contrast with a mere abstract or summary, repeating the skeleton of the previous chapters, can one point out any pattern of fresh significance which enables him to discriminate between the big and the little within the evidence? What tendencies show vigor enough to project themselves into the future and thus to forecast the further progress of the church?

Again, at what point can anything be done about it? For, as shown in the Introduction, the hope of modifying the present practice and possibly suggesting some control of the future of the church was a large part of the motivating purpose of the studies now being summarized. What, then, are the policies to which the total data most strongly point?

The present chapter attempts, first, to present the chief conclusions to be drawn from the data with a view to the reader's final orientation and general outlook upon the church; and, secondly, to summarize the church's institutional prospects at specific points and the corresponding policies indicated for church strategy and administration.

### THE GENERAL OUTLOOK

The general outlook has three major aspects.

#### OBTRUSIVENESS OF THE TRANSCENDENTAL ASPECT

The first grand impression emerging from a prolonged scrutiny of the phenomenon of the church is that its transcendental aspect exercises a great and persistent influence upon its institutional organization and life. From the viewpoint of this book the scientific study of religion constitutes a branch of the social sciences. The studies which have been summarized herein have used the logical and technical instruments of these sciences. As defined, however, by their best exponents, all these sciences have "at the center . . . a core of substantial data and inference; on the periphery . . . an uncertain borderland where all merge in a transcendent interest."[1]

---

[1] Beard, Charles A., *A Charter for the Social Sciences in the Schools,* Part I of the Report of the Commission on the Social Studies (New York, Charles Scribner's Sons, 1932), p. 18.

In other words, the persistence of the transcendent interest in the case of the church differentiates it only in type, not in kind, from the other social studies. All social science is based upon philosophic implications, avowed or unavowed. The peculiarity of the scientific study of religion is merely that it is so continuously and obtrusively invaded by the transcendent elements of the situation.

This has been evidenced, first, by the naïve attitudes and judgments of the masses of religious adherents, who, as the first chapter showed, are highly critical of an approach to the church which, even methodologically, ignores or minimizes its supra-mundane aspects. To religious people the church is first of all an object of faith, rather than an object of scientific scrutiny.

Even stronger evidence is perhaps found in the steady continuance of the financial support of the church on a voluntary basis. The most revealing factor in human economics is the spending of material resources upon ideals and passions rather than upon necessities. It is as the fulfillment of a dream rather than as the maintenance of a particularly efficient instrument that the believing masses, from generation to generation, continue to pour out their substance upon the church. Consequently, the masses are not greatly impressed either by the magnitude of the social institution or by the vast sums which the church costs. Compared to the glory of God which the church reflects these things are as the small dust of the balance.

Other evidences have come from revelations of the habitual consciousness of the ministry. Paradoxically, while the laity are not impressed by the church's strength, the ministry is not deterred by its weakness, of which it is all too poignantly aware. Ministers' sons flock into the ministry in exceedingly disproportionate numbers, in spite of its many vicissitudes, including the impossible economic situation which dooms the majority of local churches to relative inefficiency and failure, if not to death. All this does not shake the minister's confidence in his high and holy vocation, based as it is in half of the reported cases on the personal consciousness of a divine "call," nor cause him to want essentially to change its methods. Neither have these things really embittered him, although the discrepancy between the faith and the reality does tend to divide his mind and to skew his psychological characteristics.

Last of all comes the evidence of the church's persistent and unwavering insistence upon worship and symbolic observances as its supreme function. Notwithstanding the demands which all other functions make upon it, it continues to find the climax of its life in transactions which have no utilitarian value but which merely constitute appropriate conduct in the presence of a world that faith accepts as supra-mundane; which do not feed the poor but only express in ritual the sense of the fitness of things derived from what is believed to be experience in the characteristics and values of that realm.

To repeat, then, the church which is the object of scientific scrutiny is at the same time and primarily something apprehended by the faith of religious people; and that faith strongly influences and indeed is integral with its objective quality as an institution. The church puts on a character in order to celebrate and interpret the supra-mundane world; yet its off-stage character, so to speak, turns out highly consistent with the character it takes to act its religious part.

DOMINANT CHARACTERISTICS OF THE CHURCH AS A SOCIAL INSTITUTION

A second major feature of the total evidence emerges when one shifts to the specifically scientific basis of approach. One is now concerned with the church as a social institution, and legitimately subject to scientific scrutiny. In this capacity many of its aspects are beyond control. They reflect inherent characteristics of social institutions and the results of the actual historical evolution which the church has experienced as such an institution. The consequences of these are unescapable. For example, the conditioning of the local church by its environment, as shown in chapters iv and xi; its almost complete subjection to the results of the mobility of urban populations; the all but indissoluble bonds between the present fortunes of the church and the fortunes of the community—all these are things which no virtue or artfulness on the church's part can get away from.

Pure science may describe, measure and compare these phenomena. It may also possibly alleviate the bitterness of the situation by setting up the expectation of change, so that the church need not be surprised when such trials overtake it. But pure science cannot suggest anything to be done about these inevitables of the social situation except for the church to change along with its environment—incidentally to pointing out that while some changes bring disadvantages, others bring advantages.

Other objective aspects of the church to a considerable extent, and indeed most of its aspects to some extent, are amenable to rational control. This is true, in part, for the reason that they furnish alternative methods. The city, for example, offers the church other types of human association as a basis for its fellowship in exchange for the old parochial pattern which it has destroyed. To some extent, also, the church can continue to use both old and new methods, because social change is never instantaneous nor complete. It may even play one method over against the other. In the large, however, the realm of successful policy is limited. Applied science can add something to the arts of churchmanship. A certain precision may be substituted for the rule of thumb in church administration. Within these limits, as the first chapter pointed out, but only within them, scientific studies of the church have distinct practical value and help to satisfy some part of the desire of adherents and officials to improve church conditions.

The validity and importance of this analysis is further established when one considers its consequences for some of the particular phenomena which earlier chapters have investigated. The sphere of deliberate control is narrowly limited. The urban church, to repeat the example previously cited, carries over from the country the assumption of the neighborhood parish. But half of urban church people go out of their neighborhoods to church. On the whole there is really nothing for the church to do but to accept the situation. Again, the nation is unable to support anything like the present number of churches on the basis of standards which the churches are willing to admit. If, then, there are not fewer churches, those that exist will continue to be relatively poor. There is no escape from this alternative. Still again, denominations grow where they have the advantage of large rural reinforcements. A denomination which lacks such reinforcements on the whole is powerless to alter the situation. Once more, a successful grouping of churches into a "larger parish" can take place only upon an authentic community basis. There must ordinarily be a pre-existent principle of unity comprehending the institutions to be unified. The penalty of omitting to observe this principle is failure. Neither the transcendent values of the church nor the stoutest exercise of human purposes can alter the fact that such social conditionings have been determinative of the church's fortunes in the past and will continue to dominate its fortunes in the future.

ORIENTATION ON THREE LEVELS

The foregoing analysis shows why the final orientation of thinking with respect to the church must take place on three levels at once. It must take account of the ever-obtrusive and inescapable sense of transcendental social relations which so deeply colors the institutional life of the church, and weaves out of the two aspects a seamless robe of objective phenomenon. This factor, imponderable as it is, is none the less of high significance in an attempt at a sociological understanding of religion as institutionalized in the church.

At the same time, in justice to the truth, the invariable consequences flowing out of the nature of social grouping and the inherent institutional behaviors of the church must be continuously insisted upon. These can no more be ignored than can its religious characteristics. And it is these features, of course, that it is the peculiar business of social science to bring out.

Finally, in accordance with the ultimate practical purpose of the scientific studies under review, an adequate summary must point out—as this has already undertaken to do—major consequences for church policy. It is entirely possible for wise action to secure some of the church's immediate objectives. At this point, particularly, research helps to distinguish between the practicable and the impracticable and to set the church in the way of successful programizing.

HOW THE INTELLECTUAL CLIMATE AFFECTS THE CHURCH

The discovery that the church represents three strands of fact, each running through the total phenomena and maintaining its own pattern, yet all woven into one fabric with a master pattern, suggests that the great factors external to the church which universally condition it, must in turn influence the church in all three aspects. This applies to the intellectual climate of an age, and its changes, which so obviously and fundamentally affect the churches.

Consideration on all three levels of the phenomena involved in the intellectual climate reinforces the distinction made in chapter xiii between spells of weather and genuine climatic shifts. Particularly does it give one to doubt whether temporary re-shufflings of ideas have any great pertinence as compared with institutionally registered trends.

A more superficial view imagines that there might be a direct and immediate impact of transcendental insights and contents upon mundane affairs, if only the right religious conditions pertained. It vexes itself over the bondage of the church to the shifting winds of transient interest. Expounding his own theological evolution from 1911 on, an influential minister now approaching middle life writes, "Since then, things have happened. Things are still happening. And religion has gone through many a change of phase; from the social gospel in 1911-13, romantic pacifism in 1914-16, wild war madness in 1917-18, idealistic internationalism in 1919-20, and complacent 'normalcy' in 1921-29, to a kind of apocalyptic mysticism in 1930 until now."[2]

Religion in general, this writer thinks, has "followed with exact precision the changes of mood and circumstance which have taken place in the social environment as a whole." It has been little more than a burning glass focusing these changes in a peculiar manner; or at best has merely sublimated "something which was crassly material in its foundation." In some better future, he hopes, creative religion will emerge straight from the transcendental realm to enter the field of human affairs as a directly exercised power, and will control in its own right rather than merely intensifying current feelings and rationalizing current policies.

But is this a fair or illuminating account of what has happened to organized religion in the last quarter century or an inspired prophecy of

---

[2] Bradley, Dwight J., "Where Does Religion Come In?" in *The Oberlin Alumni Magazine* (Oberlin, Ohio, Feb. 1, 1934), Vol. XXX, No. 5, p. 134.

what ever ought to happen? First, did organized religion reflect in any such servile fashion the moods and circumstances of the changing days? Doubtless all of them could be traced in the sermons of the more ebullient and "progressive" clergy. But what of the rank and file of the church? Granting their rather real response to the world-war psychology and to the later reaction against it, in the light of a fuller understanding of the institutional characteristics of the church was not what truly happened something like the following?

The social gospel, at least, and possibly also "idealistic internationalism," projected certain ideas and values into the mind of the church and asked tradition to move over and give them room. For some of them tradition did move over. Next, the more persistent survivors demanded place in the institutional structure of the churches, and ultimately got it. Now, while unadjusted or even inconsistent ideas may, for a long time, more or less peacefully coincide in the same minds or in different parties of the same church, institutional structures and practices are objective entities which crowd and jostle one another. There are practical limits to the growth of organization by accretion. There is not time enough for the separate expression of each separately formulated interest. Hence, whether logically conflicting or not, as organized concerns and "units of transactions" they become competitors. Finally, the indefinite clutter of resulting social machinery breaks down. Consequently, the problem of the integration of the old and new structures and practices arises. The struggles and tensions incident to such a readjustment (which is by no means over for many of the ideas introduced within the last quarter century) become the really efficient and compelling agents for the re-examining and final readjusting of ideas. When these thorough-going processes are completed trends will have changed. There has been, for example, a decline of dogmatism in the churches. But its proof is found in objectively modified practices, in the inclusion of new institutional structures like forums and educational classes, together with the discussion method in education and the reorganization of the policy of the church so as to accommodate these things. The proof is not found in fulminations against dogmatism, nor in the floating about in the air of liberal ideas.

The marks of a significant change in the intellectual climate accordingly are from the objective standpoint, (1) the survival of a new idea in spite of contrary tradition; (2) its institutional lodgment; (3) its projection of a tentative structure to express itself; (4) the conflict of the new structures and their practices with the old which produces new situations; (5) the growth of power to challenge and compel institutional reorganization and mutually appreciative adjustment of old and new vehicles of ideas in the light of these practical necessities.

Is there any likelihood that transcendental religion will in the future take any shorter cut in bringing about the church's changes? Or that a new idea will in any briefer fashion discover its own meaning? The writers doubt it. While from the very outset of a new movement prophetic souls must risk, not only their ecclesiastical futures but their eternal destinies as well, on being right, the church at large cannot be expected to base its policies upon novelties before they have registered their influence upon the apperceiving institutional mass and have won a distinguishable place in the resulting transformation—God still not being in so much of a hurry as critics and reformers are.

A 60,000-ton liner cannot come about as quickly as a boy's sailboat can, but it is a more significant type of craft. This is simply a shortened way of saying that ways in which men group themselves religiously, the practices of these groups and the thinking incident to changes in grouping and practices, are the significant things in the religious pattern: not thinking which has not yet affected such changes or which may have passed away without having affected them.

In the light of such a general outlook, consideration may now turn to the church's prospects in some of the specific aspects in which this book has considered them and to the particular phases which are suggested by the dominant trends in each as ascertained.

## TRADITIONAL CENTRAL ACTIVITIES

Beginning with its traditional central activities, six aspects are to be reviewed. As the chief form of its activity the law of purposeful social grouping makes the local church a congregation. The tradition of the transcendent world makes it a worshipping congregation. There is little reason to suppose that either of these characteristics will grow less. With religious people there is very considerable agreement as to what constitutes appropriate group behavior in the conscious realization and celebration of supra-mundane relationships. This fits in with the essential characteristics of a voluntary face-to-face group. When it comes to explanations differences arise. Whether the minister is regarded as priest or as popularly elected representative, whether the sacrament be accepted as a sacrifice or as a memorial, the typical forms and more generic meanings of common worship have all but universal acceptance in the church. Except, then, when secondary rationalizations are insisted upon there is large agreement as to central activities.

Here there are aspects of religious activity likely to remain generically the same a century hence. The church will congregate for worship and attach the public proclamations and teaching of religion to its central ritual acts.

But will this spell the triumph or the defeat of vital religion? Do the conventional activities of the religious group reflect the strength of irrational tradition too resistent even for the "acids of modernity"? Or did the long religious evolutions of mankind hit upon a permanent and classic manner of expressing its central meanings? Is this one among the few things which the race's experience has made timeless

"And granted them an equal date,

"With Andes and with Ararat."

Decision on this point is obviously beyond any objective evidence. Faith may contrast the kings and empires which "want and come" with the church, "praying yet, a thousand years the same"; but it is more scientific to project trends a hundred years at a time, and to base the prospects of the church's central activities upon their contemporary social utility as satisfying a profound instinct of the religious group and greatly contributing to its cohesion and morale.

When it comes to the content of meaning which will be poured into these dividing forms, it is more than likely that modifications already under way will continue. Some of these have been noted as modifications of religious climate. To be timeless in form is not to be changeless in attitude. Even the Roman Catholic Church recognizes the likelihood that fresh implications of Christianity will emerge.

Thus the "social gospel" was discovered during the last generation. It managed to insert itself, with greater or less conflict, into the contemporary version of popular religion. Its ideas took on definiteness culminating in formal pronouncements. They came to be provided with institutionalized vehicles as part of the church's accepted routine. They got a rural version added to the first industrial one; and finally became nationalized in the teaching of the local church and the training of youth. The writer has just watched the constituency of a great church trying to tell what the church is for, in response to a widely circulated questionnaire. The most frequent answer is an effort to say that the modern Christian recognizes both a personal and a social aspect of religion and that somehow the two hang together. In brief, the novelty of a generation ago has become indigenous in popular religious thinking.

In the realm of the central activities of the church deliberate policy has two main phases. It can improve the technical and aesthetic standard of old functions (as shown in chapter vii) and it can facilitate the "application" of accepted novelties in thinking and teaching.

Nearly all branches of the church, moreover, wisely recognize extensive possibilities of flexibility in secondary aspects of their life and work. The church took over many primitive practices and many devout usages from Jewish sources. In every age it has inclined to reflect the prevalent pattern of civil and communal organization of contemporary civilization. Thus conservative immigrant churches in the United States have repeatedly remodeled their governments after the representative form here prevalent; while wide freedom in the setting up of supplementary ecclesiastical forms is exercised under almost all types of polities.

In this realm of secondary values church policy is free to be "progressive," to adopt new physical vehicles like the radio, or new organizational devices like the every-member canvass or church cabinet. The church may even profit by a reasonable interest in shifting ecclesiastical fashion. It may profit by a restrained use of whatever "catches on," even though the novelty has no better warrant than momentary mob psychology. But far more important it is to make the church's worship noble and profound and to elaborate the implications of its message for its age.

## ORGANIZATION

In contrast with a rigid tradition derived from some inherited version of the claims of a society held to be supra-mundane, and in contrast with the paper devices of ecclesiastical schemers, church organization gets its actual workability by agreeing with the laws implicit in spontaneous social organization. The story of the natural organization of the church, in its larger outline, has had repeated telling in previous paragraphs. Organization grows by accretion. Novelties which persist in spite of tradition and which have enough utility to survive competition, compel old ways to make room for them. Such persistent novelties have changed the pattern of church organizations very significantly during the past generation. Their multiplication inevitably results in a demand for concentration and simplification of structure. This raises problems of still further integration.

Thus the modern church has had to deal with a strong and valid tendency of organization to express all its fundamental interests according to an age and sex gradation or method; for example, the effort to combine all young people's interests under one scheme of organization, all women's interests under another, etc. Society in general and education in particular have greatly sharpened their provisions for the separate treatment of distinctive age and sex problems. At the same time the church has had to deal with a tendency on the part of each major and compelling interest to try to exercise the direct leadership of the entire constituency, from the top down. This results in a cutting across of all the grades and strata which the former tendency develops. Home and foreign missions, for example, insist on separate agencies. Each important tendency and value creates an organizational structure and develops special agencies of promotion. Urban life has broken up the family and face-to-face groups and has proceeded to reorganize society along such special interest lines.

Where two interests cross in any field of the church's life, say that of missions, duplication and conflicts of responsibility arise. There are not really enough zealous partizans to back each separate interest and leaders begin to drag on reluctant followers by the device of fictitious rivalries with other groups.

Contemporary church policy is generally a compromise between these two trends, as witness the "reorganization" of almost any denomination, church federation, or local church today. While struggling with these conflicting organizational tendencies, church policy has had also to consider that all grouping, whether formal or informal, involves and is greatly complicated by a highly sensitive set of leader-follower relationships according to which individuals blessed with "personality" or prestige are imitated, accumulate admirers and constitute centers of social force. These spontaneous groupings about natural leaders are sociologically profounder and more valid than much of the ecclesiastical machinery.

All such generic issues get one particular version in an urban environment, another in a rural one. Consequently, organization in some measure reflects environment. The various types of city churches described in chapter vii are authentic expressions of this principle.

Again, the law of unequal development of elements in any larger group, like a denomination (complicated as it is by differences between city and country and between geographical regions), determines that three-way variations shall ordinarily appear with reference to its modal tendency. One faction will press on ahead of it in the line of its own historical development. Another will diverge in the direction of novel development; while a third element pulls back in the interests of reaction.

Here then are persistent patterns of social arrangement which underlie and determine organization. With respect to novelties of organization, wise policy can avoid the cruder forms of solving their problems, such as their suppression by authority, exposure to the naked test of survival under unlimited competition, or hasty acceptance under pressure of mass psychology. Moving along with forces which it can partially steer but not control, deliberate churchmanship may save lost motion, avoid too great strain of morale in connection with change, and hasten legitimate decisions by substituting experimentation for emotion and planned progress for rule of thumb. Research avoids prejudices, analyzes situations objectively and gets data on the precise points that matter. Conclusions from experimental research have the maximum probability of being sound and workable; and in time evolve into an incipient philosophy founded on experience.

With respect to the reorganization necessary to find place for new elements which have at least tentatively justified themselves to experience, a wise policy may choose between varied solutions. Provided organizational simplification and concentration are aimed at, one may try out various alternatives, no one of which is inherently more right than another.

No solution based on policy, however, is adequate which forgets that the church always exists under the three aspects that the initial analysis of the chapter discovered. Take, for example, the peculiar witches' brew presented by an issue over a church choir. Here is involved the social psychology of a group, profoundly entangled with artistic susceptibilities, popular tastes and technical functions. At the same time the choir represents the church's chief auxiliary ministry in the celebrating of the unseen world. From the practical standpoint it is one of the church's chief attractions or distractions and is frequently a major expense. Churchmanship may very well be judged to have reached its height when it can find a happy solution for a local choir problem in all three aspects.

## Religious Education

Compared with the church's central activities where the continuance of traditional forms is in prospect, religious education is a realm in which revolutionary changes of pattern have been proposed and are ultimately probable. No such large agreement exists here as was found with respect to worship and preaching; and theory and practice are far apart. Compared with the field of organization, whose difficulties arise out of conflicting but equally natural ways of integrating groups and arranging their affairs, the difficulties of religious education largely spring from diverse understandings of the nature of the unseen world and how human beings are brought into right relations with it.

This is urgently manifest in countries where conflict of church and state has developed. Here the issue comes to be whether the human being is essentially a member of the civil order or of a supra-mundane society, and which viewpoint shall have the chief—if not the sole—chance to fix the mental pattern of childhood and youth.

But current uncertainty and doubts within the religious educational field itself rest on a similar problem. Is its business to communicate from generation to generation an authoritative version of belief and conduct which God has elaborated in detail in "revelation" and committed to the church as guardian; or is it to teach individual after individual, through his own experience and that of his normal group relations, to judge and evaluate moral issues and situations in the light of "liberal" religious interpretations?

Now, in practice, even progressive education indulges in a sort of gentle reinforcement of impulses to kindly and harmonious group relations by appeal to conventional religious ideas which do not generally originate in the church school. A child confronted by the picture of a kneeling Indian already knows that the Indian is praying. The teacher wonders whether he is not "thanking God for the blue sky." The child volunteers, "perhaps also for the warm sun." This, it is explained, is to "suggest the existence of realities not always obvious or demonstrable in class-room situations." This mild reliance upon the common fund of religious ideas is obviously in sharp contrast with formal indoctrination in catechism, creed and church rites, or in evangelical dogmatism.

Now rigid indoctrination is at outs with the age's intellectual climate. On the other hand, religious education is too unsure of the efficiency of its own methods, and too scientifically honest and critical, to want to base the religious future of the generations upon these in their present stage of development.

Meanwhile, as sociologically viewed, the transmission of religious culture without deliberation goes on as one of the most certain and binding of social realities. An acquaintance of the writer grew up in a rural hamlet where the church was never opened except briefly in the summer with an inferior supply pastor. He has no consciousness of having ever received any formulated content of religion from his early teachings and never took literally the version of the creeds popularly held in the community. Nevertheless, the demeanor of people in church, the unwonted facial expressions, the quiet Sunday hands of the hard-working neighborhood, the aloof and empty church building, the hymns, and the memories of community rituals such as "Decoration Day," registered powerfully and indelibly in the mind. Here were impressions which set themselves apart as derived from another than the work-a-day world. Such elements of a culture contrive to get transmitted from generation to generation for better or for worse. They have deep roots in the folk-ways of the "Christian" peoples. They are among the most dependable forces of human existence.

Compared with these inevitable processes deliberate efforts at religious education are efficacious only within very narrow limitations. They are less steadily successful than are the church's efforts in more traditional fields. Because they are more dominated by rationalization, the more theoretical and self-conscious methods of transmitting religious culture have also been most susceptible to the results of shifts in the religious climate and have shared the fate of delicate hybrids in the plant and animal world. Their processes have been confused by rapid changes in viewpoint. The scientific investigation of their results has reached, on the one hand, rather negative conclusions, or has seriously lacked relevancy on the other. Meanwhile a highly significant revulsion against religious education in its official versions has appeared within the rank and file of the church. In response to questionnaires a representative section of the religious public finds that religious education, as that public knows it, has less strength than weakness. The most frequent complaints are "too high-brow" and "not sufficiently religious."

For the moment, then, the first problem of religious education is to get the church at large genuinely to accept the A. B. C.'s of its thinking. For the moment experimentation in getting pupils to Sunday school and in including teachers to use moderately progressive plans is far more necessary than finding out how to affect pupils' attitudes, say, toward characters in history.

Fortunately these problems relate to a realm which is quite capable of going on with the one without leaving the other undone, a realm, moreover, which is inured to change and confusion. No one seriously suggests to bring education to a halt because educators are notoriously unsure as to both their means and their objective. It is, in the main, the contrast between the certainty of theology and the usages of the frankly experimental educational world that makes the difficulty appear acute in the field of religious education.

## SOCIAL WELFARE ACTIVITIES

The concern of the church for the social welfare of the people is a direct consequence, though not an exclusive one, of its vision of a supra-mundane society. The reign of good-will, righteousness and peace in the Kingdom of God has been the most persuasive of the Utopias. The church's ethical authority for trying to understand the possibilities of human society in the light of this ideal is as nearly inherent as is its consciousness of personal religious values. For all peoples who maintain an activist version of religion this concern is unquenchable. Unless American attitudes toward life utterly change it is likely to be as integral an interest of religion a century hence as it is today.

The actual conditions of human welfare, on the contrary, are highly debatable. Something negative appears to have been established by history and social experience; such as that happiness cannot come by force, by tyranny, or by the dominance of the human spirit by fear and ignorance. But the question of exactly what social changes will produce the happiest human relations at a given time is always clouded by a large measure of uncertain and complicated phenomena and conflicts of opinion. The church's newer social convictions have achieved a working authority without fully manifesting their implications in detail. In the midst of this confusion, which only the total experience of mankind can solve, the most authentic voice for the church is found in her convictions of the primary value of human personality, in her own experience of the inherent importance of group life for social morale, in the simple naturalness of mutual aid between churches and their members, in the contribution of religious sentiment toward the steadying of social situations, and in her sense of the duty of maintaining community effort along with the other constructive forces of society.

As a deliberate policy, church welfare activity in the realm of social service stands on most certain ground when it selects forms of service that are most in accordance with the peculiar pastoral genius of the church and that lean heavily on direct religious motivation and inspirational strength for their solutions. Second to this comes the bringing up of social-service methods and workers to established technical standards, and the maintenance of most complete coöperative relationships with the other social forces of the community.

In the realm of social ideals and convictions the church's major function is to bring social questions into the forum of educational discussion, without dogmatism, and to register tentative agreements as they may then be evolved. The churches have done this with conspicuous success in the so-called social creeds adopted by most of the denominations and by the Federal Council, paralleled as they are by various similar bodies of conviction registered by Jewish and Roman Catholic church authorities.

## THE MINISTRY

The case of the ministry has already been cited as impressive evidence of the power of the transcendent aspect of the church to color the external institutional situation. The ministerial order in contrast with the laity, recognized by almost all churches, is essentially a defining of status with reference to a supra-mundane social system. A shade of priestly character creeps in upon the ministries even of the most democratic of churches. This sacerdotal tendency is itself an important datum derived from observation of the church and is really one of the solidest of its objective facts. Stabilized by tradition growing out of its supra-mundane functions, the actual work of the ministry is in large degree unresponsive to external conditions. It is essentially the same in country as in city, in its applications to farmers as to industrial workers.

On the other hand, the strictly environmental control of the forces which fix the fortunes of the local church, and consequently of its professional leaders, is most convincingly demonstrable. In their ups and downs, the church and its community are inextricably entwined. Sociologically speaking, the ministry is in the grip of an impossible situation on account of the over-multiplication of local units which has brought economic crisis to the church.

In spite also of its strong traditional conservatism, the characteristics of the urban church are forcing functional changes upon the work of the ministry. The presence of associate ministers in staff relations and the novel functions forced upon urban churches in order to survive, are modifying the vocation in practice.

On the psychological side, the imperative requirement of the church as a voluntary society competing with others for time, attention and support, is for professional leaders with engaging social qualities. The practice of the church in choosing ministers for their very human "personality" qualifications is consequently at war with its profession; and the ministry is torn between forces pulling in opposite directions. On the side of formal education the trend of the ministry is regrettably downward.

The improvement of the ministry by deliberate effort must in many respects wait upon its changed social fortunes. Thus it is doubtful whether any appeal to heroism will bring city youths into the ministry in due proportion, or greatly improve the quality of recruits generally, without a reorganization of the church which will first reduce sectarian competition, secondly, produce fewer and better churches, and thus finally improve conditions of labor, incidentally increasing remuneration. Voluntary effort may, however, accomplish something at all these points; and, indeed, considerable progress has been evidenced by data presented in the preceding pages. Improvements of curriculum and of educational methods are important objectives still within the limits of possibility, if the concrete data on which they are based have been preceded by a sufficiently unconventional analysis of the problems. Particularly at points where the tradition is not yet fixed, as illustrated, for example, by the functions, status, conditions of labor and the remuneration of assistants and lay ministers, is it possible for the application of intelligence and conscience to make the situation very much better than it is.

The ministry, however, as compared with the other institutional phases of the church, presents this difference that, while in the case of its institutional structure and function discrepancies raise only the problem of inconsistence and impracticability, in the case of the ministry they result in internal tensions attacking foundations of personal balance. All the church's perplexities and confusions focus upon the minister as a person. He knows the church's best and worst and finds the two experiences hard to integrate. Even so, ministerial morale is quite as good as the objective prospects of the church which the minister serves.

### Coöperation and Federation

The demand for the unity of the church arising out of its transcendental nature is very powerful. As an instinct, in contrast with a doctrinaire requirement, this motive makes widespread appeal to the laity and constantly appears in lay thinking. It is the ideal picture of the church as a mirror of a fraternal society of Christians that must directly condemn sectarianism and denominational division. The idealistic compulsion on behalf of a united church is not less strong than the authoritarian requirement alleged by high-churchmen, and has much greater currency with the American religious public.

The social characteristics of the American people and the evolution of the ecclesiastical life of the nation conspire with religious motive to make the movement for greater unity in the church inescapable. The homogeneity of the religious population is increasing. The common Christian type has been established. The various denominations are repeating one another's experiences and reaching nearly identical conclusions. The social pressures; the economic compulsions; the concessions to unity already made by the denominations; the cumulative historic movement toward unity combined with current sociological and psychological conditions, all converge to make further progress inevitable. Denominationalism has already been greatly modified as a working mode of the organization of the church. While as yet the indices oblige one to distinguish three classes of denominations—an excluded, an included and a marginal class—the next chapter will present data which, to the writers' belief, opens the prospect of a further extensive merging of American Protestant churches into a single or a closely federated unit.

When the religious and social forces reinforce one another, the path of deliberate policy is made smooth. Significant progress is being made in two fields already separately reviewed; namely, (1) that of comity, which places and maintains denominational churches so as to avoid overlapping and competition, and at the same time so as to serve communities adequately; and (2) that of partial church union, which has already united some dozens of denominations and is at present a live issue with scores of additional ones; so that probably nine-tenths of all American Protestants are currently involved in union movements of greater or less significance. The final chapter of this book projects these trends into the future and foresees the probable union of a large majority of Protestants in a single church.

### Determination of the Church's Function

Here, then, are forces on three levels whose varying energies, from point to point, finally determine the church's fortunes. What the church does under the stress of these forces, in all the spheres in which it operates, and when all are put together, defines the church's functions as a social institution.

From a realistic standpoint there is and can be no such thing as a grand strategy for the church, based directly on the wise adaptations of means to the furtherance of rational ends. In the first place, decided conflicts of conviction exist with respect to the nature and scope of the church's functions. These are in part an outgrowth of varying interpretations of extra-mundane affairs. No solution of these deep-rooted theological and historical differences can be reached upon a merely rational level. No one can go about deliberately to make the church exactly according to some "pattern shown in the mount."

From the standpoint of objective social science, on the contrary, the primary function of the church as an institution is to satisfy the inherent requirements of group life and to work according to social laws and processes. But these inherent social forces do not all work in the same direction. The church has, therefore, to recognize, understand and devise fitting attitudes toward these conflicts and confusions as well as toward the elements of order which they present. It has, for example, to acquire a proper sense of behavior with respect to the dangling adherent whose remote connection with the spiritual core of the church's purpose is all too manifest. These attenuations of religious relationship, nevertheless, have a certain social validity. It is the function of the tree to bear fruit according to its kind. This is not to be confused with the gardener's functions of pruning the tree and picking the fruit.

In contrast with the determination of function by the nature of the church as a social institution, is its determination by the church's nature as a religious institution. Here the function of the church is to symbolize and serve the supra-mundane realities to which it testifies and which it strives to mirror. Considerations derived from this source call for the revision of many ecclesiastical situations growing out of the natural social pattern. The church, consequently, must persistently attempt to create the social psychology and sense of the situation which matches the transcendent order. It must keep redefining and clarifying all its meanings with reference to its religious assumptions. As repeatedly noted, it persistently makes worship its central activity, although worship has no utilitarian value.

In contrast both with the function of realizing the church's own ends as a social institution and of serving its ideal values through symbols, stands churchmanship as the deliberate exercise of human purpose in the service of the church's immediate ends. It is the function of churchmanship to attempt to bring the social fact and the religious symbol together, and to gain practical results while retaining all possible values drawn from both spheres. This necessitates the modification of one viewpoint by the other and requires the church to rationalize the total situation with a view to consequent changes in policy. The fact that, in some sense, the two viewpoints are conflicting and competitive, involves the church in the difficulty of evaluating each particular activity and program as to the degree to which basic values are actually conserved and expressed. In addition to this, churchmanship develops its own particular criteria of quality and practicability, devises its techniques, and trains its experts.

All told, then, the church's function is determined, first, by what the social group is and by the things which its nature requires it to do. Secondly, the church's function is determined by what its transcendental insight and relationships demand, and is interpreted, on the one hand, by accepted tradition and on the other, by the innovating prophetic consciousness. Thirdly, the church's concrete functioning is the work of thoughtful experimentation which devises and sets before the church its practical program. It is the function of the church to be and to do all things which the co-working of these three-fold forces brings forth as its total expression in the modern world.

### Church Planning and Administration

It remains to say a final word about the general conclusion of the studies with reference to their most specific purpose. That purpose has to do with the responsible planning and direction of the church as an institution. Most of the Institute's studies on which this book is based were suggested by and undertaken in behalf of churchmen. Their total result, consequently, is a contribution to applied churchmanship. Their largest applicability relates to such practical policies as the placement and maintenance of churches, the operation of their several units from the local church to the denominational and interchurch agency, and their success as objective undertakings.

Since organized religion is at present chiefly denominational in organization it is fair to say that one important interest of the studies was to help the denominational churches succeed.

From this viewpoint it is worth reiterating that the chief contribution of the book has been to point out the consequences of dependence of churchmanship upon social determinism. It is possible to plan wisely and successfully in the church's behalf just because the church, in spite of its higher religious values, is nevertheless a type of social organization which works according to its own institutional nature, subject to objective conditionings. Thus, to illustrate, a larger proportion of churches recently founded die than was the case with churches founded before 1870. The era of expansion is over and the fortunes of the church are increasingly precarious. The moral is not to start so many new churches. This fact lays down the law to the extension policies of the denominations.

Or again, consider the fortunes of urban churches. Objective studies have revealed some of the changing conditions which determine their destinies. By taking thought a few "down-town" churches may survive to serve; but only a few. There are positively not people enough left downtown for all the churches that previously existed. The path of churchmanship, accordingly, is hedged my many difficulties and limitations. The well-churched city depends upon knowing what constitutes enough churches and religious institutions, when they are in the right places, what sorts are needed, what quality of ministry and what precise product is required by adequate standards, and what are the relationships between particular churches and between all churches and other constructive agencies. Objective tests can measurably tell when these specifications are satisfied.

But objective evidence goes still farther and points out that deliberate adaptation is rarely an all-round success, while spontaneous or compulsory adaptation is often highly successful. The essential limitation upon adaptation is that it usually has to deal with those elements in the population which are most completely dislocated from their old traditions and standards, and which have not yet reached easy familiarity with and inner acceptance of new standards. In short, there is something artificial about its solution. The authenticity, for example, of the Southern mountaineer's religion for the Southern mountaineer leads him to designate mission institutions and missionaries from the outside as "furrin" and "furriners." After all, this is a rather scientific way of judging the situation. In religion, as in secular culture, pluralism appears to have the last word. The growth of social homogeneity all along the line must precede the integration of groups into new wholes. Education may pioneer, but formal education cannot run far in advance of inward preparation for it.

Accordingly, it is in the conduct of institutions for populations that are already essentially homogeneous that deliberate churchmanship finds its greatest scope. This includes the great mass of the churches and denominations of the long-established American stock. Here it is perfectly possible to have fewer and better churches, a condition on which so much else depends—ministerial standards, educational processes, adequate finances and institutional efficiency. Ecclesiastical control of the situation through the recognition or non-recognition of local churches, as well as through the control of subsidies, puts it quite within the power of the official conscience and determination to improve matters greatly. It is not too much to say that the major practical message of the entire book is the need of a relentless reorganization of American Protestantism along these lines.

While, then, the first great lesson of the scientific study of the church is the need of humility on the part of the churchman, the second lesson is to teach him to magnify his offices. In harmony with social forces he can do much. And as the religious version of his calling keeps reminding him, God works through the thoughtful and earnest decisions of men. If, for the moment, objective evidence and inspiration both fail, the churchman, like any other practical man, will have to do the best he can and see what comes of it. But he should first exhaust all his resources both of religious and of scientific insight and wisdom. He can improve greatly at both these points.

# CHAPTER XV

*The Promise of Unity*

The movement for church unity is backed by powerful emotional and practical attitudes widely diffused throughout the nation, in all regions, among both clergy and laity and including persons of virtually all denominations.

In nearly every Institute study denominational differences with respect to whatever phenomenon was under consideration have been meticulously traced and statistically measured. A considerable number of such comparisons have appeared in the present volume. Rarely have they furnished the major explanatory clue to any field or phenomenon under investigation. Denominational differences are generally not determinative. Generalization about the American church is thus not arbitrary. Its validity rests in the very large measure of homogeneity in the thought and life of the separate churches. The truthfulness of a unified picture of the church as an institution is itself an evidence of the church's inner unity.

Chapter xii traced in detail the particular integrative movements falling short of formal union which have marked the trends of the present century and generation. Collectively, these have built communicating arcades between the separate churches and denominations, until a considerable measure of practical unity has been achieved, while an over-arching structure of unitive attitude and habit of mind is becoming increasingly concrete and visible in joint planning, federative organizations and coöperative programs. Meanwhile partial unions have knitted up some scores of fractures within the ecclesiastical body.

PARTIAL UNIONS

An increasing number of union, federated, or community churches are appearing in local communities. These were treated in chapter xii as examples of growing religious coöperation. Strictly speaking, however, they are cases of partial ecclesiastical union. Partial union appears even more conspicuously in denominational mergers, of which ten have occurred since 1900, finally reducing twenty-three denominations to eight. Other mergers, involving twenty denominations to a total number of forty-six times, have been under discussion during the same period. About half of them may be regarded as being at present in the stage of hopeful negotiation. These movements for partial union have involved virtually all the significant denominations in the United States. For example, the Presbyterian Church in the U. S. A. has been concerned seven times, the Methodist Episcopal five times, etc. These movements have the approval of the vast majority of American Christians, who look with expectancy for their further progress.

The general significance of these phenomena is that the major churches of America have passed over from a mood of opposition to one of accommodation resulting in many forms of combination and alliance.

## GROUNDS OF HOPE FOR UNION

In popular thinking no clear distinction is made between the more broadly integrative processes, or the partial unions previously described, and the actual union of the church as a whole. The expectancy is that there will be further advance in unity, that coöperation will move on beyond mere coöperation, that the present versions and agencies of federation will widen their scope, that integration will proceed by stages until it reaches the point of substantial union, covering at least the joint functioning of denominations in such matters as a general system of philanthropies and religious education, the joint conduct of home and foreign missionary operations, and systematic common action in behalf of social morality.

Very fundamental grounds for confidence that such preliminary phases may lead up to a strong union movement are to be found; for example, in the overwhelming conviction of representative constituencies that such a movement is timely. The preponderant judgment on the subject, as derived from nearly 3,000 questionnaires, is that "a few more years of frank discussion [of union] will reveal ways by which many difficulties apparently now insuperable can ultimately be overcome" and that "discussions during recent years have disclosed basic agreements as outweighing disagreements."

Other grounds of confidence are the similar assertions by representative constituencies that the church already possesses the spiritual unity necessary to vitalize unity in organization; the recognition that the plea of "conscientious conviction" must not be allowed to set up barriers to discussion and the possible modification of positions; and the final conclusion that there is, therefore, no need or further excuse for delay.

These findings are made on the basis of many thousands of individual returns and are amply documented in special studies of unity movements.[1]

## THE CHURCH UNION BALLOT

The attitudes just set forth were more often implicit than explicit. Investigation finds them everywhere, but until they are drawn out by some specific process they ordinarily find little overt expression.

---

[1] Douglass, *Church Unity Movements in the United States* (New York: Institute of Social and Religious Research, 1934), pp. xxii, 176 and 198.

A BALLOT ON CHURCH UNION

In 1932, however, a widely-circulated church union ballot secured a well-distributed response from more than 16,000 persons.  Its result was strongly in favor of some form of union as over against the existing denominational system.  The form of the ballot as circulated and the results of the vote appear in Table XIII.

TABLE XIII — RESULTS OF THE CHURCH UNION BALLOT

| Questions | Votes Favoring | |
|---|---|---|
| | Number | Per Cent. |

If you had to decide now what the religious people of the United States should do about church union—would you

| | | |
|---|---|---|
| (1) Continue essentially the present system of separate denominations? | 5,477 | 33.5 |
| (2) Unite the various church bodies into one church?............... | 5,191 | 31.7 |
| (3) Adopt some form of permanent and binding federal union of denominations, after the analogy of the state and Federal Government in the United States?........................................ | 4,951 | 30.3 |
| Mixed ballots (more than one vote on the ballot).................. | 736 | 4.5 |
| Total.................................................. | 16,355 | 100.00 |

Table XIV shows how the vote went in the major denominations.

TABLE XIV — BALLOT ON CHURCH UNION BY PRINCIPAL DENOMINATIONS

| Denomination | Present Denominational Order | Per Cent. Favoring General Union | Federal Union | Mixed Ballots |
|---|---|---|---|---|
| Missouri Synod Lutheran............ | 89.5 | 7.5 | 1.5 | 1.5 |
| Lutheran (All)..................... | 60.0 | 17.0 | 20.5 | 2.5 |
| Baptist (Southern Conv.)........... | 58.4 | 19.7 | 19.7 | 2.2 |
| Presbyterian, U. S. ................ | 52.9 | 22.2 | 23.3 | 1.6 |
| United Lutheran................... | 51.4 | 20.1 | 26.9 | 1.6 |
| Baptist (Northern Conv.).......... | 44.9 | 24.9 | 28.6 | 1.6 |
| Friends........................... | 43.2 | 22.7 | 33.5 | 0.6 |
| Unitarian......................... | 40.6 | 23.1 | 31.0 | 3.3 |
| Methodist Episcopal, South........ | 40.3 | 31.1 | 26.8 | 1.8 |
| Protestant Episcopal.............. | 40.2 | 27.7 | 29.3 | 2.8 |
| Reformed in America.............. | 36.0 | 28.0 | 35.5 | 0.5 |
| Methodist Protestant.............. | 34.2 | 39.1 | 23.3 | 3.4 |
| Evangelical....................... | 33.2 | 29.7 | 35.6 | 1.5 |
| United Brethren................... | 27.9 | 35.0 | 34.5 | 2.6 |
| Disciples.......................... | 24.7 | 51.1 | 21.6 | 2.6 |
| Methodist Episcopal............... | 23.1 | 37.5 | 33.0 | 6.4 |
| Congregational-Christian........... | 21.1 | 33.8 | 39.9 | 5.2 |
| Presbyterian, U. S. A. ............. | 20.9 | 35.4 | 36.4 | 7.3 |
| No denomination.................. | 18.4 | 48.0 | 28.5 | 5.1 |
| Reformed, U. S. .................. | 14.7 | 27.6 | 50.9 | 6.8 |
| Evangelical Synod................. | 10.1 | 37.2 | 45.7 | 7.0 |
| All denominations.............. | 33.5 | 31.7 | 30.3 | 4.5 |

Denominations favoring the continuance of the present denominational system by a more than 50 per cent. vote included three groupings of Lutherans and two distinctly Southern bodies. Those giving less than 25 per cent. approval to the present order include the Disciples, whose historical emphasis on unity is well known, together with a group of denominations which has most frequently participated in movements for partial union. The Protestant Episcopal church occupies almost exactly middle ground.

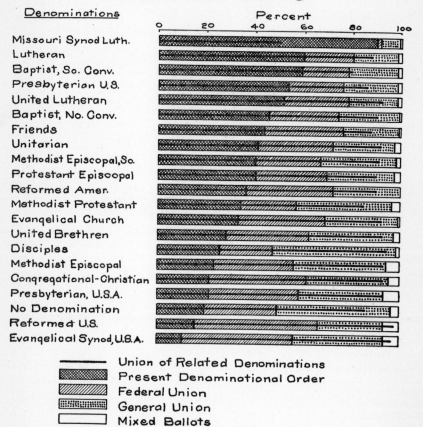

CHART XL—DISTRIBUTION OF CHURCH UNION BALLOTS BY PRINCIPAL DENOMINATIONS

Ministers favored unions somewhat more frequently than laymen; but the difference was not extreme.

Correlating the results of this ballot with the indices of religious prejudice based on about 14,000 individual returns from questionnaires,[2] it is found

[2] See p. 259.

that denominations which have the greatest prejudice strongly incline to vote for the existing denominational system, while those with the least prejudice are most strongly for union.

Adding the evidence of the vast number of free expressions of sentiment concerning unity collected by various studies, it appears certain that a strong preponderance of sentiment in favor of church union exists among all strata of American religious people.

It is, however, one thing to favor union and quite another to unite. Theory is easier than practice. While, therefore, strongly diagnostic of existing tendencies, the data presented over-simplify the actual situation.

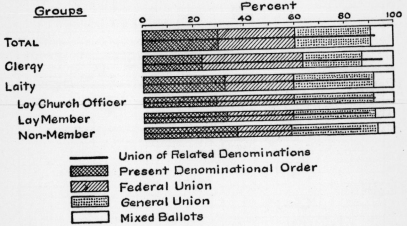

CHART XLI—DISTRIBUTION OF CHURCH UNION BALLOTS BY STATUS IN THE CHURCH OF
PERSONS BALLOTING

Taken by themselves they make the prospects of union seem more immediate than they actually are.

The ecclesiastically formulated positions and proposals to which the denominations are historically committed separate into opposite camps multitudes of people who have no substantial sense of difference and thus erect barriers against the getting of any unity movement actually under way. All war is like that.

## The Exploration of Differences

The promise of unity, therefore, cannot be established except by a prior exploration of differences. One must ask who they are that stand in real opposition to others, the precise points of such opposition, and the measure of it. Such an exploration constitutes the main concern of the present chapter. When it is completed the prevalence of agreement will have been demonstrated and the possibility of union made evident.

CONFLICTING VERSIONS OF UNITY

Opposing ecclesiastical positions as to unity involve conflicting philosophies of religion, especially as they concern the place and authority of the church and the finality of the forms under which the church is alleged to have been originally established.

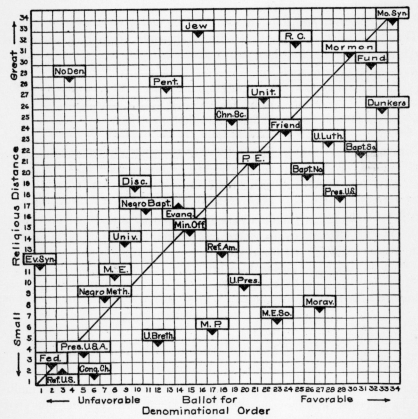

CHART XLII—CORRELATION BETWEEN BALLOT FOR THE PRESENT DENOMINATIONAL ORDER AND DEGREE OF RELIGIOUS DISTANCE-FEELING, BY DENOMINATION

Positions which call for the visible unity of the church as an institution rest upon three general types of sanction; namely, the dogmatic, the pragmatic, and the idealistic. The dogmatic argument for unity rests upon the conviction that divine authority has fixed the proper pattern of the church, which remains as revealed, unchanging. All existing churches are summoned to accept and return to this sole authentic version of unity. The various Catholic communions, Eastern Orthodox, Roman and Anglo-

Catholic, each claims that it is the only true and valid center for such a reunion.

Pragmatic unity, on the contrary, starts with the practical need of union in order to give the divided churches stronger influence in society and to enable them to present a united front to the world. This is the essential common ground occupied by the great bulk of American denominations whose slight prejudice, large desire for union, and habitual participations in actual movements of coöperation and federation have been revealed in earlier pages. This corresponds with the position of the rank and file of the church, whose common-sense attitudes have been shown to determine the tone of American religion generally.

The mediating versions of unity are idealistic without being dogmatic. They find a powerful sanction for union in a devout attachment to the ideal of continuity in the church's institutional life as well as in its spiritual experience. This is the clue to that strand of conviction in the Protestant Episcopal Church which clings to the historic episcopate yet does not make it the formal principle of the church's life. A somewhat different mediating position, with which the more liberal wing of the Disciples of Christ and the Christian Unity League are identified, derives a profound ethical sanction for union from the conviction that the alternative, division, involves not merely institutional weakness and waste, but an inherently divisive spirit and unbrotherly attitudes and deeds as between Christians.

Each of these three major positions appears in subordinate versions not easy to harmonize; so that the movement for practical church union in the United States is as yet without a well-established center of gravity.

PARTICULAR POINTS OF DIFFERENCE

Can any such center of gravity be found? To throw light on this subject one must explore further the prevalent issues which divide the churches.

If the matter of church union were primarily one of theoretical oppositions, the conflicting Catholic and Protestant philosophies of religion would assuredly represent the last ditch of controversy. Even on this issue so influential a leader as Bishop Manning of New York maintains that "the divisions among Christians . . . were caused more by human passion and prejudice . . . than by any irreconcilable differences between opposed positions." Expanding this thesis Bishop Manning writes:

"While the Episcopal Church is fundamentally and essentially Catholic, she is also truly Protestant in the original and historic meaning of that word. . . . The great spiritual truths which Protestantism has emphasized and vindicated will never be lost or obscured, but it is coming more and more to be realized that the principle which Catholicism emphasizes is not contradictory, but balancing and complementary. . . . It is not that one of these principles is true and the other false, but that both are true, both represent vital elements of the Gospel, both are needed for the full life and power of the Church of God."[3]

A condensed statement of Bishop Manning's opinion in the following form was submitted to a representative group of Protestant leaders: "The basis of church union must be looked for in the combination of Catholic and Protestant principles which in large measure are complementary rather than contradictory, since both reflect the experience and consciousness of bodies admittedly Christian. Well-distributed replies were received from 624 persons representing thirty-two denominations. A very large plurality of those replying (42 per cent.) held that Protestant and Catholic principles are not irreconcilable, while only 13.3 per cent. branded the proposition as

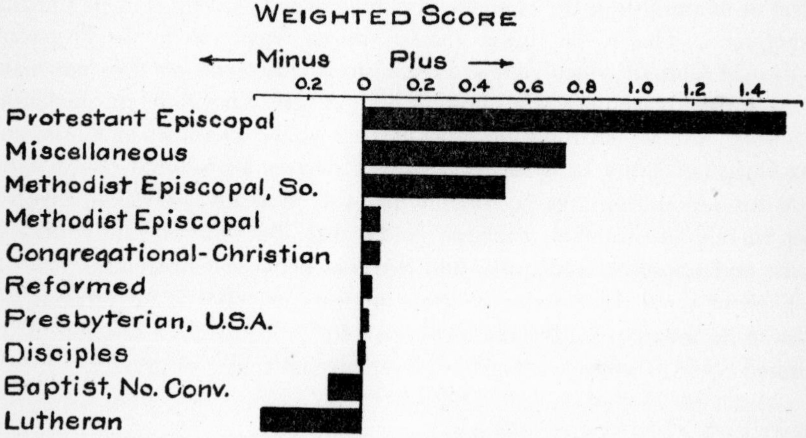

WEIGHTED SCORE

CHART XLIII—OPINION OF CHURCH LEADERS WITH RESPECT TO THE PROPOSITION THAT CATHOLIC AND PROTESTANT PRINCIPLES ARE COMPLEMENTARY RATHER THAN CONTRADICTORY, BY DENOMINATIONS

certainly false. The main differences in denominational reactions to that test are shown graphically in Chart XLIII. Leaders of the Disciples of Christ were divided half and half on this issue. Methodist Episcopal, Congregational-Christian, Reformed and Presbyterian opinions by slight majorities approved the proposition that Protestant and Catholic principles are complementary and capable of combination. Lutheran opinion was most opposed. The Protestant Episcopal position on this issue registers the ambition of that church to function as a bridge between the two extreme positions.

---

[3] Manning, "The Protestant Episcopal Church in the United States and Its Relation to the Movement for Christian Reunion," in Marchant, *The Reunion of Christendom* (New York: Henry Holt and Company, 1929), pp. 220-221.

The most striking feature of the test, however, was the large area of indecision (25 per cent. on the average) which the replies revealed. On this issue opinion has reached no finality. While the majority of American church leaders are not ready to approve a formula of possible Protestant-Catholic agreement, the way to change their minds is still open; and there is quite enough approval to justify further effort to bring it to pass on the part of those who believe in the possibility.

Responses to thirty similar issues bearing upon church union were secured from the 624 church leaders of nine representative denominational types. As in the example just presented, Protestant Episcopal and Lutheran opinions varied most widely, while those of the majority of denominations were in large general agreement.

PATTERN OF MAXIMUM DIVERGENCE

An examination of the thirty propositions in detail shows that Protestant Episcopal leaders are in radical opposition to all others on the following points: (1) in the conviction just exhibited that Protestant and Catholic principles are not contradictory; (2) in their scant approval of the proposition that the church is to be identified exclusively by spiritual rather than institutional marks; (3) in their denial that it is essentially an invisible society; and (4) in their approval of the proposition (which all other denominations doubt) that, since there is but one Christ, there can be but one church. (5) Protestant Episcopal opinion also diverges radically from that of the group as a whole in holding that episcopal ordination constitutes ministers a separate order in the church, and (6) that apostolic succession is necessary for the existence of a valid ministry.

LUTHERAN DIVERGENCES

Lutheran leaders, in turn, stand in radical opposition to all others (1) on the assumption that the church is founded upon a fixed body of revealed truth; (2) in refusing to approve that variations in religious emphasis should be controlled by fellowship rather than by authority; (3) also in much smaller than average support for the proposition that inward experience, and not its creedal expression, presents the essential reality of faith; (4) in denying that experimental common worship looking toward the intercommunion of denominations is desirable; (5) also in its relatively faint approval of federation movements as a substitute for division in the church; (6) in similar faint approval of coöperation in evangelism and brotherly service; and finally (7) in the bare approval accorded to the union of churches on foreign-mission fields.

Finally, both Protestant Episcopal and Lutheran leaders show maximum divergence from all others (1) in the decisiveness of their assertion that the church is both spiritual and external; (2) in the small faith which they put in the proposition that its proper unity is a unity in diversity; (3) in the relatively low value that they put upon the pragmatic argument that unity is necessary to "convince the world"; (4) in their denial that federation presents a satisfactory method of achieving church union; (5) in their unwillingness to admit that the ancient creeds are not sufficiently comprehensive; (6) in the rigidity with which they affirm that the authority to administer the sacraments depends on the proper ordination of ministers; (7) and that coöperation in "life and work" alone is not significant for genuine union; also (8) in their opposition to the lay opinion that ecclesiastical formulation of church-union issues are frequently unconvincing. On these twenty-one points out of a total of thirty, Protestant Episcopalians or Lutherans or both are in radical divergence from all the rest. This is the most arresting feature of the pattern of the thinking of denominational leaders.

Most of these differences obviously arise in the greater insistence by Lutheran and Episcopal leaders that unity has to be realized in the sphere of faith or order or both, and not merely, as the pragmatic view often holds, in the sphere of life and work. These, then, are the issues that separate.[4]

MITIGATIONS AND ACCENTUATIONS

Happily for the prospects of union the attitudes of the larger Protestant Episcopal constituencies—including its laity—are not so far apart from those of the churches of the central group as their leaders are. Besides this, there is the nearer as well as the farther wing of the Episcopal church. These, as a subsequent section will show, serve to locate the Protestant Episcopal Church within the zone of possible union. Some Lutheran bodies as well stand much closer to the central group than others; and on certain issues Lutheran opinion generally is quite at one with the characteristic thinking of the central group.

Lutheran leaders naturally reaffirm characteristic Protestant doctrine as developed in the original controversy with the Catholic Church and shared by all Protestant sects. On these issues, consequently, they stand at the head of the Protestant column. Nevertheless, Lutheran instinct and habit are conservative, and, compared with churches of sectarian origins, churchly. Consequently, on other issues Lutheran opinions swing to the Catholic end of the scale.

Going back over the thirty issues in which the opinion of denominational

---

[4] The foregoing condensed statements of issues obviously could not cover the full and exact meaning of the thirty propositions submitted to the leaders. For index to text and data see Douglass, "Church Unity Movements in the United States," Appendix A(3) and Appendix Table 38.

leaders is compared, a very extraordinary additional difference is brought to light. Propositions on which the Protestant Episcopal leaders are in opposition to all others constitute a group on which all others register less than half the usual amount of agreement among themselves, and propositions concerning which the percentage of neutral opinion reaches twice the average. This means that Protestant Episcopal leaders differ extremely from others where others already differ considerably among themselves, or where they don't know what to think.

In sharpest contrast, propositions on which Lutheran leaders are in opposition to all others constitute a group in which all others register very much more than average agreement and fifty per cent. less than average neutrality. In short, Lutheran leaders differ extremely from others on points in which all others agree. Propositions on which both Protestant Episcopal and Lutheran leaders differ radically from all the rest show somewhat nearly average total agreement and about average neutrality.

While, then, as will subsequently be shown, the aggregate distance between Protestant Episcopal leaders and Lutheran leaders and all others is not far from equal, it is the solid sentiment of all the rest with which Lutheran opinion conflicts, while Protestant Episcopal opposition is against the more divided sentiment and the uncertainty of many who have not fully made up their own minds. This, together with the relatively higher Lutheran prejudice scores recorded in chapter xii, makes Lutheran differences more serious obstacles to union than are Episcopal differences.

The much larger number of differences shown between Protestant Episcopal and Lutheran leaders and the central group also amply explain the difficulty found by the former two in accepting full participation in coöperative movements or in unity efforts under the leadership of the Federal Council of Churches.[5]

POINTS OF MINIMUM DIFFERENCE

Turning now from extreme differences to small or rare ones which separate even the nearest denominations, one finds that one or more denominations, whose opinions normally agree, break away and take a decisively deviant position on about one-third of the thirty propositions.

These occasional disagreements of those who usually agree merit particular attention.

On seven propositions one or more denominations of the congregational type shift to the right, that is to say, adopt a more nearly high-church viewpoint. Thus on the proposition, "One Christ, one church," Disciples' thinking contradicts its own major tendency by taking the high-church side, as it also does in insisting on the necessity of organic union, in its stand against

---

[5] P. 270.

the formula that the church is the sum of the denominations, and in doubting that the church's true unity is a unity in diversity. Here explanation appears simple. While Disciples in the main share the characteristics and position of churches of the sectarian, congregational type, on the issue of church union, to which they are historically committed, they gravitate to an essentially high-church position.

Again, in its hesitating support of union on mission fields Northern Baptist opinion takes the opposite side from that with which it is habitually associated in the total body of thinking.

Certain propositions were calculated by their very terms to break the habitual grouping of denominational reactions. Thus, a proposition that episcopal, presbyterial and congregational elements should all be associated in the government of a united church was essentially a high-church concession to churches of the congregational type; while a proposition calling for a constitutional episcopate tended to bring Methodist practice and high-church views under a common category. Both propositions were bait thrown out in particular directions. Both were nibbled at and partially succeeded in dragging those for whom they were intended out of their usual positions, in the high-church direction.

Now while, even in the essentially like-minded denominations, some leaders may doubtless be found ready to take a stand upon occasional differences and to magnify them into permanent excuses for separation, neither by their number nor by their character would the differences seem ominous. Any sensible version of unity in variety could easily allow for so much of variation within a united church.

## MEASUREMENTS OF DENOMINATIONAL DIFFERENCES

The foregoing exposition of difference between denominations, in its bearings upon the promise of unity, has now passed through two analytical stages. First, the more widely deviant denominations were identified and contrasted with the more homogeneous group; second, the points of difference, many and few, were discovered. A third stage is now reached, namely that of measurement of difference.

One knows, of course, that the sum of many differences, however small, may finally equal a great difference. One can judge from the nature of the points of rare difference as noted that they were generally small as well. But can one know with any degree of accuracy just how near or how far any two churches are with reference to one another?

### DIFFERENCES BETWEEN LEADERS

The statistical processes connected with the studies of church leaders' opinions went on to compute the differences between each of the nine denominations and every other on each of the thirty propositions in terms of standard deviation intervals. The method of deriving these intervals is too complicated for explanation in this brief chapter, but the procedure is exactly as though one compared in inches the difference between Jack's height and that of Tom, Dick, and Harry. Jack is two inches taller than Tom, one inch taller than Dick, and one inch shorter than Harry. The sum of these differences is four inches. The gaps between Tom, Dick, and Harry and each of the other three have next to be measured. Then the aggregate difference in the height of the group is reached by addition. The difference in opinions between the leaders of each denomination and every other on the thirty items of the questionnaire and the total aggregate difference in the 624 leaders' opinions have actually been compiled after this fashion, and the results are shown comparably in Table XV; the greatest difference,

TABLE XV — DIFFERENCES BETWEEN LEADERS OF NINE DENOMINATIONS IN PERCENTAGE OF PROTESTANT EPISCOPAL-LUTHERAN LEADERS DIFFERENCES

| Denominations | | Per Cent. |
|---|---|---|
| Protestant Episcopal | vs. Lutheran | 100.0 |
| Protestant Episcopal | " Baptist (North) | 96.4 |
| Lutheran | " Congregational-Christian | 96.0 |
| Protestant Episcopal | " Disciples | 93.5 |
| Protestant Episcopal | " Congregational-Christian | 92.1 |
| Lutheran | " Methodist Episcopal | 91.1 |
| Lutheran | " Disciples | 91.0 |
| Lutheran | " Methodist Episcopal, South | 88.1 |
| Lutheran | " Baptist (North) | 85.1 |
| Lutheran | " Presbyterian, U. S. A. | 81.7 |
| Protestant Episcopal | " Methodist Episcopal | 80.9 |
| Lutheran | " Reformed | 80.0 |
| Protestant Episcopal | " Methodist Episcopal, South | 77.3 |
| Protestant Episcopal | " Reformed | 68.4 |
| Protestant Episcopal | " Presbyterian, U. S. A. | 66.1 |
| Disciples | " Methodist Episcopal, South | 40.0 |
| Baptist (North) | " Reformed | 36.7 |
| Disciples | " Reformed | 36.3 |
| Congregational-Christian | " Methodist Episcopal, South | 35.3 |
| Baptist (North) | " Methodist Episcopal, South | 34.9 |
| Disciples | " Presbyterian, U. S. A. | 34.0 |
| Baptist (North) | " Presbyterian, U. S. A. | 33.7 |
| Congregational-Christian | " Reformed | 32.7 |
| Reformed | " Methodist Episcopal, South | 32.3 |
| Congregational-Christian | " Presbyterian, U. S. A. | 30.6 |
| Methodist Episcopal | " Methodist Episcopal, South | 28.6 |
| Methodist Episcopal, South | " Presbyterian, U. S. A. | 27.9 |
| Congregational-Christian | " Disciples | 27.3 |
| Methodist Episcopal | " Reformed | 27.1 |
| Disciples | " Methodist Episcopal | 26.8 |
| Baptist (North) | " Methodist Episcopal | 26.7 |
| Baptist (North) | " Congregational-Christian | 25.3 |
| Baptist (North) | " Disciples | 23.8 |
| Methodist Episcopal | " Presbyterian, U. S. A. | 23.6 |
| Congregational-Christian | " Methodist Episcopal | 18.2 |
| Reformed | " Presbyterian, U. S. A. | 18.0 |

namely, that between Protestant Episcopal and Lutheran leaders, being taken as the basis of comparison.

The outstanding points that emerge from a study of this table in the main only reiterate phenomena made familiar through previous comparisons. They are, however, crucial evidence as to the promise of church union and will bear restatement.

(1) The greatest absolute distance between any two denominations is that between the two which are in turn most different from all the rest: namely, the Protestant Episcopal and Lutheran. This negatives any live possibility that the two might get together and present an effective minority position anything like as strong as the majority. Taking this maximum difference as a basis of comparisons for smaller ones Table XV shows the relative difference between every pair of denominations included in the comparison.

(2) The Lutheran and Protestant Episcopal churches are eliminated from hope of leadership in the type of union favored by the majority of the American religious public. Their leaders' thinking stands at a much greater distance from the total thinking of the group than that of any other denomination. All cases of difference reaching 66 per cent. or more of the scale of comparison concern these two denominations. Presbyterian and Methodist Episcopal thinking, on the contrary, shows the smallest aggregate difference from that of the group as a whole.

(3) Of the largest denominations, the Presbyterian, U.S.A., and Methodist Episcopal also turn out to stand nearest to each other. Both have groups of close affiliates, the Presbyterian showing close affinity for the Reformed and Methodist Episcopal, South, churches, and the Methodist for these and also for the three churches of the congregational type. This reaffirms earlier evidence of an actual nucleus of like denominations about which union movements might rally.

(4) The smallest difference between any two denominations is that between Presbyterian and Reformed, which historically belong to the same denominational family and have recently been engaged in union negotiations. Next smallest, however, is that between Congregational and Methodist Episcopal—this in spite of the fact that they do not belong to the same denominational family, and differ in forms of church government.

(5) Each relationship between denominations deserves individual study. It is a striking fact that the thinking of the Methodist Episcopal Church, South, stands a little nearer to that of the Presbyterian leaders than it does to that of its sister denomination, the Methodist Episcopal.

While the churches of the congregational type always stand near one another, the Congregational-Christian is closer to the Methodist than it is to either of the two other congregationally organized churches. This must be due to difference in temper, since none of consequence is presumed to exist in the realms of belief or of organization. One is strongly led to suspect that it is not so much the factors of common historic antecedents or tradition that determine common thinking and govern the probabilities of union, but rather affinities of a more contemporary, subtle and vital sort.[6]

On the basis of these comparisons of 624 leaders' opinions one would judge that all the denominations involved, except the Protestant Episcopal and Lutheran, might easily get together. In order, however, to test the matter further, two other publics were circularized and their attitudes toward church unity determined by means of questionnaires. One, termed the "select constituency," consisted of 2,274 persons known to have some special knowledge of church unity issues by reasons of their positions in the church, their attendance on church unity conferences, etc. The other, representing the rank and file of the church without selection, consisted of 14,278 persons, predominantly laymen and largely young people, who returned schedules. The geographical and denominational distribution of both of these publics was such as to make them thoroughly representative.

### DIFFERENCES IN SELECT CONSTITUENCY THINKING

The select constituency was nearly four times as large as the leaders' group. These greater numbers furnished sufficient cases to permit the statistical comparison of twenty-five denominations and groups.

The method of measuring denominational differences employed in the case of the select constituency, was to calculate the number of possible times that each was separated from another by an interval equaling one-half or more of a ranking scale, on any of seventy-eight arguments. This afforded a very drastic measure of oppositions.

The most general result of this comparison was to reveal tendencies to extreme deviations from the central position in three directions. Congregationalists, for example, showed frequent instances of extreme opposition because they are so far ahead of the central position; high-church Episcopalians because they are so far behind it in the direction of dogmatic unity; and Southern Baptists because they are so far behind it in the direction of dogmatic sectarianism.

The maximum of opposition was found, however, in three groups representing parties or attitudes within denominations, rather than separate denominations; namely, the high-church, Fundamentalist and Federated church groups. These three represent extremely different types of variation.

---

[6] A supplemental instrument dealing with the assumed consequence of church union was also submitted to denominational leaders. While their answers disclosed remarkably few radical deviations (only ten of two intervals or more out of a total of 111), all ten represented the Protestant Episcopal or Lutheran denominations.

The high-church position represents extreme variation in the ecclesiastical field, the Fundamentalist extreme variation in the theological field, and the Federated extreme variation in the field of practical adjustments, in which it stands in opposition to both the others.

Other things being equal, denominations which do not often stand in extreme opposition to any others offer higher probability of uniting than those which are found habitually arrayed against others at many points. Consequently, the crucial point of the comparisons is found by noting frequency of opposition between particular denominations.

FREQUENCY OF OPPOSITION BETWEEN PARTICULAR DENOMINATIONS

More than a third of the time definite opposition between any two denominations occurs on not more than five arguments out of the seventy-eight, and in another third of the cases it does not occur more than ten times. This reminds one again that extreme opposition is infrequent.

Eleven denominations, however, take a position diametrically opposed to at least two other denominations twenty times or more, as shown in Table XVI. These constitute the most antithetical cases. It would be most difficult to get together into a united church denominations which differ so radically on so many points.

TABLE XVI—DENOMINATIONS WHOSE SELECT CONSTITUENCIES TAKE OPPOSITE POSITIONS FROM OTHER DENOMINATIONS 20 TIMES OR MORE ON 78 ARGUMENTS

| Denomination | Number of Times Opposed to Other Denominations |
|---|---|
| Lutheran | Congregational (34); Methodist Episcopal (28); Disciples (26); Federated Churches (26); Reformed, U. S. (25); Evangelical Synod (22). |
| Baptist (Southern Conv.) | Congregational (29); Methodist Episcopal (29); Disciples (26); Reformed, U. S. (25); Evangelical Synod (24); Federated Churches (22). |
| United Presbyterian | Congregational (34); Methodist Episcopal (25); Disciples (24); Protestant Episcopal (22). |
| Disciples | Lutheran (26); Baptist, South (26); Unitarian (24); United Presbyterian (24). |
| Congregational-Christian | Lutheran (34); United Presbyterian (34); Baptist, South (29). |
| Methodist Episcopal | Baptist, South (29); Lutheran (28); United Presbyterian (25). |
| Federated Churches | Lutheran (26); Baptist, South (22). |
| Reformed, U. S. | Lutheran (25); Baptist, South (25). |
| Evangelical Synod | Baptist, South (24); Lutheran (22). |
| Protestant Episcopal | Unitarian (26); United Presbyterian (22). |
| Unitarian | Protestant Episcopal (26); Disciples (24). |

The first noteworthy results of this comparison of select constituency attitudes is that it gives quite a different picture from that which the comparison of leaders' opinions gave. The attitudes of this wider Protestant Episcopal constituency do not often throw that denomination into extreme opposition to any other. On the contrary, the enlarged roll of denominations brings to light other frequent sources of extreme opposition; among

342       *The Protestant Church as a Social Institution*

them Southern Baptist, United Presbyterian, and Disciples; also less frequently, Unitarian.

Now to be in diametrical opposition on thirty-four occasions out of seventy-eight as Congregational-Christian and Lutheran attitudes are, or on twenty-nine occasions as is true of Methodist Episcopal attitudes with respect to those of their Southern Baptist brethren, is manifestly too frequent for peace. These habitual oppositions identify denominations as belonging to different systems and universes of thought and attitude, and demand the drawing of boundary lines so as to put them in different zones with respect to prospects of union.

RARE OPPOSITION

On the other hand, there is a considerable list of denominations between whom frequent opposition is never found. This does not mean that the "near" denominations are never in opposition. The Presbyterian, U.S.A., and Reformed, U.S., churches, however, are both surrounded by very considerable bodies of denominations with which they are never in diametrical opposition on more than two arguments of the entire seventy-eight. The Methodist Episcopal, Methodist Episcopal, South, Reformed in America, and United Brethren churches (together with Minor Officials) are similarly at all but perfect peace with important groups of their brethren.

These relationships are shown in Table XVII.

TABLE XVII—DENOMINATIONS WHOSE SELECT CONSTITUENCIES TAKE OPPOSITE SIDES FROM OTHER DENOMINATIONS TWICE OR LESS ON 78 ARGUMENTS

| Denomination | Denominations and Times Opposed |
|---|---|
| Presbyterian, U. S. A....... | Federated Churches (1); United Brethren (1); Methodist Episcopal (0); Reformed, U. S. (0); Presbyterian, U. S. (2); Methodist Episcopal, South (1); Baptist, North (2); Congregational (2); Disciples (2); Evangelical (2). |
| Reformed, U. S............ | Federated Churches (1); Presbyterian, U. S. A. (0); Evangelical (2); Methodist Episcopal (2); Methodist Episcopal, South (2); Minor Officials (2); United Brethren (2). |
| Methodist Episcopal....... | Congregational (1); Methodist Episcopal, South (1); Presbyterian, U. S. A. (0); Federated Churches (2). |
| Reformed in America....... | Baptist, North (1); Friends (1); Fundamentalist (1); Minor Officials (1). |
| United Brethren........... | Presbyterian, U. S. A. (1); Federated Churches (2); Minor Officials (2); Reformed, U. S. (2). |
| Methodist Episcopal, South. | Congregational (1); Baptist, North (2); Federated Churches (2). |
| Minor Officials........... | Evangelical (1); Fundamentalist (0); Baptist, South (2). |

Since these denominations never or hardly ever take opposite sides on unity issues they must already enjoy unity and should be easy to unite.

Comparing the maximum opposition with the minimum opposition lists, it is significant that only the Methodist Episcopal and Reformed, U.S., denominations appear as principals in both. They occasionally have profound conflicts and also many close affinities. Of the larger denominations only the Baptist (North) appears on neither list. Its relationships are just the reverse of the Methodist Episcopal's. It keeps close to the middle of the road, having slight differences with all denominations but great differences with none.

### MEASUREMENT OF OPPOSITION ON RANK AND FILE JUDGMENT

In passing to the comparison of denominations with respect to the frequency of opposition in the judgments of their rank and file constituency, it should be kept in mind that this body of data concerns a different type of question from those submitted to the judgment either of denominational leaders or of the select constituency. The present questions—108 in number—were more concrete and practical; the former were more involved in theological and ecclesiastical viewpoints and formulations. A still longer list of denominations—thirty-six in all—is available for comparison. When the number of cases is calculated in which each of the thirty-six denominations stands in a position of extreme opposition to any of the others, one has a rough measure of the difficulty of reaching practical adjustments between their average constituents.[7]

#### MAXIMUM OPPOSITION

Table XVIII shows the frequency of opposition between the nine denominations which show the greatest total frequency and those with which they are chiefly in conflict, while Table XIX shows, in turn, the same factors for the nine denominations which show the smallest total frequency of opposition.

Four-fifths of the particular cases of extreme opposition noted in the maximum list are between the nine denominations which show maximum total opposition. One notes that some of these are ultra-conservative, while others are ultra-liberal theologically; others are "peculiar" from the viewpoint of the Christian majority, or, as in the case of the Jews, are non-Christian. The other twenty-seven denominations all together account for only one-fifth of the instances of extreme opposition.

This list of maximum oppositions very largely coincides with the "very remote" denominations as classified by the religious distance test in chapter xii, and very definitely identifies religious bodies which offer no present prospects of union.

---

[7] The basis of this calculation was a deviation by one denomination in one direction equaling or exceeding 50 per cent. of the mean, while the opposing denomination deviated by a similar amount in the other direction.

TABLE XVIII—MAXIMUM OPPOSITION OF DENOMINATIONS OVER 108 ANSWERS CONCERNING 18 INCIDENTS AND SITUATIONS—DENOMINATIONS RANKING IN UPPER QUARTILE ACCORDING TO NUMBER OF CASES OF EXTREME OPPOSITION

| Denominations Registering Maximum Opposition | Times in Opposition | In Extreme Opposition To: |
|---|---|---|
| Unitarian.......... | 20 and over | Mo. Synod Lutheran (31). |
| | 15–19 | Latter Day Saints (19); All Lutheran (19); Fundamentalist (16); United Lutheran (15). |
| | 10–14 | Dunkers (14); Moravian (14); United Presbyterian (13); Roman Catholic (12); Minor Officials (11). |
| Universalist........ | 20 and over | Mo. Synod Lutheran (26). |
| | 15–19 | All Lutheran (17); Roman Catholic (15). |
| | 10–14 | Fundamentalist (14); Latter Day Saints (13); Dunkers (13); Moravian (12); United Lutheran (10); Miscellaneous (10). |
| Mo. Synod Lutheran | 20 and over | Unitarian (31); Universalist (26). |
| | 15–19 | No Denomination (18); Jews (16). |
| | 10–14 | Friends (14); Christian Scientist (13); Reformed U. S. (12). |
| Latter Day Saints... | 15–19 | Unitarian (19). |
| | 10–14 | Universalist (13); No Denomination (11); Friends (10). |
| Friends............ | 10–14 | Mo. Synod Lutheran (14); All Lutheran (13); Roman Catholic (11); Fundamentalist (11); Latter Day Saints (10). |
| Jews............... | 15–19 | Mo. Synod Lutheran (16). |
| | 10–14 | United Presbyterian (12); Pentecostal (11); All Lutheran (10). |
| All Lutheran....... | 15–19 | Unitarian (19); Universalist (17). |
| | 10–14 | Friends (13); No Denomination (11); Jews (10); Christian Scientist (10). |
| No Denomination... | 15–19 | Mo. Synod Lutheran (18). |
| | 10–14 | Latter Day Saints (11); All Lutheran (11); United Presbyterian (11). |
| Christian Scientist.. | 10–14 | Mo. Synod Lutheran (13); All Lutheran (10). |

MINIMUM OPPOSITION

Table XIX, on the contrary, shows denominations which register the smallest total opposition and the particular denominations with which their opposition is least frequent.

It is particularly noteworthy that none of the denominations listed in Table XIX as showing minimum opposition ever occur in extreme opposition to those showing maximum opposition, with the sole exception of the miscellaneous group in one case. Substantially all extreme opposition is thus confined to widely separated groups.

It is little less than sensational that on 108 judgments the middle-of-the-road Northern Baptists are found only once in extreme opposition to any of thirty-five other denominations. Still more significant, however, is the fact that many denominations which frequently stand in polar opposition on church unity issues register only one or two such oppositions on the practical judgments of the rank and file. These judgments, as has already been explained, had to do broadly with the integration of the churches

TABLE XIX—MINIMUM OPPOSITION OF DENOMINATIONS OVER 18 INCIDENTS
AND SITUATIONS—DENOMINATIONS RANKING IN LOWER QUARTILE ACCORDING
TO NUMBER OF CASES OF EXTREME OPPOSITION TOWARD 35 OTHERS

| Denomination | Times in Opposition | In Extreme Opposition to: |
|---|---|---|
| Baptist (Northern | none | 34 denominations. |
| Convention) | 1 | Pentecostal. |
| Methodist Episcopal, | none | 25 denominations. |
| South | 1 | Mo. Synod Lutheran; Latter Day Saints; All Lutheran; Roman Catholic; Fundamentalist; United Lutheran; Baptist, South; Protestant Episcopal; Negro Baptist; Miscellaneous. |
| Methodist Episcopal | none | 23 denominations. |
| | 1 | Unitarian; Universalist; Friends; No Denomination; Pentecostal; Evangelical Synod; United Presbyterian; Federated Churches; Baptist, South; United Brethren; Presbyterian, U. S.; Reformed in America. |
| Disciples.......... | none | 10 denominations. |
| | 1 | Unitarian; Universalist; Latter Day Saints; Friends; No Denomination; Pentecostal; Roman Catholic; Congregational-Christian; Evangelical Synod; Baptist, South; Minor Officials; Miscellaneous; Reformed in America. |
| | 2 | Mo. Synod Lutheran; Jews; All Lutheran; Dunkers; Methodist Protestant; United Presbyterian; Moravian; Fundamentalist; United Lutheran; Negro Methodist; Protestant Episcopal; Evangelical Church. |
| Presbyterian, U. S. A. | none | 15 denominations. |
| | 1 | No Denomination; Christian Scientist; Pentecostal; United Presbyterian; Negro Methodist; Evangelical Church; Negro Baptist. |
| | 2 | Methodist Protestant; Moravian; United Lutheran; Minor Officials; Protestant Episcopal. |
| | 3 | Mo. Synod Lutheran; Latter Day Saints; All Lutheran; Dunkers; Roman Catholic; Fundamentalist; Baptist, South; Miscellaneous. |
| Reformed in America | none | 12 denominations. |
| | 1 | Pentecostal; Moravian; Fundamentalist; Disciples; Methodist Episcopal. |
| | 2 | Mo. Synod Lutheran; Friends; All Lutheran; Dunkers; Roman Catholic; Federated Churches; Baptist, South; Negro Baptist. |
| | 3 | Universalist; Latter Day Saints; Christian Scientist; Methodist Protestant; Protestant Episcopal. |
| | 4 | No Denomination; Congregation-Christian; Negro Methodist. |
| | 5 | Unitarian; Jews. |
| Presbyterian, U. S... | none | 12 denominations. |
| | 1 | Mo. Synod Lutheran; All Lutheran; Roman Catholic; Moravian; Fundamentalist; United Brethren; Negro Baptist; Methodist Episcopal. |
| | 2 | Dunkers; Evangelical Synod; Negro Methodist; Protestant Episcopal. |
| | 3 | Latter Day Saints; No Denomination; Christian Scientist; Federated Churches. |
| | 4 | Reformed, U. S.; Methodist Protestant. |
| | 5-10 | Friends (5); Universalist (6); Unitarian (7); Jews (7); Congregational-Christian (7). |

TABLE XIX (*Continued*)

| Denomination | Times in Opposition | In Extreme Opposition to: |
| --- | --- | --- |
| Miscellaneous...... | none | 13 denominations. |
| | 1 | No Denomination; Dunkers; Negro Methodist; Protestant Episcopal; Evangelical Church; Negro Baptist; Disciples; Methodist Episcopal, South. |
| | 2 | Latter Day Saints; Methodist Protestant. |
| | 3 | Pentecostal; Federated Churches; Presbyterian, U. S. A. |
| | 4 | Christian Scientist; Evangelical Synod; United Brethren. |
| | 5–10 | Jews (5); Reformed, U. S. (6); Unitarian (7); Congregational-Christian (7); Friends (9); Universalist (10). |
| Negro Baptist...... | none | 7 denominations. |
| | 1 | Jews; No Denomination; Congregational-Christian; Fundamentalist; Federated Churches; Miscellaneous; Presbyterian, U. S.; Presbyterian, U. S. A.; Methodist Episcopal, South. |
| | 2 | Christian Scientist; Moravian; Reformed in America. |
| | 3 | Latter Day Saints; All Lutheran; Evangelical Synod; Methodist Protestant; United Lutheran; Minor Officials. |
| | 4 | Unitarian; Mo. Synod Lutheran; Friends; Dunkers; Pentecostal; United Presbyterian; United Brethren; Evangelical Church. |
| | 5–10 | Universalist (6); Reformed, U. S. (6). |

rather than narrowly with their unification. The denominations, then, are in far greater agreement on the lesser than on the more complete form of unity, and their masses are less controversially minded than are their leaders.

CONCLUSIONS ESPECIALLY AS BEARING UPON STRATEGY IN BEHALF OF UNION

From the foregoing exploration of the attitudes of denominations as separately revealed by their three different types of constituencies, eight general conclusions emerge.

(1) There is a vast area, relating both to the theory and to the practice of church relationships, with respect to which many denominations register no extreme differences. These denominations, though differing in minor emphases, never clash on the great majority of issues. Their tendencies of thinking and action are too much alike.

(2) Contrasting with this first area is another characterized by very extreme differences between denominations. Here many denominations habitually clash on a wide range of issues, both with the like-minded majority of the first area and with other deviants like themselves.

(3) Yet with none of the three constituencies do these clashes of absolutely opposing opinion occur on a majority of issues. There is a generic common Christianity inclusive of even the most extreme differences. This central core is defined by the large number of attitudes and judgments on which all agree. When expressed graphically even the most extreme differences appear generally as variations upon the common trend. This common ele-

ment defines a larger unity even of denominations whose corporate union is for the present practically impossible.

(4) Occasional real differences occur within the major group of like-minded denominations, but they are both rare and relatively incidental. A first step in strategy is manifestly to try to compose such differences.

(5) Still other real differences occur as to the availability of denominations for leadership within the zone of union. In listing denominations which register minimum disagreement, the present chapter has furnished a preliminary identification of the logical leaders for union movements, and of the denominations normally affiliating with them. The network of relationships of which they are the center constitutes the actual groundwork for union.

(6) Certain churches are found in a marginal position with respect to the central group and consequently not in frequent opposition to it, and these churches do not even get much opposition from either of the more widely sundered wings. It is possible for these to serve somewhat as bridge churches linking the extremes together. Part of their linkage with the extremes is due to common historical antecedents. These may be developed strategically. More important, however, are common attitudes and tendencies which make even the most divergent denominations in many respects like those with which they more generally disagree.

(7) Actual though not extreme differences have been demonstrated between the three publics. Radical opposition between denominations is less frequent with the larger and more representative constituencies than with the leaders. The friendlier attitude of the rank and file is perhaps partly due to the less searching issues submitted to its judgment, but also partly due to an impression on the part of the rank and file that the bitterness of extreme difference oftener arises in a clerical hairsplitting than in inherently inevitable conflicts of conviction or of reality.

(8) Issues differ with respect to the rigidity with which opinion about them is held. About some no finally fixed opinion has yet developed. Denominations remain more or less teachable and the final balance of decisions in one direction or another is still subject to deliberate pressure.

### THE PREVALENCE OF AGREEMENT AND ITS GROUNDS

Passing beyond the explanation of differences, the evidence warrants the positive assertion that, both in the doctrinal and in the practical fields, agreement between most denominations greatly outweighs their disagreements. Most differences are relatively slight and extreme differences occur at relatively few points. This has now been proved by answers from some 15,000 people representing a fair cross-section of the religious public, to a total of more than 250 explicit questions or issues.

THE FACT OF AGREEMENT

Combining this evidence with that of previous chapters, one may affirm a strong tendency toward agreement which runs throughout the data. The most natural evidence to recall is that of the church union ballot,[8] which showed two-thirds of those voting agreeing in the desire to substitute some form of union for the present denominational order, and more than nine-tenths advocating the union of related denominations.

On the battery of incidents and situations covering a varied set of practical adjustments between the church's denominations, the replies were strongly dominated by willingness to change the status quo. Over three-fourths of the denominations showed this common trend on this test, which reflected common-sense attitudes and preponderant lay viewpoint of the rank and file of the church. The extreme views were rarely far apart.

Again, on the battery of current issues on church unity responded to by a more competent church constituency, selected on the basis of some special contact with the problem of unity, a strong modal tendency to adopt a mediating position or to a trend moderately in the direction of diversity as opposed to uniformity was characteristic. Three-fourths of the denominations united in this trend in opposition to extreme positions at either end of the scale.

Still again, measured by the opinions of church leaders on thirty propositions covering the major areas of church unity, more than 75 per cent. agreement for or against the proposition was shown in seventeen of the thirty cases.

Out of twenty-three assumed consequences of church unity, there was 75 per cent. agreement or more with respect to more than half, while on only three was there less than two-thirds agreement. With respect to the approval of the expected consequences, there was more than two-thirds agreement in all twenty-three cases.

All along the line, then, relatively little sharp difference of opinion is left. That difference has just been located and measured. There is, however, a good deal of variation between one field of interest and another as to the degree of agreement and disagreement. Thus, agreement is strongest with respect to the more general notions of the church's unity, and weakest on particular aspects of unity in the fields of faith and order. A still further difficulty lies in the fact that the various points of agreement and disagreement vary greatly in weight. How much actual tendency to integration or division is represented at any of the points canvassed cannot be told unless its relative value can be determined. This, of course, is beyond mere statistics.

---

[8] P. 328.

It is nevertheless possible to arrive at a generalization of the situation by systematic use of the objective tests previously presented. The agreements and disagreements discovered lie in definable directions and the multifarious details are capable of being combined into a definite pattern.

DIRECTIONS OF AGREEMENT

The general directions of agreement, as generalized from the varied tests previously presented, is indicated in Chart XLIV.

On dial A, position U stands for the advocacy of extreme unity on the dogmatic basis. Position D stands for the similar dogmatic defense of sectarian division, while M stands for a position half way between. Intermediate positions are inserted as follows: UT stands for a tendency toward unity, not going to the extreme, and DT for a similar moderate tendency toward diversity as reflected in denominational divisions.

The strongly preponderant attitude of the American church as a whole is indicated by the position of the hand on the dial. It points in the mediating direction, but appreciably more in the direction of diversity than of external unity.

Summarizing the total evidence, one finds that the kind of unity which the American church wants is "unity in diversity," according to which neither complete creedal agreement nor agreement upon a fixed form of the church's order is regarded as necessary to make the church the valid channel of divine grace, but under which a considerably stronger type of organizational union than that furnished by present church federations is expected. Briefly defined, this is union of the pragmatic type reinforced by idealistic but not authoritarian considerations.

Dial B indicates a similar scale running from the conservative to the progressive extreme. It registers the direction of Protestant rank and file conviction in matters concerning the changing of the church's structure and customs in behalf of practical strength and utility, and the adjusting of relations between denominations accordingly. The preponderant attitude of the American Protestant public with respect to such issues is very strongly progressive. Even the most belated denominations tend more in the progressive direction than in any other.

Returning to dial A, one should note the direction of the secondary hand. This locates the chief area of uncertainty in the thinking of the Protestant religious constituency. It is concretely illustrated by such a proposition as that "Catholic and Protestant principles are complementary rather than contradictory" (as already noted), upon which 25 per cent. of the church leaders replying declared themselves to be undecided. A similar high percentage of indecision is shown on most of the propositions that represent concessions proposed by the high-church wing of Protestantism in the effort

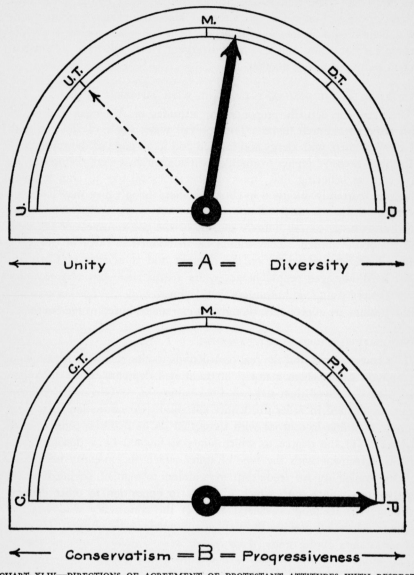

CHART XLIV—DIRECTIONS OF AGREEMENT OF PROTESTANT ATTITUDES WITH RESPECT
TO CHURCH UNITY AND PROGRESSIVENESS

to compose its differences with the majority group. While the majority does not accept these concessions, neither does it reject them. It is rather in large measure undecided about them. Here the evidence again points out a definite sphere for hopeful negotiations, in which opinion has not become hard and fast, and in which divergent views still have a chance to become tempered to one another.

PREVALENCE OF THE DOMINANT TENDENCY WITH DIFFERENT CLASSES

These are the actually preponderant attitudes of American Protestants with respect to church union. They prevail with people of all ages, with men and women, with clergy and laymen and in all parts of the country.

In their extensive replies to questionnaires, church leaders themselves are on record as believing that "most of the issues relative to church union which are currently discussed in church bodies, though they may have had meaning in the past and still appear important to the ecclesiastical mind, are unconvincing or fall entirely outside of the consciousness of the rank and file of the church. They should be abandoned in favor of considerations which take vital hold on the thought and conscience of Christians today." Middle-aged people, however, are a little more favorable to union than the very young, and ministers than laymen, while the northeastern and western states are appreciably, though not extremely, ahead of the South.

DENOMINATIONS WHICH OUGHT TO UNITE

This leaves one to find the real obstructions to church union where popular opinion locates them, namely, in traditional denominational differences which have outlived their day. A final battery of considerations was consequently devised in order to identify specifically denominations that show promise of union in contrast with those that do not. These considerations included: (1) the degree to which unity is favored by a denomination; (2) its agreement with the type of unity which the majority believe in; (3) its availability for leadership in a union movement (defined by the relative infrequency with which it stands in opposition to other denominations); (4) its progressiveness; and (5) the consistency with which it occupies a habitual position throughout the whole series of tests. Utilizing the entire data of the study, these criteria were employed to rank the denominations according to their readiness for actual union. The results are shown graphically in Chart XLV.

This process results in demonstrating that the central position in a practical movement for church union is held by the Methodist Episcopal and the Presbyterian, U.S.A., churches.

The Federated, Congregational-Christian, Reformed, U.S., and Evangeli-

ZONE OF UNION

Federated
Reformed, U.S.   Congregational-Christian

Evangelical Synod

PRAGMATIC UNION
CORPORATE        FEDERAL
Presbyterian, U.S.A.        Methodist Episcopal
Methodist Episcopal, So.
Reformed Amer.        UNION OF RELATED
Evangelical   DENOMINATIONS

OFFICIAL ANGLICAN        NATIONAL & LOCAL
Protestant Episcopal        CHURCH FEDERATIONS
Disciples        Baptist, No. Conv.
CHRISTIAN UNITY LEAGUE        United Brethren

Negro Methodist        Negro Baptist
Moravian
ZONE OF
COOPERATION

Friends
United Presbyterian   Universalist
LUTHERAN
United Lutheran
Presbyterian, U.S.
Unitarian
NON-COOPERATION
Pentecostal

EASTERN ORTHODOX        Baptist, So. Conv.
ANGLO CATHOLIC        Dunkers        No Denomination
High Church Episcopal
Jewish
All Lutheran
ROMAN CATHOLIC        EXTREME SECTARIANISM

Fundamentalist

DOGMATIC UNITY        DOGMATIC DIVERSITY

Missouri Synod Luth.
ZONE OF NON-COOPERATION

CHART XLV—DENOMINATIONAL POSITIONS WITH RESPECT TO CHURCH UNION cal Synod churches are even more favorable to union, but are less available for leadership, because they are too far ahead of the procession.

Not far behind the Presbyterian, U.S.A., and Methodist Episcopal stand the Reformed in America, Methodist Episcopal, South, Evangelical, Protestant Episcopal (in its official position and as measured by the attitudes of its majority constituencies), Disciples, Baptist (Northern Convention), and United Brethren Churches; and, except for considerations of racial separateness, the great bodies of Negro Methodists and Baptists. The positions of all of these denominations locate them within a zone of union in which some form of actual union, going beyond the weak confederations now in existence, is indicated at an early date.

### INCLUSION WITHIN A COMMON SYSTEM

This judgment is based not merely upon the fact that these denominations are not far apart in thinking and feeling on separate issues, but rather on the more positive ground that their whole attitude toward religion and the world, emotionally, intellectually, and volitionally, belongs to a coherent and interrelated system of tendencies whose correlations have been statistically demonstrated in specialized studies of unity movements.

### MARGINAL AND EXCLUDED CHURCHES

This verdict has to leave out certain important bodies of Protestants which, for the present at least, demonstrably fail to share this common coherent position. Some of them are close enough to be classified as marginal, and thus as hopeful subjects for some form of integration less complete than actual union. Others, including the more extremely Catholic, the more emotional and the more radically non-evangelical bodies, remain outside of the zone of present unification as actually defined by the attitudes and convictions of the major religious constituencies.

So far as expressed in distinct movements, integration has limited itself in the main to evangelical Protestant bodies. While the term "evangelical" is not closely defined, both integrative conduct and attempted definition tend to exclude non-evangelical together with non-Christian and Roman Catholic bodies. But they also tend to exclude others like the Holiness-Pentecostal bodies and Mormons, who occupy a generally Protestant position but differ radically from the dominant national type, either in belief or in cultural characteristics or both. Religious "distance-feeling" between the dominant type and these variants is still strong and mutual. The like-minded majority defends proselyting from such variant groups on the general ground that their version of religion is not vital and effective. A considerable minority holds, however, that it would be better to make common cause with the variant churches, expecting them to reform themselves from the inside; while a slender stream of Protestant opinion even calls for the immediate inclusion of Catholics and Jews in a comprehensive conception of religious unity. In the main, however, the integrative movement is not conscious of being all-inclusive or syncretic as concerns the three great historic faiths.

THE PROBABILITY OF CHURCH UNION

The hope of turning these possibilities of union into actualities is bound up with the strength and probability of the entire integrating process. Of elements in this process to which the entire discussion bears witness the following seem to be clear and demonstrable. (1) A historic trend toward unity has existed over a long period of time and is profoundly rooted in the national life. (2) This trend is in harmony with the deep-rooted traits of the American people. (3) The antipathies between denominations which it has to overcome have been worn thin and are rapidly diminishing. (4) A strong and convergent set of movements for integration, in aspects falling short of actual union, has come into being; and (5) very extensive partial unions have been accomplished or are in prospect. (6) The preponderant religious constituency of the nation shows practical attitudes favorable to further union. (7) Its agreements greatly outweigh its disagreements even in the realm of theological and ecclesiastical thinking. (8) These factors do not stand singly but are a part of a system of favorable convictions and attitudes. On all these counts the prospect of actual union appears to be good.

The strategy necessary to make such a union effective will naturally start with the churches occupying the central position in the zone of union, and should rapidly progress by drawing in those who are slightly ahead of the procession and those which are only slightly behind the central bodies. This should be possible through a series of mutual compromises and adjustments which the experience of the United Church of Canada and similar extensive unions elsewhere have proved to lie well within the bounds of precedent.

AN IMMEDIATE STEP

In saying this one must in candor confess that church-union movements in the United States are not developed and implemented in any way commensurate with the authenticity and potential power of the underlying forces of integration.

The most needed as well as the most immediately hopeful contribution to the cause of union would consequently be the creation and setting up of educational processes by means of which the implicit attitudes favorable to union, cherished by the American religious public, can be liberated and prepared for action. Adequate awareness on the part of the public of the broad sweep to integrative tendencies of which it is actually a part would clothe union movements with new force; and thus the preponderance of favorable feeling and conviction which has been proved to exist would be brought actually to bear upon the situation.

# BIBLIOGRAPHY

## CHAPTER I

Abel, Theodore, *Protestant Home Missions to Catholic Immigrants* (1933).
Athearn, Walter S., *Indiana Survey of Religious Education* (1924) Vol. II.
Brunner, Edmund de S., *Churches of Distinction in Town and Country* (1923).
Brunner, Edmund de S., *Immigrant Farmers and Their Children* (1929) chapter vi.
Brunner, Edmund de S., *Surveying Your Community* (1925-27-30).
Brunner, Edmund de S., *Village Communities* (1927-28), chapter vi.
Douglass, H. Paul, *The Church in the Changing City* (1927).
Douglass, H. Paul, *Church Unity Movements in the United States* (1934), chapter i.
Douglass, H. Paul, *How to Study the City Church* (1928).
Douglass, H. Paul, *1,000 City Churches* (1926), Introduction.
Douglass, H. Paul, *The St. Louis Church Survey* (1924).
*Fact Finders' Reports, Laymen's Foreign Missions Inquiry*—4 volumes, (New York: Harper and Brothers, 1933).
Fry, C. Luther, *Diagnosing the Rural Church* (1924).
Fry, C. Luther, *The Technique of Social Investigation* (New York: Harper and Brothers, 1934).
Hallenbeck, Wilbur C., *Urban Organization of Protestantism* (1934).
Hartshorne, Hugh and Miller, J. Quinter, *Community Organization in Religious Education* (New Haven: Yale University Press, 1932), chapter x.
Hooker, Elizabeth R., *Religion in the Highlands* (New York: Home Missions Council, 1933).
Lynd, Robert S. and Helen Merrell, *Middletown* (New York: Harcourt, Brace and Company, 1928).
May, Mark A. and Others, *The Education of American Ministers*, Vol. III, "The Institutions That Train Ministers" (1934).
May, Mark A. and Shuttleworth, Frank K., *The Education of American Ministers*, Vol. IV, "Appendices" (1934).
Mays, B. E. and Nicholson, J. W., *The Negro's Church* (1932), chapter i.
Morse, Hermann N., and Brunner, Edmund de S., *Town and Country Churches in the United States* (1923).
Sanderson, Ross W., *The Strategy of City Church Planning* (1932).

## CHAPTER II

Brunner, *Churches of Distinction in Town and Country*, chapter xiv.
Brunner, Edmund de S., *Larger Parishes* (1934), chapter i.

Douglass, *The Church in the Changing City.*

Douglass, *Church Unity Movements in the United States,* chapter ii.

Douglass, *1,000 City Churches,* chapter iv.

Douglass, H. Paul, *Protestant Coöperation in American Cities* (1930), chapter iii.

Douglass, *The St. Louis Church Survey,* chapter i.

Douglass, *The Springfield Church Survey,* chapter ii.

Fry, *Diagnosing the Rural Church,* Part III.

Hallenbeck, *Urban Organization of Protestantism,* chapter ii.

Hooker, Elizabeth R., *Hinterlands of the Church* (1932), chapters iv and v.

Hooker, *Religion in the Highlands,* chapter i.

Mays and Nicholson, *The Negro's Church,* chapter ii.

Silcox, Claris Edwin, *Church Union in Canada* (1933), Parts I and II.

Silcox, Claris Edwin and Fisher, Galen M., *Catholics, Protestants and Jews* (1934), chapter i.

### Chapter III

Brunner, *Immigrant Farmers and Their Children.*

Brunner, *Surveying Your Community,* chapter v.

Brunner, Edmund de S. and Kolb, J. H., *Rural Social Trends* (New York: McGraw-Hill Book Company, 1933), chapter viii.

Douglass, *The Church in the Changing City.*

Douglass, *How to Study the City Church,* Part I.

Douglass, *The St. Louis Church Survey,* chapter iii.

Douglass, *The Springfield Church Survey,* chapter iv.

Fry, C. Luther, "Changes in Religious Organizations," chapter xx in *Recent Social Trends in the United States,* Part II (New York: McGraw-Hill Book Company, 1933).

Fry, *Diagnosing the Rural Church,* chapters iv and v.

Fry, C. Luther, *The U. S. Looks at Its Churches* (1930), chapters ii and v.

Hartshorne, Hugh and Ehrhart, E. V., *Church Schools of Today* (New Haven: Yale University Press, 1933), chapters viii and xviii.

Hartshorne and Miller, *Community Organization in Religious Education,* chapter v.

Mays and Nicholson, *The Negro's Church,* chapters v and xii.

Morse and Brunner, *Town and Country Churches in the United States,* chapters v, ix, and x.

Sanderson, *The Strategy of City Church Planning,* chapter iii.

### Chapter IV

Brunner, Edmund de S., *Industrial Village Churches* (1930).

Brunner, *Larger Parishes,* chapter vi.

Brunner, *Surveying Your Community,* chapter iii.

Brunner and Kolb, *Rural Social Trends,* chapters iv and v.

Douglass, *The Church in the Changing City,* Introduction.

Douglass, *How to Study the City Church,* chapters vi and vii.

Douglass, *1,000 City Churches,* chapter xii.
Douglass, *The St. Louis Church Survey,* chapters iii and viii.
Douglass, *The Springfield Church Survey,* chapters ix and x.
Hallenbeck, Wilbur C., *Minneapolis Churches and Their Comity Problems* (1929).
Hooker, *Hinterlands of the Church.*
Sanderson, *The Strategy of City Church Planning.*
Silcox, *Church Union in Canada,* chapter xi.

### CHAPTER V

Abel, *Protestant Home Missions to Catholic Immigrants,* chapters ii and v.
Brunner, *Larger Parishes.*
Brunner, Edmund de S., *Tested Methods in Town and Country Churches* (1923-24-28-30), chapter vii.
Brunner and Kolb, *Rural Social Trends,* chapter viii.
Douglass, *The Church in the Changing City.*
Douglass, *Protestant Coöperation in American Cities,* chapters v and vi.
Douglass, *The St. Louis Church Survey,* chapters v and x.
Douglass, *The Springfield Church Survey,* chapters v and vii.
Fact Finders' Reports, *Laymen's Foreign Missions Inquiry.*
Fry, "Changes in Religious Organizations," in *Recent Social Trends in the United States,* chapter xx.
Hallenbeck, *Urban Organization of Protestantism,* Introduction and Part I.
Lynd, *Middletown.*
May and others, *The Education of American Ministers,* Vol. III, "The Institutions That Train Ministers," Part V.

### CHAPTER VI

Abel, *Protestant Home Missions to Catholic Immigrants,* chapter iv.
Brown, William Adams, *The Education of American Ministers,* Volume I, "Ministerial Education in America—Summary and Interpretation," (1934) Part II.
Brunner, *Larger Parishes,* chapter v.
Brunner and Kolb, *Rural Social Trends,* chapter viii.
Douglass, *The Church in the Changing City.*
Douglass, *Protestant Coöperation in American Cities,* chapter xvii.
Fact Finders' Reports, *Laymen's Foreign Missions Inquiry.*
Fry, *The U. S. Looks at Its Churches,* chapter vii.
Hartshorne and Miller, *Community Organization in Religious Education,* chapter vii.
May, Mark A., *The Education of American Ministers,* Volume II, "The Profession of the Ministry—Its Status and Problems," Parts II and III; and Volume III, "The Institutions That Train Ministers," Part III.
Mays and Nicholson, *The Negro's Church,* chapters iii, iv, and xiii.

CHAPTER VII

Brunner, *Larger Parishes,* chapter iii.

Brunner, *Tested Methods in Town and Country Churches,* chapters i, ii, and iv.

Brunner and Kolb, *Rural Social Trends,* chapter viii.

Douglass, H. Paul, *Church Comity* (1929).

Douglass, *The Church in the Changing City.*

Douglass, H. Paul, *How Shall Country Youth Be Served?* (1926).

Douglass, *1,000 City Churches.*

Douglass, *Protestant Coöperation in American Cities,* chapters vii and ix.

Douglass, *The St. Louis Church Survey,* chapter vi.

Douglass, *The Springfield Church Survey,* chapter viii.

Fry, "Changes in Religious Organizations," *in Recent Social Trends in the United States,* chapter xx.

Fry, *Diagnosing the Rural Church,* chapter viii.

Hallenbeck, *Urban Organization of Protestantism,* chapter iii.

Hartshorne and Miller, *Community Organization in Religious Education,* chapter xiv.

Hooker, *Hinterlands of the Church,* chapters viii and ix.

Hooker, *Religion in the Highlands,* chapters vi-viii.

Lindquist, G. E. E., *The Red Man in the United States* (1923, 1924).

Mays and Nicholson, *The Negro's Church,* chapters vii, viii, and xxiv.

Morse and Brunner, *Town and Country Churches in the U. S.,* chapters ii and vi.

CHAPTER VIII

Abel, *Protestant Home Missions to Catholic Immigrants,* chapter ii.

Athearn, *Indiana Survey of Religious Education.*

Beach, Harlan P. and Fahs, Charles H., *World Missionary Atlas* (1925).

Brown, William Adams, *The Education of American Ministers,* Volume I, "Ministerial Education in America—Summary and Interpretation," Parts II and IV.

Brunner, *Larger Parishes,* chapter iv.

Brunner, *Tested Methods in Town and Country Churches,* chapter iii.

Brunner and Kolb, *Rural Social Trends,* chapter viii.

Daniel, W. A., *The Education of Negro Ministers* (1925).

Douglass, *The Church in the Changing City.*

Douglass, *Protestant Coöperation in American Cities,* chapter xix.

Douglass, *The St. Louis Church Survey,* chapter vii.

Douglass, *The Springfield Church Survey,* chapter vi.

Edwards, R. H., Artman, J. M., and Fisher, Galen M., *Undergraduates* (1928).

*Fact Finders' Reports, Laymen's Foreign Missions Inquiry.*

Fry, *The U. S. Looks at Its Churches,* chapter vi.

Hartshorne and Ehrhart, *Church Schools of Today.*

Hartshorne, Hugh and Lotz, Elsa, *Case Studies of Present-Day Religious Teaching* (New Haven: Yale University Press, 1932), Part II.

Hartshorne, Hugh and May, Mark A., *Studies in Deceit* (New York: The Macmillan Company, 1928).

Hartshorne, Hugh and May, Mark A., *Studies in Service and Self-Control* (New York, The Macmillan Company, 1929).

Hartshorne and Miller, *Community Organization in Religious Education*, chapter ix.

Hartshorne, Hugh and Shuttleworth, Frank K., *Studies in the Organization of Character* (New York: The Macmillan Company, 1930).

Hartshorne, Hugh, Stearns, Helen R., and Uphaus, Willard E., *Standards and Trends in Religious Education* (New Haven, Yale University Press, 1933), Parts I and II.

Hooker, *Religion in the Highlands*, chapter ix.

Kelly, Robert L., Theological Education in America (1924).

May, Mark A., *The Education of American Ministers*, Volume II, "The Profession of the Ministry—Its Status and Problems," Parts I and IV.

May, Mark A. and others, *The Education of American Ministers*, Volume III, "The Institutions that Train Ministers."

Morse and Brunner, *Town and Country Churches in the United States*, chapter vii.

Silcox and Fisher, *Protestants, Catholics and Jews*, chapters v and vi.

### CHAPTER IX

Brunner, *Tested Methods in Town and Country Churches*, chapter ix.

Douglass, *The Church in the Changing City*.

Douglass, *Protestant Coöperation in American Cities*, chapters xx and xxi.

Douglass, *The St. Louis Church Survey*, chapter ix.

Douglass, *The Springfield Church Survey*, chapter xi.

*Fact Finders' Reports, Laymen's Foreign Missions Inquiry*.

Hartshorne and Miller, *Community Organization in Religious Education*, chapter xv.

Mays and Nicholson, *The Negro's Church*, chapter ix.

Silcox and Fisher, *Protestants, Catholics and Jews*, chapter iv.

### CHAPTER X

Abel, *Protestant Home Missions to Catholic Immigrants*, chapter iii.

Brunner, *Tested Methods in Town and Country Churches*, chapters v and vi.

Brunner and Kolb, *Rural Social Trends*, chapter viii.

Douglass, *The Church in the Changing City*.

Douglass, *Protestant Coöperation in American Cities*, chapter xxiii.

Douglass, *The Springfield Church Survey*, chapter ix.

*Fact Finders' Reports, Laymen's Foreign Missions Inquiry*.

Fahs, Charles H., *Trends in Protestant Giving* (1929).

Fry, *Diagnosing the Rural Church*, chapters ii, iii and vii.

Fry, *The U. S. Looks at Its Churches*, chapters viii and ix.

Hallenbeck, *Urban Organization of Protestantism*, chapters iii and iv.
Hartshorne and Miller, *Community Organization in Religious Education*, chapter viii.
Mays and Nicholson, *The Negro's Church*, chapters vi, x, and xv.
Morse and Brunner, *Town and Country Churches in the U. S.*, chapter viii.

## Chapter XI

Beach and Fahs, *World Missionary Atlas*.
Brunner and Kolb, *Rural Social Trends*, chapter viii.
Douglass, *The Church in the Changing City*, Introduction.
Douglass, H. Paul, *How Shall Country Youth Be Served?* (1926), Part I.
Douglass, *1,000 City Churches*, chapters iv and xii.
Douglass, *The St. Louis Church Survey*, chapters iv and xii.
Douglass, *The Springfield Church Survey*, chapter ix.
*Fact Finders' Reports, Laymen's Foreign Missions Inquiry*.
Fahs, *Trends in Protestant Giving*.
Fry, C. Luther, *American Villagers* (1926).
Fry, *The U. S. Looks at Its Churches*, chapter iv.
Hallenbeck, *Minneapolis Churches and Their Comity Problems*.
Hooker, *Hinterlands of the Church*, chapter i and appendix iv.
Hooker, *Religion in the Highlands*, chapters ii to v.
Morse and Brunner, *Town and Country Churches in the U. S.*, chapters i and iv.
Sanderson, *Strategy of City Church Planning*.

## Chapter XII

Brunner, *Tested Methods in Town and Country Churches*, chapter ix.
Brunner and Kolb, *Rural Social Trends*, chapter viii.
Douglass, *Church Comity* (1929).
Douglass, *Church Unity Movements in the United States*, Part I.
Douglass, *Protestant Coöperation in American Cities*.
Douglass, *The St. Louis Church Survey*, chapter ix.
Fahs, Charles H., *Coöperation and Union Enterprises Abroad* (1934).
Fry, "Changes in Religious Organizations" in *Recent Social Trends in the United States*, chapter xx.
Fry, *The U. S. Looks at Its Churches*, chapter iii.
Hallenbeck, *Minneapolis Churches and Their Comity Problems*, chapter vi.
Hallenbeck, *Urban Organization of Protestantism*, chapter v.
Hartshorne and Miller, *Community Organization in Religious Education*, Part I and chapter xvi.
Hooker, Elizabeth R., *United Churches* (1926, 1928).
Mays and Nicholson, *The Negro's Church*, chapter xi and xvi.
Sanderson, *The Strategy of City Church Planning*, chapter vii.
Silcox, *Church Union in Canada*.
Silcox and Fisher, *Protestants, Catholics and Jews*, chapter ix.

CHAPTER XIII

Abel, *Protestant Home Missions to Catholics,* chapter i.
Brown, *The Education of American Ministers,* "Ministerial Education in America
    —Summary and Interpretation," Volume I.
*Fact Finders' Reports, Laymen's Foreign Missions Inquiry.*
Fry, "Changes in Religious Organizations," *in Recent Social Trends in the
    United States,* chapter xx.
Hooker, *Religion in the Highlands.*

CHAPTER XIV

Abel, *Protestant Home Missions to Catholic Immigrants,* chapter vi.
Brown, *The Education of American Ministers,* "Ministerial Education in America
    —Summary and Interpretation," Volume I.
Brunner, *Larger Parishes,* chapter vi.
Brunner, *Tested Methods in Town and Country Churches,* chapter x.
Brunner and Kolb, *Rural Social Trends,* chapter viii.
Douglass, *Church Comity,* chapter viii.
Douglass, *1,000 City Churches,* chapter xiv.
Douglass, *The St. Louis Church Survey,* chapters xi and xiii.
Douglass, *The Springfield Church Survey,* chapters i and xii.
Fry, *Diagnosing the Rural Church,* chapter xii.
Hallenbeck, *Urban Organization of Protestantism,* chapter vii.
Hartshorne and Miller, *Community Organization in Religious Education,* chapter xvii.
Mays and Nicholson, *The Negro's Church,* chapter xvii.
Silcox, *Church Union in Canada,* chapter xvi.

CHAPTER XV

Douglass, *Church Unity Movements in the United States.*
Douglass, *Protestant Coöperation in American Cities,* chapter ii.
Silcox, *Church Union in Canada.*

# INDEX

## H

Hartshorne, Hugh, 174-177, 179, 294
Holiness-Pentecostal churches, 353
Holy Rollers, 13
Home mission aid, 222-225, 325
Home Mission Councils, vi, 188, 264, 265-266, 279, 283
Homogeneous areas, in cities, 251
Hooker, Elizabeth, 278
Hospitals, 185, 186, 192, 196
Hutchinson, Paul, 292, 298

## I

Immigration and Immigrants, 19, 21, 27, 28, 55
Indoctrination, 182
Industrial villages, 41, 150
Inflation and deflation, Monetary, 218
Institute of Social and Religious Research, v, 3, 12, 139
Institutionalized Religion, 3, 13-16, 33, 103, 185, 201
*See also* Anti-institutionalism
Intellectual climate, 311
Interchurch agencies, 99, 164, 179
Interchurch World Movement, v, 265
Interfaith coöperation, 169
International Council of Religious Education, 165, 174, 188, 264, 267-268
Internationalism, 311-312

## J

Jewish attitudes and positions, 169-320
Jewish churches, 28, 195, 202, 343
Juvenile delinquency, 187

## L

Lake, Kirsopp, 9
Lambeth Quadrilateral, 264
Larger parish, 67, 103, 123, 310
Latter Day Saints, 56, 353
Lay attitudes, 329-330
Lay church workers, employed, 93, 123-127
official, 95, 227, 330
volunteer, 93, 128, 159, 196
Laymen's Foreign Missions Inquiry, 11
Laymen's Foreign Missions Movement, 264
Leader-follower patterns and relationships, 316
Lent, 151
Lippmann, Walter, 290
Lutheran churches, 23, 41, 52, 112, 145, 167, 201, 261, 285, 329, 332-336, 339-340

## M

Manning, William T., 332
Marriage and sex, 299
May, Mark, 114, 121, 177, 247-248
McPherson, Aimee Semple, 148
Members and constituents, church, active and inactive, 43
admission, rate of, 56
age and sex groupings, 42, 72, 90, 101, 137, 243
degree of attachment, 49, 76, 155, 243, 323
distance traveled in attending church, 71
gains and losses of, 43
indeterminate adherents, 34
non-member adherents, 34, 72
non-resident members, 43
records of, 60
rural and urban, 37-44
transfer of, 54, 77, 257-258
varieties of, 34, 255
Men and Religion Forward Movement, 264
Men's organizations, 136-137
Mencken, H. L., 292
Methodist churches, 52, 107, 109, 145, 167, 261, 275, 284, 291, 327, 333, 339, 342, 343, 351, 353
*Middletown*, 93, 147, 150, 291, 293, 297, 298
Ministers and the ministry, abandonment of, 117-118
age upon entering, 115-116
conceptions of, 112
characteristics, 104-105
demand for replenishment of, 105
duties of, 91, 96, 118-120, 122-123, 133-134
education, 25, 107-115, 169-173, 243
employment, 116, 120
improvement, 321
non-parochial types, 132
non-residence, 114, 120
number, 83, 104
ordination, 115
psychology and attitudes, 131, 320-321, 330
recruiting of, 106
rural concentration of, 29
rural vs. urban, 111
sources of, 37, 106-107, 308
subordinate types of, 123-125
supervision of, 116
types of, 121
Missionary Education Movement, 268
Missions, Home and Foreign, 101, 196-197, 221-222, 224-225
Mission schools, 167-168
Mission study, 161-162

L.B.

a summary picture 96

churches want a successful salesman C D enterprises

preaching ability - only one in four churches 105

visitation evangelism 150

man of religious education is traditional 177    religious education not religious

    but brain 318

modern relig education has overtones of disillusion a reaction 178

youth + age 291

conversion 302

duplication in interests & conflicts 315